Shakespeare
LEGALLY SPEAKING

Shakespeare
LEGALLY SPEAKING

The Law in
Shakespeare's
Plays

Thomas W. Thrash

To Meg, Drew, and Maggie

CONTENTS

Introduction

"The first thing we do let's kill all the lawyers" (*Henry VI, Part 2*, 4.2.68). This is Shakespeare's most famous line about the law and lawyers. It has adorned coffee mugs, T-shirts, and is the title of a book on Shakespeare and the law. As is the case with many of the Bard's most famous quotations, this one is almost always quoted without regard to context. It is what Professor Marjorie Garber refers to as a "celebrated floating quotation."[1] It is often quoted as expressing Shakespeare's opinion that there are too many lawyers, that we would be better off without lawyers, and that lawyers are a pestilence upon society.

But considered in the context of the drama in which it occurs, exactly the opposite is true. It is from one of Shakespeare's earliest plays. First performed between 1590 and 1591, *Henry VI, Part 2*, is set in the late 1400s, just before the bloody conflict over the English throne between the House of Lancaster and the House of York known as the Wars of the Roses. Shakespeare's Henry VI (as he was in real life) is a pious, but weak and ineffectual king. The great lords—Gloucester, Suffolk, Salisbury, Warwick, Buckingham, and York—control vast private armies and rule the realm. At the start of the play, as they quarrel among themselves, England is in turmoil. The rule of law has broken down at all levels of society.

A mob of disaffected tenant farmers and mechanics has gathered in Kent under the leadership of a charlatan named Jack Cade. The mob is in open rebellion against the rule of the nobility and the

---

[1] Marjorie Garber, *Shakespeare After All* (Anchor Books, 2005), 102.

manor courts that were the primary source of law in the countryside. Cade pretends to be a descendant of the powerful Mortimers and claims to be the legitimate heir to the kingship of England. He lies about who he is and what he will do when he becomes king. The bigger the lies, the greater the enthusiasm he gets from the mob. Shakespeare uses the story of Jack Cade and his mob to illustrate the horrific consequences of a breakdown of the rule of law.

By the mid-sixteenth century, the law permeated English culture. The great common law judges such as Sir Edward Coke believed that adherence to the rule of law was essential to a stable social, economic, and political system. Cade and his followers know that lawyers have a special responsibility to support and uphold the rule of law. He and his mob cannot have their anarchic revolution if they allow the lawyers to live. This is not, like the American Revolution, a revolution to enforce their rights as Englishmen. So, first thing, they must kill all the lawyers. Therefore, I have chosen to cite Jack Cade and his mob in my introduction to this book on Shakespeare and the law. I will return to *King Henry VI, Part 2*, in a later chapter where I will again consider the rule of law in the trials and tribulations of the good Humphrey, Duke of Gloucester, the king's uncle, and the Lord Protector of England.

I am a federal trial judge. In more than twenty-five years on the bench, I have seen thousands of cases involving the crimes and follies of humankind. Many involve mostly good people doing very bad things. Shakespeare said it more poetically: "The web of our life is of a mingled yarn, good and ill together: our virtues would be proud, if our faults whipped them not; and our crimes would despair, if they were not cherished by our virtues" (*All's Well That Ends Well*, 4.3.66–69). This is a profound truth that animates much of his work and mine.

There is a great affinity between Shakespearean drama and the trials that occur in courtrooms such as mine. In a trial, the lawyers and the witnesses are the players, who tell conflicting stories to the jury. In a play, it is the actors who perform for the audience. In a trial, questions of motive, intention, credibility, and perception versus reality abound as in a Shakespearean tragedy. Rhetoric and oratory are the tools of the trade of the trial lawyer and the actor. The trial jury must use its imagination to recreate a dramatic event such as a violent crime—just as the theater audience uses its imagination to bring life to the action of a play. In a trial, there is a director (the judge) who keeps the proceeding moving toward a resolution. There is the drama of the jury returning to the courtroom to deliver its verdict. It is this aspect of a trial as a drama that I wrote about in a patent case (usually dreadfully dull cases) that had gone to trial: "This is an ordinary commercial dispute which skillful counsel turned into a melodrama filled with heroes and villains."

In part, it is this common theatricality of the stage and the courtroom that has made Shakespeare such a favorite for lawyers over the ages. In the histories, particularly in the great tragedies, Shakespeare brilliantly displays the psychology of crime: think of *Othello* and *Macbeth*. This is one more reason that lawyers and judges such as me, who are involved in the criminal justice system, return to Shakespeare over and over.

For the many years that I have been a trial lawyer and a judge, William Shakespeare has been a companion, teacher, and an inspiration. Forty years ago, as a young Assistant District Attorney, in my closing argument in a murder case, I quoted the ghost of Hamlet's father: "Remember me, remember me" (*Hamlet* 1.5.91) when I asked the jury to remember the young prostitute victim in my court whom the defendant had strangled to death while they were having sex. Just a few years ago, as a federal judge, I began a particularly messy *habeas corpus* case opinion with: "There is something rotten in Denmark" (*Hamlet*, 1.4.90).

But there is much more to Shakespeare than familiar quotations. In recent years, I have given several Continuing Legal Education talks on lessons of ethics and professionalism from the plays of William Shakespeare. Afterward, there has almost always been a lawyer or two who come up to me and say that after my talk he or she wants to go back and read Shakespeare with a new perspective and interest.

My ambition for this book is to spread the message to a wider audience of law students, law professors, practicing attorneys, judges, students of law and literature, and lovers of Shakespeare in general.

Shakespeare was not a lawyer. But he knew a lot about the law and said a lot about the law in his plays. He displays much more than a superficial knowledge of the law and its language in his plays. Other than obvious metaphors there is little, if any, nonstandard use by Shakespeare of the legal terminology of his time. The occasional confusion between "dowry" and "dower" may well have been introduced by the printers.

In Shakespeare's day, the English language was undergoing a profound transformation. The freedom it gave to a poet (or a lawyer) for expression was expanding rapidly. However, the law is not generally known as a fertile field for poetic expression. It is truly remarkable that Shakespeare, with the greatest vocabulary of anyone ever writing in the English language, would so persistently turn to the language of the law for poetic expression. One Shakespearean scholar has speculated that before his father's financial difficulties, Shakespeare was a student at one of the Inns of Court and had his introduction to the theater and to performing plays there.

There were few law books in Shakespeare's time. The best way to acquire a working knowledge of the law was to attend an Inn of Court. So the idea that Shakespeare attended one has a lot of appeal. In addition to his authoritative use of legal terminology, Shakespeare writes often about the law and trials and justice. In many of the plays, law or a legal proceeding provides the framework of the plot. There are formal trials in *The Merchant of Venice*, *The Winter's Tale*, and *Henry VIII* (two in this play). Trial by battle is featured in *Richard II*, *King Lear*, and *Henry VI, Part 2*. Henry V says that he will go to war with France only if he has a valid claim to be the lawful King of France. In *Henry VI, Part 1*, the Wars of the Roses are foreshadowed by an argument in the garden of one of the Inns of Court. Many of the comedies begin with a law that prevents lovers from marrying. There is a lot of material here.

Indeed, my argument is that an understanding of Shakespeare's use of the language of the law is helpful—if not essential—to a full understanding of the plays. I do not intend to enter what is called the authorship controversy over whether Shakespeare actually wrote the plays and poems attributed to him. Of course he did. For those interested in the evidence of Shakespeare's authorship, I commend Jonathan Bate's, *The Genius of Shakespeare*. As he says, "The Anti-Stratfordian position begins from incredulity at the idea of a provincial grammar-school boy being the greatest artistic genius the world has ever seen."[2]

In the essays that follow, I will explore the legal concepts, terminology, and structures in the plays. My hope is to provide the reader—legally trained or not—with a deeper understanding of the richness and genius of William Shakespeare. My subject matter is broader than the law as it is taught in law schools or that is the business of the courts. It is law in the broader sense of how we order and govern our society.

So I will address larger issues, such as political legitimacy under the law, as they are dramatized in the plays. I will also discuss Shakespeare's recurring use of legal terminology and legal procedures in the plays, and his extraordinary use of the law as a metaphor for the human condition. The language of the law is pervasive in Shakespeare's plays. Enhancing the reader's understanding of this is the object of this work. Although I will not attempt to relate the plays to ever-changing current events, I hope that these reflections will demonstrate the continuing relevance of Shakespeare to the eternal virtues and follies of humanity.

This is not meant to be a work of literary criticism. It is also not simply a catalogue or dictionary of legal terms in Shakespeare. One goal of this book is to provide a companion to someone who is seeing Shakespeare in performance. Some of Shakespeare's legal allusions and metaphors may be hard to appreciate without advance warning. And some of the best can occur so fast that it is difficult to appreciate how brilliant they are. For example, the

---

[2] Jonathan Bate, *The Genius of Shakespeare* (Picador, 1997), 68.

hilarious scene in *Much Ado About Nothing* in which the character Dogberry presents his prisoners to the magistrate for arraignment is strewn with legal malapropisms that may be missed unless you know they are coming.

Each chapter will discuss one play. There will be a summary of the plot and extensive quotations from the speeches or dialogue to put in context the legal allusions or metaphors and the use of legal procedures to structure the movement of the play.[3] With a few notable exceptions (*A Midsummer Night's Dream* and *Measure for Measure*), the law in Shakespeare's plays was almost always consistent with the law in late Tudor and early Stuart England regardless of the setting in time and place of the play. Shakespeare's friend and rival Ben Jonson said of him: "He was not of an age, but for all time." There is no question that this accounts for the great appeal of Shakespeare down through the ages.

But the legal system Shakespeare knew was that of a particular time and place. For example, in Shakespeare's time, criminal defendants accused of a felony or treason were not allowed to be represented at trial by a lawyer. This is why Buckingham defends himself in his treason trial in *Henry VIII*. Also, marriage is central to many of the comedies. The law of marriage in Shakespeare's time was confused and evolving. It was much different from that of our own day.

Given the pervasiveness of legal references and metaphors in the plays, I hope that even the serious Shakespearean scholar may gain new insights and a better understanding of the legal landscape in Shakespeare's England.

Nineteen plays are discussed, more or less in the chronological order scholars generally think Shakespeare wrote them. This will allow me to follow Shakespeare's use of legal metaphors and legal structures as they progress over time. Because the three *Henry VI* plays were written close together in time, I've arranged them in

---

[3] Unless otherwise noted, all quotations are from *Shakespeare Online*, https://www.shakespeare-online.com.

historical chronological order, although *Henry VI, Part 2* may have been written first. I do not apologize for the lengthy quotations from the plays. I agree with Shakespeare scholar Emma Smith, who has said: "The language of the plays and poems *is the thing* itself, not a vehicle for something else, and therefore it is forever irreducible to paraphrase."[4]

Focusing upon Shakespeare's language itself also shows his incomparable insight into the psychological and moral inner life of his characters as well as their actions. Each chapter stands on its own and can serve as a guide to the reader of the play, or one who is about to attend a live performance.

In the end, I hope the reader will not think the effort has been much ado about nothing.

---

[4] Emma Smith, *The Cambridge Introduction to Shakespeare* (Cambridge University Press, 2007), 72.

CHAPTER 1

HENRY VI, PART 1

*H*enry VI, Part 1, was one of the earliest (if not the earliest) of the history plays written by Shakespeare. It contains far fewer legal allusions and metaphors than any of the other history plays. Indeed, this might be support for the argument made by many nineteenth century critics that very little of the play should be attributed to the pen of Shakespeare. There seems to be scholarly agreement that Shakespeare wrote the Temple-garden scene and the beautiful speeches leading up to the death of the character Talbot. Other portions of the play may have been written by unknown collaborators.

In any event, it is clear that Shakespeare and his collaborators took many liberties with historical facts to compress the action for dramatic effect. For example, England's loss of the towns of Paris, Rouen, and Orleans did not occur until years after the death of Henry V in 1422.

The play is Shakespeare's telling of the origins of the political chaos known as the Wars of the Roses that he brilliantly depicted in the two other *Henry VI* plays. Shortly after World War II, Harold Goddard would write prophetically of Shakespeare's Henry VI: "Shakespeare seems to have sensed very early—what the world at large has still to learn—that he who cannot rule himself is not entitled to rule a city, still less a nation."[5]

---

[5] Harold C. Goddard, *The Meaning of Shakespeare* (University of Chicago Press), Vol I, 30.

When King Henry VI was born, England and France had been at war for almost one hundred years. King Philip IV of France had three sons who died without producing a male heir. The Hundred Years War began when England's King Edward III, whose mother was the daughter of Philip IV, declared himself to be King of France.

Initially the war went very well for the English, with smashing victories at Crecy and Poitiers. As a result of the peace treaty after Poitiers, England acquired large swaths of land in southwestern France. In Edward's later years, the war went badly and English possessions in France were reduced to only the coastal towns of Calais, Bordeaux, and Bayonne.

Edward's great-grandson, King Henry V, fought the French at Harfleur and won the spectacular victory at Agincourt. He then conquered large portions of France, including Normandy, which had been lost by the English in the reign of King John (1199–1216). After months of negotiation with Charles VI of France, the Treaty of Troyes in 1420 recognized Henry V as heir to the French throne, and he married Charles's daughter, Catherine of Valois.

Everything seemed to point to the formation of a union between the kingdoms in the person of Henry V, although the disinherited Dauphine continued the war against English conquest. However, Henry V died two years later and was succeeded by his son, the infant King Henry VI. Shakespeare's play begins with the funeral procession of King Henry V.

[Dead March. Enter the Funeral of KING HENRY the Fifth, attended on by Dukes of BEDFORD, Regent of France; Gloucester, Protector; and EXETER, Earl of Warwick, the BISHOP OF WINCHESTER, Heralds, &c]

BEDFORD   Hung be the heavens with black, yield day
to night!
Comets, importing change of times and states,
Brandish your crystal tresses in the sky,
And with them scourge the bad revolting stars

That have consented unto Henry's death!
King Henry the Fifth, too famous to live long!
England ne'er lost a king of so much worth.

GLOUCESTER   England ne'er had a king until his time.
Virtue he had, deserving to command:
His brandish'd sword did blind men with his beams:
His arms spread wider than a dragon's wings;
His sparking eyes, replete with wrathful fire,
More dazzled and drove back his enemies
Than mid-day sun fierce bent against their faces.
What should I say? his deeds exceed all speech:
He ne'er lift up his hand but conquered.
(Henry VI, Part 1, 1.1.1–16)

Humphrey, Duke of Gloucester, the younger brother of Henry V, was the son of Henry IV and the grandson of John of Gaunt and his first wife, Blanche of Lancaster.

Henry Beaufort, Bishop of Winchester, was the illegitimate son of John of Gaunt and his mistress Katherine Swynford, who became his third wife. Their bastard children were eventually legitimized by an act of Parliament, but Henry IV added an addendum to the act that excluded them from the line of succession to the throne. Taking the name of Beaufort after a castle and lordship in France owned by Gaunt, they were a force in English politics for the next century. The Tudors would claim their right to inherit the throne as descendants of Margaret Beaufort, daughter of John Beaufort, Duke of Somerset.

Although a lawyer, Henry Beaufort spent his entire career in the church. He was also Chancellor under Henry IV and Henry V. Immensely wealthy, he made large loans to the Exchequer. His European ambitions to be pope were never realized.

Gloucester and Winchester were bitter political rivals and dominated the Regency Council during Henry's minority. The quarrels of young Henry's older relatives overlay the conflict between the

English and the French. Gloucester headed the court faction that favored aggressive prosecution of the war against the French. Winchester and the Duke of Bedford led the faction that favored making peace.

Shortly after the play begins, Gloucester and the Bishop of Winchester erupt into a vicious quarrel as Henry V's casket is led to the church. The Bishop attributes the success of Henry V to the prayers of the church. Gloucester attributes his death to the lack of prayer because Winchester wanted only an "effeminate prince" (1.1.35) who could be controlled by the ambitious Bishop.

In London, the men at arms of Gloucester and Winchester brawl on the streets in front of the Tower. When Gloucester and his men arrive at the Tower to survey the weapons stored there, Winchester and his men bar Gloucester from entering. Their men fight until the Mayor of London arrives and has his officer read the riot act.

MAYOR   Naught rests for me in this tumultuous strife
But to make open proclamation:
Come, officer; as loud as e'er thou canst,
Cry.

OFFICER   All manner of men assembled here in arms this day
against God's peace and the king's, we charge and
command you, in his highness' name, to repair to
your several dwelling-places; and not to wear,
handle, or use any sword, weapon, or dagger,
henceforward, upon pain of death.

GLOUCESTER   Cardinal, I'll be no breaker of the law:
But we shall meet, and break our minds at large.

BISHOP OF WINCHESTER   Gloucester, we will meet; to thy cost,
be sure.

(1.3.70–81)

In a separate quarrel, Suffolk and Somerset take sides against Richard Plantagenet (soon to be Duke of York). They began by arguing over some point of law in the Temple Hall of the Inns of Court. They then take their argument out into the Temple Garden where the two sides choose the red (Lancaster) and the white rose (York) as badges of their allegiance.

London. The Temple-garden.
[Enter the Earls of Somerset, Suffolk, and Warwick; Richard Plantagenet, VERNON, and another Lawyer]

RICHARD PLANTAGENET   Great lords and gentlemen, what
means this silence?
Dare no man answer in a case of truth?

SUFFOLK   Within the Temple-hall we were too loud;
The garden here is more convenient.

RICHARD PLANTAGENET   Then say at once if I maintain'd the
truth;
Or else was wrangling Somerset in the error?

SUFFOLK   Faith, I have been a truant in the law,
And never yet could frame my will to it;
And therefore frame the law unto my will.

SOMERSET   Judge you, my Lord of Warwick, then, between us.
                    (2.4.1–10)

Suffolk is definitely in the "might makes right" camp. Warwick also demurs. "But in these nice sharp quillets of the law, / Good faith, I am no wiser than a daw" (2.4.17–18).

The word "law" is Norse, not Anglo-Saxon. It is one of many words that entered the English language as a result of the Viking invasions of the tenth century, and the Danish occupation of much of northern, eastern, and southern England. This area was known as the Danelaw. We are never told what the question of law was that started the argument. This does not matter, because this is not an occasion to decide who is right about the law; it is one for picking sides to the political quarrel that will become the Wars of the Roses.

RICHARD PLANTAGENET   Since you are tongue-tied and
    so loath to speak,
    In dumb significants proclaim your thoughts:
    Let him that is a true-born gentleman
    And stands upon the honour of his birth,
    If he suppose that I have pleaded truth,
    From off this brier pluck a white rose with me.

SOMERSET   Let him that is no coward nor no flatterer,
    But dare maintain the party of the truth,
    Pluck a red rose from off this thorn with me.

WARWICK   I love no colours, and without all colour
    Of base insinuating flattery
    I pluck this white rose with Plantagenet.

SUFFOLK   I pluck this red rose with young Somerset
    And say withal I think he held the right.
                (2.4.25–38)

Somerset refuses to continue the argument on the grounds that Richard is a mere yeoman because his father was convicted of treason (a subplot in Shakespeare's *Henry V*) and forfeited his title and any claim by his heirs to nobility.

SOMERSET   By him that made me, I'll maintain my words
    On any plot of ground in Christendom.
    Was not thy father, Richard Earl of Cambridge,
    For treason executed in our late king's days?

And, by his treason, stand'st not thou attainted,
Corrupted, and exempt from ancient gentry?
His trespass yet lives guilty in thy blood;
And, till thou be restored, thou art a yeoman.

RICHARD PLANTAGENET   My father was attached,
    not attainted,
Condemn'd to die for treason, but no traitor;
And that I'll prove on better men than Somerset,
Were growing time once ripen'd to my will.

                    (2.4.89–100)

Richard Plantagenet's father, the Earl of Cambridge, was executed
for plotting to kill King Henry V. He was the subject of an Act of
Attainder by Parliament which led to the confiscation of his lands.
The conviction for treason also caused "corruption of the blood,"
which disinherited his descendants as well. Somerset and his parti-
sans depart in anger. Warwick declares; "And here I prophesy: this
brawl to-day, / Grown to this faction in the Temple-garden, / Shall
send between the red rose and the white / A thousand souls to death
and deadly night" (2.4.125–28).

Thus, this quarrel in the Temple Garden over the obscure question of law and then as to Richard Plantagenet's right to inherit his
father's nobility has set the stage for the Wars of the Roses in the
next two plays of the first Henriad.

At this stage of the quarrel between the houses of Lancaster and
York, the red and white roses represent the opposing factions within
the court rather than rival claims to the throne. Warwick promises
that the next Parliament will restore Richard Plantagenet as Duke
of York. For whatever reason, Vernon and the other unnamed
lawyer have taken the side of the white rose; they then disappear
from the play except for a brief brawl at court between Vernon and
one of Somerset's men.

The play continues with the quarrelling of the lords at court and
the war in France. The tide turns against the English when Joan La

Pucelle ("Joan the Maid," known to us as Joan of Arc) arrives on the scene to lead the French forces. Suffolk captures Margaret of Anjou and is instantly captivated by her. But he already has a wife. Suffolk proposes marriage between Margaret and Henry, while making it clear to her that she can be both Queen of England and his lover. She agrees to his proposal.

Joan La Pucelle is captured by the Duke of York. Without the formality of a trial, York condemns Joan as a witch and orders her burnt at the stake. Joan seeks to avoid execution by claiming that she is not the daughter of a shepherd, but of noble birth. Her father, the shepherd, denies this. Joan declares that she is a virgin and will be avenged by heaven. York is unmoved. Joan is desperate and starts to change her story.

YORK   Ay, ay: away with her to execution!

WARWICK   And hark ye, sirs; because she is a maid,
Spare for no faggots, let there be enow:
Place barrels of pitch upon the fatal stake,
That so her torture may be shortened.

JOAN LA PUCELLE   Will nothing turn your unrelenting hearts?
Then, Joan, discover thine infirmity,
That warranteth by law to be thy privilege.
I am with child, ye bloody homicides:
Murder not then the fruit within my womb,
Although ye hale me to a violent death.

YORK   Now heaven forfend! the holy maid with child!

WARWICK   The greatest miracle that e'er ye wrought:
Is all your strict preciseness come to this?

YORK   She and the Dauphin have been juggling:
I did imagine what would be her refuge.

WARWICK   Well, go to; we'll have no bastards live;
    Especially since Charles must father it.
(5.4.55–72)

No, Joan declares. The father was the Duke of Alencon. Then she says it was Reignier, King of Naples. Joan is claiming the privilege at common law for a pregnant woman condemned to death to have her execution delayed until the birth of her child. York is not moved. "Strumpet, thy words condemn thy brat and thee: / Use no entreaty, for it is in vain" (5.4.85–86). Joan is led off to be burned at the stake. The French see Joan as a heroine and savior. The English see her as a whore and a witch. Notably, Shakespeare expresses no moral judgment upon Joan.

The brave English warriors Bedford, Salisbury, and Talbot are now dead as a result of fighting the French. The fate of the English cause is now in the hands of squabbling politicians.

In the English camp, Winchester enters with letters from the King proclaiming that the war is over. York is outraged that after so many men have been lost the war is concluded by an "effeminate peace" (5.4.108).

Suffolk returns to England. He gives King Henry such "wondrous rare description" (5.5.1) of Margaret that he agrees to the marriage if the Protector Gloucester will give his consent. Gloucester is not enthusiastic.

GLOUCESTER   So should I give consent to flatter sin.
    You know, my lord, your highness is betroth'd
    Unto another lady of esteem:
    How shall we then dispense with that contract,
    And not deface your honour with reproach?
(5.5.26–30)

This contract of marriage with another would in that time be a legal impediment to marriage with Margaret. Suffolk brushes the objection aside on the grounds that the other is just a "poor earl's daughter" (5.5.35). Exeter argues that the daughter of the Earl of Armagnac will come with "a liberal dower" (5.5.47). Margaret is the daughter of the impoverished King of Naples and Jerusalem. But Suffolk prevails with Henry after expressing an uncharacteristic attitude toward the importance of dowries in royal marriage alliances.

SUFFOLK   A dower, my lords! disgrace not so your king,
   That he should be so abject, base and poor,
   To choose for wealth and not for perfect love.
   Henry is able to enrich his queen
   And not seek a queen to make him rich:
   So worthless peasants bargain for their wives,
   As market-men for oxen, sheep, or horse.
   Marriage is a matter of more worth
   Than to be dealt in by attorneyship;
   Not whom we will, but whom his grace affects,
   Must be companion of his nuptial bed.
                 (5.5.49–59)

The impulsive and immature King is infatuated by Suffolk's description of Margaret and agrees to the disastrous marriage. He tells Suffolk to go to France: "Agree to any covenants, and procure / That Lady Margaret do vouchsafe to come / To cross the seas to England and be crown'd / King Henry's faithful and anointed queen" (5.5.88–91).

Gloucester laments: "Ay, grief, I fear me, both at first and last" (5.5.103).

In the event, Gloucester was right to fear grief, both at first and last, as we will see in the next two *Henry VI* plays. Thus, the play ends. But not the war between England and France, and the conflict between the Houses of York and Lancaster.

To me, the fictional scene in Temple Garden where the red and white roses become emblems of the York and Lancastrian factions in the Wars of the Roses is an illustration of the importance of the law and legal institutions such as the Inns of Court in Shakespeare's work.

In the sixteenth century, the royal courts sat in Westminster Hall in the suburb of Westminster just west of London. Four times a year at term time, lawyers came to Westminster to attend the royal courts—and they needed somewhere to stay. In the western suburbs of London near Westminster were great town houses of the magnates who attended the courts and Parliament. A number of these great houses off Holborn, Fleet Street, and Chancery Lane were acquired by societies of lawyers and became known as the Inns of Court. They apparently began as places to eat, sleep, and hold chambers. The Inns of Court did not hold royal charters and were never incorporated.

The origins of the Inns as educational institutions are rather obscure. This may have started as a means of bringing in more revenue. By the late fourteenth century, the Inns of Court (completely independent of Oxford and Cambridge Universities) were functioning as law schools for attorneys practicing in the common law courts. By the sixteenth century, they were sometimes referred to as the Third University of England.

When Shakespeare was writing his plays, the Inns of Court were at the height of their glory. The most important of the Inns were the Inner Temple, the Middle Temple, Gray's Inn, and Lincoln's Inn. The serjeants had their own Serjeant's Inn. The great halls of the Inns of Court were important venues for the performance of Shakespeare's plays.

The young men of Shakespeare's day who came to the Inns of Court were the beneficiaries of the radical expansion of humanistic education in the grammar schools and universities of England. This humanistic education involved a profound shift in emphasis away from scholastic logic and toward rhetoric and classical literature. In the grammar schools of the Tudor period, the young scholars would learn the rhetorical skills needed for participation in the legal training provided by the Inns of Court.

In a Tudor grammar school like that attended by Shakespeare, the students would have studied logic, grammar, and rhetoric (including the ability to argue both sides of a case), as well as the classical authors of Greece and Rome. They would have read Terence, Cicero, Sallust, Virgil, and Ovid's *Metamorphoses*. The works of Cicero were particularly important because of their use in the grammar schools for the teaching of Latin grammar.

The poet and dramatist Ben Jonson described the Inns of Court as "the noblest nurseries of humanity, and liberty, in the kingdom." Many sons of the landed gentry attended the Inns of Court without any intention of practicing law, but to prepare them for managing their estates or business activities. Typically, they would be in residence for only a couple of years. Attendance at an Inn of Court was considered good preparation for later service as a local Justice of the Peace, such as Shakespeare's foolish Justice Shallow, whose boasts of brawls with trade apprentices were not unrealistic.

These educated young gentlemen with money and leisure were prime candidates for filling Elizabethan playhouses. Play going was their favorite form of recreation. Unlike the dons of Oxford and Cambridge, the senior leaders (known as "benchers") of the Inns of Court did not discourage their students from attending plays. Shakespeare expected them to be in the audience and to understand his legal allusions and metaphors. Well-versed in the rhetoric and repartee of the Inns of Court moots, they would have appreciated clever Shakespearean dialogue and wordplay.

In the taverns and ale houses that surrounded the theater district, they could also be counted upon to provide lively company to young Will Shakespeare. Holiday revels at the Inns of Court included banquets, elaborate masques, and plays performed by members of the Inns and public companies of players such as the Lord Chamberlain's Men. In the 1594 holiday revels at Gray's Inn, *The Comedy of Errors* was performed. In 1602, the Middle Temple featured *Twelfth Night* in its hall during the holidays.

Lawyers associated with the Inns of Court played a significant role in the cultural and literary life of sixteenth century London. Thomas Sackville, along with Thomas Norton (both of the Inner Temple) wrote *Gorboduc*, the first great Elizabethan tragedy in blank verse. Norton translated John Calvin's *Institutes of the Christian Religion* into English. Sir Thomas North of Lincoln's Inn published the first English translation of Plutarch's *Lives*, which Shakespeare brought to the stage in *Julius Caesar, Coriolanus, Timon of Athens*, and *Antony and Cleopatra*. Sir Thomas Elyot, who wrote the influential *The Boke Named the Governour*, was a member of the Middle Temple and had close connections to Sir Thomas More and Thomas Cromwell.

A collaborative of men from the Inns produced the influential *A Mirror for Magistrates* that documented the consequences of abandoning the rule of law. The dramatist Francis Beaumont, whose father was a Justice of the Court of Common Pleas, joined his two brothers in the Inner Temple; he composed theatrical productions for the Inner Temple and Gray's Inn. Later, he became well-known for his collaboration with John Fletcher in writing plays for the public theaters.

The playwright John Ford was admitted to Middle Temple where his great uncle, John Popham, Chief Justice of the King's Bench, was Treasurer. Thomas Lodge of Lincoln's Inn wrote erotic poetry and defended plays and the theaters against attacks from the Puritans. His *Rosalynde* was the source for Shakespeare's *As You Like It*. Jasper Heywood of Gray's Inn translated into English three of the plays of the Roman author Seneca.

In addition to serving as Henry VIII's Lord Chancellor, Sir Thomas More of Lincoln's Inn wrote *Utopia* and had plays performed at his estate in Chelsea. In his *Utopia*, there were few laws and lawyers were banished. As Chancellor, More made no significant proposals for law reform as might have been expected from the author of *Utopia*. His biography of Richard III (generally considered to be mostly Tudor propaganda) was Shakespeare's main source for his play *Richard III*. John Donne of Lincoln's Inn was one of the great poets of the age.

There was an enormous increase in the number of practicing attorneys during Shakespeare's lifetime. By the mid-sixteenth century, the law was supplanting the church as the means by which an able young man without a title of nobility could seek wealth and power. The civil lawyers educated at Oxford and Cambridge practiced the civil, or canon law, in the conciliar and ecclesiastical courts. They were far exceeded in numbers, wealth, and prestige by the lawyers practicing in the common law courts.

The Inns of Court were the great gateway to upward mobility. Early in this period, the boundaries between the legal work performed by an attorney or solicitor and a barrister were ill-defined. By the middle of the sixteenth century, the leadership of the senior Inns of Court were excluding mere attorneys and solicitors from membership in the Inns. By the end of the sixteenth century, a call to the bar at an Inn of Court was a prerequisite to practice as a barrister in the central and circuit courts.

Eventually, the Inns prohibited their members from practicing as solicitors. By the end of Shakespeare's life, the modern distinction between barristers as advocates in court and solicitors was largely in place. In general, solicitors were the initial point of contact for the client. The solicitor worked up the case, and prepared a "brief" of the evidence and argument for the barrister to use in argument of the case in the royal courts such as the Court of Common Pleas and Court of Kings Bench.

The educational functions of the Inns did not survive the years of the Civil War (1642–1661) when admissions declined to almost nothing and the Inns virtually ceased to function. Efforts to resume the educational functions of the Inns after the Restoration were unsuccessful. The increased availability of legal textbooks and reports probably contributed to the collapse of the oral teaching traditions of the Inns. Apprenticeships then became the primary path to professional qualification for both barristers and solicitors.

CHAPTER 2

Henry VI, Part 2

The court of King Henry VI, son of Henry V and grandson of the mad King Charles VI of France, is a nest of political intrigue. The King is no longer a child, but merely childlike. Henry describes himself as surrounded by furious peers. He is an incompetent ruler, and his mental instability threatens to lead to political instability as well. Amid this turmoil, his uncle Humphrey, Duke of Gloucester, is the one beacon of loyalty to the King. He also stands in sharp contrast to Jack Cade, whom we met in the Introduction.

Gloucester embodies respect for the rule of law—even when it condemns his own wife. He is also a strong advocate for pursuing the war in France. Although the tide of the Hundred Years' War in France has turned against them, the English still hold Normandy, Maine, and Anjou in the north, as well as Calais and the area around Bordeaux in the southwest.

Suffolk, who is of the peace party, has negotiated a truce with the King of France. He has returned from France where he has married by proxy Lady Margaret Anjou, daughter of the impoverished King of Naples and niece of the King of France, to King Henry.

The play begins as Suffolk presents Margaret to Henry, who is delighted with her. He thanks God: "For thou hast given me in this beauteous face / A world of earthly blessings to my soul, / If sympathy of love unite our thoughts" (*Henry VI, Part 2*, 1.1.21–23). Margaret is to come with no dowry, which is the money or property

15

paid to the husband by the bride's family. For her, England is to give up Anjou and Maine in France. During a truce, the Duke of York is to be removed as regent of France. As the articles of the marriage contract are read, Gloucester knows that Suffolk has paid too heavy a price for Margaret's hand.

GLOUCESTER   Brave peers of England, pillars of the state,
    To you Duke Humphrey must unload his grief,
    Your grief, the common grief of all the land.
    What! did my brother Henry [*Henry V*] spend his youth,
    His valour, coin and people, in the wars?
    Did he so often lodge in open field,
    In winter's cold and summer's parching heat,
    To conquer France, his true inheritance?
    And did my brother Bedford toil his wits,
    To keep by policy what Henry got?
    Have you yourselves, Somerset, Buckingham,
    Brave York, Salisbury, and victorious Warwick,
    Received deep scars in France and Normandy ... ?
    And shall these labours and these honours die?
    Shall Henry's conquest, Bedford's vigilance,
    Your deeds of war and all our counsel die?
    O peers of England, shameful is this league!
    Fatal this marriage, cancelling your fame,
    Blotting your names from books of memory,
    Razing the characters of your renown,
    Defacing monuments of conquer'd France,
    Undoing all, as all had never been!
                (1.1.75–88, 96–100)

Gloucester has other troubles known and unknown to him. His wife Eleanor is ambitious to be Queen and is vexed that he will not cooperate because of his "base and humble mind" (1.2.62). Unknown to Gloucester, she enlists a conjuror to tell her the fate of Henry VI. In Shakespeare's day, this sort of prophesy about the fate of the King had been prohibited by Henry VIII, Edward VI, and Queen Elizabeth.

There is a tremendous conjuring scene in which a Spirit arises to tell the fate of the King: "The duke yet lives that Henry shall depose; / But him outlive, and die a violent death" (1.4.31–32). The conjuror writes this down on paper. This is the sort of ambiguous prophecy we will later encounter in *Macbeth*. Is the Duke to depose Henry? Or is the King to depose the Duke? Who outlives whom? Who dies a violent death?

The conjuration is interrupted by the Duke of York, who has learned of the affair. He has Eleanor arrested for imagining the death of the King. York reads from the paper: "The duke yet lives, that Henry shall depose; / But him outlive, and die a violent death.' / Why, this is just '*Aio te, AEacida, Romanos vincere posse*" (1.4.60–63). The Latin phrase was the famous prophecy given by Apollo to the Greek King Pyrrhus before a battle with the Romans. It is ambiguous because it can mean he "shall conquer the Romans" or "the Romans shall conquer him." Pyrrhus heard what he wanted to hear. He fought the Romans and won the famous Pyrrhic victory whereby he won the battle but lost the war. Shakespeare does not call this an "equivocation" here. But he will by the time we get to *Macbeth*, and his audience will understand the word.

Gloucester and Henry Beaufort, Cardinal of Winchester, continue their quarrels. Gloucester was popular with the people who came to him seeking redress of grievances: "What though the common people favour him, / Calling him 'Humphrey, the good Duke of Gloucester' " (1.1.158–60). Suffolk and Cardinal Beaufort are bent upon supplanting Gloucester as Protector of the Realm. Beaufort accuses Gloucester of being disloyal to the King: "Consider, lords, he is the next of blood, / And heir apparent to the English crown" (1.1.151–52).

Shakespeare is a little off here. An "heir apparent" is one who succeeds to his kinsman's estate simply by outliving him. An "heir presumptive" is one whose inheritance could be defeated by some other event such as the birth of a child to the kinsman. Gloucester is an heir presumptive because his claim to the throne could be defeated by the birth of a male child to the King.

Buckingham and Somerset are allies of the Cardinal. The Duke of York agrees to join forces with Salisbury (not the same one who was killed in *Henry VI, Part 1*) and his son Warwick. When he is alone on stage, York reveals to us his true ambition is to take the Crown from Henry: "A day will come when York shall claim his own; / And therefore I will take the Nevils' parts / And make a show of love to proud Duke Humphrey, / And, when I spy advantage, claim the crown, / For that's the golden mark I seek to hit" (1.1.240–45). The ambitious York will attempt to reach out and grab power out of the chaos created by Henry's feckless reign. Suffolk and Cardinal Beaufort have the active support of Queen Margaret—both in opposition to Gloucester and for peace with France.

The nobles quarrel over who should be regent in France. Margaret objects to Gloucester continuing as Protector after Henry has come of age. Suffolk accuses Gloucester of mismanaging the war in France and affairs in England. Buckingham accuses him of abusing his power to administer justice: "Thy cruelty in execution / Upon offenders, hath exceeded law, / And left thee to the mercy of the law" (1.3.130–32). He is saying Gloucester should be impeached for abusing the law.

Gloucester is outraged at these charges and storms off the stage. When he returns, he offers to submit his case to the law: "As for your spiteful false objections, / Prove them, and I lie open to the law" (1.3.153–54). Gloucester is challenging his accusers to present evidence against him in an impeachment trial. If convicted, he agrees to submit to the judgment and punishment of the law.

The argument over who is to be Regent in France is interrupted when Suffolk produces Peter, an apprentice who has accused Horner, his master, of "high treason" for saying that York is the true King of England. Suffolk: "His words were these: that Richard, Duke of York, / Was rightful heir unto the English crown / And that your majesty was a usurper" (1.3.181–83). York urges the

King to subject the master to "all the rigor of the law" (1.3.194).
The inept King turns to Gloucester to pronounce judgment in
the case.

KING HENRY VI   Uncle, what shall we say to this in law?

GLOUCESTER   This doom, my lord, if I may judge:
    Let Somerset be regent over the French,
    Because in York this breeds suspicion:
    And let these have a day appointed them
    For single combat in convenient place,
    For he hath witness of his servant's malice:
    This is the law, and this Duke Humphrey's doom.

SOMERSET   I humbly thank your royal majesty.

HORNER   And I accept the combat willingly.

PETER   Alas, my lord, I cannot fight; for God's sake, pity
    my case. The spite of man prevaileth against me. O
    Lord, have mercy upon me! I shall never be able to
    fight a blow. O Lord, my heart!

GLOUCESTER   Sirrah, or you must fight, or else be hang'd.

KING HENRY VI   Away with them to prison; and the day
    of combat shall be the last of the next month. Come,
    Somerset, we'll see thee sent away.
                    (1.3.202–19)

Gloucester's judgment is that the apprentice and his master will
have a trial by battle to see who is telling the truth. Trial by combat
was a method of trying an accused person or of settling a dispute
by a personal fight between the two parties involved, or, in some
circumstances, their permitted champions. It was introduced to
England after the Norman Conquest and abolished in 1819.

When "an appeal of felony" was made, the accuser and the accused had to fight in person. If the appellant prevailed in an appeal of felony or treason and the appellee remained alive, he was immediately executed by hanging. However, if the appellee defeated his opponent, or if he were able to fend off his opponent from sunrise to sunset, he would go free. If the appellant said, "I am vanquished" and gave up the fight, he was to be declared infamous, deprived of the privileges of a freeman, and was liable for damages to his successful opponent.

Trial by battle was not allowed between persons of different social rank. Women, priests, minors, and those who were lame, blind, or over sixty years of age were exempt and could be represented by champions.

Before we witness the low comedy of this trial by combat, Gloucester's wife is caught by York using witchcraft to assist her ambitions to have her husband placed upon the throne of England.

In the meantime, the King's party has gone into the country for the sport of falconry. Gloucester and the Cardinal continue their quarrels and agree to a secret duel. This high-level intrigue is unexpectedly interrupted by cries of "A miracle! a miracle!" (2.1.69). The King's party is told that a man blind since birth has received his sight at St. Alban's shrine. The feckless, naive Henry immediately accepts the report that there has been a miracle: "Now, God be praised, that to believing souls / Gives light in darkness, comfort in despair!" (2.1.74–75). But Gloucester is skeptical, and his suspicion increases as the formerly blind man is brought forward and questioned by the King.

[Enter the Mayor of Saint Alban's and his brethren, bearing Simpcox, between two in a chair, Simpcox's Wife following]

CARDINAL   Here comes the townsmen on procession,
To present your highness with the man.

KING HENRY VI   Great is his comfort in this earthly vale,
Although by his sight his sin be multiplied.

GLOUCESTER   Stand by, my masters: bring him near the king;
    His highness' pleasure is to talk with him.

KING HENRY VI   Good fellow, tell us here the circumstance,
    That we for thee may glorify the Lord.
    What, hast thou been long blind and now restored?

SIMPCOX   Born blind, an't please your grace.

WIFE   Ay, indeed, was he.

SUFFOLK   What woman is this?

WIFE   His wife, an't like your worship.

GLOUCESTER   Hadst thou been his mother, thou couldst have
    better told.
                        (2.1.76–90)

Here we see Gloucester's talent for poking holes in phony stories. We learn that Simpcox is also lame because he (while blind)
has climbed up and fallen out of a plum tree. This sets the stage for
Gloucester's spectacularly successful cross-examination of Simpcox.
It is both a comic and a forensic masterpiece.

GLOUCESTER   A subtle knave! but yet it shall not serve.
    Let me see thine eyes: wink now: now open them:
    In my opinion yet thou seest not well.

SIMPCOX   Yes, master, clear as day, I thank God and Saint
    Alban.

GLOUCESTER   Say'st thou me so? What colour is this cloak of?

SIMPCOX   Red, master; red as blood.

GLOUCESTER   Why, that's well said. What colour is my
gown of?

SIMPCOX   Black, forsooth: coal-black as jet.

KING HENRY VI   Why, then, thou know'st what colour jet is of?

SUFFOLK   And yet, I think, jet did he never see.

GLOUCESTER   But cloaks and gowns, before this day, a many.

WIFE   Never, before this day, in all his life.

GLOUCESTER   Tell me, sirrah, what's my name?

SIMPCOX   Alas, master, I know not.

GLOUCESTER   What's his name?

SIMPCOX   I know not.

GLOUCESTER   Nor his?

SIMPCOX   No, indeed, master.

GLOUCESTER   What's thine own name?

SIMPCOX   Saunder Simpcox, an if it please you, master.

GLOUCESTER   Then, Saunder, sit there, the lyingest knave in
Christendom. If thou hadst been born blind, thou
mightest as well have known all our names as thus to
name the several colours we do wear. Sight may
distinguish of colours, but suddenly to nominate them
all, it is impossible. My lords, Saint Alban here

hath done a miracle; and would ye not think his
cunning to be great, that could restore this cripple
to his legs again?

SIMPCOX   O master, that you could!

GLOUCESTER   My masters of Saint Alban's, have you not bea-
dles in your town, and things called whips?

MAYOR   Yes, my lord, if it please your grace.

GLOUCESTER   Then send for one presently.

MAYOR   Sirrah, go fetch the beadle hither straight.

[Exit an Attendant]

GLOUCESTER   Now fetch me a stool hither by and by. Now, sirrah,
if you mean to save yourself from whipping, leap me
over this stool and run away.

SIMPCOX   Alas, master, I am not able to stand alone:
You go about to torture me in vain.
[Enter a Beadle with whips]

GLOUCESTER   Well, sir, we must have you find your legs. Sirrah
beadle, whip him till he leap over that same stool.

BEADLE   I will, my lord. Come on, sirrah; off with your
doublet quickly.

SIMPCOX   Alas, master, what shall I do? I am not able to stand.

*[After the Beadle hath hit him once, he leaps over the stool
and runs away; and they follow and cry, 'A miracle!']*

KING HENRY VI   O God, seest Thou this, and bearest so long?

QUEEN MARGARET   It made me laugh to see the villain run.
(2.1.119–165)

This trial of Saunder Simpcox is the first of an extraordinary number of trials and trial-like scenes in this play.

At this moment of triumph for the Protector, word comes that his wife has been accused of treason by witchcraft against King Henry. Buckingham tells the King that Eleanor and other conjurors have been "apprehended in the fact" (2.1.182), meaning they were caught in the act of committing the crime of using witchcraft to predict the life and death of the King and "other of your highness' privy-council" (2.1.185).

In the sixteenth and early seventeenth centuries, witchcraft was an ecclesiastical offense punishable by burning at the stake as well as a crime at common law. In response to the taunts of Queen Margaret, Gloucester nobly reaffirms his loyalty and his commitment to the rule of law.

QUEEN MARGARET   Gloucester, see here the tainture of thy nest.
And look thyself be faultless, thou wert best.

GLOUCESTER   Madam, for myself, to heaven I do appeal,
How I have loved my king and commonweal:
And, for my wife, I know not how it stands;
Sorry I am to hear what I have heard:
Noble she is, but if she have forgot
Honour and virtue and conversed with such
As, like to pitch, defile nobility,
I banish her my bed and company
And give her as a prey to law and shame,
That hath dishonour'd Gloucester's honest name.

KING HENRY VI   Well, for this night we will repose us here:

To-morrow toward London back again,
To look into this business thoroughly
And call these foul offenders to their answers
And poise the cause in justice' equal scales,
Whose beam stands sure, whose rightful cause prevails.

(2.1.198–215)

When Gloucester says if she is guilty he will "banish her my bed and company" he is referring to a divorce *a mensa et thoro*, or divorce from board and bed, which would not terminate the marriage. Legally, he would have to obtain such a separation from a church court. Under William the Conqueror, jurisdiction over spiritual matters was taken from the local courts and given to the church courts such as the consistory courts presided over by the bishops. The church courts had jurisdiction over moral behavior and religious conformity. This jurisdiction extended to the collection of tithes, marriage and bastardy, inheritance of personal property, and punishment of moral offenses, such as fornication and adultery.

Under canon law, there could be no divorce if a couple were validly married. The church courts could grant an annulment of a marriage, a divorce *a vinculo matrimony*, if they found an "impediment" to the marriage. This meant that the marriage was *void ab initio* and the parties were free to remarry.

We will return shortly to Gloucester and his marital and political troubles.

As we will see throughout the history plays, Shakespeare and his audiences were intensely interested in the question of how to resolve disputes over competing claims to royal sovereignty and power. The dreadful Wars of the Roses had ended within the memory of the generation born just before Shakespeare.

In Act II of the play, York sets the stage for the Wars of the Roses when he lays out his claim to be the rightful heir to the throne of England, as opposed to Henry and the House of Lancaster. York makes this claim to the preeminent members of the Neville family: the Earl of Salisbury and his son, the Earl of Warwick. York bases his claim to the throne upon his descent from Lionel, the third son of Edward III. Henry VI was the great-grandson of the fourth son of Edward III. York claims that Henry IV had usurped the Crown from Richard II and his heirs.

This account of the descent of the Duke of York is historically accurate and gave him a claim to the Crown under English law—if one disregards the strict application of the law of primogeniture. York is making a claim as a descendant of Lionel's daughter.

Warwick agrees that York is his "rightful sovereign" (2.2.62). York urges the Nevilles to keep "silent secrecy" (2.2.69) as to his claim to the throne until Gloucester's powers have been destroyed and the way cleared for him to claim the throne.

As is seen throughout the history plays, Shakespeare's underlying constitutional theory of sovereignty is one of strictly hereditary succession. York claims the throne as his inheritance. He does not appeal to the will of the people or the Council or Parliament. York is not yet ready to openly claim the Crown: "We thank you, lords. But I am not your king / Till I be crown'd and that my sword be stain'd / With heart blood of the house of Lancaster" (2.2.65–67). However, the stage is set for the bloody Wars of the Roses between the Houses of York and Lancaster that Shakespeare will chronicle in the history plays up through the reign and downfall of Richard III.

The first stage of the fulfillment of York's prophesy occurs off stage when Gloucester's wife is tried and convicted of treason by witchcraft. Her sentence is then pronounced by the King.

KING HENRY VI   Stand forth, Dame Eleanor Cobham,
Gloucester's wife:
In sight of God and us, your guilt is great:
Receive the sentence of the law for sins
Such as by God's book are adjudged to death.
You four [*Eleanor's accomplices*], from hence to prison back again;
From thence unto the place of execution:
The witch in Smithfield shall be burn'd to ashes,

And you three shall be strangled on the gallows.
You, madam, for you are more nobly born,
Despoiled of your honour in your life,
Shall, after three days' open penance done,
Live in your country here in banishment,
With Sir John Stanley, in the Isle of Man.

DUCHESS   Welcome is banishment; welcome were my death.

GLOUCESTER   Eleanor, the law, thou see'st, hath judged thee:
I cannot justify whom the law condemns.
[*Exeunt* DUCHESS *and other prisoners, guarded*]
Mine eyes are full of tears, my heart of grief.
Ah, Humphrey, this dishonour in thine age
Will bring thy head with sorrow to the ground!
I beseech your majesty, give me leave to go;
Sorrow would solace and mine age would ease.
                    (2.3.1–20)

This is an eloquent statement of Gloucester's submission to the rule of law. Even a person of his high rank and in the case of his own spouse must submit to the judgment of the law. The King commands him to give up his staff and the office of Protector, making him vulnerable to his enemies. King Henry loses a wise and prudent counselor. His expectation that God will guide him through the political quagmire that is his court is predictably disastrous.

Shakespeare then escapes from the high-level court intrigue to give us the trial by combat between the armorer and his apprentice. But it is more like trial by farce. Horner's neighbors ply him with drink until he is too drunk to fight. Incredibly, Peter then strikes him a lucky blow with a club and kills him. Clueless, King Henry proclaims God's justice: "Go, take hence that traitor from our sight; / For his death we do perceive his guilt: / And God in justice hath revealed to us / The truth and innocence of this poor fellow" (2.3.95–98). Having a serious charge of treason determined in a drunken brawl does not inspire confidence in English justice.

It gets worse.

A Parliament is convened at Bury St Edmonds. Gloucester, not suspecting treachery, is late. The Queen, Suffolk, York, and the Cardinal continue to scheme against Gloucester and denounce him as a traitor. Part of their specious claim is that he has subverted the law. Cardinal: "Did he not, contrary to form of law, / Devise strange deaths for small offences done?" (3.1.58–59). Henry declares his belief in Gloucester's innocence: "Our kinsman Gloucester is as innocent / From meaning treason to our royal person / As is the sucking lamb or harmless dove" (3.1.70–72).

But when Gloucester arrives, contrary to the weak King's wishes, Suffolk, with the Queen's support, arrests him for high treason.

[Enter Gloucester]

GLOUCESTER   All happiness unto my lord the king!
Pardon, my liege, that I have stay'd so long.

SUFFOLK   Nay, Gloucester, know that thou art come too soon,
Unless thou wert more loyal than thou art:
I do arrest thee of high treason here.

GLOUCESTER   Well, Suffolk, thou shalt not see me blush
Nor change my countenance for this arrest:
A heart unspotted is not easily daunted.
The purest spring is not so free from mud
As I am clear from treason to my sovereign:
Who can accuse me? wherein am I guilty?

YORK   'Tis thought, my lord, that you took bribes of France,
And, being protector, stayed the soldiers' pay;
By means whereof his highness hath lost France.

(3.1.94–107)

Gloucester vigorously denies the charges that he has subverted the law. The spineless King stands by while Suffolk commits loyal Gloucester to the Cardinal to await his trial. After the tearful King leaves the stage, Margaret and the plotters decide on their next step. The Cardinal thinks they must find an excuse to have Gloucester convicted in a court of law: "That he should die is worthy policy; / But yet we want a colour for his death: / 'Tis meet he be condemn'd by course of law" (3.1.237–39).

Suffolk says the evidence against Gloucester is weak, that the King will support him, and that the "commons" (3.1.242) would rise up to save his life. They agree the only sure solution to achieve their ends is to have Gloucester murdered. The Cardinal: "And I'll provide his executioner" (3.1.278). The bloody Cardinal is as good as his word. He procures two murderers who smother Gloucester in his bed on the eve of his trial.

As the Lords gather in a room of state at Bury St Edmunds, King Henry sends Suffolk to summon Gloucester for his trial. It is clear that Henry intends Gloucester to have a fair trial by his peers the lords.

KING HENRY VI   Lords, take your places; and, I pray you all,
Proceed no straiter 'gainst our uncle Gloucester
Than from true evidence of good esteem
He be approved in practise culpable.
                    (3.2.19–22)

An "approver" was someone who had been indicted but not convicted of a crime, who then accuses by means of an appeal of felony an accomplice or coconspirator of also being involved in the crime. If that person was convicted, the approver would escape the death penalty in exchange for imprisonment or abjuring the realm. Henry is using the term "approved" loosely, as to say convicted.

The cynical and guilty Queen Margaret tells Henry: "Pray God he may acquit him of suspicion!" (3.2.25). Suffolk returns with the shocking news that Gloucester is dead in his bed. True to form, the spineless King responds by fainting. Suffolk and the Cardinal are immediately suspected of murder.

> *[Noise within. Enter Warwick, SALISBURY, and many Commons]*

WARWICK   It is reported, mighty sovereign,
That good Duke Humphrey traitorously is murder'd
By Suffolk and the Cardinal Beaufort's means.
The commons, like an angry hive of bees
That want their leader, scatter up and down
And care not who they sting in his revenge.
Myself have calm'd their spleenful mutiny,
Until they hear the order of his death.

KING HENRY VI   That he is dead, good Warwick, 'tis too true;
But how he died God knows, not Henry:
Enter his chamber, view his breathless corpse,
And comment then upon his sudden death.

WARWICK   That shall I do, my liege. Stay, Salisbury,
With the rude multitude till I return.

(3.2.123–36)

I think Warwick's reference to the "commons" is a reference to members of the House of Commons. In an earlier scene, a herald had summoned Gloucester "to his majesty's parliament, / Holden at Bury the first of this next month" (2.4.71–72).

According to Shakespeare's source, Parliament met in in 1447 in Bury St Edmunds. The country gentlemen, merchants, and professionals who made up the House of Commons were an increasingly influential political force. Bury St Edmunds was in the heart of Suffolk's territory. Gloucester's popularity with the commons would explain why Parliament did not meet in Westminster, near London. This would account for the proximity of influential commoners to the King at Bury St Edmunds. That there is no explicit reference to the House of Commons by Shakespeare may reflect concern about censorship in Tudor and early Stuart England with respect to "mutiny" against the king by Parliamentarians.

In the scene that follows, Shakespeare has Warwick return and report on the first forensic autopsy in English literature. His testimony will ring true to any lawyer who has ever prosecuted or defended a murder case. After viewing the body, Warwick tells the Lords that Gloucester was murdered.

WARWICK   Come hither, gracious sovereign, view this body.

KING HENRY VI   That is to see how deep my grave is made;
For with his soul fled all my worldly solace,
For seeing him I see my life in death.

WARWICK   As surely as my soul intends to live
With that dread King that took our state upon him
To free us from his father's wrathful curse,
I do believe that violent hands were laid
Upon the life of this thrice-famed duke.

SUFFOLK   A dreadful oath, sworn with a solemn tongue!
What instance gives Lord Warwick for his vow?

WARWICK   See how the blood is settled in his face.
Oft have I seen a timely-parted ghost,
Of ashy semblance, meagre, pale and bloodless,
Being all descended to the labouring heart;
Who, in the conflict that it holds with death,
Attracts the same for aidance 'gainst the enemy;
Which with the heart there cools and ne'er returneth
To blush and beautify the cheek again.
But see, his face is black and full of blood,
His eye-balls further out than when he lived,

Staring full ghastly like a strangled man;
His hair uprear'd, his nostrils stretched with struggling;
His hands abroad display'd, as one that grasp'd
And tugg'd for life and was by strength subdued:
Look, on the sheets his hair you see, is sticking;
His well-proportion'd beard made rough and rugged,
Like to the summer's corn by tempest lodged.
It cannot be but he was murder'd here;
The least of all these signs were probable.

SUFFOLK   Why, Warwick, who should do the duke to death?
Myself and Beaufort had him in protection;
And we, I hope, sir, are no murderers.

WARWICK   But both of you were vow'd Duke Humphrey's foes,
And you, forsooth, had the good duke to keep:
'Tis like you would not feast him like a friend;
And 'tis well seen he found an enemy.

QUEEN MARGARET   Then you, belike, suspect these noblemen
As guilty of Duke Humphrey's timeless death.

WARWICK   Who finds the heifer dead and bleeding fresh
And sees fast by a butcher with an axe,
But will suspect 'twas he that made the slaughter?
(3.2.150–191)

Warwick then asks the King to "view" the body. In the sixteenth century, the local coroner played an important role in initiating criminal charges in homicide cases. The coroner's first task was to "view" the body. The coroner would look at the body for signs of foul play. In effect, Warwick is asking Henry to make an inquest upon the cause of Gloucester's death.

As counsel for the prosecution, Warwick is magnificent in laying out the evidence that Gloucester has been murdered. Suffolk is outraged. Warwick and Suffolk draw their swords and are on the verge of mortal combat in the presence of Henry when Salisbury and the "commons" break in and demand the death or banishment of Suffolk. Suffolk is unrepentant: "'Tis like the commons, rude unpolish'd hinds, / Could send such message to their sovereign" (3.2.274–75).

The weak King is overwhelmed and banishes Suffolk. Margaret pleads for her lover but to no avail. For once, Henry stands firm. Left alone on the stage, Margaret and Suffolk part with eloquence and passion. On his way to the Continent, Suffolk is captured by pirates. The pirate captain accuses Suffolk of treason and orders him beheaded when he refuses to respond to the accusations. "O that I were a god, to shoot forth thunder / Upon these paltry, servile, abject drudges!" (4.1.108–09). Suffolk is then beheaded by the pirates. At the court, Cardinal Beaufort is repentant and dies in agony over his guilt in the murder of Gloucester.

It is after this breakdown of the rule of law among the highborn nobility that Shakespeare portrays the revolt of Jack Cade and the low-born mechanics and tenants of Kent. Cade was the fifteenth century equivalent of a populist demagogue. As I said in the Introduction, Shakespeare does a magnificent job of using Cade's rebellion to show the consequences of a total breakdown of the rule of law. In this, Shakespeare appears as a conservative supporter of the establishment. Certainly, he says nothing about the abuses of government under Henry VI that actually spurred the revolt, such as the forcible requisitioning of property from the common people to support the royal household and the subversion of the royal courts. Cade begins his speech to the mob by boasting of his own bravery and of the lower-class utopia he will create. Dick, the butcher of Ashford, provides a skeptical commentary:

CADE   I fear neither sword nor fire.

SMITH   [Aside] He need not fear the sword; for his coat is
    of proof.

DICK   [*Aside*] But methinks he should stand in fear of
  fire, being burnt i' the hand for stealing of sheep.

CADE   Be brave, then; for your captain is brave, and vows
  reformation. There shall be in England seven
  halfpenny loaves sold for a penny: the three-hooped
  pot; shall have ten hoops and I will make it felony
  to drink small beer: all the realm shall be in
  common; and in Cheapside shall my palfrey go to
  grass: and when I am king, as king I will be,–

ALL   God save your majesty!

CADE   I thank you, good people: there shall be no money;
  all shall eat and drink on my score; and I will
  apparel them all in one livery, that they may agree
  like brothers and worship me their lord.
      (4.2.56–67)

Dick the butcher says that Cade has been "burnt i' the hand for stealing of sheep." This is a reference to the peculiar English legal custom of "benefit of clergy." In the Middle Ages, the English secular courts were not allowed to impose capital punishment upon members of the clergy who committed a felony. A person who could read and write was presumed to be a member of the clergy, because almost everyone else was illiterate. The privilege was later extended to anyone who could read. The thief who could read (or recite from memory) a certain Bible verse (usually Psalm 51, Verse 1, the "neck verse") would have his thumb branded with a T to prevent him from claiming benefit of clergy more than once. Shakespeare's friend and rival Ben Johnson was branded with an M (probably manslaughter rather than murder) for killing a fellow actor in a duel.

Here, Dick the butcher is saying that Cade had been convicted of stealing sheep. He escaped hanging by invoking benefit of clergy and was branded as a thief. Under the early common law, felonies were crimes involving moral turpitude, that is, those which violated the moral standards of a community. Later, however, crimes that did not involve moral turpitude became included in the definition of a felony. All felonies were punished by hanging or other forms of capital punishment. Under Cade's rule, private property is to be abolished.

Wearing "one livery" is a reference to the sumptuary laws which regulated the fabrics and types of clothing that could be worn by different social classes and tradesmen. For example, under the Act of Apparel of 1483, garments of purple or velvet were forbidden to be worn by lawyers.

Dick the butcher then salutes Cade with the famous line about killing all the lawyers:

> DICK   The first thing we do, let's kill all the lawyers.
> CADE   Nay, that I mean to do. Is not this a lamentable
> thing, that of the skin of an innocent lamb should
> be made parchment? that parchment, being scribbled
> o'er, should undo a man? Some say the bee stings:
> but I say, 'tis the bee's wax; for I did but seal
> once to a thing, and I was never mine own man
> since.
>
> (4.2.68–75)

Important legal documents were often written on vellum, a fine parchment made from calfskin, lambskin, or kidskin. This is what Cade is referring to as "the skin of an innocent lamb."

The practice of affixing wax seals to legal documents was introduced into England by the Normans. When Cade refers to sealing "once to a thing," he is probably referring to the sealing of an indenture binding him as an apprentice for a term of years.

"Kill all the lawyers." Undoubtably, Shakespeare's audiences laughed—as do modern audiences—at Dick's lawyer joke. It is a joke, isn't it? And lawyer jokes are meant to be funny. But things turn dark in a hurry. Some of Cade's men come in with the Clerk of Chatham.

[Enter some, bringing forward the Clerk of Chatham]

SMITH   The clerk of Chatham: he can write and read and
cast accompt.

CADE   O monstrous!

SMITH We took him setting of boys' copies.

CADE   Here's a villain!

SMITH Has a book in his pocket with red letters in't.

CADE   Nay, then, he is a conjurer [*conveyancer*].

DICK   Nay, he can make obligations, and write court-hand.
(4.2.76–83)

"Court-hand" refers to a style of cursive handwriting used in
the English law courts of the time. Then as now, the first stage in a
formal criminal prosecution was the arraignment of the accused in
which a plea of guilty or not guilty would be entered. Shakespeare's
dark humor is evident in Cade's confused arraignment of the Clerk:

CADE   I am sorry for't: the man is a proper man, of mine
honour; unless I find him [*not*] guilty, he shall not die.
Come hither, sirrah, I must examine thee: what is thy name?

CLERK   Emmanuel.

DICK   They use to write it on the top of letters: 'twill
go hard with you.

CADE   Let me alone. Dost thou use to write thy name? or
hast thou a mark to thyself, like an honest
plain-dealing man?

CLERK   Sir, I thank God, I have been so well brought up
that I can write my name.

ALL   He hath confessed: away with him! he's a villain
and a traitor.

CADE   Away with him, I say! hang him with his pen and
ink-horn about his neck.
(4.2.84–98)

This is a parody of the commitment procedure for arraigning
felons adopted during the reign of Queen Mary. Cade and the mob
have condemned the Clerk of Chatham to be hanged because he can
read and write. The illiterate mob is threatened and victimized by the
new skill of literacy. Cade does not promise education for the masses.
He promises destruction of the educated and the elite. Cade: "But
then are we in order when we are most out of order" (4.2.177–178).
    Maybe this is not a joke after all.
    Cade and his mob then defeat a royal army led by Sir Humphrey
Stafford and his brother William. Both are killed in battle. Cade
summons his loyal lieutenant Dick the butcher.

CADE   Where's Dick, the butcher of Ashford?

DICK   Here, sir.

CADE   They fell before thee like sheep and oxen, and thou
behavedst thyself as if thou hadst been in thine own
slaughter-house: therefore thus will I reward thee,
the Lent shall be as long again as it is; and thou
shalt have a licence to kill for a hundred lacking one.

DICK   I desire no more.

CADE   And, to speak truth, thou deservest no less. This

monument of the victory will I bear;

[Putting on SIR HUMPHREY'S brigandine]

and the bodies shall be dragged at my horse' heels
till I do come to London, where we will have the
mayor's sword borne before us.

DICK   If we mean to thrive and do good, break open the
gaols and let out the prisoners.

CADE   Fear not that, I warrant thee. Come, let's march
towards London.

(4.3.1–18)

A license is the permission granted by authorities to do something that would otherwise be forbidden. Cade is referring to the
statutes enacted under Queen Elizabeth forbidding butchers to sell
meat during Lent. A license could be given to allow some exceptions
to sell meat to the sick who were thought to need it to regain their
health. Such a license would be very useful to a butcher. In addition
to killing all the lawyers, Dick the butcher suggests that all prisoners
are to be set free, and anarchy will reign in England under Cade's rule.

In London, the royal court is in turmoil because of the beheading
of Suffolk, Queen Margaret's lover. After Cade and the mob take
London Bridge, King Henry and Margaret flee the city. At Smithfield,
the forces of the King are again defeated. Cade gives the orders that
will result in the overthrow of all of England's legal institutions.

CADE   So, sirs: now go some and pull down the Savoy;
others to the inns of court; down with them all.

DICK   I have a suit unto your lordship.

CADE   Be it a lordship, thou shalt have it for that word.

DICK Only that the laws of England may come out of your
mouth.

HOLLAND [*Aside*] Mass, 'twill be sore law, then; for he was
thrust in the mouth with a spear, and 'tis not whole
yet.

SMITH [*Aside*] Nay, John, it will be stinking law for his
breath stinks with eating toasted cheese.

CADE I have thought upon it, it shall be so. Away, burn
all the records of the realm: my mouth shall be
the parliament of England.

HOLLAND [*Aside*] Then we are like to have biting statutes,
unless his teeth be pulled out.

CADE And henceforward all things shall be in common.
(4.7.1–16)

The Inns of Court (as described at length earlier) were the law
schools for the common law courts as well as gentlemen's clubs for
the sons of the nobility and the landed gentry. Thus, the lawyers are
to be killed and the law schools are to be destroyed so that there will
be no more lawyers.

In the actual Peasants' Revolt of 1381 during the reign of Richard
II, the rebels were peasants who sought to destroy the "copyhold"
records that bound them as serfs to work the land for the lord of
their manor. As a result of successive waves of the Black Death,
there was a severe labor shortage in rural England. Men who could
escape the manor hired themselves out as free laborers at much
higher wages. The rebels in the Peasants' Revolt were largely those
who had not been able to escape from serfdom. Their anger was
particularly directed against the lawyers and manor stewards who
kept records of their bondage.

It appears that Shakespeare appropriated this aspect of the Peasants' Revolt into Cade's rebellion. Shakespeare's source, *Holinshed's Chronicles*, stated that the leader of the Peasant's Revolt said he would "put to death all lawyers, escheaters, and other which by any office had to doo with the law." The Peasants' Revolt mob invaded London and beheaded John Cavendish, Chief Justice of the Court of King's Bench. Cade's Rebellion took place much later, in 1450.

Shakespeare combines elements of the two in his play. All records of property ownership and crime and punishment are to be burned. Indeed, the intent and purpose of Cade and his followers is the complete overthrow of the rule of law. All law is to come from the mouth of the demagogue Jack Cade. The mob is so angry at the establishment that it prefers to be ruled by a populist demagogue rather than a democratically elected Parliament. The fearsome consequences of this are soon seen.

As the King and Queen flee London before the onslaught of the mob, Lord Say remains. He is captured and brought before Cade:

MESSENGER   My lord, a prize, a prize! here's the Lord Say,
which sold the towns in France; he that made us pay
one and twenty fifteens, and one shilling to the
pound, the last subsidy.

[Enter BEVIS, with Lord SAY]

CADE   Well, he shall be beheaded for it ten times. Ah,
thou say, thou serge, nay, thou buckram lord! now
art thou within point-blank of our jurisdiction
regal. What canst thou answer to my majesty for
giving up of Normandy unto Mounsieur Basimecu, the
dauphin of France? Be it known unto thee by these
presence, even the presence of Lord Mortimer, that I
am the besom that must sweep the court clean of such
filth as thou art. Thou hast most traitorously
corrupted the youth of the realm in erecting a

grammar school; and whereas, before, our forefathers
had no other books but the score and the tally, thou hast caused
printing to be used, and, contrary to the king, his crown and
dignity, thou hast built a paper-mill. It will be proved to thy face
that thou hast men about thee that usually talk of a noun and
a verb, and such abominable words as no Christian
ear can endure to hear. Thou hast appointed
justices of peace, to call poor men before them
about matters they were not able to answer.
Moreover, thou hast put them in prison; and because
they could not read, thou hast hanged them; when,
indeed, only for that cause they have been most
worthy to live. Thou dost ride in a foot-cloth, dost thou not?

SAY   What of that?

CADE   Marry, thou oughtest not to let thy horse wear a
    cloak, when honester men than thou go in their hose
    and doublets.

DICK   And work in their shirt too; as myself, for example,
    that am a butcher.

SAY   You men of Kent,–

DICK   What say you of Kent?

SAY   Nothing but this; 'tis 'bona terra, mala gens.'

CADE   Away with him, away with him! he speaks Latin.
                        (4.7.17–55)

"Be it known unto thee by these presence" is a parody of the traditional opening language of a deed of real property: "Be it known
by these presents." Cade is here protesting the great expansion of

English grammar schools in the sixteenth century. It was in the grammar school of Stratford-upon-Avon that Shakespeare learned to read and write and studied logic, rhetoric, and the classics of ancient Greece and Rome. Widespread literacy and the enormous expansion of printing in the sixteenth century made it possible for Shakespeare to have a successful career as a poet and playwright.

A justice of the peace was a judicial officer with limited power whose duties included hearing cases that involved small civil controversies, preserving the peace, hearing minor criminal complaints, and committing offenders accused of felonies. There is again a reference to the benefit of clergy, which was available only to those who could read and write; the illiterate masses were hanged for committing felonies.

Lord Say is condemned to die because he established schools and can speak Latin. What began as a lawyer's joke has suddenly become very dark. Lord Say pleads eloquently for his life because of his good works for the people.

Cade is unrelenting.

CADE Nay, he nods at us, as who should say, I'll be even
    with you: I'll see if his head will stand steadier
    on a pole, or no. Take him away, and behead him.

SAY Tell me wherein have I offended most?
    Have I affected wealth or honour? speak.
    Are my chests fill'd up with extorted gold?
    Is my apparel sumptuous to behold?
    Whom have I injured, that ye seek my death?
    These hands are free from guiltless bloodshedding,
    This breast from harbouring foul deceitful thoughts.
    O, let me live!

CADE [Aside] I feel remorse in myself with his words;
    but I'll bridle it: he shall die, an it be but for
    pleading so well for his life. Away with him! he

has a familiar under his tongue; he speaks not o'
God's name. Go, take him away, I say, and strike
off his head presently; and then break into his
son-in-law's house, Sir James Cromer, and strike off
his head, and bring them both upon two poles hither.

ALL   It shall be done.

(4.7.86–105)

After Lord Say is lead away to execution and his son-in-law
murdered, Cade and his mob parade through the streets of London
with their heads on long poles, stopping at each corner to have the
two heads engage in a grotesque kiss. Jack Cade will make England
great again. Or not.

The wheel of fortune, however, continues to turn. In a recurring Shakespearean theme, the fickle mob soon abandons Cade. It
disburses, and the feudal order of King and his nobility is restored.
Cade flees with a reward of a thousand crowns upon his head. After
five days of hiding in the forest, Cade climbs into the garden of
Alexander Iden seeking something to eat. Iden enters and speaks of
the sublime pleasures of membership in the landed gentry: "Lord,
who would live turmoiled in the court, / And may enjoy such
quiet walks as these? / This small inheritance my father left me /
Contenteth me, and worth a monarchy" (4.10.17–20).

Is Shakespeare speaking through Alexander Iden, describing his
idea of the good life? It certainly sounds like the life Shakespeare
chose in 1610 when he retired from London and the theater to live
the life of a wealthy gentleman in Stratford. Shakespeare amassed
considerable wealth from his work as an actor and playwright
and as a sharer in the proceeds of performances at the Globe and
Blackfriars theaters. He invested this capital in real estate in Stratford
and London. Iden's pleasant estate and role in a hierarchical society
based upon ownership of property would be obliterated by Jack
Cade and his mob. In any event, his reverie is interrupted by the
discovery of the intruder. Cade says: "Here's the lord of the soil

come to seize me for a stray, for entering his fee-simple without leave" (4.10.25–26).

"Fee simple" referred to ownership of full title to real property such that the land could be sold, devised by will, and inherited by the heir of the owner. A conveyance of land to a purchaser (or inheritor) "and his heirs" conveyed a fee simple estate. Lawyers in the audience would have appreciated the turn of phrase. Although the poor who come to his gate are well treated, Iden springs to the defense of his property against a trespasser. They fight, and Iden kills Cade with his sword. Iden drags the body to a dunghill and cuts off his head to take to the King.

York brings an army from Ireland, ostensibly to thwart Somerset and fight Cade. He agrees to disband his army when Buckingham tells him that the King has sent Somerset to the Tower. But Queen Margaret has freed him and brought him back to court. Upon seeing Somerset, York drops all pretense of loyalty to Henry.

Although York says Henry is not "fit" to rule, his primary claim is that he is entitled to be king by the will of God. Somerset accuses York of being a traitor: "O monstrous traitor! I arrest thee, York, / Of capital treason 'gainst the king and crown; / Obey, audacious traitor; kneel for grace" (5.1.107–09). York refuses to surrender and is supported in arms by his sons and Warwick and Salisbury.

Thus, in this early play Shakespeare confronts the question of how a society governed by law deals with an incompetent or tyrannous king. In the play, the response is armed rebellion by the nobility. The opposing forces meet on the field of St. Albans, where York kills Lord Clifford and York's son Richard kills Somerset. Henry flees to London. The Wars of the Roses have begun.

York has won the opening battle. He goes after the fleeing King to London where the King intends to call a Parliament. York: "Let us pursue him ere the writs go forth" (5.3.27). Parliament would be summoned by the Chancellor issuing writs of election. This is a tiny hint that Parliament might have a role to play in a dispute about dynastic succession. Thus, the play ends with York's victory in the battle of St. Albans. But King Henry VI is free, and it is not clear whether York can prevail if he declares himself King.

Henry VI, Part 2, is a magnificent but unappreciated work of genius. It is seldom performed and generally overlooked in the critical literature. But for anyone interested in the intersection of law, politics, history, and literature it is a masterpiece.

It is worth noting that Shakespeare significantly downplays the role of Parliament, and particularly the House of Commons, in the story he tells in the play. Parliament met a month after the fall of Normandy's capital of Rouen in October 1449, for which Suffolk was blamed. After taking a break for Christmas, it reconvened in Westminster in January 1450. Suffolk appeared before it, and denounced the accusations being made against him in the Commons. Suffolk and his small group of courtiers who surrounded the King were largely abandoned by the Lords. Four days after Suffolk's speech, the Commons demanded that Suffolk be arrested until formal charges could be brought against him. In February 1450, the House of Commons impeached him for "high, great heinous and horrible treasons." The most serious of the charges was that he had passed military and diplomatic secrets to France and had invited it to invade England.

In March 1450 the King invited the Lords and Suffolk to his private chambers in the palace of Westminster. There, Suffolk denied the charges. He waived his rights to trial by the Lords and threw himself on the mercy of the King. The King declared Suffolk innocent of treason but found him guilty of a few minor offenses. Rather than condemn him to death for treason, Henry ordered him banished. This institutional role of the House of Commons in the banishment of Suffolk is glossed over in a reference by Shakespeare to "the commons."

The next play of the Henry VI trilogy will begin in Parliament.

CHAPTER 3

Henry VI, Part 3

In *Henry VI, Part 3*, Shakespeare chronicles the triumph of the house of York in the bloody Wars of the Roses. The play opens in the Parliament House in London. York and Warwick wonder how King Henry VI escaped capture in the battle of St. Albans. With Warwick's encouragement, York takes the throne as King of England.

Henry enters with Clifford and others to find York sitting on the throne. Clifford and Northumberland urge an immediate armed attack upon the Yorkists. The ever-timorous Henry will not allow it, and is determined to use "frowns, words and threats" (Henry VI, Part 3, 1.1.72) as his weapons. King Henry: "Thou factious Duke of York, descend my throne, / and kneel for grace and mercy at my feet" (1.1.74–75). Henry and York's allies accuse the others of being traitors for following a false king.

Henry claims to be King because his grandfather and father were kings. He inherited the throne. The Yorkists counter that his grandfather, Henry IV (Henry Bolingbroke), usurped the Crown.

Henry says in an aside: "I know not what to say; my title's weak" (1.1.135). Henry is the son and heir of Henry V who was recognized universally as the legitimate King of England. Henry's title is "weak" only upon the strictest application of the rule of hereditary succession. Prior to York's revolt, Henry had been universally recognized as the de facto and de jure king. But Henry's legalistic defense of his crown soon falls to pieces.

KING HENRY VI   Tell me, may not a king adopt an heir?

YORK   What then?

KING HENRY VI   An if he may, then am I lawful king;
    For Richard, in the view of many lords,
    Resign'd the crown to Henry the Fourth,
    Whose heir my father was, and I am his.

YORK   He rose against him, being his sovereign,
    And made him to resign his crown perforce.

WARWICK   Suppose, my lords, he did it unconstrain'd,
    Think you 'twere prejudicial to his crown?

EXETER   No; for he could not so resign his crown
    But that the next heir should succeed and reign.

KING HENRY VI   Art thou against us, Duke of Exeter?

EXETER   His is the right, and therefore pardon me.

YORK   Why whisper you, my lords, and answer not?

EXETER   My conscience tells me he is lawful king.

KING HENRY VI   [*Aside*] All will revolt from me, and turn
    to him.

                    (1.1.125–52)

Exeter's argument here is that under the law of primogenitor,
if Richard resigned the Crown, it would descend under the law of
inheritance to his nearest male heir. Henry Bolingbroke's [Henry
IV's] claim to the throne involved a less direct line of descent from
Edward III. Therefore, York is claiming a more direct line of descent

than Henry VI, Bolingbroke's grandson. The entire argument depends upon Henry IV being an illegitimate king. Exeter has obviously forgotten that Richard had no children and Bolingbroke was the most direct male heir of Edward III.

Richard II and Henry VI were undone by Edward III's success in having five male heirs live to maturity thereby creating rival claimants to the throne. He married them into the upper tiers of English and European nobility and made them the first English dukes. Exeter declares that his "conscience" tells him that York is King. Warwick threatens to fill the Parliament with soldiers and write York's title to the throne "with usurping blood" (1.1.170). Henry then makes a desperate offer.

KING HENRY VI   My Lord of Warwick, hear me but one word:
Let me for this my life-time reign as king.

YORK   Confirm the crown to me and to mine heirs,
And thou shalt reign in quiet while thou livest.

KING HENRY VI   I am content: Richard Plantagenet,
Enjoy the kingdom after my decease.
                    (1.1.171–76)

This is shocking. In the chaos of the Wars of the Roses, even loyalty to family is breaking down. The King has just disinherited his own son.

Henry's spineless surrender is not received well by the nobles of his party. Westmoreland: "Base, fearful and despairing Henry!" (1.1.179). Henry sighs audibly. "Not for myself, Lord Warwick, but my son, / Whom I unnaturally shall disinherit. / But be it as it may: I here entail / The crown to thee and to thine heirs for ever" (1.1.194–97). "Entail" is a technical term of early modern English property law that meant to abridge or limit succession to real property. An entailed estate was one whose succession is limited to certain people (usually the eldest male descendant) rather than being passed to all heirs. Strictly speaking, granting a fee entail applied only to land. But here it is a beautiful expression. York takes an oath acknowledging Henry as King during his lifetime. Prince Edward and Queen Margaret enter. She is enraged at what Henry has done to her and her son.

PRINCE EDWARD   Father, you cannot disinherit me:
    If you be king, why should not I succeed?

KING HENRY VI   Pardon me, Margaret; pardon me, sweet son:
    The Earl of Warwick and the duke enforced me.

QUEEN MARGARET   Enforced thee! art thou king, and wilt
    be forced?
    I shame to hear thee speak. Ah, timorous wretch!
    Thou hast undone thyself, thy son and me;
    And given unto the house of York such head
    As thou shalt reign but by their sufferance. . . .
    But thou preferr'st thy life before thine honour:
    And seeing thou dost, I here divorce myself
    Both from thy table, Henry, and thy bed,
    Until that act of parliament be repeal'd
    Whereby my son is disinherited.
                    (1.1.229–54)

Margaret is referring to the divorce *a mensa et thoro* or divorce from board and bed discussed earlier. Legally, Margaret would have to go to a church court to obtain such a separation.

Not only are familial loyalties breaking down, but gender roles are reversing. Margaret is now the head of her family and the leader of the Lancastrian party. She has an army loyal to her and she means to use it on behalf of her son.

In the next scene in the Yorkist camp, Henry's settlement is also rejected by York's sons, who urge him to claim the Crown immediately. At first York demurs because "I took an oath that he should quietly reign" (1.2.15). Edward bluntly says he would break a thousand oaths to be King for one year. Clever Richard (later Duke of Gloucester) comes up with a shrewd argument to relieve York of his oath of allegiance to Henry.

Richard: "An oath is of no moment, being not took / Before a true and lawful magistrate, / That hath authority over him that swears" (1.2.22–24). Henry had no authority over York because he was a usurper. Richard: "Then, seeing 'twas he that made you to depose, / Your oath, my lord, is vain and frivolous" (1.2.26–27). York is persuaded and declares that he will be King or die.

Before York goes into open rebellion, the Queen and her northern allies approach with an army of twenty thousand men to besiege York in Sandal Castle. Although he is outnumbered four to one, York recklessly goes out to meet the Queen's army. At Wakefield, bloody Clifford finds Rutland, York's seventeen-year-old-son, and murders him. "Thy father slew my father; therefore, die" (1.3.48).

Family loyalty now just means cold-blooded murder of a defenseless youth. Despite the heroic efforts of his sons Richard and Edward, York is defeated and captured. He is brought before the Queen who mocks him and sets a paper crown upon his head. Margaret: "What! was it you that would be England's king? / Was't you that revell'd in our parliament, / And made a preachment of your high descent?" (1.3.70–72). Margaret gives him a napkin soaked in Rutland's blood to dry his cheek. She then makes the mistake of allowing York to make a final speech before his execution. Famously, he brands her as the "she-wolf of France" (1.4.111). Clifford and Margaret then stab York to death. Margaret orders his head be chopped off and mounted on the gates of York.

Young Edward Plantagenet is now the Duke of York and the Yorkist claimant to be the King of England. King Henry remains in the custody of Edward and Warwick. At a second battle at St. Albans, Margaret defeats Warwick and regains King Henry. At York, where he sees the impaled head of the Duke of York, Henry frets that Margaret is causing him to break his word. Henry: "Withhold revenge, dear God! 'tis not my fault, / Nor wittingly have I infringed my vow" (2.2.7–8). When the opposing forces meet at Towton, they make the usual legalistic arguments about who is the legitimate king.

EDWARD [OF YORK]   Now, perjured Henry! wilt thou kneel
    for grace,
    And set thy diadem upon my head;
    Or bide the mortal fortune of the field?

QUEEN MARGARET   Go, rate thy minions, proud insulting boy!
    Becomes it thee to be thus bold in terms
    Before thy sovereign and thy lawful king?

EDWARD   I am his king, and he should bow his knee;
    I was adopted heir by his consent:
    Since when, his oath is broke; for, as I hear,
    You, that are king, though he do wear the crown,
    Have caused him, by new act of parliament,
    To blot out me, and put his own son in.

CLIFFORD   And reason too:
    Who should succeed the father but the son?
                                                            (2.2.81–94)

Margaret has apparently obtained a law from Parliament declaring the rightful succession to be in the House of Lancaster, that is, from Henry VI to his son Prince Edward. At Towton, the battle rages back and forth while Henry sits alone on a molehill. Musing upon the sorrows of his life, Henry sees a son who has unwittily killed his father and a father who has unwittily killed his son in the battle. "O piteous spectacle! O bloody times!" (2.5.73). This is symbolic of the total breakdown of society.

By this point, Henry is an impotent spectator to the horrors of a civil war brought about due to his ineptitude as King. Clifford is killed, and the forces of the Queen are defeated in a vicious battle.

The triumphant Yorkists march on London where the Duke of York is proclaimed King by a council of the nobility. Margaret and Prince Edward flee to France.

Henry seeks refuge in Scotland but is captured in Northern England when he returns in disguise and is recognized by two foresters. They say that they will take him to London and surrender him to King Edward. Henry accuses them of breaking their oath of allegiance to him: "I was anointed king at nine months old; / My father and my grandfather were kings, / And you were sworn true subjects unto me: / And tell me, then, have you not broke your oaths?" (3.1.76–79). They say no; they were his subjects only when he was King. Henry is taken to London and "conveyed" to the Tower.

Warwick is dispatched to France to win the Lady Bona, sister of the French King, in marriage to King Edward. At the English court, Lady Elizabeth Grey comes to ask the King that the lands of her dead husband be restored to her. Edward and his brothers agree that the lands of her husband who fought for the House of York should be restored. But Edward is interested in more than doing "justice" (3.2.5). Richard, now Duke of Gloucester, says in an aside to his brother Clarence: "I see the lady hath a thing to grant, / Before the king will grant her humble suit" (3.2.11–12).

The King's brothers rightly suspect that the lecherous Edward will seek sexual gratification from Lady Grey as the price of granting her suit. But she refuses him.

KING EDWARD IV   To tell thee plain, I aim to lie with thee.

LADY GREY   To tell you plain, I had rather lie in prison.

KING EDWARD IV   Why, then thou shalt not have thy husband's lands.

LADY GREY   Why, then mine honesty shall be my dower; For by that loss I will not purchase them.

KING EDWARD IV   Therein thou wrong'st thy children
  mightily.

LADY GREY   Herein your highness wrongs both them and me.
  But, mighty lord, this merry inclination
  Accords not with the sadness of my suit:
  Please you dismiss me either with 'ay' or 'no.'

KING EDWARD IV   Ay, if thou wilt say 'ay' to my request;
  No if thou dost say 'no' to my demand.

LADY GREY   Then, no, my lord. My suit is at an end.
  (3.2.80–92)

Lady Grey's reference to her "dower" is the widow's right of a life interest in one-third of the lands of her deceased husband. This is an example of Shakespeare using the term in its correct legal sense. Elsewhere in the plays the term is used interchangeably and incorrectly with "dowry."

Edward refuses to take no for an answer and offers to make her his Queen. He then astonishes his brothers by announcing he will marry Lady Grey. Richard is left alone on the stage and in a long speech reveals his lust for the Crown and his determination to gain it at all costs:

GLOUCESTER   Ay, Edward will use women honourably.
  Would he were wasted, marrow, bones and all,
  That from his loins no hopeful branch may spring,
  To cross me from the golden time I look for!
  And yet, between my soul's desire and me–
  The lustful Edward's title buried–
  Is Clarence, Henry, and his son young Edward,
  And all the unlook'd for issue of their bodies,
  To take their rooms, ere I can place myself:
  A cold premeditation for my purpose!

Why, then, I do but dream on sovereignty;
Like one that stands upon a promontory,
And spies a far-off shore where he would tread,
Wishing his foot were equal with his eye,
And chides the sea that sunders him from thence,
Saying, he'll lade it dry to have his way:
So do I wish the crown, being so far off;
And so I chide the means that keeps me from it;
And so I say, I'll cut the causes off,
Flattering me with impossibilities.
My eye's too quick, my heart o'erweens too much,
Unless my hand and strength could equal them.

(3.2.140–161)

Richard says he must have the throne, because there is no other source of pleasure for him: "Why, love forswore me in my mother's womb" (3.2.169). He has a shriveled arm and a hump upon his back. His legs are not of equal length. No woman could love such a man.

GLOUCESTER   And am I then a man to be beloved?
O monstrous fault, to harbour such a thought!
Then, since this earth affords no joy to me,
But to command, to cheque, to o'erbear such
As are of better person than myself,
I'll make my heaven to dream upon the crown,
And, whiles I live, to account this world but hell,
Until my mis-shaped trunk that bears this head
Be round impaled with a glorious crown.
And yet I know not how to get the crown,
For many lives stand between me and home:
And I,–like one lost in a thorny wood,
That rends the thorns and is rent with the thorns,
Seeking a way and straying from the way;
Not knowing how to find the open air,
But toiling desperately to find it out,–

Torment myself to catch the English crown:
And from that torment I will free myself,
Or hew my way out with a bloody axe.
Why, I can smile, and murder whiles I smile,
And cry 'Content' to that which grieves my heart,
And wet my cheeks with artificial tears,
And frame my face to all occasions.
I'll drown more sailors than the mermaid shall;
I'll slay more gazers than the basilisk;
I'll play the orator as well as Nestor,
Deceive more slily than Ulysses could,
And, like a Sinon, take another Troy.
I can add colours to the chameleon,
Change shapes with Proteus for advantages,
And set the murderous Machiavel to school.
Can I do this, and cannot get a crown?
Tut, were it farther off, I'll pluck it down.
                    (3.2.179–211)

This is Shakespeare's first powerful soliloquy (another is in Act 5). It is an astonishingly vivid and chilling self-portrait of the narcissistic personality and morbid ambition of a Machiavellian villain. Richard will destroy his brother Clarence if he stands in the way of gaining the throne. "I have no brother, I am like no brother; / And this word 'love,' which graybeards call divine, / Be resident in men like one another / And not in me: I am myself alone" (5.6.80–83).

Richard is the ultimate expression of the disintegration of loyalty to family and kin. Unlike Iago in *Othello*, Richard at least gives his deformity and his ambition as credible motivations for his villainy. Thus, the stage is set here for the psychological melodrama of Shakespeare's *Richard III*.

In France, Margaret pleads her cause before Louis IX to restore her husband to the throne of England. Margaret: "With this my son, Prince Edward, Henry's heir, / Am come to crave thy just and lawful aid; / And if thou fail us, all our hope is done" (3.3.32–34).

Louis seems inclined to help until Warwick enters with his offer to make the Lady Bona Edward's wife and Queen of England. Margaret knows this dooms her cause. Warwick and the exiled Earl of Oxford again debate whether the usurpation of Henry IV undermines Henry VI's claim to be the lawful King of England. Warwick persuades Louis that Edward is the lawful King of England. Louis and Lady Bona then consent to the proposal. Louis begins the negotiation over the terms of the marriage: "Then, Warwick, thus: our sister shall be Edward's; / And now forthwith shall articles be drawn / Touching the jointure that your king must make, / Which with her dowry shall be counterpoised" (3.3.137–140).

A jointure was an agreement by the wife to accept certain property upon the death of the husband in lieu of dower. In the fifteenth century, the wife's dowry and the property settled upon her by a jointure were often roughly equal.

Margaret's cause seems lost until letters arrive announcing that Edward has married Lady Grey. Warwick is outraged at Edward's treachery. He renounces Edward and pledges to Margaret to restore the Crown to Henry. Louis agrees to send five thousand men to England to revenge the shame to his sister. In pledge of his loyalty, Warwick gives his daughter in marriage to Prince Edward. As in so many of the plays, the Third Act is the pivot upon which the action and the plot turn.

In Act Four, Edward's brothers are not happy. They worry about the alliance of France and Warwick. Lord Hastings, with one short speech, shows the rewards of sycophancy at Edward's court. Edward dismisses any concern that he is abusing his power to reward his favorites: "Ay, what of that? it was my will and grant; / And for this once my will shall stand for law" (4.1.49–50). Richard and Clarence object to Edward rewarding the relatives of his new wife.

Thus, political differences have joined with familial jealousy to create dissension at court. Clarence declares that he will desert the King and marry Warwick's younger daughter. Another breakdown in family loyalty. Richard does not follow. He tells us: "Not I: / My thoughts aim at a further matter; I / Stay not for the love of Edward, but the crown" (4.1.125–26).

In Warwickshire, as his men advance on the invading French and Warwick, Edward is careless in the disposition of his forces and is captured in his tent by Warwick and French soldiers. Edward is held as prisoner in the custody of Warwick's brother, the Archbishop of York. Warwick marches on London to free King Henry. Queen Elizabeth and her infant son seek sanctuary. Elizabeth: "To save at least the heir of Edward's right / There shall I rest secure from force and fraud" (4.4.31–32).

Sanctuary is a place of refuge, where the process of the law cannot be executed. At this time in England, religious houses afforded protection from arrest to all persons, whether accused of crime or pursued for debt. This right of sanctuary dates from early Anglo-Saxon kingships. Richard and Hastings go to Yorkshire where they rescue Edward. He flees to Flanders where he will seek aid from the Duke of Burgundy.

In London, Warwick rescues Henry from the Tower. The grateful Henry turns his government over to Warwick and the treacherous Clarence. They agree that "Edward be pronounced a traitor, / And all his lands and goods be confiscate" (4.6.54–55). So much for brotherly affection and loyalty on the part of Clarence.

Having learned nothing from all of his travails, Henry does not understand why the people do not support him. It does not occur to Henry that the people want a leader who will deliver them from all the turmoil and bloodshed. King Henry declares that the young Earl of Richmond, Henry Tudor, "will prove our country's bliss" (4.6.71).

Shakespeare's audience would know that Henry Tudor was the future Henry VII, grandfather of Queen Elizabeth I. He was the strong political leader who ended the chaos arising out of Henry's ineptitude as king. For now, Richmond is sent to Brittany in case Edward is restored to the throne. Indeed, with forces from Burgundy, Edward returns to England, marches on London, and again seizes Henry. Perfidious Clarence deserts Warwick and rejoins his brothers.

In the battle of Barnet, Warwick is killed. Warwick: "Why, what is pomp, rule, reign, but earth and dust? / And, live we how we can, yet die we must" (5.2.27–28). Queen Margaret returns to England with a French army and meets Edward at Tewksbury. It is Edward who triumphs upon the field. Margaret and Prince Edward are captured. Somerset is summarily condemned to beheading. The young Prince defies his captors. Margaret: "Ah, that thy father had been so resolved!" (5.5.22). It does not end well for the young Prince. First Edward and then Gloucester stab him. Margaret cries out: "O, kill me too!" (5.5.41). Edward restrains his brother from killing her: "Hold, Richard, hold; for we have done too much" (5.5.43). But Richard is not done. He rushes off to London to kill Henry in the Tower. In the end, Henry has a dignity and a presence he lacked until the very end of his life. He faces a Richard who has "neither pity, love, nor fear" (5.6.68) and murders Henry. Richard has killed Henry and his son. But Richard is not done: "Clarence, thy turn is next, and then the rest, / Counting myself but bad till I be best" (5.6.90–91).

Edward is once more King. In the palace, he invites his brothers to kiss his new-born son. Richard does so, but in an aside tells us: "To say the truth, so Judas kiss'd his master, / And cried 'all hail!' when as he meant all harm" (5.7.33–34). Richard is warning us of what he is capable of doing in order to seize the Crown.

The Wars of the Roses have ended in a complete triumph for Edward and the House of York. Edward declares: "Sound drums and trumpets! farewell sour annoy! / For here, I hope, begins our lasting joy" (5.7.45–46).

But there is Richard.

In these plays, there is little of the idea of the King as God's anointed sovereign as we will hear later in *Richard II*. Fortunes ebb and flow. Battles are won and lost. Fathers are savagely killed and sons seek revenge. Sons are savagely killed and fathers seek revenge. Brothers turn against brothers. Kings are crowned and uncrowned.

The king who sits on the throne is the one who is supported by the stronger force of lords and their fighting men.

When we read *Richard II*, are we to think that all this bloody slaughter was inevitable due to the overthrow of an anointed king?

CHAPTER 4

RICHARD III

Shakespeare's next play, *Richard III*, was as popular in the poet's day as it is in ours. The play was written early in Shakespeare's career and probably completed by 1593. Sir Thomas More's biography of Richard III (a brilliant piece of Tudor propaganda retold by Holinshed and Hall one of the most consulted history textbooks of the age) was his main source. This was one of Shakespeare's first great hits. At least five quarto versions of the play were produced during Shakespeare's lifetime.

In a couple of scenes in *Henry VI, Part 3*, Shakespeare employed the dramatic technique of using a soliloquy to explore Richard's internal thoughts. In *Richard III*, Shakespeare's use of the technique goes wild. As Richard shares his thoughts directly with us, we are captivated, intoxicated, and seduced as he carries out his villainy.

Richard is ambitious, narcissistic, outrageously charming, self-mocking, flattering, deceitful, exciting, eloquent, ruthlessly dangerous, and a consummate actor. "And thus I clothe my naked villany / With odd old ends stolen out of holy writ; / And seem a saint, when most I play the devil" (*Richard III,* 1.3.334–36). Richard's thoughts are Shakespeare's script for the play. Shakespeare's friend and fellow actor Richard Burbage delighted audiences at the Globe with his portrayal of the villainous Richard.

The play begins with the famous "winter of our discontent" soliloquy by Richard, Duke of Gloucester: "Now is the winter of our discontent / Made glorious summer by this sun of York" (1.1.1–2).

His brother King Edward is indulging his insatiable appetites for sexual pleasure. Richard once again laments that his deformed body makes love impossible for him. Richard: "And therefore, since I cannot prove a lover, / To entertain these fair well-spoken days, / I am determined to prove a villain / And hate the idle pleasures of these days" (1.1.28–31).

This is an interesting use of the words "to prove." We normally think of this to mean to demonstrate the truth of something by evidence or argument. For example, that is what is meant to prove something in court. Shakespeare is using "to prove" in the now obsolete sense of meaning to become something. He does it twice in the same sentence. This is an example of Shakespeare borrowing a word from the language of the law to create a vivid expression.

Richard uses his deformity and his isolation from others as an excuse and cloak for his villainy. If his deformity denies him the normal pleasures of humanity, he denies any obligation on his part to conform to the norms of morality and law that govern others. Unlike Iago in *Othello*, Richard at least gives his deformity and his ambition as credible motivations for his villainy. This honesty adds to Richard's initial charm.

Richard convinces Edward that their brother Clarence will again betray him. Edward, who is sick, has Clarence arrested and confined to the Tower. Richard knows Edward must live until Clarence has been eliminated because if alive, as the elder brother, Clarence would succeed Edward as King. Richard plots to advance his cause by marrying Warwick's daughter Anne.

In the second scene, the open coffin of King Henry VI is brought on stage accompanied by the Lady Anne, the youngest daughter of Warwick and the dead king's daughter-in-law. In *Henry VI, Part 3*, Richard murdered King Henry and his son, Anne's husband, Edward, Prince of Wales. She mourns the dead king and her dead husband. She curses Richard: "Cursed be the hand that made these fatal holes! / Cursed be the heart that had the heart to do it! / Cursed the blood that let this blood from hence!" (1.2.14–16).

Richard enters and orders the bearers to set down Henry's coffin. Anne continues her execrations.

LADY ANNE   Foul devil, for God's sake, hence, and trouble us not;
For thou hast made the happy earth thy hell,
Fill'd it with cursing cries and deep exclaims.
If thou delight to view thy heinous deeds,
Behold this pattern of thy butcheries.
O, gentlemen, see, see! dead Henry's wounds
Open their congeal'd mouths and bleed afresh!
Blush, Blush, thou lump of foul deformity;
For 'tis thy presence that exhales this blood
From cold and empty veins, where no blood dwells;
Thy deed, inhuman and unnatural,
Provokes this deluge most unnatural.
(1.2.50–61)

"Cruentation" was a medieval form of trial by ordeal in which the accused was brought to the corpse of the deceased and forced to place his hands on the dead body. If the corpse began to bleed, this was evidence of God's judgment that the accused was guilty. Cruentation was used more in continental Europe than in England, where trial by jury replaced trial by ordeal in the thirteenth century.

Richard declares that he will "acquit" (1.2.77) himself. He cleverly turns Anne's curses into legalistic accusations that Richard's talent for sophistry may exploit. It is the most extraordinary wooing scene in all of literature.

LADY ANNE   Didst thou not kill this king?

GLOUCESTER   I grant ye.

LADY ANNE   Dost grant me, hedgehog? then, God grant me too
Thou mayst be damned for that wicked deed!
O, he was gentle, mild, and virtuous!

GLOUCESTER   The fitter for the King of heaven, that hath him.

LADY ANNE   He is in heaven, where thou shalt never come.

GLOUCESTER   Let him thank me, that holp to send him thither;
For he was fitter for that place than earth.

LADY ANNE   And thou unfit for any place but hell.

GLOUCESTER   Yes, one place else, if you will hear me name it.

LADY ANNE   Some dungeon.

GLOUCESTER   Your bed-chamber.

(1.2.102–14)

This is outrageous. Richard has killed Anne's husband and her
father-in-law. It is a measure of Richard's enormous ego that he thinks
he can get away with this. Richard now tells Anne that he killed King
Henry and Prince Edward because he was captivated by her beauty.

GLOUCESTER   Is not the causer of the timeless deaths
Of these Plantagenets, Henry and Edward,
As blameful as the executioner?

LADY ANNE   Thou art the cause, and most accursed effect.

GLOUCESTER   Your beauty was the cause of that effect;
Your beauty: which did haunt me in my sleep
To undertake the death of all the world,
So I might live one hour in your sweet bosom.

LADY ANNE   If I thought that, I tell thee, homicide,
   These nails should rend that beauty from my cheeks.
(1.2.121–30)

In essence, Richard is accusing Anne of being an accessory to the murder of her husband and her father-in-law. In criminal law, an accessory is one who aids, abets, commands, or counsels another in the commission of a crime. However, an accessory must knowingly promote or contribute to the crime. In other words, she must aid or encourage the offense deliberately, not accidentally. Anne certainly did not deliberately aid or encourage Richard to commit murder. Therefore, she cannot be guilty of the offense. He cannot shift the guilt from his shoulders onto hers. She rightly accuses him of being a "homicide."

Richard claims to have killed Prince Edward to get Anne a better husband. When Richard says he would be a better husband for her, she spits in his face. Richard gives her his sword and bares his breast to let her kill him. This theatrical gesture shows Richard's skill at play acting. But she cannot do it and bids him to kill himself. She at least knows Richard's gesture is just an act.

LADY ANNE   Arise, dissembler: though I wish thy death,
   I will not be the executioner.

GLOUCESTER   Then bid me kill myself, and I will do it.

LADY ANNE   I have already.

GLOUCESTER   Tush, that was in thy rage:
   Speak it again, and, even with the word,
   That hand, which, for thy love, did kill thy love,
   Shall, for thy love, kill a far truer love;
   To both their deaths thou shalt be accessary.

LADY ANNE   I would I knew thy heart.

GLOUCESTER   'Tis figured in my tongue.

LADY ANNE   I fear me both are false.

GLOUCESTER   Then never man was true.

LADY ANNE   Well, well, put up your sword.

GLOUCESTER   Say, then, my peace is made.

LADY ANNE   That shall you know hereafter.

GLOUCESTER   But shall I live in hope?

LADY ANNE   All men, I hope, live so.
                           (1.2.182–99)

Sensing that she is giving way to the force of his will, he gets Anne to take a ring. He tells Anne to come to him after he has buried Henry. Anne then leaves the stage. Although Richard said he was not fit for love, he has just done something extraordinary in the field of love. He has seduced Anne—as well as the audience. When Richard is alone on the stage, he gives us a review of his performance.

GLOUCESTER   Was ever woman in this humour woo'd?
    Was ever woman in this humour won?
    I'll have her; but I will not keep her long.
    What! I, that kill'd her husband and his father,
    To take her in her heart's extremest hate,
    With curses in her mouth, tears in her eyes,
    The bleeding witness of her hatred by;
    Having God, her conscience, and these bars against me,
    And I nothing to back my suit at all,
    But the plain devil and dissembling looks,
    And yet to win her, all the world to nothing!
    Ha!
                           (1.2.221–30)

Richard is the ultimate con man. He has won Anne—and us, the audience—at least temporarily. Anne is a frightened, vulnerable young woman who has lost everything. She has no male protector. Warwick, King Henry, and Prince Edward are all dead. Richard does a masterful job of exploiting her fears and insecurities. Perhaps she naively thinks she will be safe with Richard from further calamities. Indeed, she will soon find herself crowned Queen of England. Poor Anne!

At the palace, Queen Elizabeth speaks with her brother, Lord Rivers, and her son from her first marriage, Lord Gray. She worries what will happen to her if the sick King Edward should die. Will her young son (with King Edward) be put under the protection of Gloucester, who hates her and her family? Richard enters and immediately quarrels with Rivers. Richard accuses the Queen of having Clarence imprisoned in the Tower. Old Queen Margaret, King Henry's widow, enters and magnificently curses all of them, particularly Richard.

All but Richard leave the stage to attend to the King. Richard is very pleased with himself and how his schemes are sowing dissension and discord within the court. And very soon, one of the obstacles between Richard and the Crown will be removed.

GLOUCESTER   And thus I clothe my naked villany
    With odd old ends stolen out of holy writ;
    And seem a saint, when most I play the devil.

[Enter two Murderers.]

But, soft! here come my executioners.
How now, my hardy, stout resolved mates!
Are you now going to dispatch this deed?

FIRST MURDERER   We are, my lord; and come to have
    the warrant
    That we may be admitted where he is.

GLOUCESTER   Well thought upon; I have it here about me.

[Gives the warrant.]
When you have done, repair to Crosby Place.
(1.3.334–43)

A warrant is a written order issued by a judicial officer or other authorized person commanding a law enforcement officer to perform some act in furtherance of the administration of justice, such as executing an arrest warrant. Here, it is apparently an order to Clarence's jailers to allow the murderers to take custody of the prisoner. It is not clear what authority the Duke of Gloucester had to issue such an order, since Clarence was in custody on the order of the King.

In the Tower, Clarence has a wonderful speech in which he describes to his jailer a dream in which he escapes from the Tower and is on a ship in the Channel when Richard accidentally knocks him overboard and he drowns. Clarence again sleeps, and the murders enter and show the jailer their "commission."

[A paper is delivered to BRAKENBURY who reads it.]

BRAKENBURY   I am, in this, commanded to deliver
The noble Duke of Clarence to your hands:
I will not reason what is meant hereby,
Because I will be guiltless of the meaning.
There lies the duke alseep–and there the keys,
I'll to the king; and signify to him
That thus I have resign'd to you my charge.

FIRST MURDERER   You may sir, 'tis a point of wisdom:
fare you well.
(1.3.91–98)

It is surprising that Shakespeare spills this much ink on the rather mundane requirement for a written order to admit the murders to Clarence's cell. Brakenbury knows the thugs are about to murder Clarence. Is he "guiltless" because he is obeying orders? Is this not always the excuse of those who have aided the rise of tyrants? One of the murderers has an attack of conscience—until he is reminded of the reward they will receive from the Duke of Gloucester's purse. When Clarence awakes and sees the murders, he proclaims his innocence until convicted in accordance with the law.

CLARENCE   Are you call'd forth from out a world of men
 To slay the innocent? What is my offence?
 Where are the evidence that do accuse me?
 What lawful quest have given their verdict up
 Unto the frowning judge? or who pronounced
 The bitter sentence of poor Clarence' death?
 Before I be convict by course of law,
 To threaten me with death is most unlawful.
 I charge you, as you hope to have redemption
 By Christ's dear blood shed for our grievous sins,
 That you depart and lay no hands on me
 The deed you undertake is damnable.
     (1.3.191–202)

Clarence rightfully protests that he cannot be killed without a trial and judgment by a lawful court. The murderers declare they act on the order of the King. Clarence appeals to the murderers not to break God's law by obeying the command of the King set forth in the warrant. The first murderer stabs Clarence and then drowns him in a barrel of Malmsey wine. Thus, Clarence's dream of death by drowning is fulfilled.

At the palace, the sick King Edward tries to make peace among his squabbling lords and relations. When the Queen speaks of Clarence, Richard shocks the court by announcing that Clarence is dead. Edward protests that his order was "reversed." But Richard says the second order came too late.

In the next scene, King Edward has died. Richard and Buckingham plot to be the first to take charge of young Edward, the Prince of Wales, and his younger brother. Richard orders that the

Queen's son and brother, Lords Grey and Rivers, be taken as prisoners to Pomfret Castle. The Queen knows this means the downfall of her house: "Come, come, my boy; we will to sanctuary" (2.4.70).

At common law, the right of sanctuary was the right to claim exemption from service of civil or criminal process while the offender was in a church. A fugitive in sanctuary was immune from arrest, generally for forty days. During this time, the fugitive had to choose between standing trial or adjuring the realm—leaving the country forever. As hostility to special privileges for the clergy grew, the right of sanctuary was abolished in 1540 for murder, rape, burglary, robbery, and arson.

In London, Richard and Buckingham welcome young Prince Edward. Hastings enters with the news that the Queen and Prince Edward's younger brother, the Prince of York, have taken sanctuary. Buckingham protests that the Prince cannot claim sanctuary; he has done nothing to merit it. Buckingham: "This prince hath neither claim'd it nor deserved it; / And therefore, in mine opinion, cannot have it" (3.1.51–52). He orders Cardinal Bourchier to seize the boy from his mother. Hastings and the Cardinal leave to fetch the young Prince. Richard tells Edward he should stay in the Tower until his coronation.

Richard has been playing a dangerous game by locking up the Queen's relations. But he will go further. When the Princes leave, Richard and Buckingham instruct their henchman Sir William Catesby to sound out Hastings on Richard's scheme to take the throne from young Edward. If Hastings will not cooperate, Richard has a bloody plan: Richard makes no pretense of following the law. He will murder Hastings and confiscate his lands without a trial or lawful process. Lord Stanley sends a messenger to warn Hastings against Richard. But Hastings scoffs: "Tell him his fears are shallow, wanting instance" (3.2.24).

Hastings is too excited by the news of the downfall of his enemies at court to believe he is in any danger. He trusts that his loyal friend Catesby will warn him of danger. Catesby arrives, but on another errand. When he solicits Hastings to join in Richard's plot to seize the Crown, Hastings refuses: "But, that I'll give my voice on Richard's side, / To bar my master's heirs in true descent, / God knows I will not do it, to the death" (3.2.52–54). Hastings hates the Woodvilles but remains loyal to Edward's children. He does not know it, but he is doomed.

At Pomfret Castle, Rivers, Grey, and Vaughan are summarily executed. Here in Act III, Scene 3, Richard and his accessories have abandoned any pretense of honoring the rule of law.

Hastings, Buckingham, and others gather in the Tower to discuss the coronation of Prince Edward. Richard enters, makes small talk, and has the Bishop of Ely send for strawberries. Hastings is confident he is secure in Richard's favor. "I know he loves me well" (3.4.15). But Hastings reveals how little insight he has into Richard's true character: "I think there's never a man in Christendom / That can less hide his love or hate than he; / For by his face straight shall you know his heart" (3.4.55–57). This naive error in judgment about Richard's ability to deceive will prove fatal to Hastings. Aside, Buckingham tells Richard that Hastings will not support his claim to the throne at the expense of King Edward's young sons.

When Richard returns to the room, he swiftly condemns Hastings, declaring him a traitor and ordering his execution. No one tries to stop Richard. Are they all cowards? Clearly, by this point, Richard has shown that he will not be restrained by the rule of law. Hastings now realizes he has helped create a monster: "O bloody Richard! miserable England!" (3.4.107).

Richard is well aware that ordering Hastings's execution without a trial is illegal. He demands unquestioned loyalty but shows no gratitude to those who have supported him.

Shortly thereafter, the Mayor of London appears before Richard and Buckingham, who are on the battlements of the Tower. Lovel and Ratcliff enter with the head of Hastings. Richard feigns grief at Hastings's treachery. "So smooth he daub'd his vice with show of virtue, / That, his apparent open guilt omitted, / I mean, his conversation with Shore's wife, / He lived from all attainder of suspect" (3.5.29–32).

To justify his summary execution, Buckingham proclaims that Hastings was a traitor who had planned to murder Buckingham and Richard in the council chamber. Richard and Buckingham plot to spread the word among the Parliament men of London that Edward's sons are bastards. Richard wants to go even further and accuse his own mother of adultery in conceiving Edward while the Duke of York was away in France. "But touch this sparingly, as 'twere far off, / Because you know, my lord, my mother lives" (3.5.93–94). Richard, anxious to legalize the murder of Hastings, has an indictment drawn up.

[Enter a Scrivener, with a paper in his hand.]

SCRIVENER   This is the indictment of the good Lord Hastings;
    Which in a set hand fairly is engross'd,
    That it may be this day read over in Paul's.
    And mark how well the sequel hangs together:
    Eleven hours I spent to write it over,
    For yesternight by Catesby was it brought me;
    The precedent was full as long a-doing:
    And yet within these five hours lived Lord Hastings,
    Untainted, unexamined, free, at liberty
    Here's a good world the while! Why who's so gross,
    That seeth not this palpable device?
    Yet who's so blind, but says he sees it not?
    Bad is the world; and all will come to nought,
    When such bad dealings must be seen in thought.
                  (3.6.1–14)

Buckingham had assured Richard that he could play his part to persuade Londoners of Richard's rightful claim to the throne. But at Baynard's Castle, Buckingham reports to Richard that the Londoners were unmoved by his claims of the illegitimacy of Edward and his sons. Buckingham says he had proclaimed the bastardy of Edward's children by alleging that he was not lawfully married to Elizabeth: "I did; with his contract with Lady Lucy, / And his contract by deputy in France" (3.7.5–6). This is the claim that the marriage contract with Lady Lucy made Edward a bigamist when he married Elizabeth and made their children bastards.

The pre-Reformation church courts would invalidate a marriage as bigamous whenever either party was shown to have a prior contract for marriage with another. This was so controversial that a statute under Henry VIII prohibited the church courts from invalidating marriages on this ground.

Buckingham summons the Mayor and the London citizens to the courtyard at Barynard's Castle. Richard appears on the wall above between two churchmen reading a book of prayer. Buckingham urges Richard to take the Crown for the good of his country. Richard feigns indifference: "Alas, why would you heap these cares on me? / I am unfit for state and majesty" (3.7.203–04). Buckingham swears that his brother's son will never be king, and leaves with the mayor and citizens. Buckingham and the citizens immediately return and Richard, with pretended reluctance, accepts their plea for him to take the Crown. Buckingham: "Then I salute you with this kingly title – / Long live Richard, England's royal king!" (3.7.238–39).

So Richard has schemed, conspired, lied, slandered, and murdered his way to the Crown of England. Shakespeare makes no mention of any role of Parliament in proclaiming Richard as King, and in this instance, there was none. Parliament was not to be called into session until after the coronation of Edward V. Instead, a hastily gathered group of lords, bishops, and Londoners assembled in Westminster Hall. They declared Edward IV's marriage to Elizabeth Grey invalid on the grounds of a previous marriage. His sons were excluded from the succession as bastards and Richard was proclaimed King.

As soon as Richard becomes King, the wheel of fortune begins to turn against him, and he loses his wicked charm. He gained the throne by murder and now he cannot stop. It begins with his co-conspirator Buckingham. Richard now wears the crown, but he believes that he cannot be assured of being King while Prince Edward and his younger brother live. He begins to confide in Buckingham, who does not seem to understand what Richard in hinting at. Richard then is blunt: "Shall I be plain? I wish the bastards dead; / And I would have it suddenly perform'd" (4.2.18–19).

Buckingham asks for time to think about it. This enrages Richard. Now that he is King, his ability to manipulate all of those around him seems to be fading. He tells Catesby to spread the rumor that Anne is sick and about to die. Richard learns that Elizabeth's son from her first marriage, the Marquis Dorset, has fled to France to join Henry Tudor, the Earl of Richmond. He then engages Sir James Tyrrel to murder the Princes in the Tower.

Buckingham asks to be given the Earldom of Hereford that he was promised. But Richard says he is not "in the giving vein to-day" (4.2.118). Remembering the fate of Hastings, Buckingham decides to flee London.

In the next scene, Tyrrel reports to Richard that he has murdered the Princes. The chaplain of the Tower has buried their bodies. Although Richard believes he is now safely on the throne, the wheel of fortune continues to turn. At this moment Richard learns that the Bishop of Ely has fled to Richmond in France and Buckingham has an army in the field in rebellion.

Queen Margaret, Queen Elizabeth, and the Duchess of York join in cursing Richard. After a long speech in which Queen Margaret recites all of Richard's crimes, the Duchess of York asks, "Why should calamity be full of words?" (4.4.126). Queen Elizabeth responds: "Windy attorneys to their client woes, / Airy succeeders of intestate joys, / Poor breathing orators of miseries!" (4.4.127–29). This is a particularly vivid use by Shakespeare of the language of the law as metaphor.

Richard starts to get desperate. His wife, Anne, is sick. Richard comes up with a desperate plan to marry his brother Edward's daughter to enhance his claim to the throne. "Murder her brothers, and then marry her! / Uncertain way of gain! But I am in / So far in blood that sin will pluck on sin: / Tear-falling pity dwells not in this eye" (4.2.62–64).

Richard denies being subject to any ordinary human moral obligations. He attempts to obtain Elizabeth's daughter in marriage by using the same trick he used with Anne. He says to Elizabeth, "Say that I did all this for love of her" (4.4.293). This is even more outrageous than his proposal to Anne. Richard has just killed Elizabeth's two little boys. He now proposes that Elizabeth consent to him marrying their sister. Richard: "If I have kill'd the issue of your womb, / To quicken your increase, I will beget / Mine issue of your blood upon your daughter" (4.4.301–03).

This is truly monstrous. To protect herself, Elizabeth promises to speak to her daughter. But she secretly intends her daughter to wed the Earl of Richmond. Richard's manner of wooing is no longer working. Is he losing his touch?

Richard learns that Richmond has sailed for England and the rebellion has spread. Buckingham, however, has been defeated by forces loyal to Richard and has been captured. Buckingham admits that he is now the victim of the course of lawless murder he orchestrated to put Richard on the throne. He remembers Margaret's curse as he is taken to the block for execution: "Now Margaret's curse fall heavy on my neck" (5.1.26).

Richmond leads his invading army deep into England until only a day's march separates him and Richard, who is camped at Bosworth Field. In the night before the battle, the ghosts of all of Richard's murdered victims appear to him in a dream. Then he awakens. "Methought the souls of all that I had murder'd / Came to my tent; and every one did threat / To-morrow's vengeance on the head of Richard" (5.3.204–06).

Richmond also sees the ghosts, who bless his cause. He speaks eloquently to his men on the morning of the battle about Richard: "A bloody tyrant and a homicide; / One raised in blood, and one in blood establish'd" (5.3.245–46). Richmond proclaims Richard to be God's enemy. This justifies rebellion against him. "Then, if you fight against God's enemy, / God will in justice ward you as his soldiers; / If you do sweat to put a tyrant down, / You sleep in peace, the tyrant being slain" (5.3.252–55).

The battle begins, and Richard fights bravely. He seeks man-to-man combat with Richmond. But he is undone when his horse is slain: "A horse! a horse! my kingdom for a horse!" (5.4.7). Richard and Richmond meet and exit the stage, fighting. Lord Stanley enters. He announces that Richard is dead, and proclaims Richmond to be King. Richmond pledges to end the bloody War of the Roses by marrying Elizabeth of York.

RICHMOND   Inter their bodies as becomes their births:
Proclaim a pardon to the soldiers fled
That in submission will return to us:
And then, as we have ta'en the sacrament,
We will unite the white rose and the red:
Smile heaven upon this fair conjunction,
That long have frown'd upon their enmity!
Now civil wounds are stopp'd, peace lives again:
That she may long live here, God say amen!
                    (5.5.15–21, 40–41)

Henry Tudor is crowned King on the battlefield. The terrible Wars of the Roses are over, and the Tudor dynasty has begun with the reign of Richmond as Henry VII. His granddaughter would reign in Shakespeare's time as Elizabeth, the Virgin Queen.

The thirty years of the Wars of the Roses was a period of near total breakdown of the rule of law. It was a bloody time when might made right. Henry VI was a bad king because he was incapable of governing. At least in Shakespeare's play, Richard III was a bad king because he was a murderer and a tyrant. The deposition of Richard was clearly inconsistent with the doctrine of hereditary succession and rule by divine right.

But the removal of a murderer and tyrant was the right thing on so many levels that Shakespeare meant his audience to approve of it. Rebellion against a tyrant doesn't look so bad after all. Although Henry Tudor's claim to the throne through heredity was slim, there was no serious question as to the legitimacy of his successor, his son Henry VIII, who was a grandson of Edward IV.

As I said at the beginning, *Richard III* represents a new level of sophistication in Shakespeare's plays. It was the sustained use of the soliloquy—thinking out loud—as a means of exploring the psychology and motivation of a character that we see first in *Richard III*. Shakespeare would refine the technique until the famous "To be or not to be" speech of Hamlet and the agonizing monologues of Lear.

CHAPTER 5

THE TAMING OF THE SHREW

The *Taming of the Shrew* is set in Padua, a city in northeastern Italy about twenty miles west of Venice. In Shakespeare's day, Padua was part of the Venetian Republic. The first great medieval university was established in nearby Bologna in 1088. In the thirteenth century, a group of professors broke away and established a competing university at Padua. Both universities had great law schools that revived the study and practice of Roman law.

As the play begins, Lucentio, the young son of a merchant, and his servant Tranio have traveled to Padua from their home in Pisa. Lucentio seeks to study virtue and philosophy that will allow him to know true happiness. "Tranio, since for the great desire I had / To see fair Padua, nursery of arts, / I am arrived for fruitful Lombardy, / The pleasant garden of great Italy" *The Taming of the Shrew* (1.1.1–4). Tranio responds: "Let's be no stoics nor no stocks, I pray; / Or so devote to Aristotle's cheques /As Ovid be an outcast quite abjured" (1.1.31–33).

The Roman poet Ovid wrote the famous *Metamorphoses* that Shakespeare would have studied in grammar school. He also wrote *The Art of Love*, which taught the art of seduction. It is to this work that Tranio appears to be referring.

Tranio wants to have a little fun. Baptista, a rich gentleman of Padua, enters with his two daughters, Katharina and Bianca, along with Bianca's suitors, Gremio and Hortensio. Baptista sets the plot in motion by telling the suitors that Katharina, his eldest daughter, must marry first. That presents a problem—because no one wants to marry Katharina. Gremio says, "she's too rough for me" (1.1.55). Hortensio says, "no mates for you, / Unless you were of gentler, milder mould" (1.1.59–60).

Lucentio is immediately smitten by Bianca. But she submits to the will of her father. Gremio and Hortensio discuss the possibility of finding a husband for Katharina. Gremio says, "I had as lief take her dowry with this condition, to be whipped at the high cross every morning" (1.1.131–33). Dowry was the money and property that came with the bride when she married.

They agree to cooperate in attempting to find a husband for Katharina because of a "bar in law" (1.1.135). Under the imaginary law of Padua, a daughter could not marry without the consent of her father. In Shakespeare's England, an adult female could marry without the consent of her father. But the father could refuse to offer a dowry—as Page proposes in *The Merry Wives of Windsor* if his daughter Anne marries the courtier Fenton without his consent: "No, he shall not knit a knot in his fortunes with the finger of my substance: if he take her, let him take her simply; the wealth I have waits on my consent, and my consent goes not that way" (*The Merry Wives of Windsor*, 3.2.51–53).

In Scene 2, Petruchio, a gentleman of Verona (a nearby city also part of the Venetian Republic), has come to Padua to visit his friend Hortensio. When the friends meet, Petruchio announces his purpose in coming to Padua is to seek a wife.

In jest, Hortensio says he knows of one who would be very rich but "a shrewd ill-favour'd wife" (1.2.58). Petruchio responds that if she is rich enough he will take her, notwithstanding her faults. Hortensio replies: "I would not wed her for a mine of gold" (1.2.90). Hortensio tells Petruchio that her father is Baptista, who was well known to Petruchio's father. Petruchio vows to see Katharina before he sleeps. Tranio and Lucentio meet Petruchio and Hortensio. Tranio introduces himself as a wooer of Bianca. Hortensio introduces Petruchio as the wooer of Katharina. Tranio responds:

TRANIO   Sir, I shall not be slack: in sign whereof,
  Please ye we may contrive this afternoon,
  And quaff carouses to our mistress' health,
  And do as adversaries do in law,
  Strive mightily, but eat and drink as friends.

BIONDELLO   O excellent motion! Fellows, let's be gone.
                    (1.2.276–281)

Sadly, this relationship of civility among adversaries was greater in Shakespeare's day than in our own. Shakespeare undoubtedly witnessed lawyers eating and drinking as friends in the taverns around the Globe Theatre.

Petruchio goes to Baptista's house with Hortensio, who is disguised as a music teacher. As soon as he meets Baptista, Petruchio boldly introduces himself as a suitor of Katharina. Before even meeting the girl he quickly gets to the question of her dowry: "Then tell me, if I get your daughter's love, / What dowry shall I have with her to wife?" (2.1.121–22). Baptista responds: "After my death the one half of my lands, / And in possession twenty thousand crowns" (2.1.123–24). This is a reasonably generous offer. Because Baptista has no sons, upon his death his two daughters would ordinarily each inherit half of his estate. He will pay now twenty thousand crowns. Under the law of England at the time, they would belong to her husband. Clearly, he sees Petruchio as an appropriate husband for his eldest daughter. Petruchio responds to the offer:

PETRUCHIO   And, for that dowry, I'll assure her of
  Her widowhood, be it that she survive me,
  In all my lands and leases whatsoever:
  Let specialties be therefore drawn between us,
  That covenants may be kept on either hand.
                    (2.1.125–129)

A specialty was a written agreement that is sealed. Thus, Petruchio agrees to the financial arrangements. For many readers, Petruchio seems to view marriage as purely a financial transaction for his benefit. In fact, however, Petruchio's offer is one of extraordinary generosity. Under the English common law, his widow would ordinarily receive as her dower a life interest in only one third of his real property. The would-be husband could bargain for a jointure providing less.

As I read the passage quoted above, Petruchio—without bargaining—is proposing a jointure that gives Katharina a life interest in everything (real and personal property such as leases) when he dies. If he was merely proposing that she receive as her dower rights a life interest in one third of his real property, there would be no reason to have "specialties" drawn to document his side of the bargain. Baptista responds to this generous offer by telling Petruchio that he must get Katharina's love first. Petruchio says, "that is nothing: for I tell you, father, / I am as peremptory as she proud-minded" (2.1.133).

The disguised Hortensio and Lucentio are introduced into the Baptista household as teachers for his daughters. A servant leads them into the house. When Hortensio re-enters the stage, his head bloodied, he tells Baptista and Petruchio that Katharina hit him with his lute. Although he has not yet met her, Petruchio responds: "Now, by the world, it is a lusty wench; / I love her ten times more than e'er I did" (2.1.163–64). Baptista agrees to send Katharina to him. Alone on stage, Petruchio tells us of his plan for wooing Katharina.

PETRUCHIO   I will attend her here,
And woo her with some spirit when she comes.
Say that she rail; why then I'll tell her plain
She sings as sweetly as a nightingale:
Say that she frown, I'll say she looks as clear
As morning roses newly wash'd with dew:
Say she be mute and will not speak a word;

Then I'll commend her volubility,
And say she uttereth piercing eloquence:
If she do bid me pack, I'll give her thanks,
As though she bid me stay by her a week:
If she deny to wed, I'll crave the day
When I shall ask the banns and when be married.
But here she comes; and now, Petruchio, speak.
                    (2.1.172–185)

The "banns" were the formal announcement in church of an intended marriage. They were generally made on three successive Sundays in the home church of the bride and the groom. This gave anyone the chance to object to the marriage if there was an impediment. Petruchio's wooing does not go well. After many insults, Katharina hits him (this is the only physical violence between the two in the play) and he threatens to hit her back. She responds: "So may you lose your arms: / If you strike me, you are no gentleman; / And if no gentleman, why then no arms" (2.1.228–231). This apparently refers to the social norms of the day that a gentleman did not strike a lady. Only gentlemen were entitled to bear arms, such as a sword.

After much angry quarrelling, Petruchio tells her what he thinks of her: "I find you passing gentle. / 'Twas told me you were rough and coy and sullen, / And now I find report a very liar" (2.1.249–50). Petruchio then tells her she is to marry him. When Baptista enters, Petruchio says Kate is to marry him on Sunday. Katharina responds: "I'll see thee hang'd on Sunday first" (2.1.307). Petruchio responds: "I will unto Venice, / To buy apparel 'gainst the wedding-day" (2.1.323–24).

After Katharina and Petruchio leave, Gremio and Tranio bid for Bianca's hand. This time it is Baptista who sees his younger daughter's marriage purely in monetary terms: "'Tis deeds must win the prize; and he of both / That can assure my daughter greatest dower / Shall have my Bianca's love" (2.1.352–354).

Dower is the wife's share of her husband's real property after his death. The aged Gremio's opening offer is his house and its rich furnishings and his farm. Tranio offers three or four houses in Pisa, "Besides two thousand ducats by the year / Of fruitful land, all which shall be her jointure" (2.1.379–80).

A "jointure" was a property settlement that the wife agreed to in lieu of her dower rights. Ships are then added to the initial offers. The hard bargaining between Gremio and Tranio is quite a contrast to Petruchio's generosity. Baptista accepts Tranio (disguised as Lucentio) as the highest bidder—provided that his father consents to Bianca's endowment.

On Sunday, the time for the wedding comes—but Petruchio is not there. Katharina feels shame and leaves the stage weeping. Is she just ashamed or has she fallen for the bold Petruchio? When Petruchio finally shows up, he is wearing old clothes unsuitable for a wedding. Baptista protests. But Petruchio responds: "To me she's married, not unto my clothes: / Could I repair what she will wear in me, / As I can change these poor accoutrements, / 'Twere well for Kate and better for myself" (3.2.116–19).

Katharina must accept him as he is. The wedding then occurs off stage in a church. Gremio describes Petruchio's outlandish behavior during the ceremony to Tranio. Petruchio has made a mockery of the wedding ceremony required by the "book" (the English Book of Common Prayer). Then, over the protests of everyone, Petruchio insists upon leaving before he and Katharina partake of the wedding feast. At first Katharina refuses to go but she is eventually carried away by Petruchio. Before they leave, Petruchio declares that Katharina is his property. Others may enjoy the wedding feast, but she will go with him: "I will be master of what is mine own. / She is my goods, my chattels; she is my house" (3.2.231–32). This is the doctrine of "coverture" under the common law where the husband and wife are one person and the legal existence of the wife is incorporated in the husband.

On the road to Petruchio's country house, Katharina falls off her horse into the mud. At the house, Petruchio beats the servants. He throws away the newlyweds' supper on the grounds that it is not good enough for her. Petruchio keeps her up awake all night.

Petruchio: "This is a way to kill a wife with kindness; / And thus I'll curb her mad and headstrong humour. / He that knows better how to tame a shrew, / Now let him speak: 'tis charity to show" (4.1.196–99).

In the morning, Petruchio refuses to accept Katharina's wedding garments. He insists on returning to Baptista's house. On the road, Petruchio insists that Katharina call the sun the moon and the moon the sun. When she "crosses" him, Petruchio threatens to turn around and go back to his house. She relents and calls the sun the moon. Petruchio has won his bride.

Lucentio runs off with Bianca and marries her. The play ends with Katharina's famous speech about the duty that wives owe their husbands. "Thy husband is thy lord, thy life, thy keeper, / Thy head, thy sovereign" (5.2.158–59). Petruchio responds: "Why, there's a wench! Come on, and kiss me, Kate" (5.2.192).

Katharina has come to accept that Petruchio loves her, and she now loves him. Modern readers and theatergoers tend to view Katharina's speech, if genuine, as one of female submission and oppression in marriage. However, the law of marriage and property in Shakespeare's time made the husband the supreme and dominant partner in a completely unequal relationship.

As usual, Shakespeare does not tell us what to think.

CHAPTER 6

ROMEO AND JULIET

Romeo and Juliet is Shakespeare's great play about young love. I agree with literary critic Harold Bloom that "*Romeo and Juliet* is unmatched, in Shakespeare and in the world's literature, as a vision of an uncompromising mutual love that perishes of its own idealism and intensity."[6]

Juliet is the great heroine of the play. Like Rosalind and Cleopatra, Juliet overshadows her male lover, who does not seem quite good enough for her. Although magnificent in the last scene, Romeo is often whiny and self-pitying. But Juliet, who, when performed well, begins as a wide-eyed teenage girl, then quickly matures into a courageous and determined young woman who defies her bullying father and is willing to face death rather than abandon the young man she loves.

In the background: the political problem of how to govern a city beset by two warring factions (the Montagues and the Capulets), and young men who go about armed and are quick to draw the rapier rather than submit to the law.

The play begins on a street in Verona. Two of the Capulet men, Gregory and Sampson, stroll along trading quips about fighting the Montague men and seducing their women. Two Montague men appear, and Gregory suggests that they provoke a fight. But

---

[6] Harold Bloom, *Shakespeare: The Invention of the Human* (Riverhead Books, 1998), 89.

Sampson is cautious: "Let us take the law of our sides; let them begin" (*Romeo and Juliet*, 1.1.28).

Under the common law, it was legal to use force, even lethal force, in self-defense. Sampson is suggesting that they provoke the Montague men to start the fight. When Montague's men, Abraham and Baltazar, come on stage, Sampson bites his thumb. At the time, this was some sort of insulting gesture: "I will bite my thumb at them; which is a disgrace to them, if they bear it" (1.1.31–32).

[Enter ABRAHAM and BALTHASAR]

ABRAHAM   Do you bite your thumb at us, sir?

SAMPSON   I do bite my thumb, sir.

ABRAHAM   Do you bite your thumb at us, sir?

SAMPSON   *[Aside to GREGORY]* Is the law of our side, if I say ay?

GREGORY   No.

SAMPSON   No, sir, I do not bite my thumb at you, sir, but I bite my thumb, sir.

GREGORY   Do you quarrel, sir?

ABRAHAM   Quarrel sir! no, sir.

SAMPSON   If you do, sir, I am for you: I serve as good a man as you.

(1.1.33–42)

Both sides draw swords and fight. Romeo's cousin Benvolio enters and temporarily stops the fight. But Tybalt, cousin to Juliet, enters and draws on Benvolio. "What, drawn, and talk of peace! I hate the word, / As I hate hell, all Montagues, and thee: / Have at thee, coward!" (1.1.57–59).

The fight resumes. More men come from both houses and join the fight. The noise attracts the elderly Lords Capulet and Montague. They try to join the fray but are restrained by their wives. The Prince of Verona enters and orders the fighting to cease. This is the third time the two houses have fought in the streets, and the Prince sentences anyone who again disturbs the peace to die: "If ever you disturb our streets again, / Your lives shall pay the forfeit of the peace" (1.1.83–84).

In England since the reign of Edward I, the King's justices of the peace and sheriffs were bound to preserve the peace of the kingdom. They did this by committing to custody those who broke the peace or by binding them with sureties to keep the peace. That is what the Prince does here to Montague and Capulet. Capulet: "But Montague is bound as well as I, / In penalty alike; and 'tis not hard, I think, / For men so old as we to keep the peace" (1.2.1–3).

As in *The Comedy of Errors*, the play begins with a law or decree that is harsh and unbending with the punishment of death for the offender. In *The Comedy of Errors*, the Duke of Ephesus in the end forgives the merchant Aegeon, and everyone lives happily ever after—which is what happens in comedies. In *Romeo and Juliet*, the Duke's decree leads to tragedy and the death of both young lovers.

The story of the "star-cross'd lovers" occupies the rest of the play and is well-known. Shakespeare in this play writes some of the most beautiful poetry up to this point in his career. After the opening scene, there are only a few references to the law or use of legal terms as metaphors. Before Romeo and his friends crash the Capulet feast late in Act I, Romeo's friend Mercutio regals them with his fantastic tale of the Fairy Queen Mab. She is the fairies' midwife: "And in this state she gallops night by night / Through lovers' brains, and then they dream of love; / O'er courtiers' knees, that dream on court'sies straight, / O'er lawyers' fingers, who straight dream on fees" (1.4.74–77).

In the famous balcony scene, Juliet blushes at the words she has overheard and asks if Romeo loves her faithfully rather than commit "lovers' perjuries" (2.2.92). Romeo begins to swear that he is faithful. But Juliet stops him. She says: "I have no joy of this contract to-night" (2.2.117). Juliet recognizes that they have entered into a contract of marriage. Under the English common law, they were married if their words were seen as mutual declarations of present intention to marry.

But during Elizabeth's reign, whether the law would recognize such a marriage without church solemnization became somewhat muddled. So they go the following day to Friar Laurence's cell, where he performs the church ceremony offstage. The English Church frowned upon a "clandestine" marriage such as this without two witnesses.

Another reference to law: Before Mercutio fights with Tybalt, Benvolio says to him: "An I were so apt to quarrel as thou art, any man should buy the fee-simple of my life for an hour and a quarter" (3.1.30–31). Under the common law, to hold land in "fee simple" meant the owner had full title to the land and the right to exclusively possess it, dispose of it by deed or will, and profit from any income derived from it. A fee simple interest represented as close to absolute ownership of land as there was under common law. Shakespeare is using the term here metaphorically to mean that Benvolio's entire life would worth only an hour and a quarter were he as quarrelsome as Mercutio.

After Romeo fights Tybalt and kills him to avenge the death of Mercutio, Lady Capulet demands that the Prince condemn Romeo to death. "I beg for justice, which thou, prince, must give; / Romeo slew Tybalt, Romeo must not live" (3.1.175). The Prince responds: "Romeo slew him, he slew Mercutio; / Who now the price of his dear blood doth owe?" (3.1.178–79). The Prince banishes Romeo.

The distinction between murder and manslaughter was in flux during Shakespeare's time. One mitigating factor was whether a homicide was committed "in chance medley"—meaning during the heat of a quarrel. This became the offense of manslaughter. The punishment for this might be banishment rather than hanging. That is what the Prince does here. His final comment is: "Bear hence this body and attend our will: / Mercy but murders, pardoning those that kill" (3.1.192–93). He is concerned that undue leniency will encourage further violence.

After the tragic deaths of Romeo and Juliet in the crypt, Capulet and Montague are reconciled. The last lines of the play are spoken by the Prince.

PRINCE   A glooming peace this morning with it brings;
    The sun, for sorrow, will not show his head:
    Go hence, to have more talk of these sad things;
    Some shall be pardon'd, and some punished:
    For never was a story of more woe
    Than this of Juliet and her Romeo.
(5.3.304–9)

The Prince is still thinking of punishments and pardons. No one remembers his name (Escalus). But the names of Romeo and Juliet are immortal because of this beautiful tragedy. Shakespeare does not write a romantic comedy that allows the young lovers to escape to Mantua and live happily ever after. Instead, they are destroyed by their love. Characteristically, he then declines to pass judgment upon the catastrophe.

As Harold Bloom says, "Shakespeare stands back from assigning blame, whether to the feuding older generation, or to the lovers, or to fate, time, chance, and the cosmological contraries."[7]

This sets the stage for the great tragedies that were to follow, beginning with *Hamlet*.

---

[7] Bloom, *Shakespeare*, 93.

CHAPTER 7

RICHARD II

When he takes the Shakespearean stage, Richard II is an impulsive, self-absorbed, erratic King with a guilty conscience.

Richard of Bordeaux was a mere ten years old when he was crowned King upon the death of his grandfather, Edward III. Richard's father, the legendary Edward the Black Prince, had died one year earlier. At this time, the law of primogeniture strictly dictated the hereditary succession of the Crown. Rule by a child could have been avoided (and would have been in earlier days) by crowning another of Edward III's three living sons as King. Doing so in 1377, however, would have created serious questions as to the legitimacy of the King.

With his elaborate coronation ceremony, Richard of Bordeaux could be excused from thinking he had been chosen by God to be King of England. A series of councils ruled in Richard's name during his minority. Richard's uncle Old John of Gaunt proclaimed his loyalty to Richard (notwithstanding his minority) and made no effort to seize the throne for himself.

The Hundred Years' War in France, border conflicts with Scotland, and the economic consequences of the Black Death made for a troubled reign. Heavy taxes were spent on unsuccessful military adventures on the Continent. During Richard's teenage years, England's Angevin Empire in France was lost—except for Calais and a small strip on the Atlantic coast in Gascony. In 1385 Richard led a disastrous military campaign into Scotland. Conflicts between peasants and landowners culminated in the Peasants' Revolt. As the rebel mob took over London, Richard was besieged in the Tower. But then he personally led the forces that ultimately defeated the rebels.

As Richard came into his own as King, his small circle of courtiers and upstarts alienated the established nobility. Richard's coercion of the royal judges into declaring Parliamentary opposition to Richard as treason was the last straw. A group known as the Lords Appellant—which included Henry Bolingbroke (the son of John of Gaunt) and Thomas de Mowbray—led a revolt against Richard's favorites. The leader of the Lords Appellant was Richard's uncle Thomas of Woodstock, Duke of Gloucester.

Many of the King's favorites and supporters were executed (including the Chief Justice of the King's Bench) or exiled by the Lords Appellant. His favorite, the Earl of Oxford Robert de Vere, was banished. To stem the revolt and avoid deposition, Richard promised to seek peace with France and lessen the crushing burden of taxation. This settlement resulted in eight years of peaceful rule. John of Gaunt remained a staunch supporter of the King. Bolingbroke and Mowbray also eventually switched sides and also became supporters of the King. But Richard never forgave Gloucester for the banishment of de Vere.

The period referred to as the "tyranny" of Richard II began with the arrest in 1397 of the Duke of Gloucester. He put his detested uncle in the custody of Thomas Mowbray, who held him in his castle in Calais. While awaiting his trial for treason by Parliament, Gloucester died in Mowbray's castle—probably killed on Richard's orders to avoid a trial and the execution of a prince of the blood. Shakespeare's audience may have been familiar with an anonymous play titled *Thomas of Woodstock,* written around the same time as *Richard II,* which told the story of the murder of the Duke of Gloucester.

Heavy fines were levied on the supporters of the Lords Appellant and their lands were unlawfully confiscated. Richard became increasingly paranoid. In 1398, Richard summoned a Parliament to Shrewsbury. It declared that the laws passed by the Lords Appellant were null and void, and that Parliament had no power to restrain the King. The Parliament of Shrewsbury delegated all parliamentary power to a committee of twelve lords and six commoners chosen from the King's friends. This made Richard an absolute ruler, at least for the time being. He considered the lives and property of his subjects to be disposed of at his pleasure.

Shakespeare's play *Richard II* (written between 1595 and 1596), is set in 1399, the year after the Parliament of Shrewsbury. It begins with two furious lords, Henry Bolingbroke and Thomas Mowbray, accusing each other of treason. Richard has summoned them to court to explain the reasons for the quarrel.

He first addresses himself to Bolingbroke's father, John of Gaunt, the Duke of Lancaster, and the oldest of Edward III's surviving sons.

KING RICHARD II   Old John of Gaunt, time-honour'd
    Lancaster,
    Hast thou, according to thy oath and band,
    Brought hither Henry Hereford thy bold son,
    Here to make good the boisterous late appeal,
    Which then our leisure would not let us hear,
    Against the Duke of Norfolk, Thomas Mowbray?

JOHN OF GAUNT   I have, my liege.

KING RICHARD II   Tell me, moreover, hast thou sounded him,
    If he appeal the duke on ancient malice;
    Or worthily, as a good subject should,
    On some known ground of treachery in him?

JOHN OF GAUNT   As near as I could sift him on that argument,
    On some apparent danger seen in him
    Aim'd at your highness, no inveterate malice.

KING RICHARD II   Then call them to our presence; face to face,
    And frowning brow to brow, ourselves will hear

The accuser and the accused freely speak:
High-stomach'd are they both, and full of ire,
In rage deaf as the sea, hasty as fire.

                     (1.1.1–20)

Richard's reference to an "appeal" refers to an "appeal of felony" which was an accusation by a private citizen of the commission of a felony such as murder or treason. There were no appeals as we know them today from the royal courts. As explained below, trial of an appeal of felony was trial by combat. An appeal of felony based upon malice rather than commission of a felony or treason would fail. The accused had the right to submit the appeal to twelve knights to determine whether the appeal was based upon malice. This had a significant role in the emergence of trial by jury in criminal cases.

At this time, the last thing Richard wants is to have these men speak freely. He knows he is suspected of ordering Mowbray to murder his uncle Gloucester. If the accusation is made against Mowbray, the only defense he can make is that he obeyed an order of the King. When summoned to Richard's presence, Bolingbroke begins the furious accusations.

HENRY BOLINGBROKE   First, heaven be the record to my
    speech!
In the devotion of a subject's love,
Tendering the precious safety of my prince,
And free from other misbegotten hate,
Come I appellant to this princely presence.
Now, Thomas Mowbray, do I turn to thee,
And mark my greeting well; for what I speak
My body shall make good upon this earth,
Or my divine soul answer it in heaven.
Thou art a traitor and a miscreant,
Too good to be so and too bad to live,
Since the more fair and crystal is the sky,
The uglier seem the clouds that in it fly.

Once more, the more to aggravate the note,
With a foul traitor's name stuff I thy throat;
And wish, so please my sovereign, ere I move,
What my tongue speaks my right drawn sword may prove.
(1.1.31–47)

In other words, Bolingbroke, being of equal rank with the Duke of
Norfolk, is challenging him to a trial by combat (a trial of an appeal
of felony). Trial by combat (also called a wager of battle, trial by battle,
or judicial duel) was a method of Germanic law to settle accusations
in the absence of witnesses or a confession. The two parties to the
dispute fought in single combat; the winner was proclaimed to be
in the right. If the accused was vanquished but not killed, he would
be hanged. In essence, it was a judicial- and church-sanctioned duel.
The last known trial by battle in England occurred in 1446 when a
servant accused his master of treason. The master drank too much
wine before the battle and was slain by the servant.

Shakespeare includes such a trial by combat in *Henry VI, Part 2*.
Here, Mowbray responds in kind to Bolingbroke:

THOMAS MOWBRAY   Let not my cold words here accuse
    my zeal:
'Tis not the trial of a woman's war,
The bitter clamour of two eager tongues,
Can arbitrate this cause betwixt us twain;
The blood is hot that must be cool'd for this:
Yet can I not of such tame patience boast
As to be hush'd and nought at all to say:
First, the fair reverence of your highness curbs me
From giving reins and spurs to my free speech;
Which else would post until it had return'd
These terms of treason doubled down his throat.
Setting aside his high blood's royalty,
And let him be no kinsman to my liege,
I do defy him, and I spit at him;

Call him a slanderous coward and a villain:
Which to maintain I would allow him odds,
And meet him, were I tied to run afoot
Even to the frozen ridges of the Alps,
Or any other ground inhabitable,
Where ever Englishman durst set his foot.
Mean time let this defend my loyalty,
By all my hopes, most falsely doth he lie.

(1.1.48–69)

Each of the angry lords accepts the challenge to trial by combat by picking up the glove thrown by the other at his feet. When Richard asks for the particulars of Bolingbroke's accusations, by far the most serious is that Mowbray was complicit in the murder of the Duke of Gloucester: "That he did plot the Duke of Gloucester's death, / Suggest his soon-believing adversaries, / And consequently, like a traitor coward, / Sluiced out his innocent soul through streams of blood" (1.1.100–03). Mowbray's response is curiously ambiguous: "For Gloucester's death, / I slew him not; but to my own disgrace / Neglected my sworn duty in that case" (1.1.133–35).

Richard seeks to pacify the situation because the accusation of complicity in the murder of Gloucester comes too close to his own person.

In a later scene, we learn that John of Gaunt also had some "part" in Gloucester's death. This could not have happened without Richard's assent. Gaunt says to Gloucester's widow: "God's is the quarrel; for God's substitute, / His deputy anointed in His sight, / Hath caused his [Gloucester's] death" (1.2.38–40).

Mowbray responds to the King that he cannot forgive and forget because Bolingbroke's accusations have stained his honor. Richard persists, and Mowbray gives a passionate and eloquent defense of his honor.

KING RICHARD II   Norfolk, throw down [*the glove*], we bid;
there is no boot.

THOMAS MOWBRAY   Myself I throw, dread sovereign,
   at thy foot.
My life thou shalt command, but not my shame:
The one my duty owes; but my fair name,
Despite of death that lives upon my grave,
To dark dishonour's use thou shalt not have.
I am disgraced, impeach'd and baffled here,
Pierced to the soul with slander's venom'd spear,
The which no balm can cure but his heart-blood
Which breathed this poison.

KING RICHARD II   Rage must be withstood:
   Give me his gage: lions make leopards tame.

THOMAS MOWBRAY   Yea, but not change his spots: take
   but my shame.
And I resign my gage. My dear dear lord,
The purest treasure mortal times afford
Is spotless reputation: that away,
Men are but gilded loam or painted clay.
A jewel in a ten-times-barr'd-up chest
Is a bold spirit in a loyal breast.
Mine honour is my life; both grow in one:
Take honour from me, and my life is done:
Then, dear my liege, mine honour let me try;
In that I live and for that will I die.

                    (1.1.166–88)

Richard replies: "We were not born to sue, but to command" (1.1.199). Bolingbroke is equally insistent that only a fight to the death can vindicate his honor. He certainly knows that Richard ordered the murder of Gloucester. He cannot attack the King directly, so he attacks Mowbray.

After John of Gaunt, Bolingbroke was next in line for the kingship if Richard, who was childless, died without a male heir.

If Bolingbroke defeated Mowbray in single combat, he would be a greater threat to the King. Richard says he could command them not to fight but does not do so. Reluctantly, Richard sets the time and place for a trial by combat. "At Coventry, upon Saint Lambert's day: / There shall your swords and lances arbitrate / The swelling difference of your settled hate" (1.1.202–04).

In historical fact, the dispute was referred to a committee of Parliament and then to a Court of Chivalry that ordered the men to fight at Coventry. The belief at the time was that God determined the outcome in a trial by battle. Therefore, God would judge between Mowbray and Bolingbroke.

In the lists at Coventry, the trial begins as almost any modern court proceeding does, with the presiding judge (here the King) calling upon the adverse parties to identify themselves.

[The trumpets sound, and KING RICHARD enters with his nobles, JOHN OF GAUNT, BUSHY, BAGOT, GREEN, and others.
When they are set, enter THOMAS MOWBRAY in arms, defendant, with a Herald.]

KING RICHARD II   Marshal, demand of yonder champion
The cause of his arrival here in arms:
Ask him his name and orderly proceed
To swear him in the justice of his cause.

LORD MARSHAL   In God's name and the king's, say who thou art
And why thou comest thus knightly clad in arms,
Against what man thou comest, and what thy quarrel:
Speak truly, on thy knighthood and thy oath;
As so defend thee heaven and thy valour!

THOMAS MOWBRAY   My name is Thomas Mowbray,
Duke of Norfolk;

Who hither come engaged by my oath—
Which God defend a knight should violate!—
Both to defend my loyalty and truth
To God, my king and my succeeding issue,
Against the Duke of Hereford that appeals me
And, by the grace of God and this mine arm,
To prove him, in defending of myself,
A traitor to my God, my king, and me:
And as I truly fight, defend me heaven!
                    (1.3.8–26)

Thus, the formalities of the opening of a trial are followed, although everyone present knew who the combatants were. A similar challenge is given to Bolingbroke, who responds in kind.

Afterward, Mowbray says he is going to "prove" Bolingbroke's guilt. When the herald formally announces Mowbray, he uses the word "approve." Second Herald: "Here standeth Thomas Mowbray, Duke of Norfolk, / On pain to be found false and recreant, / Both to defend himself and to approve / Henry of Hereford, Lancaster, and Derby, / To God, his sovereign and to him disloyal" (1.3.111–15).

An "approver" was someone who had been indicted but not convicted of a crime, who then accuses by means of an appeal of felony an accomplice or coconspirator of also being involved in the crime. If that person was convicted, the approver would escape the death penalty in exchange for imprisonment or abjuring the realm. The use of the word seems a little out of place here. It basically means the same as "prove."

Bolingbroke and Mowbray are handed their lances, take their positions in the lists, and the charge is sounded. But just before the deadly collision of lances upon the armored knights, the King throws out his staff, halting the trial. In a long, high-sounding speech, the King accuses both men of disturbing the peace of the kingdom. And with no pretense of legality other than a hasty consultation with his "council," the King announces that he is banishing Bolingbroke from England for ten years.

This sentence of banishment without a trial is directly contrary to the guarantee of Section 39 of Magna Carta. Mowbray (who we remember had some role in the murder of Gloucester) receives a heavier sentence: banishment for life. Mowbray protests that the sentence is one of speechless death: "Within my mouth you have engaol'd my tongue, / Doubly portcullis'd with my teeth and lips; / And dull unfeeling barren ignorance / Is made my gaoler to attend on me" (1.3.167–70).

Richard ignores Mowbray's eloquent plea for more just treatment. Richard believes banishment gets rid of both these dangerous, troublesome men. Yet, as if to emphasize the arbitrary and capricious nature of his administration of justice, Richard reduces Bolingbroke's banishment from ten years to six—because he notices the "sad aspect" (1.3.210) of John of Gaunt.

By the end of Act I, Scene 3, Richard's reliance upon personal whim rather than the law is apparent. He has arbitrarily interrupted the trial by combat between Bolingbroke and Mowbray. He has banished both without trial, contrary to Magna Carta. He arbitrarily sentences Mowbray to banishment for life while he banishes Bolingbroke, who started the quarrel, to banishment for only six years.

Old Gaunt accurately predicts that he will not survive his son's banishment. But after the King leaves, he gives Bolingbroke sound advice: "There is no virtue like necessity. / Think not the king did banish thee, / But thou the king" (1.3.280–82). Bolingbroke rejects his father's advice to imagine that banishment will not be so bad. Bolingbroke: "O, who can hold a fire in his hand / By thinking on the frosty Caucasus?" (1.3.296–97). He is a realist, unlike Richard, who thinks he can solve a problem by imagining himself playing a role that provides a solution or by invoking divine intervention. Bolingbroke never speaks of himself as an instrument of God. He is always the practical politician.

At court in the next scene, Richard, thinking he is now safe from the threat posed by Bolingbroke's popularity with the commons, says, "As were our England in reversion his, / And he our subjects' next degree in hope" (1.4.36–37). He reveals that he will personally lead a campaign against Irish rebels. The campaign will be expensive. And he knows "our coffers, with too great a court / And liberal largess, are grown somewhat light" (1.4.44–45). He vows to issue "blank charters" to his officers to extort large sums of money from the wealthy.

At this moment, one of his courtiers enters with news: "Old John of Gaunt is grievous sick, my lord, / Suddenly taken; and hath sent post haste / To entreat your majesty to visit him" (1.4.55–57).

Richard declares that if God will hurry John of Gaunt to the grave, he will take Gaunt's riches to finance his Irish war: "The lining of his coffers shall make coats / To deck our soldiers for these Irish wars. / Come, gentlemen, let's all go visit him: / Pray God we may make haste, and come too late!" (1.4.62–65). This is Richard in his worst tyrannical self-absorption. We have no sympathy for Richard at this point in the play.

On his deathbed, John of Gaunt wishes to see Richard to give him wholesome advice. His brother the Duke of York tells him this is useless. John of Gaunt responds with his famous "scepter'd isle" speech. He thinks because he is dying that he can tell Richard what he is doing to his kingdom. Significantly, Gaunt does not suggest that any of Richard's misguided policies justify rebellion against him. Richard arrives, and his dying uncle gives him harsh and blunt advice. Although Gaunt is ill, he says that Richard is dying: "Thy death-bed is no lesser than thy land. / Wherein thou liest in reputation sick" (2.1.96–97). He accuses Richard of being England's landlord rather than its king: "Landlord of England art thou now, not king: / Thy state of law is bondslave to the law" (2.1.114–15).

John of Gaunt represents the old nobility whose tenants held the traditional copyhold estates rather than a leasehold. To be a mere landlord was to be less than noble. Richard refuses to listen and accuses his uncle of being a "lunatic lean-witted fool" (2.1.116). Richard threatens Gaunt with more arbitrary injustice: "Wert thou not brother to great Edward's son, / This tongue that runs so roundly in thy head / Should run thy head from thy unreverent shoulders" (2.1.122–24).

Gaunt dies, and Richard immediately declares that he will confiscate all of his dead uncle's property to pay for the war in Ireland. "And for these great affairs do ask some charge, / Towards our assistance we do seize to us / The plate, corn, revenues and moveables, / Whereof our uncle Gaunt did stand possess'd" (2.1.159–62).

Richard's uncle the Duke of York (now the last surviving son of Edward III) protests this unlawful confiscation of what under the law is now the property of Henry Bolingbroke.

DUKE OF YORK   O my liege,
Pardon me, if you please; if not, I, pleased
Not to be pardon'd, am content withal.
Seek you to seize and gripe into your hands
The royalties and rights of banish'd Hereford?
Is not Gaunt dead, and doth not Hereford live?
Was not Gaunt just, and is not Harry true?
Did not the one deserve to have an heir?
Is not his heir a well-deserving son?
Take Hereford's rights away, and take from Time
His charters and his customary rights;
Let not to-morrow then ensue to-day;
Be not thyself; for how art thou a king
But by fair sequence and succession?
Now, afore God–God forbid I say true!–
If you do wrongfully seize Hereford's rights,
Call in the letters patent that he hath
By his attorneys-general to sue
His livery, and deny his offer'd homage,
You pluck a thousand dangers on your head,
You lose a thousand well-disposed hearts
And prick my tender patience, to those thoughts
Which honour and allegiance cannot think.

KING RICHARD II   Think what you will, we seize into
our hands
His plate, his goods, his money and his lands.
(2.1.189–213)

York is protesting that Bolingbroke, as a loyal subject, is entitled to inherit John of Gaunt's property and titles according to the
common law.

Letters patent were official documents conferring some benefit or
title to property. Although it is not mentioned in the play, Richard
had given Bolingbroke a patent preserving his right to his property and his inheritance during his banishment. A lawful seizure
of property occurs when it follows the judgment of a competent
tribunal such as Parliament or a court of law. Richard's seizure of
his uncle's property is manifestly illegal because neither John of
Gaunt nor Bolingbroke have been attainted or convicted of a felony.

York makes the argument that it is the law that made Richard
King. "Be not thyself; for how art thou a king / But by fair sequence
and succession?" (2.1.201–02).

Richard acts here again as a tyrant who ignores the law when it
suits his purpose. He rashly ignores the law of succession that gave
him the right to the Crown. Does this give Bolingbroke the right
to argue that resistance to the unlawful seizure of his property is
not treason? How may Richard's subjects respond to a tyrannical
king? As the Duke of York says, this will end badly.

After Richard leaves the room, the remaining lords openly
express their grievances against his tyranny and misrule. Then
Northumberland announces that Bolingbroke has set sail from
France with a group of rebellious lords and six thousand soldiers.
The revolt against Richard has begun.

Richard rashly goes to Ireland to put down a revolt of his Irish
subjects. At court, the Queen is sad without knowing the cause of
her sadness. "'Tis in reversion that I do possess; / But what it is,
that is not yet known; what / I cannot name; 'tis nameless woe, I
wot" (2.2.38–40). A "reversion" was the right to a future succession

to property. She is using the word in the sense that some calamity
lies in the future.

One of Richard's courtiers arrives and tells the Queen that
Bolingbroke has landed in England and the rebellion has widened
to include Lord Northumberland and other powerful lords. The
Duke of York is left to command the King's forces. He remains loyal
to Richard even though he disagrees with the lawless behavior that
spawned the rebellion. But York is old, weary, and has no money
to pay for soldiers. Outside of Berkeley Castle, York confronts his
rebellious nephew. To the accusation that he is committing treason,
Bolingbroke responds that he seeks only his lawful rights as the
Duke of Lancaster.

HENRY BOLINGBROKE   As I was banish'd, I was banish'd
    Hereford;
    But as I come, I come for Lancaster.
    And, noble uncle, I beseech your grace
    Look on my wrongs with an indifferent eye:
    You are my father, for methinks in you
    I see old Gaunt alive; O, then, my father,
    Will you permit that I shall stand condemn'd
    A wandering vagabond; my rights and royalties
    Pluck'd from my arms perforce and given away
    To upstart unthrifts? Wherefore was I born?
    If that my cousin king be King of England,
    It must be granted I am Duke of Lancaster.
    You have a son, Aumerle, my noble cousin;
    Had you first died, and he been thus trod down,
    He should have found his uncle Gaunt a father,
    To rouse his wrongs and chase them to the bay.
    I am denied to sue my livery here,
    And yet my letters-patents give me leave:
    My father's goods are all distrain'd and sold,
    And these and all are all amiss employ'd.
    What would you have me do? I am a subject,

And I challenge law: attorneys are denied me;
And therefore, personally I lay my claim
To my inheritance of free descent.

(2.3.114–137)

Bolingbroke is making the same argument that York made: The law of hereditary succession is what made Richard King and Bolingbroke Duke of Lancaster.

"Distraint" for rent in arrears was a self-help remedy whereby the landlord could seize the tenant's chattels to secure payment of rent. Shakespeare does not seem to be using the word in this technical sense here. Bolingbroke is saying his father's goods have been seized and sold by the King. Treason was a crime at common law. But the substantive law of treason was unusual in that very early it was defined by statute. A statute of Edward III in 1352 defined treason as to "compass or imagine the death of our lord the king, of our lady his Queen, or of their eldest son and heir; . . . to levy war against the king in his realm or adhere to the king's enemies and be provably attaint of it by men of the offender's own condition. . . ."

The statue was intended by Parliament to limit what royal judges could charge as treason. Up to this point, Bolingbroke has not committed treason as defined by the 1352 statute. He has not threatened the King. Arguably, his violation of the King's decree of banishment is not an act of rebellion. He has not claimed the kingship for himself.

York does not attempt to defend the unlawful acts of Richard. He is loyal to the legitimate King, but he wearily replies that he is too weak to force Bolingbroke and his confederates into obedience to the King. So he invites them into Berkeley Castle for the night. Bolingbroke vows to go to Bristol Castle, which is held by Bushy and Bagot, two of Richard's courtiers: "The caterpillars of the commonwealth, / Which I have sworn to weed and pluck away" (2.3.167–68).

In Act III, Richard, returning from Ireland, lands on the coast of Wales to confront Bolingbroke and his rebellion. The Bishop of

Carlisle assures him that God is on his side. But Richard must use the means that heaven provides. Richard responds with a beautiful speech on the power of a king appointed by God.

KING RICHARD II   Discomfortable cousin! know'st thou not
    That when the searching eye of heaven is hid,
    Behind the globe, that lights the lower world,
    Then thieves and robbers range abroad unseen
    In murders and in outrage, boldly here;
    But when from under this terrestrial ball
    He fires the proud tops of the eastern pines
    And darts his light through every guilty hole,
    Then murders, treasons and detested sins,
    The cloak of night being pluck'd from off their backs,
    Stand bare and naked, trembling at themselves?
    So when this thief, this traitor, Bolingbroke,
    Who all this while hath revell'd in the night
    Whilst we were wandering with the antipodes,
    Shall see us rising in our throne, the east,
    His treasons will sit blushing in his face,
    Not able to endure the sight of day,
    But self-affrighted tremble at his sin.
    Not all the water in the rough rude sea
    Can wash the balm off from an anointed king;
    The breath of worldly men cannot depose
    The deputy elected by the Lord:
    For every man that Bolingbroke hath press'd
    To lift shrewd steel against our golden crown,
    God for his Richard hath in heavenly pay
    A glorious angel: then, if angels fight,
    Weak men must fall, for heaven still guards the right.
                    (3.2.36–62)

As God's appointed deputy, Richard may not be deposed by mere mortal men. Disobedience to Richard is disobedience to God.

Shakespeare's audience would recognize this belief from the letter of St. Paul to the Romans.

> Let every soul submit himself unto the authority of the higher powers; for there is no power but of God; the powers that be, be ordained of God. Whosoever therefore resisteth the power resisteth the ordinance of God: but they that resist shall receive to themselves damnation.[8]

Immediately, however, Richard is told he will need angels to fight for him because his Welsh forces have abandoned him. Richard's sun is not rising but setting. But there is more of woe. Bushy, Green, and Wiltshire have all lost their heads at Bristol. Richard's response to death and abandonment is Shakespeare showing the power of his poetic genius. When Richard is asked where is the Duke of York with his powers, he wails at his abandonment by his those who should be supporting him.

KING RICHARD II   No matter where; of comfort no man speak:
    Let's talk of graves, of worms, and epitaphs;
    Make dust our paper and with rainy eyes
    Write sorrow on the bosom of the earth,
    Let's choose executors and talk of wills:
    And yet not so, for what can we bequeath
    Save our deposed bodies to the ground?
    Our lands, our lives and all are Bolingbroke's,
    And nothing can we call our own but death
    And that small model of the barren earth
    Which serves as paste and cover to our bones.
    For God's sake, let us sit upon the ground
    And tell sad stories of the death of kings;
    How some have been deposed; some slain in war,
    Some haunted by the ghosts they have deposed;

---

[8] Romans 13:1–2

Some poison'd by their wives: some sleeping kill'd;
All murder'd: for within the hollow crown
That rounds the mortal temples of a king
Keeps Death his court and there the antic sits,
Scoffing his state and grinning at his pomp,
Allowing him a breath, a little scene,
To monarchize, be fear'd and kill with looks,
Infusing him with self and vain conceit,
As if this flesh which walls about our life,
Were brass impregnable, and humour'd thus
Comes at the last and with a little pin
Bores through his castle wall, and farewell king!
Cover your heads and mock not flesh and blood
With solemn reverence: throw away respect,
Tradition, form and ceremonious duty,
For you have but mistook me all this while:
I live with bread like you, feel want,
Taste grief, need friends: subjected thus,
How can you say to me, I am a king?
               (3.2.144–177)

This speech was a favorite of President Lincoln, perhaps a reflection of the fatalism and depression to which he was prone.

In an orgy of self-pity and despair, Richard orders his forces discharged. He will "[g]o to Flint castle: there I'll pine away; / A king, woe's slave, shall kingly woe obey" (3.2.210–211). Richard is the ultimate victim of his own theory of kingship. He is anointed by God and omnipotent, but his subjects have rebelled against him. The divine right of kings has failed. Therefore, he is not a king. He is nothing.

When Bolingbroke arrives at Flint Castle, he sends Northumberland to tell Richard that he seeks only his lawful rights as Duke of Lancaster. His message to the King alternates between submission and brutal threats of what he will do if the King does not yield to his demands.

Richard is unnerved and is now determined to make a martyr of himself: "What must the king do now? must he submit? / The king shall do it: must he be deposed? / The king shall be contented: must he lose / The name of king? o' God's name, let it go" (3.3.145–48). Marjorie Garber says of this speech: "If the king is not God's anointed representative, but only a man chosen by other men, then everything that follows is role-playing."[9] Still playing a role, Richard chooses to play the role of martyr. He comes down from the castle wall and meekly submits to an astonished Bolingbroke. Richard is not only restoring to him his inheritance, Richard is giving Bolingbroke the Crown.

Because Shakespeare never has Bolingbroke tell us what he is thinking, we don't know whether he intended this all along, or he just accepts the gift of kingship from Richard.

They all set off for London. At London's Westminster Hall York announces that "Great Duke of Lancaster, I come to thee / From plume-pluck'd Richard; who with willing soul / Adopts thee heir, and his high sceptre yields / To the possession of thy royal hand" (4.1.109–12). Bolingbroke is proclaimed King Henry IV: "Ascend his throne, descending now from him; / And long live Henry, fourth of that name!" (4.1.113–14).

But his ascent to the throne is challenged by the Bishop of Carlisle. He presents the argument in favor of an absolutist hereditary monarchy. He denies the right of ordinary men to sit in judgment of a king. As an anointed King, Richard was God's deputy and cannot be deposed by mortal men. He predicts that Bolingbroke's rebellion will lead to other rebellions and civil war.

HENRY BOLINGBROKE   In God's name, I'll ascend the regal throne.

BISHOP OF CARLISLE   Marry. God forbid!
Worst in this royal presence may I speak,

---

[9] Garber, *Shakespeare After All*, 261.

Yet best beseeming me to speak the truth.
Would God that any in this noble presence
Were enough noble to be upright judge
Of noble Richard! then true noblesse would
Learn him forbearance from so foul a wrong.
What subject can give sentence on his king?
And who sits here that is not Richard's subject?
Thieves are not judged but they are by to hear,
Although apparent guilt be seen in them;
And shall the figure of God's majesty,
His captain, steward, deputy-elect,
Anointed, crowned, planted many years,
Be judged by subject and inferior breath,
And he himself not present? O, forfend it,
God, That in a Christian climate souls refined
Should show so heinous, black, obscene a deed!
I speak to subjects, and a subject speaks,
Stirr'd up by God, thus boldly for his king:
My Lord of Hereford here, whom you call king,
Is a foul traitor to proud Hereford's king:
And if you crown him, let me prophesy:
The blood of English shall manure the ground,
And future ages groan for this foul act;
Peace shall go sleep with Turks and infidels,
And in this seat of peace tumultuous wars
Shall kin with kin and kind with kind confound;
Disorder, horror, fear and mutiny
Shall here inhabit, and this land be call'd
The field of Golgotha and dead men's skulls.
O, if you raise this house against this house,
It will the woefullest division prove
That ever fell upon this cursed earth.
Prevent it, resist it, let it not be so,
Lest child, child's children, cry against you woe!
(4.1.115–151)

Shakespeare's audience, hearing this speech, would remember the turmoil and rebellions of King Henry IV's reign, and the calamitous Wars of the Roses during the reign of Henry VI.

Carlisle says Bolingbroke is a traitor and not a legitimate king. But he is the de facto king and rebellion against him is treason. There is no response to Carlisle's speech except to arrest him for treason. Northumberland: "Well have you argued, sir; and, for your pains, / Of capital treason we arrest you here. / My Lord of Westminster, be it your charge / To keep him safely till his day of trial" (4.1.152–54).

Thus, with Bolingbroke firmly in power, the forms of the law rather than summary execution (as in the case of Bushy *et al.*) must be observed. Bolingbroke insists that Richard be brought forth to publicly yield up the crown "that in common view / He may surrender; so we shall proceed / Without suspicion" (4.1.158–60).

Bolingbroke is the practical politician who wants all to see that there is an apparently legitimate transfer of power from Richard to himself. Richard, however, is not done with role-playing and drama. When he comes onstage, Richard demands to know why he is sent for. He will not give up the crown without one last scene of theatrical pathos.

KING RICHARD II   Alack, why am I sent for to a king,
    Before I have shook off the regal thoughts
    Wherewith I reign'd? I hardly yet have learn'd
    To insinuate, flatter, bow, and bend my limbs:
    Give sorrow leave awhile to tutor me
    To this submission. . . .
    God save the king! Will no man say amen?
    Am I both priest and clerk? well then, amen.
    God save the king! although I be not he;
    And yet, amen, if heaven do think him me.
    To do what service am I sent for hither?

DUKE OF YORK   To do that office of thine own good will
    Which tired majesty did make thee offer,

The resignation of thy state and crown
To Henry Bolingbroke.

KING RICHARD II   Give me the crown. Here, cousin, seize
the crown;
Here cousin:
On this side my hand, and on that side yours.
Now is this golden crown like a deep well
That owes two buckets, filling one another,
The emptier ever dancing in the air,
The other down, unseen and full of water:
That bucket down and full of tears am I,
Drinking my griefs, whilst you mount up on high.

HENRY BOLINGBROKE   I thought you had been willing
to resign.

KING RICHARD II   My crown I am; but still my griefs are mine:
You may my glories and my state depose,
But not my griefs; still am I king of those.

HENRY BOLINGBROKE   Part of your cares you give me with
your crown.

KING RICHARD II   Your cares set up do not pluck my cares
down.
My care is loss of care, by old care done;
Your care is gain of care, by new care won:
The cares I give I have, though given away;
They tend the crown, yet still with me they stay.

HENRY BOLINGBROKE   Are you contented to resign the crown?

KING RICHARD II   Ay, no; no, ay; for I must nothing be;
Therefore no no, for I resign to thee.

Now mark me, how I will undo myself;
I give this heavy weight from off my head
And this unwieldy sceptre from my hand,
The pride of kingly sway from out my heart;
With mine own tears I wash away my balm,
With mine own hands I give away my crown,
With mine own tongue deny my sacred state,
With mine own breath release all duty's rites:
All pomp and majesty I do forswear;
My manors, rents, revenues I forego;
My acts, decrees, and statutes I deny:
God pardon all oaths that are broke to me!
God keep all vows unbroke that swear to thee!
Make me, that nothing have, with nothing grieved,
And thou with all pleased, that hast all achieved!
Long mayst thou live in Richard's seat to sit,
And soon lie Richard in an earthly pit!
God save King Harry, unking'd Richard says,
What more remains?

(4.1.165–169, 175–224)

Verbally, Richard reverses his ceremony of coronation. But the coronation of a king anointed by God was supposed to last forever. Northumberland tries to force Richard to sign a paper confessing his crimes against the state in order to satisfy the "commons" that he has been lawfully deposed. Richard responds that his eyes are too full of tears to read the paper. Bolingbroke orders Richard to be conveyed to the Tower. Richard responds: "O, good! convey? conveyers are you all, / That rise thus nimbly by a true king's fall" (4.1.323–25).

A conveyance was an instrument such as a deed transferring title to property. Richard is protesting the treatment of his royal person as if he was nothing more than property.

On October 1, 1399, with Richard in the Tower, the reign of the last Plantagenet king ends. Bolingbroke announces that his coronation will be the following Wednesday.

Bolingbroke is now King Henry IV. The reign of the House of Lancaster has begun. But the means by which this has happened are not settled. York wanted Richard to voluntarily yield up the Crown. Richard does not do so. Northumberland wants Richard to confess to crimes against the state so that he may be impeached by Parliament. Richard refuses to sign the confession. Bolingbroke asks Richard: "Are you contented to resign the crown?" (4.1.204). He then takes the crown.

In the play, there is no accepted legal or political theory as to how Bolingbroke has become King. The question of how Henry IV could be a legitimate king after usurping the place of a king chosen by God would haunt Henry and his successors of the Lancastrian dynasty. This is foreshadowed in the farewells between Richard and his Queen. She waits in a street leading to the Tower as he is led there by Northumberland and guards. She asks Northumberland if Richard can be banished to France with her.

QUEEN   And must we be divided? must we part?

KING RICHARD II   Ay, hand from hand, my love, and heart from heart.

QUEEN   Banish us both and send the king with me.

NORTHUMBERLAND   That were some love but little policy.

QUEEN   Then whither he goes, thither let me go.

KING RICHARD II   So two, together weeping, make one woe.
   Weep thou for me in France, I for thee here;
   Better far off than near, be ne'er the near.
                    (5.1.81–88)

Northumberland is saying the King cannot be exiled to France with the Queen ("little policy") where they could have a son who would further threaten the legitimacy of King Henry IV and his heirs. Edward III had five sons who lived to maturity and whose descendants could make some claim to the throne. It is an irony of history that his grandson Richard II had no male heirs.

Imprisoned at Pomfret Castle, Richard imagines how he "may compare / This prison where I live unto the world: / And for because the world is populous / And here is not a creature but myself, / I cannot do it; yet I'll hammer it out" (5.5.1–5). He laments that "I wasted time, and now doth time waste me" (5.5.49). Richard is murdered in prison by one seeking favor with the new king.

At the last, Richard dies bravely and with dignity.

[Enter EXTON and Servants, armed]

KING RICHARD II   How now! what means death in this rude assault?
Villain, thy own hand yields thy death's instrument.

[Snatching an axe from a Servant and killing him]

Go thou, and fill another room in hell.

[He kills another. Then Exton strikes him down]

That hand shall burn in never-quenching fire
That staggers thus my person. Exton, thy fierce hand
Hath with the king's blood stain'd the king's own land.
Mount, mount, my soul! thy seat is up on high;
Whilst my gross flesh sinks downward, here to die.

[Dies]

EXTON   As full of valour as of royal blood:
Both have I spill'd; O would the deed were good!
For now the devil, that told me I did well,
Says that this deed is chronicled in hell.
(5.5.104–116)

Exton puts Richard's body in a coffin and takes it to the King, where his deed is not well received: "Exton, I thank thee not; for thou hast wrought / A deed of slander with thy fatal hand / Upon my head and all this famous land" (5.6.34–36). He banishes Exton. Henry's wish for Richard's death was too well known for him to deny it. So, Henry declares: "I'll make a voyage to the Holy Land, / To wash this blood off from my guilty hand" (5.5.49–50).

The play began with Richard banishing Mowbray and Bolingbroke. It ends with Henry banishing the Bishop of Carlisle and Exton. It begins and ends with disputes over the responsibility for the murder of the Duke of Gloucester. Richard's guilty response to the question ultimately led to his downfall.

King Henry handles the issue with an acute sense of the most practical solution to the problem. However, the deposition and murder of Richard will haunt the kingship of Henry, just as the murder of Gloucester had haunted that of Richard. Ultimately, we will see the prophesy of the Bishop of Carlisle come true.

Richard II was written and first performed between 1595 and 1596. Five or so years later, the Earl of Essex, a former favorite of Queen Elizabeth, returned from Ireland after a disastrous military campaign against the rebel Tyrone. After a trial before the Privy Council, he was dismissed from office and put under house arrest. The foolhardy Essex and a small band of followers then concocted an insane plan to storm the palace, kidnap Elizabeth, and rule England in her name. Allies of Essex commissioned a performance by the Lord Chamberlain's Men of the old play *Richard II* on February 7, 1601.

The idea was that this play about the overthrow of a king would inspire the London populace to rise up and rally to Essex. The day after the performance, on February 8, 1601, Essex and his armed followers rode into London to carry out this insane plan. But the performance did not have the intended effect; Londoners barricaded their streets against Essex. The pathetic little rebellion was quickly smashed by forces loyal to the Queen under the command of the Bishop of London.

As his followers fled after an attack by the Bishop's pikemen, Essex returned to his mansion. With his house surrounded by a company of cavalry, Essex burned his papers and surrendered. He was quickly tried for treason in Westminster Hall before the Lord High Steward, the common law court judges (including Chief Justice Popham, who had briefly been held as a hostage at Essex House), and a jury of Peers. Sir Edward Coke and Sir Francis Bacon (Essex's former protégé) prosecuted him. Sir Walter Raleigh commanded forty members of the Queen's Guard in attendance.

Essex was convicted and sentenced to death. On the scaffold he proclaimed his innocence: "I entreat that all men would have a charitable opinion of me. We never, I protest to God, intended violence or harm to her Majesties person or dignity." Essex was beheaded, but many of his small band of followers were spared, including Shakespeare's patron, the Earl of Southampton.

Shakespeare was approaching dangerous ground in telling the story of the deposition of a legitimate monarch. Under the Tudors, the idea of deposing a lawful king was unthinkable. The Tudor sense of order was embodied in the opening of the Anglican *Sermon of Obedience* that was preached regularly during Shakespeare's lifetime.

Almighty God hath created and appointed all things, in heaven, earth, and waters, in a most excellent and perfect order. In heaven he hath appointed distinct Orders and states of Archangels and Angels. In the earth he has assigned Kings, princes, with other governors under them, all in good and necessary order. . . . Take away Kings, Princes, Rulers, Magistrates, Judges and such states of God's order , no man shall ride or go by the high way unrobbed, no man shall sleep in his own house or bed unkilled, no man shall keep his wife, children, and possessions in quietness, all things shall be common, and there must needs follow all mischief and utter destruction, both of souls, bodies, goods and commonwealths.

After Shakespeare wrote *Richard II*, the lawyer John Hayward was accused by the Queen of sedition for writing a history (dedicated to the Earl of Essex) of Henry IV in which he told the story of the deposition of Richard II. Hayward was tried in the Court of Star Chamber in 1599 and sent to the Tower for the rest of her reign. Hayward's book was introduced as evidence at the treason trial of the Earl of Essex in 1601. After Essex's rebellion, Queen Elizabeth said, "I am Richard II, know ye not that."

She survived because Essex was not Bolingbroke, and she was not Richard II. But this statement reflects the potentially seditious nature of Shakespeare's *Richard II*. After the Essex rebellion, one of Shakespeare's colleagues from the Lord Chamberlain's Men was summoned to appear before the Privy Council and explain the performance of the play on the eve of the rebellion. Questioned by Attorney General Edward Coke, Augustine Phillips testified that the play was old and stale, but that one of Essex's conspirators, Sir Gelly Meyrick, had paid the company forty shillings to perform it.

We do not know how close Shakespeare came to getting into serious trouble over this performance of *Richard II*. The Lord Chamberlain admonished the company for performing the play but imposed no other punishment, probably because the Lord Chamberlain's Men were favorites of Queen Elizabeth.

Convicted of treason, Sir Gelly Meyrick was soon hanged, drawn and quartered.

Under the law, it was treason to engage in rebellion against the King. But was there no means by which the country could rid itself of a lawless or tyrannical king? The Roman Church answered the question by teaching absolute obedience to the monarch. This is the argument of the Bishop of Carlisle in Act 4 of *Richard II*. York, Northumberland, and the other great lords *act* on the premise that a bad king can be forced to resign the Crown. Richard refers it to as a deposition rather than a resignation: "You may my glories and my state depose, / But not my griefs; still am I king of those" (4.1.196).

To satisfy the "commons," Northumberland tries to get Richard to sign a paper confessing to "grievous crimes" against the state.

Richard refuses to sign the document but yields the Crown to Bolingbroke. Significantly, this deposition scene was not included in the first quarto version of the play that was published during Elizabeth's reign. It appears for the first time in the *First Folio* in 1623.

In the play, the theory of the divine right of kings was eloquently stated by Richard and Carlisle. Bolingbroke and his supporters never explicitly articulate a political or constitutional theory that would justify resistance to a legitimate monarch.

Indeed, under the Tudors and the Stuarts, with their belief in the absolute divine right of kings, such a theory would have been viewed as treason. Even the suggestion that the king was subject to the law resulted in King James I dismissing Sir Edward Coke as Chief Justice of England.

Shakespeare himself seems more interested in drama and character than abstract political theories. But by the publication of the *First Folio*, a generation was coming of age that, relying on the precedent of 1399, would depose King Charles I, and after a trial behead him.

In the Glorious Revolution of 1688, the last of the absolutist Stuart kings was deposed. According to the later Whig historians such as Lord Macaulay, the principle of constitutionalism grounded upon the consent of the people as opposed to absolutism had been firmly established. The seeds of thought that led to 1688 are in Shakespeare's *Richard II*.

CHAPTER 8

KING JOHN

John was King of England from 1199 until his death in 1216. As the youngest of five sons of King Henry II and Eleanor of Aquitaine, John was not expected to succeed to the Crown. However, John's older brothers William, Henry, and Geoffrey all died young. By the time Richard I became King in 1189, young John was a potential heir to the throne. While his brother was participating in the Third Crusade, John unsuccessfully attempted a rebellion against Richard's royal administrators.

While Richard was captured and held for ransom by the Holy Roman emperor as he was attempting to return to England, John schemed with the King of France to make himself King. That effort failed when Richard was ransomed, returned to England, and regained the throne in 1194. Five years later, at the siege of a castle in Southern France, Richard was struck in the shoulder by a crossbow bolt. He developed gangrene and died on April 6, 1199, at the age of forty-one. On his deathbed, he is said to have named his brother John as his successor.

John seized the English treasury at the castle of Chinon and got himself proclaimed as Duke of Normandy. The English barons thought John was untrustworthy and were appalled by his treachery toward Richard. Despite this, and largely due to the efforts of William Marshal, 1st Earl of Pembroke, in England, and Eleanor of Aquitaine in France, John was proclaimed King of England. He was crowned by the Archbishop of Canterbury in a hastily organized ceremony on May 25, 1199.

By inheritance and marriage, King Henry II, John's father, ruled over vast stretches of French land, including Normandy, Aquitaine, and Gascony. Louis VII of France encouraged Henry's sons to rebel against him as part of his campaign to regain French territory from the English. When Louis VII died in 1180, his son Philip II continued his father's policy by fighting Henry and his sons.

In the early years of his reign, John lost the Duchy of Normandy to Philip, resulting in the collapse of most of the Angevin Empire acquired by Henry II. John was in constant conflict with Archbishop Hubert Walter, whom Richard had left to administer the state in his absence and who retained his authority under John.

As we will see in the play, Pope Innocent III forced John to accept Stephen of Langton as Walter's successor as Archbishop of Canterbury and the conflict continued. The revolt of the barons near the end of John's reign led to the signing of Magna Carta in 1215. At the time, it was not obvious that it would become one of the most important legal documents in the English common law tradition. The Magna Carta was intended to be fundamental law, binding upon John and his successors. It famously declared: "No freeman shall be taken or imprisoned, or disseised [dispossessed] of his free tenement, liberties or free customs, or outlawed or exiled or in any way destroyed . . . unless by the lawful judgment of his peers, or by the law of the land."

From the thirteenth century, the myth and legend of Magna Carta grew—until in the seventeenth century all the forces of liberalism rallied around it in the face of Stuart absolutism and tyranny. But this was long after the death of William Shakespeare. In fact, Magna Carta is not even mentioned in Shakespeare's play.

Sometimes described as a "neglected masterpiece," *King John* was written between 1596 and 1597 when England was fixated on the question of who would succeed the aging Queen Elizabeth. Another War of the Roses had to be avoided at all costs. Much of the play focuses upon John's usurpation of the throne that rightly (by the law of primogeniture) belonged to young Arthur, the son of John's older brother Geoffrey. Once again, Shakespeare frames the play around the relations between generations, here three pairs of mothers and sons.

The play begins with the French ambassador Chatillon announcing to King John that Philip II of France has recognized Arthur as England's "lawful" king.

KING JOHN   Now, say, Chatillon, what would France with us?

CHATILLON   Thus, after greeting, speaks the King of France
In my behavior to the majesty,
The borrow'd majesty, of England here.

QUEEN ELINOR   A strange beginning: 'borrow'd majesty!'

KING JOHN   Silence, good mother; hear the embassy.

CHATILLON   Philip of France, in right and true behalf
Of thy deceased brother Geffrey's son,
Arthur Plantagenet, lays most lawful claim
To this fair island and the territories,
To Ireland, Poictiers, Anjou, Touraine, Maine,
Desiring thee to lay aside the sword
Which sways usurpingly these several titles,
And put these same into young Arthur's hand,
Thy nephew and right royal sovereign.
                    (*King John*, 1.1.1–16)

Clearly, Chatillon is suggesting that John is not the lawful king of England. Upon the death of the childless Richard I, there were two possible claimants to the English throne: John, Richard's younger brother, and Arthur, the son of Geoffrey, John's deceased older brother.

Before he left on the Third Crusade, Richard declared that Arthur was his heir. On his deathbed, he was reported to have declared John as his heir. Philip II initially supported John as King of England because he had the support of the Norman barons. But he switched his support to Arthur after John abducted and married the twelve-year-old daughter of one of the leading lords of the Aquitaine.

In the play, John and his mother, Queen Eleanor, are defiant in opposing Arthur's claim to the Crown. Chatillon says there will be war. John and Eleanor don't bother to deny that under hereditary succession as the proper theory of sovereignty, John should not be king. But he is recognized in England as the de facto king: "Our strong possession and our right for us" (1.1.40). As in so many of the history plays, the backbone of the plot is built upon a struggle over title to the Crown.

Under the Norman and early Plantagenet monarchs, the king would sit with his council (known as the *Curia Regis*) to adjudicate legal disputes. After Chatillon departs, John is called upon to judge a more mundane case of disputed succession. An estate is claimed by two brothers. The Earl of Essex was John's Chief Justicar, at the time the chief legal officer of England. He introduces the Sheriff of Northampton, who brings forward the case. Although the property in dispute is in Northampton, the case is brought to London because that is where Henry II established the royal courts. Presumably, the case could also have been brought in the Court of Common Pleas at Westminster.

[Enter a Sheriff]

ESSEX   My liege, here is the strangest controversy
Come from country to be judged by you,
That e'er I heard: shall I produce the men?

KING JOHN   Let them approach.
Our abbeys and our priories shall pay
This expedition's charge.

[Enter ROBERT and the BASTARD]

What men are you?

BASTARD   Your faithful subject I, a gentleman
    Born in Northamptonshire and eldest son,
    As I suppose, to Robert Faulconbridge,
    A soldier, by the honour-giving hand
    Of Coeur-de-lion knighted in the field.
                  (1.1.45–56)

Coeur-de-lion is French for Heart of Lion. This was the name used
at court to refer to King Richard I. More than a hundred years after
the Norman Conquest the language spoken at court was Norman
French. The language spoken in the law courts was "law French,"
an amalgamation of French and English.

John demands to know who the other brother is and why he is
making a claim upon the Bastard's inheritance.

KING JOHN   What art thou?

ROBERT   The son and heir to that same Faulconbridge.

KING JOHN   Is that the elder, and art thou the heir?
    You came not of one mother then, it seems.

BASTARD   Most certain of one mother, mighty king;
    That is well known; and, as I think, one father:
    But for the certain knowledge of that truth
    I put you o'er to heaven and to my mother:
    Of that I doubt, as all men's children may.

QUEEN ELINOR   Out on thee, rude man! thou dost shame thy
    mother
    And wound her honour with this diffidence.

BASTARD   I, madam? no, I have no reason for it;
    That is my brother's plea and none of mine;
    The which if he can prove, a' pops me out

> At least from fair five hundred pound a year:
> Heaven guard my mother's honour and my land!

KING JOHN   A good blunt fellow. Why, being younger born,
Doth he lay claim to thine inheritance?

BASTARD   I know not why, except to get the land.
But once he slander'd me with bastardy:
But whether I be as true begot or no,
That still I lay upon my mother's head,
But that I am as well begot, my liege,–
Fair fall the bones that took the pains for me!–
Compare our faces and be judge yourself.
If old sir Robert did beget us both
And were our father and this son like him,
O old sir Robert, father, on my knee
I give heaven thanks I was not like to thee!

KING JOHN   Why, what a madcap hath heaven lent us here!

QUEEN ELINOR   He hath a trick of Coeur-de-lion's face;
The accent of his tongue affecteth him.
Do you not read some tokens of my son
In the large composition of this man?
                                              (1.1.57–90)

John's second question recognizes the law of primogeniture, which made the eldest son the heir of his father. This is the same law that would make Arthur King—as the son of an older brother rather than John. Robert then states his claim that King Richard sent his father as ambassador to Germany, and that Philip the Bastard was conceived while Richard was staying with his mother in England. "Upon his death-bed [*my father*] by will bequeath'd / His lands to me, and took it on his death / That this my mother's son was none of his" (1.1.111–13).

At common law, a bastard had no rights of inheritance to real property. John denies the claim of bastardy, invoking the rule of law at the time that a child born during wedlock was presumed to be legitimate.

KING JOHN Sirrah, your brother is legitimate;
Your father's wife did after wedlock bear him,
And if she did play false, the fault was hers;
Which fault lies on the hazards of all husbands
That marry wives. Tell me, how if my brother,
Who, as you say, took pains to get this son,
Had of your father claim'd this son for his?
In sooth, good friend, your father might have kept
This calf bred from his cow from all the world;
In sooth he might; then, if he were my brother's,
My brother might not claim him; nor your father,
Being none of his, refuse him: this concludes;
My mother's son did get your father's heir;
Your father's heir must have your father's land.
    (1.1.118–131)

John is saying that whoever was his father, the Bastard is his father's heir. King John's judgment was perfectly correct according to English common law of the time. This presumption of legitimacy could be overcome only by strong evidence such as the impotency of the husband or that he was "beyond the four seas" during the entire period of the pregnancy. Robert admits that his father returned to England within fourteen weeks after his mother's pregnancy. According to the law, the Bastard was legitimate and entitled to inherit his father's land. But then the case takes a strange turn.

ROBERT Shall then my father's will be of no force
To dispossess that child which is not his?

BASTARD Of no more force to dispossess me, sir,
Than was his will to get me, as I think.

QUEEN ELINOR   Whether hadst thou rather be a Faulconbridge
    And like thy brother, to enjoy thy land,
    Or the reputed son of Coeur-de-lion,
    Lord of thy presence and no land beside?

BASTARD   Madam, an if my brother had my shape,
    And I had his, sir Robert's his, like him;
    And if my legs were two such riding-rods,
    My arms such eel-skins stuff'd, my face so thin
    That in mine ear I durst not stick a rose
    Lest men should say 'Look, where three-farthings goes!'
    And, to his shape, were heir to all this land,
    Would I might never stir from off this place,
    I would give it every foot to have this face;
    I would not be sir Nob in any case.

QUEEN ELINOR   I like thee well: wilt thou forsake thy fortune,
    Bequeath thy land to him and follow me?

BASTARD   I am a soldier and now bound to France.
    Brother, take you my land, I'll take my chance.
    Your face hath got five hundred pound a year,
    Yet sell your face for five pence and 'tis dear.
    Madam, I'll follow you unto the death.
                          (1.1.132–156)

At this time, the owner of real property could not by will alter
the rules of succession with respect to title to land. But as a bastard,
Philip could not inherit property from his mother's husband.

    John knights his bastard nephew as Richard Plantagenet. Philip
gets the name Plantagenet but inherits nothing else from his deceased
father. He is a "landless knight." And as a bastard, he is entirely
out of the royal succession. Nevertheless, he is the real hero of the
play. Philip's mother enters and, after rebuking her impertinent
son, admits that Richard was his father.

LADY FAULCONBRIDGE   Hast thou denied thyself a
Faulconbridge?

BASTARD   As faithfully as I deny the devil.

LADY FAULCONBRIDGE   King Richard Coeur-de-lion was thy
father:
By long and vehement suit I was seduced
To make room for him in my husband's bed:
Heaven lay not my transgression to my charge!
Thou art the issue of my dear offence,
Which was so strongly urged past my defence.
(1.1.254–261)

A man committed the crime of seduction at common law when
he induced a female to have unlawful sexual intercourse, in this case
a married woman having sex with someone other than her husband.
Lady Falconbridge and Philip are the second mother-and-son pair,
although she has little further role to play.

In France, young Arthur and his mother, Constance (the third
mother-and-son pair), have joined forces with King Philip of France
and the Duke of Austria to lay siege to the English town of Angiers,
the capital of the County of Anjou.

Austria declares to Arthur: "Upon thy cheek lay I this zealous
kiss, / As seal to this indenture of my love. . . ." (2.1.20–21). At common
law, an indenture was a deed or written instrument between two or
more persons. A seal was necessary for the instrument to be enforced.

The French King receives the news that John and his army are
marching through France toward Angiers. Indeed, John, Eleanor,
and the Bastard meet King Philip before the walls of Angiers. Citing
the law of primogeniture and divine will, Philip declares that Arthur
is the rightful King of England. John challenges Philip's authority
to make this declaration.

After the Kings of France and England state their rival claims,
Eleanor and Constance hurl insults at each other. Eleanor accuses

Arthur of being a bastard. Of course, if Arthur were a bastard, he would have no legitimate claim to the throne as Geoffery's heir. Eleanor claims that she can "can produce / A will that bars the title of thy son." Constance responds that it will be "a canker'd grandam's will!" (2.1.197–200). Shakespeare draws a vivid picture here of two strong women, both of whom are ambitious for their sons to be King.

The play then describes the brief alliance between John and Philip to conquer the rebellious city of Angiers. Lady Constance rails against the corrupt bargain that the "perjured" kings have made to deprive her beautiful boy of his rightful inheritance. She is powerless to obtain redress.

But then her cause becomes tangled up in a legal quarrel between John and the pope over who has the authority to name the Archbishop of Canterbury. Innocent III refused to allow John's favored candidate to become Archbishop. He instead named Stephen Langton, an Englishman and a renowned scholar. John was opposed to Langton's appointment because he wanted money from the church to support his wars in France.

In a tradition going back to William the Conqueror, John considered bishops to be civil servants of the royal state and resented meddling by the pope. Langton decreed that John had forfeited the allegiance of his subjects by breaking faith with the pope, arguing "as an exponent of feudal custom in the light of those principles of law to which all human law should conform."[10]

Thus, the struggle between English monarchs and the pope did not begin with Henry VIII. Cardinal Pandulph, the legate of Pope Innocent III, arrives and excommunicates John for defying the pope's authority. This provokes Constance to declare:

CONSTANCE   O, lawful let it be
That I have room with Rome to curse awhile!
Good father cardinal, cry thou amen

---

[10] Plunknet, *A Concise History of the Common Law*, 22.

To my keen curses; for without my wrong
There is no tongue hath power to curse him right.

CARDINAL PANDULPH   There's law and warrant, lady, for
my curse.

CONSTANCE   And for mine too: when law can do no right,
Let it be lawful that law bar no wrong:
Law cannot give my child his kingdom here,
For he that holds his kingdom holds the law;
Therefore, since law itself is perfect wrong,
How can the law forbid my tongue to curse?
(3.1.183–94)

Constance acknowledges that John, as the de facto King of England, controls the machinery of justice, and that she cannot appeal to the courts to enforce her son's right to inherit the throne.

Threatened by Pandulph, the French King abandons his alliance with John. In the battle that follows, Philip the Bastard kills the Duke of Austria. The English seize Angiers, and John captures Arthur. John plots to murder Arthur, who dies trying to escape by jumping from the wall of a castle. Convinced that John murdered the boy, the barons rebel. John receives news that the French Dauphin has landed an army in England. His ever-watchful mother has died and there is no one to warn him of the impending invasion. The common people are provoked to disorder and rebellion by rumors of Arthur's death. John makes a bargain with Cardinal Pandulph to yield to the pope in exchange for the Cardinal calling off the French invasion.

Poisoned by a monk, King John dies just as the news arrives that Cardinal Pandulph has persuaded the French to retire and end the invasion. John's son Prince Henry will now become the undisputed King of England. King Henry III is the only surviving grandson of Henry II and is a descendant through the male line. The "lineal state" of dynastic succession has been restored. The play ends with a beautiful speech by Philip the Bastard.

BASTARD   O, let us pay the time but needful woe,
    Since it hath been beforehand with our griefs.
    This England never did, nor never shall,
    Lie at the proud foot of a conqueror,
    But when it first did help to wound itself.
    Now these her princes are come home again,
    Come the three corners of the world in arms,
    And we shall shock them. Nought shall make us rue,
    If England to itself do rest but true.
                (5.7.116–24)

Philip the Bastard joins John of Gaunt and Henry V as Shakespeare's most eloquent English patriots.

In this play, Shakespeare again addresses issues of legitimacy, both in a familial sense and in a political sense. John has possession of the throne but no legal right to it. Arthur has the right to rule under the law, but he is a child. He is in exile and then in captivity. Falconbridge is the noblest and most fit of those with royal blood to rule. But he is a bastard and may not succeed to the throne.

When does a tyrant forfeit the right to be king? Shakespeare's King John was a thoroughly bad man. But as usual, Shakespeare is neither judgmental nor moralistic about John.

Arguably, the historical King John was even worse. He was exceedingly cruel and rapacious. Shakespeare only hints at the First Barons' War that broke out near the end of John's reign. It was this large-scale rebellion that forced John to sign the Magna Carta. The always faithless John repudiated the Great Charter only months later, and got the pope to declared it null and void.

Upon John's death, his son succeeded him without dispute as King Henry III. Was this a happy ending for England? No, because the long reign of Henry III was one calamity after another.

In addition to Magna Carta, King John's reign was pivotable in the development of the English language. After the Norman Conquest, England was a land of three languages.

Latin was the language of the church and early literature, such as Geoffrey of Monmouth's Latin poem about the legendary King Arthur of Briton. Latin was also the language of the local church and monastery schools.

French was the language of the nobility, government, and the law courts, where it displaced Latin. Increasingly, it was also the language of romantic literature. Both were thought of as superior to English, which was the vulgar language of the peasants.

In the twelfth century, English as a written language virtually disappeared. The Angevin Empire of the early Plantagenet kings was more French than English. Neither Richard I nor John spoke English. In 1204 King Philip of France drove the English out of Normandy, and English control over the central and southern provinces collapsed. Philip demanded that the Norman barons with lands in both France and England abandon any allegiance to the English king, and John demanded that his nobles abandon any allegiance to the French king. The English Channel now separated two countries: England and France. In time, this contributed to a sense of Englishness that led to the reemergence of English as a written language.

Shortly after 1204, a West Midlands monk wrote a history of England that contained the first English version of the Arthurian legend. Chaucer and Shakespeare would follow.

Late in the reign of Henry III, the barons rebelled against his rapacious demands for money. They convened a Parliament at Oxford in 1258. This Parliament adopted the Provisions of Oxford. These were a series of constitutional reforms. A council of fifteen barons was established to rule in the name of the king and guarantee the rule of law. A proclamation describing the reforms was issued that was to be read in each of the counties. The proclamation was issued in Latin, French, and English. This was the first official government document written in English since the Norman conquest.

The ascendancy of English was accelerated by the Hundred Years War between France and England. Law French was the language spoken in the royal law courts. Because they did not understand

Norman French, the common people complained that they did not understand what was being said about them in the law courts.

In 1362, Parliament enacted the Statute of Pleading. The Act decreed that "all Pleas which shall be pleaded in [any] Courts whatsoever, before any of his Justices whatsoever, or in his other Places, or before any of His other Ministers whatsoever, or in the Courts and Places of any other Lords whatsoever within the Realm, shall be pleaded, shewed, defended, answered, debated, and judged in the English language, and that they be entered and inrolled in Latin."

After this enactment, the use of Law French steadily declined except for its use in the Inns of Court. By Shakespeare's time, Law French as a spoken language had disappeared.

CHAPTER 9

THE MERCHANT OF VENICE

The *Merchant of Venice*, written between 1596 and 1598, is Shakespeare's most legalistic play. But it does not begin that way. It begins with two people who are sad. Antonio—the merchant of Venice—begins the play by telling his companions Salarino and Salanio:

ANTONIO   In sooth, I know not why I am so sad:
   It wearies me; you say it wearies you;
   But how I caught it, found it, or came by it,
   What stuff 'tis made of, whereof it is born,
   I am to learn;
   And such a want-wit sadness makes of me,
   That I have much ado to know myself.
                     (*The Merchant of Venice*, 1.1.1–7)

His companions think Antonio is sad because of the risk to his ships at sea.

Antonio responds that his wealth is not entrusted all to one ship or bound to one destination. Salarino then suggests that Antonio is sad because he is in love, to which Antonio responds, "Fie, fie!" (1.1.46).

Salarino then gives up on a serious explanation for Antonio's sadness:

SALARINO   Not in love neither? Then let us say you are sad,
    Because you are not merry: and 'twere as easy
    For you to laugh and leap and say you are merry,
    Because you are not sad.

(1.1.47–50)

Indeed, Shakespeare intends us to understand that there is no good reason for Antonio to be sad. He is rich. He has friends. We later discover that he is highly respected in the city. But something is lacking.

I believe Antonio is afflicted with a case of self-loathing, because despite all his wealth and prestige, he feels his life has no real purpose or value. And perhaps he has some premonition that fate may be about to impose a heavy sentence upon him.

It is this interpretation of Antonio's predicament that helps me deal with the most problematic aspect of the play. While continuing to be one of the most popular of Shakespeare's plays, *The Merchant of Venice* is difficult for post-Holocaust modern audiences because of the shocking anti-Semitism of Antonio and his Venetian companions. Antonio's loathing of the Jewish moneylender Shylock is described early in the play by Shylock himself:

SHYLOCK   Signior Antonio, many a time and oft
    In the Rialto you have rated me
    About my moneys and my usances:
    Still have I borne it with a patient shrug,
    For sufferance is the badge of all our tribe.
    You call me misbeliever, cut-throat dog,
    And spit upon my Jewish gaberdine,
    And all for use of that which is mine own.

(1.2.107–14)

It is easy to dismiss this as the fault of the times. And perhaps because we never see Antonio engage in such vile acts of bigotry, my sense is that modern audiences do not lose their sympathy for Antonio at this early point in the play. My interpretation is that what Shylock has described is an expression of Antonio's own existential self-loathing which he vents at the Jewish moneylender.

Although persecuted and confined to a ghetto at night, Jews played an important role as moneylenders in Venetian trade and commerce at the time Shakespeare wrote the play.

While wars of religion swept over much of Europe in the sixteenth century, Venice was almost uniquely tolerant of religious diversity. As the preeminent trading center between Asia and Western Europe, it was full of foreigners. In England, by contrast, Shakespeare would have encountered few, if any, Jews. The Jews had been expelled from England in 1290 by Edward I; they were not allowed to return until forty years after Shakespeare's death.

But Shakespeare would have been aware of the extreme anti-Semitism of the religious and cultural environment of his times. He and his audience would have known of Dr. Roderigo Lopez, a converted Jewish physician who was physician-in-chief to Queen Elizabeth. Lopez was accused by the Earl of Essex of trying to poison the Queen in exchange for Spanish bribes. Accused of treason, he was tried and convicted in a fervent outburst of anti-Semitism. He was hanged, drawn and quartered in June 1594.

At the time, executions were public spectacles. Shakespeare could easily have been part of the mob that witnessed the execution. This notorious event would have been fresh in the mind of his audience when he was writing the play.

Modern audiences, however, struggle with the play. The best performances I have seen have presented the drama's anti-Semitism brutally and unvarnished. The play is a powerful reminder that racial and religious bigotry is not some mere harmless relic of the past. The brutal treatment of Shylock at the end of Act IV foreshadows the later "dark comedies" such as *Troilus and Cressida* and *Measure for Measure.*

As Salarino and Salanio leave, Gratiano and Bassanio greet Antonio. He responds with a familiar Shakespearean metaphor. Antonio: "I hold the world but as the world, Gratiano; / A stage where every man must play a part, / And mine a sad one" (1.1.73–75).

Gratiano says he will play the fool, then he leaves to pursue his merrymaking. Bassanio responds:

BASSANIO   Gratiano speaks an infinite deal of nothing, more
      than any man in all Venice. His reasons are as two
      grains of wheat hid in two bushels of chaff: you
      shall seek all day ere you find them, and when you
      have them, they are not worth the search.
                    (1.1.114–18)

Bassanio sounds like a trial judge such as me, one who has spent his day listening to lawyers spending hours uttering an infinite deal of nothing. Lawyers are very good at hiding grains of wheat in bushels of chaff.

Antonio then gets the action of the play moving. He asks Bassanio to tell him of the lady to whom he has made a secret pilgrimage. Before answering directly, Bassanio reminds Antonio, his largest creditor, of his dire financial circumstances. Credit had become an important commodity by the later part of the sixteenth century. Many of the familiar figures of Elizabeth's reign, including the Earl of Essex and the Earl of Southampton, owed enormous debts. Elizabeth herself borrowed money from European bankers. Venice was a place where credit could be obtained to support commercial ventures.

Antonio responds with generosity:

ANTONIO   I pray you, good Bassanio, let me know it;
      And if it stand, as you yourself still do,
      Within the eye of honour, be assured,
      My purse, my person, my extremest means,

Lie all unlock'd to your occasions.

(1.1.135–39)

Bassanio, however, has something other than a commercial venture in mind. He reveals to Antonio his plan to repair his fortune by
a high-stakes gamble to win the hand of a rich heiress in the nearby
town of Belmont.

BASSANIO   In Belmont is a lady richly left;
　　And she is fair, and, fairer than that word,
　　Of wondrous virtues: sometimes from her eyes
　　I did receive fair speechless messages:
　　Her name is Portia, nothing undervalued
　　To Cato's daughter, Brutus' Portia:
　　Nor is the wide world ignorant of her worth,
　　For the four winds blow in from every coast
　　Renowned suitors, and her sunny locks
　　Hang on her temples like a golden fleece;
　　Which makes her seat of Belmont Colchos' strand,
　　And many Jasons come in quest of her.
　　O my Antonio, had I but the means
　　To hold a rival place with one of them,
　　I have a mind presages me such thrift,
　　That I should questionless be fortunate!

(1.1.161–176)

Bassanio needs money to buy new clothes and expensive gifts for
the lady richly left in Belmont. It is this rather mercenary description
by Bassanio of the heroine Portia that has earned him the unde-
served reputation among generations of Shakespearean readers of
being merely a crass fortune hunter—totally unworthy of Portia.
For many, nothing he does later that is good or noble redeems him
from this initial impression.

　　I believe Shakespeare does this deliberately, in order to make
his character nuanced and ambiguous. But I submit, if this was

all there was to Bassanio, Portia would not fall in love with him. Antonio responds to Bassanio's request by saying he will help. But he has no ready money, and they must seek out a moneylender.

In Act I, Scene 2, we are transported to Portia's house in Belmont. Portia—like Antonio—opens the scene by saying she is sad. "By my troth, Nerissa, my little body is aweary of this great world" (1.2.1). Nerissa, her lady-in-waiting, tells Portia how fortunate she is. She is rich and beautiful, but something is missing in her life.

Portia replies to Nerissa with a speech rich in legal metaphor:

PORTIA   Good sentences and well pronounced.

NERISSA   They would be better, if well followed.

PORTIA   If to do were as easy as to know what were good to
    do, chapels had been churches and poor men's
    cottages princes' palaces. It is a good divine that
    follows his own instructions: I can easier teach
    twenty what were good to be done, than be one of the
    twenty to follow mine own teaching. The brain may
    devise laws for the blood, but a hot temper leaps
    o'er a cold decree: such a hare is madness the
    youth, to skip o'er the meshes of good counsel the
    cripple. But this reasoning is not in the fashion to
    choose me a husband. O me, the word 'choose!' I may
    neither choose whom I would nor refuse whom I
    dislike; so is the will of a living daughter curbed
    by the will of a dead father. Is it not hard,
    Nerissa, that I cannot choose one nor refuse none?
                    (2.1.11–29)

We see in this speech the rich use by Shakespeare of the law as metaphor: laws for the blood, a cold decree, and the "meshes of good counsel." We also learn that her father's will is an instrument of the law that in some fashion is constraining her choice of a husband.

Indeed, he has established a strange wager or lottery to determine who his daughter must wed. He has left three chests: one of gold, one of silver, and one of lead. Each suitor gets to pick one casket. In one of the chests there is a picture of Portia. If a suitor picks that casket, Portia must marry him.

Nerissa asks Portia what she thinks of the suitors who have already come to Belmont. In her commentary upon her current suitors—the nephew of the Duke of Saxony, the Neapolitan Prince, the Count Palatine, the French Lord, the young Baron of England, and the Scottish Lord—Portia sparkles with pithy wit and biting sarcasm. She delivers this masterpiece of a libelous put down of Saxony's nephew:

NERISSA   How like you the young German, the Duke of
    Saxony's nephew?

PORTIA   Very vilely in the morning, when he is sober, and
    most vilely in the afternoon, when he is drunk: when
    he is best, he is a little worse than a man, and
    when he is worst, he is little better than a beast:
    and the worst fall that ever fell, I hope I shall
    make shift to go without him.

NERISSA   If he should offer to choose, and choose the right
    casket, you should refuse to perform your father's
    will, if you should refuse to accept him.

PORTIA   Therefore, for fear of the worst, I pray thee, set a
    deep glass of rhenish wine on the contrary casket,
    for if the devil be within and that temptation
    without, I know he will choose it. I will do any
    thing, Nerissa, ere I'll be married to a sponge.
                    (2.1.90–108)

Because of a penalty I will describe in a moment, these wooers have told Nerissa they'll all leave if they must seek Portia's hand through the lottery of the three caskets. Portia declares that she'll honor her father's will.

We also learn of another potential suitor. Nerissa asks: "Do you not remember, lady, in your father's time, a Venetian, a scholar and a soldier, that came hither in company of the Marquis of Montferrat?" (2.1.122–24). Portia responds: "I remember him well, and I remember him worthy of thy praise" (2.1.130–31). This was Bassanio. Thus, it appears that Bassanio has a chance to win the lady if Antonio can raise the money to get him to Belmont, and if he succeeds in picking the right casket in the trust and estates trial left by Portia's father. But first, Portia must survive the trial of two new suitors: the Prince of Morocco and the Prince of Aragon.

The scene shifts back to Venice where Bassanio is negotiating with the Jewish moneylender Shylock for a loan of three thousand ducats to be guaranteed by Antonio. When Bassanio's friend enters the stage, Shylock reveals his deep-seated hatred of Antonio:

[Enter ANTONIO]

BASSANIO   This is Signior Antonio.

SHYLOCK   [*Aside*] How like a fawning publican he looks!
I hate him for he is a Christian,
But more for that in low simplicity
He lends out money gratis and brings down
The rate of usance here with us in Venice.
If I can catch him once upon the hip,
I will feed fat the ancient grudge I bear him.
He hates our sacred nation, and he rails,
Even there where merchants most do congregate,
On me, my bargains and my well-won thrift,
Which he calls interest. Cursed be my tribe,
If I forgive him!

(1.3.41–53)

Antonio and Shylock engage in a lively debate over the morality of lending money at interest. To make a point, Shylock tells the Biblical story of how Jacob obtained a greater share of his Uncle Laban's sheep by causing the striped lambs to multiply more rapidly. Antonio responds: "Mark you this, Bassanio, / The devil can cite Scripture for his purpose" (1.3.98–99).

Clearly, Shylock has more reason than mere religious prejudice to hate Antonio, who has called him a dog and spit upon him. This seems uncharacteristic of the Antonio we see in the rest of the play. But they agree on the terms of the loan, including an unusual penalty in the case of Antonio's default.

SHYLOCK   This kindness will I show.
  Go with me to a notary, seal me there
  Your single bond; and, in a merry sport,
  If you repay me not on such a day,
  In such a place, such sum or sums as are
  Express'd in the condition, let the forfeit
  Be nominated for an equal pound
  Of your fair flesh, to be cut off and taken
  In what part of your body pleaseth me.

ANTONIO   Content, I' faith: I'll seal to such a bond
  And say there is much kindness in the Jew.
                (1.3.145–55)

Bassanio shows some (generally unappreciated) nobility of character when he protests that "I'll rather dwell in my necessity" (1.3.156) than allow his friend to enter into such a bloody bargain. But Antonio assures him that there is no danger, and the loan can be repaid with ease when Antonio's ships come in a month before the bond is forfeited. Shylock then says: "Pray you, tell me this; / If he should break his day, what should I gain / By the exaction of the forfeiture?" (1.3.163–65). This statement could potentially have

furnished Antonio with a defense of fraudulent inducement, but
Shakespeare has something more dramatic in mind.

The play returns to Belmont and the trial mandated by the will
of Portia's father. When the Prince of Morocco comes to venture for
Portia's hand, we learn why other suitors have declined the wager.
Portia: "You must take your chance, / And either not attempt to
choose at all / Or swear before you choose, if you choose wrong /
Never to speak to lady afterward / In way of marriage: therefore
be advised" (2.1.38–42). Morocco agrees to the condition. After
dinner, Portia and the Prince return to the caskets for him to make
his choice:

PORTIA   Go draw aside the curtains and discover
    The several caskets to this noble prince.
    Now make your choice.

MOROCCO   The first, of gold, who this inscription bears,
    'Who chooseth me shall gain what many men desire;'
    The second, silver, which this promise carries,
    'Who chooseth me shall get as much as he deserves;'
    This third, dull lead, with warning all as blunt,
    'Who chooseth me must give and hazard all he hath.'
    How shall I know if I do choose the right?

PORTIA   The one of them contains my picture, prince:
    If you choose that, then I am yours withal.

MOROCCO   Some god direct my judgment! Let me see;
    I will survey the inscriptions back again.
    What says this leaden casket?
    'Who chooseth me must give and hazard all he hath.'
    Must give: for what? for lead? hazard for lead?
    This casket threatens. Men that hazard all
    Do it in hope of fair advantages:
    A golden mind stoops not to shows of dross;

I'll then nor give nor hazard aught for lead.
What says the silver with her virgin hue?
'Who chooseth me shall get as much as he deserves.'
As much as he deserves! Pause there, Morocco,
And weigh thy value with an even hand:
If thou be'st rated by thy estimation,
Thou dost deserve enough; and yet enough
May not extend so far as to the lady:
And yet to be afeard of my deserving
Were but a weak disabling of myself.
As much as I deserve! Why, that's the lady:
I do in birth deserve her, and in fortunes,
In graces and in qualities of breeding;
But more than these, in love I do deserve.
What if I stray'd no further, but chose here?
Let's see once more this saying graved in gold
'Who chooseth me shall gain what many men desire.'
Why, that's the lady; all the world desires her;
From the four corners of the earth they come,
To kiss this shrine, this mortal-breathing saint. . . .
Deliver me the key:
Here do I choose, and thrive I as I may!

PORTIA   There, take it, prince; and if my form lie there,
Then I am yours.

(2.7.1–38, 59–62)

Morocco unlocks the golden casket, and he is horrified at what
he sees.

MOROCCO   O hell! what have we here?
A carrion Death, within whose empty eye
There is a written scroll! I'll read the writing.

[Reads]

All that glisters is not gold;
Often have you heard that told:
Many a man his life hath sold
But my outside to behold:
Gilded tombs do worms enfold.
Had you been as wise as bold,
Young in limbs, in judgment old,
Your answer had not been inscroll'd:
Fare you well; your suit is cold.
Cold, indeed; and labour lost:
Then, farewell, heat, and welcome, frost!
Portia, adieu. I have too grieved a heart
To take a tedious leave: thus losers part.
(2.7.63–77)

Portia is relieved. The Prince of Aragon suffers the same fate when he wagers and chooses the silver casket; silver, which is the currency of commerce. But Bassanio is on his way to Belmont to seek love and fortune.

Meanwhile in Venice, Shylock's daughter, Jessica, has run off with her Christian lover, Lorenzo. Knowing her father would not consent to her marriage to a Christian and she will have no dowry, she helped herself to as much of her father's money and jewels as she could carry. She also converted to Christianity. Otherwise, her marriage to a Christian would have been a crime under English law and punishable by death.

Shylock is outraged and horrified when he discovers her elopement. Then it is with great bitterness that Shylock greets the news that all of Antonio's ships have been lost. Salarino asks if he intends to demand the pound of flesh if the bond is forfeited. Shylock's response reveals Shakespeare's great humanity as well as his understanding of the psychology of revenge. What is a pound of flesh good for asks Salarino?

SHYLOCK   To bait fish withal: if it will feed nothing else,
it will feed my revenge. He hath disgraced me, and

hindered me half a million; laughed at my losses,
mocked at my gains, scorned my nation, thwarted my
bargains, cooled my friends, heated mine
enemies; and what's his reason? I am a Jew. Hath
not a Jew eyes? hath not a Jew hands, organs,
dimensions, senses, affections, passions? fed with
the same food, hurt with the same weapons, subject
to the same diseases, healed by the same means,
warmed and cooled by the same winter and summer, as
a Christian is? If you prick us, do we not bleed?
if you tickle us, do we not laugh? if you poison
us, do we not die? and if you wrong us, shall we not
revenge? If we are like you in the rest, we will
resemble you in that. If a Jew wrong a Christian,
what is his humility? Revenge. If a Christian
wrong a Jew, what should his sufferance be by
Christian example? Why, revenge. The villany you
teach me, I will execute, and it shall go hard but I
will better the instruction.

(3.1.55–75)

Here, Shylock's eloquence in the cause of a persecuted race rivals that of Portia in her great trial scene. It is the genius of Shakespeare that he could imagine what it felt like to be a Jew. Although it is Portia's play, in this speech, Shylock seems to have gotten away from Shakespeare the way that Falstaff gets away from him a couple of years later in the *Henry IV* plays. This speech has been offered by critics such as Jonathan Bate and Peter Ackroyd as Shakespeare's powerful challenge to the anti-Semitism of his times. I am inclined to agree with them more than with Harold Bloom, who opines that "what he is saying is now of possible interest only to wavering skinheads and similar sociopaths."[11]

---

[11] Bloom, *Shakespeare*, 180.

But if Shylock is saying that revenge is an acceptable response to injustice, Jews are no better or worse than Christians. And Shylock has his opportunity for revenge. All of Antonio's ventures fail and he is unable to repay the three thousand ducats on the appointed day. The merchants and lawyers in Shakespeare's audience must have smiled at this, knowing that ships and cargoes had been regularly insured for decades. Marine insurance originated in Italy in the fourteenth century.

Shylock demands his pound of flesh. Significantly, no one contends that the sealed contract is invalid or unenforceable.

In Belmont, Bassanio and Portia confess their love for each other but abide by the terms of her father's will. In making his choice, Bassanio declares that he will not be deceived by gaudy ornament.

BASSANIO   So may the outward shows be least themselves:
The world is still deceived with ornament.
In law, what plea so tainted and corrupt,
But, being seasoned with a gracious voice,
Obscures the show of evil? In religion,
What damned error, but some sober brow
Will bless it and approve it with a text,
Hiding the grossness with fair ornament?
(3.2.73–80)

Shakespeare seems to be using the term "plea" to refer broadly to any argument in court and not in the technical sense of the response to the charges of the prosecutor in a criminal case. Again, Shakespeare makes his point—that appearances deceive—with a legal metaphor.

Bassanio wins the hand of Portia by spurning appearances and choosing the casket of lead, which contains Portia's picture. The inscription says he may claim his bride by giving her a kiss. But Bassanio again shows some nobility of character by declaring that she is not his "[u]ntil confirm'd, sign'd, ratified by you" (3.2.149).

Portia responds:

PORTIA   You see me, Lord Bassanio, where I stand,
Such as I am: though for myself alone
I would not be ambitious in my wish,
To wish myself much better; yet, for you
I would be trebled twenty times myself;
A thousand times more fair, ten thousand times more rich. . . .
Myself and what is mine to you and yours
Is now converted: but now I was the lord
Of this fair mansion, master of my servants,
Queen o'er myself: and even now, but now,
This house, these servants and this same myself
Are yours, my lord: I give them with this ring;
Which when you part from, lose, or give away,
Let it presage the ruin of your love
And be my vantage to exclaim on you.
                    (3.2.150–55, 168–76)

A married woman in England was known in the Law French of the time as a *feme covert*. Under the common law, a married woman's property became the property of her husband under the doctrine of "coverture." Shakespeare's description of Portia's property being "converted" is an extraordinarily subtle metaphor of her going from *feme sole* as an unmarried woman to *feme covert* as a married woman. The metaphor is likely to fly by a modern audience. But the lawyers and law students in Shakespeare's audience would have appreciated it.

The giving of a ring was in that day a way to symbolize the transfer of land to another. It is noteworthy that the ring is given as part of the transfer of Portia's property rather than as part of the marriage ceremony, as it would be in a ceremony performed under the rites of the Book of Common Prayer.

Portia understands that, as a married woman, her husband will have the command of her person and property under the law. Portia joyfully accepts this sacrifice because of her love for Bassanio. There are no premarital negotiations regarding a marriage settlement whereby Portia could protect some of her property, as would likely have occurred in the case of such a large estate in Tudor England. She is extraordinarily generous.

At this moment, a messenger arrives from Venice with a letter to Bassanio from Antonio telling of the disaster that has befallen Antonio's ventures. Bassanio confesses to Portia how indebted he is to Antonio. Salerio delivers more bad news, news involving Antonio's bargain with Shylock: "Besides, it should appear, that if he had / The present money to discharge the Jew, / He would not take it" (3.2.276–78).

As in so many of Shakespeare's plays, love expresses itself as generosity: Portia offers to pay Antonio's debt twice and then three times three. She tells Bassanio to go with her to church to get married and then to go immediately to Venice to rescue his friend "[f]or never shall you lie by Portia's side with an unquiet soul" (3.2.307–08). As Bassanio is dearly bought, she will love him dearly.

But she asks him to read Antonio's letter. Portia has a plan. She instructs a servant to take a letter to her cousin Doctor Bellario in Padua, and to meet her at the ferry to Venice with the notes and garments that the servant is given. Portia tells Nerissa they are going to Venice disguised as men.

Padua was a city in Venice's mainland territories in northern Italy. It had a famous university where Roman law was studied. The first of the great late-medieval universities was established in nearby Bologna. It specialized in the study of Roman and canon law. Its most advanced graduates were awarded the degree of Doctor of Laws. Writers in English referred to university educated continental lawyers as Doctors of Law. English lawyers educated at the Inns of Court might be called to the bar but were not awarded any advanced degree.

In Venice, Antonio has defaulted on his debt. Shylock has him arrested in anticipation of obtaining a judgment that the bond is forfeited. He turns a deaf ear to pleas for mercy.

SHYLOCK   Gaoler, look to him: tell not me of mercy;

This is the fool that lent out money gratis:
Gaoler, look to him.

ANTONIO   Hear me yet, good Shylock.

SHYLOCK   I'll have my bond; speak not against my bond:
I have sworn an oath that I will have my bond.
Thou call'dst me dog before thou hadst a cause;
But, since I am a dog, beware my fangs:
The duke shall grant me justice. I do wonder,
Thou naughty gaoler, that thou art so fond
To come abroad with him at his request.

ANTONIO   I pray thee, hear me speak.

SHYLOCK   I'll have my bond; I will not hear thee speak:
I'll have my bond; and therefore speak no more.
I'll not be made a soft and dull-eyed fool,
To shake the head, relent, and sigh, and yield
To Christian intercessors. Follow not;
I'll have no speaking: I will have my bond.
                   (3.3.1–17)

Under the early common law, trial by wager of law in an action for
debt could be avoided where the contract was in the form of a sealed
instrument known as a bond. Bonds typically began with the *Noverint
universi praesnti* ("Be it known unto all men by these presents") quoted
by Celia in *As You Like It*. She describes three young men as: "With
bills on their necks: 'Be it known unto all men by these presents.' "
These written instruments could be prepared by a scrivener or an
attorney. They typically included a confession of judgment, which
allowed the obligation to be recorded in the records of a court.

Antonio's friends assure him that the Duke of Venice will never
allow Shylock to have his pound of flesh. Antonio responds that
the Duke must enforce the law for the greater benefit of Venice.

SALARINO   I am sure the duke
Will never grant this forfeiture to hold.

ANTONIO   The duke cannot deny the course of law:
For the commodity that strangers have
With us in Venice, if it be denied,
Will much impeach the justice of his state;
Since that the trade and profit of the city   ,
Consisteth of all nations. Therefore, go:
These griefs and losses have so bated me,
That I shall hardly spare a pound of flesh
To-morrow to my bloody creditor.
Well, gaoler, on. Pray God, Bassanio come
To see me pay his debt, and then I care not!
                    (3.3.25–36)

Antonio recognizes that the wealth of Venice depends upon commerce, which relies upon the rule of law and the enforcement of contracts. Indeed, commerce had made Venice the richest city in Renaissance Europe. By contrast to the rest of Western Europe, differences of religion and nationality were set aside in Venice for the sake of making money.

Act IV, Scene 1, begins with the Duke sitting in his court of law. He finds Antonio at peace with himself, notwithstanding his impending death.

DUKE   What, is Antonio here?

ANTONIO   Ready, so please your grace.

DUKE   I am sorry for thee: thou art come to answer
A stony adversary, an inhuman wretch
uncapable of pity, void and empty
From any dram of mercy.

ANTONIO   I have heard
Your grace hath ta'en great pains to qualify
His rigorous course; but since he stands obdurate
And that no lawful means can carry me
Out of his envy's reach, I do oppose
My patience to his fury, and am arm'd
To suffer, with a quietness of spirit,
The very tyranny and rage of his.

                    (4.1.1–13)

Shylock is summoned. He enters with a knife and a set of scales. His appearance is a parody of the Goddess of Justice, who is generally depicted with a sword in one hand and scales in the other. The Duke tells Shylock that he is expected to relent and not insist upon a strict enforcement of his legal rights: "We all expect a gentle answer, Jew" (4.1.34). Shylock says he has taken an oath to have his bond forfeited. The Duke responds:

DUKE   How shalt thou hope for mercy, rendering none?

SHYLOCK   What judgment shall I dread, doing no wrong?
You have among you many a purchased slave,
Which, like your asses and your dogs and mules,
You use in abject and in slavish parts,
Because you bought them: shall I say to you,
Let them be free, marry them to your heirs?
Why sweat they under burthens? let their beds
Be made as soft as yours and let their palates
Be season'd with such viands? You will answer
'The slaves are ours:' so do I answer you:
The pound of flesh, which I demand of him,
Is dearly bought; 'tis mine and I will have it.
If you deny me, fie upon your law!
There is no force in the decrees of Venice.
I stand for judgment: answer; shall I have it?

                    (4.1.88–103)

Shylock is pointing out the hypocrisy of the Venetians who use the law to protect their possessions (including slaves) but who demand that he give up what is legally his. But Shakespeare is also raising the question here (and again most notably in *Measure for Measure*) of what can be done when a strict application of the law ("I stand here for law") leads to a result that is unjust, and even cruel and inhumane.

The Duke, however, has summoned a learned doctor of law to advise him on the case.

DUKE   Upon my power I may dismiss this court,
Unless Bellario, a learned doctor,
Whom I have sent for to determine this,
Come here to-day.

SALERIO   My lord, here stays without
A messenger with letters from the doctor,
New come from Padua.

DUKE   Bring us the letter; call the messenger.

BASSANIO   Good cheer, Antonio! What, man, courage yet!
The Jew shall have my flesh, blood, bones and all,
Ere thou shalt lose for me one drop of blood.

ANTONIO   I am a tainted wether of the flock,
Meetest for death: the weakest kind of fruit
Drops earliest to the ground; and so let me
You cannot better be employ'd, Bassanio,
Than to live still and write mine epitaph.
(4.1.104–120)

The critics generally again ignore this act of nobility on the part of Bassanio. Clearly, however, the nobility of character of Antonio shines through, and his existential angst of Act I is replaced with his stoical acceptance of his doom.

Our heroine, Portia—disguised as a young Doctor of Laws—then enters the court as Bellario's substitute to advise the Duke. She says she is fully informed as to the case, but then asks an astonishing question: "Which is the merchant here, and which the Jew?" (4.1.174). Of course, it is customary to ask the parties to a trial to identify themselves when the trial begins even though everyone knows who they are. I imagine the question is also intended to reinforce her pose as a stranger to Venice. She first addresses Shylock.

PORTIA   Is your name Shylock?

SHYLOCK   Shylock is my name.

PORTIA   Of a strange nature is the suit you follow;
    Yet in such rule that the Venetian law
    Cannot impugn you as you do proceed.
    You stand within his danger, do you not?

ANTONIO   Ay, so he says.

PORTIA   Do you confess the bond?

ANTONIO   I do.

PORTIA   Then must the Jew be merciful.

SHYLOCK   On what compulsion must I? tell me that.
                (4.1.176–185)

By confessing the bond, Antonio admits that he is subject to the forfeiture. Portia agrees that the law does not compel Shylock to be merciful. But she then makes the most eloquent plea for mercy ever heard in a court of law.

PORTIA   The quality of mercy is not strain'd,

It droppeth as the gentle rain from heaven
Upon the place beneath: it is twice blest;
It blesseth him that gives and him that takes:
'Tis mightiest in the mightiest: it becomes
The throned monarch better than his crown;
His sceptre shows the force of temporal power,
The attribute to awe and majesty,
Wherein doth sit the dread and fear of kings;
But mercy is above this sceptred sway;
It is enthroned in the hearts of kings,
It is an attribute to God himself;
And earthly power doth then show likest God's
When mercy seasons justice. Therefore, Jew,
Though justice be thy plea, consider this,
That, in the course of justice, none of us
Should see salvation: we do pray for mercy;
And that same prayer doth teach us all to render
The deeds of mercy. I have spoke thus much
To mitigate the justice of thy plea;
Which if thou follow, this strict court of Venice
Must needs give sentence 'gainst the merchant there.

(4.1.186–205)

The lawyers and law students in Shakespeare's audience would recognize that Portia is appealing to justice exercised in a court of equity such as the English Court of Chancery. It would refuse to enforce the penalty of a pound of flesh.

But Shylock is not moved by Portia's eloquence. He exclaims: "My deeds upon my head! I crave the law, / The penalty and forfeit of my bond" (4.1.206–07).

Portia asks if Antonio's debt can be paid, and Bassanio responds immediately and generously:

BASSANIO   Yes, here I tender it for him in the court;
Yea, twice the sum: if that will not suffice,

I will be bound to pay it ten times o'er,
On forfeit of my hands, my head, my heart:
If this will not suffice, it must appear
That malice bears down truth. And I beseech you [*Duke*],
Wrest once the law to your authority:
To do a great right, do a little wrong,
And curb this cruel devil of his will.

(4.1.209–17)

Bassanio here raises the question of whether the rigors of the law may not be tempered by justice. Shakespeare's audience would again recognize that Bassanio is appealing for an equitable remedy that could be provided by the Court of Chancery in England. But Portia says it cannot be done.

PORTIA   It must not be; there is no power in Venice
    Can alter a decree established:
    'Twill be recorded for a precedent,
    And many an error by the same example
    Will rush into the state: it cannot be.

SHYLOCK   A Daniel come to judgment! yea, a Daniel!
    O wise young judge, how I do honour thee!

PORTIA   I pray you, let me look upon the bond.

SHYLOCK   Here 'tis, most reverend doctor, here it is.

PORTIA   Shylock, there's thrice thy money offer'd thee.

SHYLOCK   An oath, an oath, I have an oath in heaven:
    Shall I lay perjury upon my soul?
    No, not for Venice.

(4.1.218–229)

Portia says that not enforcing the contact would set a bad precedent. The reference to Daniel is from the apocryphal book, *The History of Susanna of the Old Testament*. Susanna was a virtuous wife who repulsed the lustful advances of two wicked elders. They charged her with adultery. At her trial they testified to personally witnessing the crime. Daniel demanded the right to cross-examine Susanna's accusers. He asked each accuser the type of tree under which the adultery occurred. Not having agreed before the trial upon this detail, the accusers gave different answers and were obviously lying. Susanna was acquitted.

Finally, we see Shakespeare's wonderful use of the law as metaphor when Shylock asks if he commits "perjury" upon his soul by violating an oath.

After examining the bond, Portia announces that the bond is forfeited, and Shylock is entitled to his pound of flesh. At that time, this was the correct verdict for a common law court such as the Court of Common Pleas, which would enforce a forfeiture and penalty. But she once again entreats Shylock to show mercy.

PORTIA   Why, this bond is forfeit;
   And lawfully by this the Jew may claim
   A pound of flesh, to be by him cut off
   Nearest the merchant's heart. Be merciful:
   Take thrice thy money; bid me tear the bond.

SHYLOCK   When it is paid according to the tenor.
   It doth appear you are a worthy judge;
   You know the law, your exposition
   Hath been most sound: I charge you by the law,
   Whereof you are a well-deserving pillar,
   Proceed to judgment: by my soul I swear
   There is no power in the tongue of man
   To alter me: I stay here on my bond.
                    (4.1.230–242)

No doubt, Shakespeare had many of the young Inns of Court gentlemen in debt to the moneylenders squirming in their seats. The law students in Shakespeare's audience would recognize that Shylock is refusing the tender of money damages for breach of contract and is insisting upon specific performance of his bond. But they also would have known that specific performance could only be granted by a court of equity such as Chancery, which would have refused to order an unconscionable penalty. Chancery would order the creditor to accept late payment of the principal by the defaulting debtor plus damages for delay such as interest. As a dramatist, Shakespeare could ignore these technicalities of English law.

Antonio, resigned to his death, urges Portia to render judgment.

ANTONIO   Most heartily I do beseech the court
To give the judgment.

PORTIA   Why then, thus it is:
You must prepare your bosom for his knife.

SHYLOCK   O noble judge! O excellent young man!

PORTIA   For the intent and purpose of the law
Hath full relation to the penalty,
Which here appeareth due upon the bond.

SHYLOCK   'Tis very true: O wise and upright judge!
How much more elder art thou than thy looks!

PORTIA   Therefore lay bare your bosom.

SHYLOCK   Ay, his breast:
So says the bond: doth it not, noble judge?
'Nearest his heart:' those are the very words.

PORTIA   It is so.

(4.1.243–56)

When questioned by Portia, Shylock declares that he has a scale to weigh the pound of flesh. Again, with his knife and scale, Shylock is a parody of the image of blindfolded Justice. But when asked if he has a surgeon, Shylock responds with a strictly literal reading of the bond, one that will come back to haunt him.

PORTIA   Have by some surgeon, Shylock, on your charge,
To stop his wounds, lest he do bleed to death.

SHYLOCK   Is it so nominated in the bond?

PORTIA   It is not so express'd: but what of that?
'Twere good you do so much for charity.

SHYLOCK   I cannot find it; 'tis not in the bond.

(4.1.257–262)

Portia then invites Antonio to exercise what in criminal procedure is the right of allocution—the right to make a statement before sentence is pronounced. Antonio proclaims his resignation to his fate and his love for Bassanio. Bassanio responds in kind, which prompts a wicked retort by Portia.

BASSANIO   Antonio, I am married to a wife
Which is as dear to me as life itself;
But life itself, my wife, and all the world,
Are not with me esteem'd above thy life:
I would lose all, ay, sacrifice them all
Here to this devil, to deliver you.

PORTIA   Your wife would give you little thanks for that,
If she were by, to hear you make the offer.

(4.1.282–89)

Once again, Bassanio is generously offering to sacrifice himself to save his friend Antonio. Shylock demands that Portia pronounce sentence without further delay, which she does.

PORTIA   A pound of that same merchant's flesh is thine:
The court awards it, and the law doth give it.

SHYLOCK   Most rightful judge!

PORTIA   And you must cut this flesh from off his breast:
The law allows it, and the court awards it.

SHYLOCK   Most learned judge! A sentence! Come, prepare!
                                        (4.1.299–303)

Thus, the law announced by Portia is to enforce the contract in all its rigor. And Antonio must die! But just as Shylock approaches Antonio to cut out his pound of flesh, Portia shocks and astounds everybody.

PORTIA   Tarry a little; there is something else.
This bond doth give thee here no jot of blood;
The words expressly are 'a pound of flesh:'
Take then thy bond, take thou thy pound of flesh;
But, in the cutting it, if thou dost shed
One drop of Christian blood, thy lands and goods
Are, by the laws of Venice, confiscate
Unto the state of Venice.

GRATIANO   O upright judge! Mark, Jew: O learned judge!

SHYLOCK   Is that the law?

PORTIA   Thyself shalt see the act:
For, as thou urgest justice, be assured

Thou shalt have justice, more than thou desirest.

GRATIANO   O learned judge! Mark, Jew: a learned judge!
(4.1.305–313)

Portia is reading the bond just as literally as Shylock has read it. Shylock then wants to go back and accept Bassanio's offer to pay three times the debt. But Portia will not allow it: "The Jew shall have all justice; soft! no haste: / He shall have nothing but the penalty" (4.1.322–23). Portia again stresses literal compliance with the literal terms of the contract. Shylock must cut exactly a pound of flesh, not the smallest part more or less.

PORTIA   Therefore prepare thee to cut off the flesh.
Shed thou no blood, nor cut thou less nor more
But just a pound of flesh: if thou cut'st more
Or less than a just pound, be it but so much
As makes it light or heavy in the substance,
Or the division of the twentieth part
Of one poor scruple, nay, if the scale do turn
But in the estimation of a hair,
Thou diest and all thy goods are confiscate.

GRATIANO   A second Daniel, a Daniel, Jew!
Now, infidel, I have you on the hip.

PORTIA   Why doth the Jew pause? take thy forfeiture.

SHYLOCK   Give me my principal, and let me go.

BASSANIO   I have it ready for thee; here it is.

PORTIA   He hath refused it in the open court:
He shall have merely justice and his bond.

GRATIANO   A Daniel, still say I, a second Daniel!
                (4.1.325–333)

Portia would have escaped much contemporary criticism had she
stopped there. But she does not and gives an even harsher judgment.

SHYLOCK   Shall I not have barely my principal?

PORTIA   Thou shalt have nothing but the forfeiture,
    To be so taken at thy peril, Jew.

SHYLOCK   Why, then the devil give him good of it!
    I'll stay no longer question.

PORTIA   Tarry, Jew:
    The law hath yet another hold on you.
    It is enacted in the laws of Venice,
    If it be proved against an alien
    That by direct or indirect attempts
    He seek the life of any citizen,
    The party 'gainst the which he doth contrive
    Shall seize one half his goods; the other half
    Comes to the privy coffer of the state;
    And the offender's life lies in the mercy
    Of the duke only, 'gainst all other voice.
    In which predicament, I say, thou stand'st;
    For it appears, by manifest proceeding,
    That indirectly and directly too
    Thou hast contrived against the very life
    Of the defendant; and thou hast incurr'd
    The danger formerly by me rehearsed.
    Down therefore and beg mercy of the duke.
                (4.1.342-363)

Portia is not showing the mercy she had urged upon Shylock. An argument can be made that had Shylock taken his pound of flesh pursuant to a lawful judgment of the court he could not be committing a crime. But that technicality is ignored.

The Duke pardons Shylock of the penalty of death but orders half of his estate forfeited to Antonio and half forfeited to the state. When asked if he will show mercy, Antonio appears to contradict the Duke by allowing Shylock to keep half of his estate on the condition that he deed it in trust to Antonio to convey it to his estranged daughter and her Christian husband upon Shylock's death. And this small act of mercy is conditioned upon Shylock converting to Christianity.

PORTIA   Art thou contented, Jew? what dost thou say?

SHYLOCK   I am content.

PORTIA   Clerk, draw a deed of gift.

SHYLOCK   I pray you, give me leave to go from hence;
   I am not well: send the deed after me,
   And I will sign it.

(4.1.393–397)

As Shylock is leaving, he is taunted by Gratiano: "In christening shalt thou have two god-fathers: / Had I been judge, thou shouldst have had ten more, / To bring thee to the gallows, not the font" (4.1.399–401).

This is an oblique reference to the right of a criminal defendant charged with a felony in England to be tried by a jury of twelve. The penalty for conviction of felony was hanging. (In continental Europe, juries were not used in criminal cases.)

The young doctor of laws then sets the stage for the last act of the play by persuading Bassanio to give him Portia's ring in gratitude for what she has done for his friend. Again, Bassanio acts generously and gives the ring, much to his later discomfiture when he returns to his wife in Belmont.

Generations of lawyers have admired and identified with Portia for her skill in using a strict construction of contract law to free her husband's friend from a cruel judgment. Others have not been so free with praise. She is roundly criticized for not showing Shylock the same mercy she urged him to show Antonio. She has been accused of committing a fraud on the court by not revealing that she has an interest in the outcome of the case. She is also faulted for relying upon hyper-technicalities—lawyerly quibbles—when a more liberal appeal to the doctrine of unconscionability or the presumption against forfeitures should have prevailed.

This hyper-legalistic argument may be technically correct. But this misses the point that Shakespeare was a poet and writing a drama, not a legal treatise. Portia is clever, witty, resourceful, wise, eloquent, and generous in love.

I'll take Shakespeare's Portia any day.

CHAPTER 10

HENRY IV, PART 1

Shakespeare's two *Henry IV* plays are the pinnacle of his work in the genre of historical drama. In Sir John Falstaff, Shakespeare creates a character of epic comedy. Shakespeare wrote *Henry IV, Part 1,* in 1597, two years after writing *Richard II.* Although the play is named for him, King Henry IV is not the principal character of the drama. His son, Prince Hal, who is preparing himself to be King in a most unorthodox way, is the central character; he and Falstaff dominate the play. We hear of Hal near the end of *Richard II.*

HENRY BOLINGBROKE   Can no man tell me of my unthrifty son?
'Tis full three months since I did see him last;
If any plague hang over us, 'tis he.
I would to God, my lords, he might be found:
Inquire at London, 'mongst the taverns there,
For there, they say, he daily doth frequent,
With unrestrained loose companions,
Even such, they say, as stand in narrow lanes,
And beat our watch, and rob our passengers;
Which he, young wanton and effeminate boy,
Takes on the point of honour to support
So dissolute a crew.
                (*Richard II,* 5.3.1–12)

The leader of this "dissolute crew" is Shakespeare's comic masterpiece, the fat knight Sir John Falstaff. Nothing in *Richard II* (or any of the earlier plays) would have prepared the Elizabethan theater audience for Shakespeare's Falstaff.

Henry Bolingbroke was the oldest son of John of Gaunt, who was the fourth son of King Edward III. While Richard II was still alive, King Henry IV was considered by many to be a usurper with no legal claim to the throne of England. After Richard II died childless, Henry Bolingbroke was the nearest in blood to his grandfather in the direct male line of descent.

Edmund Mortimer, 5th Earl of March, was a direct descendant of Edward III through a daughter of Lionel of Antwerp, the third son of Edward III. In continental Europe, under what was known as the Salic Law (more about this is in *Henry V*) an inheritance could not pass through the female line. But under the common law, it could.

Richard II had recognized Edmund Mortimer as his heir and next in line for the throne if he died childless. Therefore, there were grounds to question the legitimacy of Henry's claim to the throne— even under the laws of primogeniture. Importantly, Parliament (only vaguely referenced in *Richard II* as "the commons") supported Henry in his claim to the throne. However, his reign was constantly troubled by revolts and rebellions by the nobility.

As Shakespeare's play opens, it is 1400, shortly after the death of Richard II. In the first line of the play Henry tell us his brief reign has not been a happy one. He speaks with an eloquence we did not hear from him in *Richard II*.

King Henry IV: "So shaken as we are, so wan with care, / Find we a time for frighted peace to pant, / And breathe short-winded accents of new broils / To be commenced in strands afar remote" (*Henry IV, Part 1*, 1.1.1–4).

Henry intends to lead a crusade to the Holy Land. But he receives news that the Welsh have revolted and defeated his Herefordshire forces. In the north, the Scots have revolted under the Earl of Douglas. They have been defeated by the gallant young Harry Hotspur, the son of Lord Northumberland. The exploits of Hotspur provoke an unhappy comparison by the King with those of his own Harry. "Yea, there thou makest me sad and makest me sin / In envy that my Lord Northumberland / Should be the father to so blest a son" (1.1.78–80).

In King Henry's speech about Hal in *Richard II* and in this speech, the stage is set for the essential conflicts of the play. Hal is pulled in opposite directions by the two father figures of the play: Falstaff of the tavern world and King Henry of the court. He also has a rival in Hotspur, one he must overcome if he is to be King.

Throughout his plays, Shakespeare addresses the question of how one generation in a family responds to that of another. This unfavorable comparison of Prince Hal with Hotspur is more than just the common complaint of a father about the behavior of his son. As I said about *Richard II*, Bolingbroke in that play does not articulate a political or legal theory that would justify the deposition of a legitimate king. In *Henry IV, Part 1*, we will see that he seems to suggest that he was right to depose Richard because he was the better man to serve as King.

But this argument presents an obvious problem when Henry himself sees Prince Hal as unfit to succeed him as King. After his usurpation, can King Henry revert back to the strict principle of hereditary succession? If the nobility is to elect the best man to serve as King, should it be Hotspur?

Trouble has already broken out from that direction over Hotspur's claim to hold on to prisoners from the recent battle. The King asserts his right under military law to receive any prisoners taken in battle by his forces. Prisoners were important, because they could be held for ransom. Hotspur, however, may have the better argument: that he was entitled to all the prisoners of lesser rank other than his most important prisoner, the Earl of Fife, who had royal blood.

Henry is as deliberate as Richard was rash and impulsive. This question of what to do with the prisoners provokes an angry clash between the King and Hotspur at the council. Hotspur quickly demonstrates that he has neither the patience nor the prudence to be a prince.

The scene shifts to Prince Hal's room in London. This is our introduction to Sir John Falstaff. When Falstaff wakes up in the middle of the day and asks the Prince what time it is, the Prince gives us a vivid description of the fat knight and his habits.

FALSTAFF   Now, Hal, what time of day is it, lad?

PRINCE HENRY   Thou art so fat-witted, with drinking of
   old sack and unbuttoning thee after supper and sleeping upon
   benches after noon, that thou hast forgotten to
   demand that truly which thou wouldst truly know.
   What a devil hast thou to do with the time of the
   day? Unless hours were cups of sack and minutes
   capons and clocks the tongues of bawds and dials the
   signs of leaping-houses and the blessed sun himself
   a fair hot wench in flame-coloured taffeta, I see no
   reason why thou shouldst be so superfluous to demand
   the time of the day.

FALSTAFF   Indeed, you come near me now, Hal; for we
   that take purses go by the moon and the seven stars, and not
   by Phoebus, he, 'that wandering knight so fair.' And,
   I prithee, sweet wag, when thou art king, as, God
   save thy grace,–majesty I should say, for grace
   thou wilt have none,–

PRINCE HENRY   What, none?

FALSTAFF   No, by my troth, not so much as will serve to
   prologue to an egg and butter.

PRINCE HENRY   Well, how then? come, roundly, roundly.

FALSTAFF   Marry, then, sweet wag, when thou art king, let not

us that are squires of the night's body be called
thieves of the day's beauty: let us be Diana's
foresters, gentlemen of the shade, minions of the
moon; and let men say we be men of good government,
being governed, as the sea is, by our noble and
chaste mistress the moon, under whose countenance we steal. . . .
And is not my hostess of the tavern a most sweet wench?

PRINCE HENRY   As the honey of Hybla, my old lad of the castle.
And is not a buff jerkin a most sweet robe of durance?

FALSTAFF   How now, how now, mad wag! what, in thy quips
and thy quiddities? what a plague have I to do with a
buff jerkin?

(2.1.1–29, 40–44)

The "buff jerkin" is a refence to the tan leather jackets worn by
the sheriff's officers who could arrest persons accused of a crime.
This is the topsy-turvey world of John Falstaff, who sleeps through
the day and steals purses at night. Falstaff is outside of time. Even
the gallows is the butt of Falstaff's humor.

FALSTAFF   –But, I prithee, sweet
wag, shall there be gallows standing in England when
thou art king? and resolution thus fobbed as it is
with the rusty curb of old father antic the law? Do
not thou, when thou art king, hang a thief.

PRINCE HENRY   No; thou shalt.

FALSTAFF   Shall I? O rare! By the Lord, I'll be a brave judge.

PRINCE HENRY   Thou judgest false already: I mean, thou shalt
have the hanging of the thieves and so become a rare hangman.

FALSTAFF   Well, Hal, well; and in some sort it jumps with my
humour as well as waiting in the court, I can tell you.

PRINCE HENRY   For obtaining of suits?

FALSTAFF   Yea, for obtaining of suits, whereof the hangman
hath no lean wardrobe.

(1.2.54–68)

News arrives of a party of wealthy travelers who may be robbed the
following night. Hal refuses to join Falstaff and his crew in robbing
the pilgrims: "Who, I rob? I a thief? not I, by my faith" (1.2.131). But
Hal and his friend Poins concoct a scheme to disguise themselves
and rob Falstaff after he and his crew have robbed the travelers.
When Hal is left alone on the stage he tells us of his plan to imitate
the sun in hiding the greatness he will have as king.

PRINCE HENRY   I know you all, and will awhile uphold
The unyoked humour of your idleness:
Yet herein will I imitate the sun,
Who doth permit the base contagious clouds
To smother up his beauty from the world,
That, when he please again to be himself,
Being wanted, he may be more wonder'd at,
By breaking through the foul and ugly mists
Of vapours that did seem to strangle him.
If all the year were playing holidays,
To sport would be as tedious as to work;
But when they seldom come, they wish'd for come,
And nothing pleaseth but rare accidents.
So, when this loose behavior I throw off
And pay the debt I never promised,
By how much better than my word I am,
By so much shall I falsify men's hopes;

And like bright metal on a sullen ground,
My reformation, glittering o'er my fault,
Shall show more goodly and attract more eyes
Than that which hath no foil to set it off.
I'll so offend, to make offence a skill;
Redeeming time when men think least I will.

(2.1.184–206)

Understanding this soliloquy is the key to understanding the character of Prince Hal. Is he a cold, calculating, manipulative, Machiavellian character who abandons his erstwhile friends after they are no longer of any use to him? Or is he a young man who, in an unorthodox manner, is trying to prepare himself to be a worthy king? Or both?

There is the Hal of the tavern world and there is the Prince who will be King. The Prince seems to be under the spell of Falstaff. But if we read his speeches carefully, he always tells the truth about his disreputable companions—particularly when he speaks to Falstaff. He wants to learn the language of the common people so that he can communicate with them and lead them when he is King.

In the Act II, Hal tells Poins that he is "sworn brother to a leash of drawers [*tapsters*]" (2.4.6–7). They say of him that he is "a lad of mettle, a good boy, by the Lord, so they call me, and when I am king of England, I shall command all the good lads in Eastcheap" (2.4.12–15). In part, his success will be because he knows their language: "To conclude, I am so good a proficient in one quarter of an hour, that I can drink with any tinker [*mender of pots*] in his own language during my life" (2.4.17–20). Unlike his father, he does not hold himself aloof from the common people. The last two lines of the Act 1 soliloquy are: "I'll so offend, to make offence a skill; / Redeeming time when men think least I will" (1.2.205–06).

Shakespeare's audience would have recognized the "redeeming time" as a paraphrase of Paul's letter to the Ephesians when he says: "See then that ye walk circumspectly, not as fools, but as wise,

Redeeming the time, because the days are evil."[12] Hal is saying he will atone for his prodigal youth by serving as a wise king. But there is plenty of material to support the critics who see Hal as a calculating, heartless politician who uses people as long as they are useful in pursuing his ambitions, after which he discards them.

At court, the King is provoked by the jealousy of Worchester and the stubbornness of Hotspur, who not only keeps his prisoners but also demands that his brother-in-law, Mortimer, be ransomed from his Welsh captors.

This sends Henry into a rage: "Let me not hear you speak of Mortimer: / Send me your prisoners with the speediest means, / Or you shall hear in such a kind from me / As will displease you" (1.2.120–23). Worcester accuses the King of ingratitude: "Our house, my sovereign liege, little deserves / The scourge of greatness to be used on it; /And that same greatness too which our own hands / Have holp to make so portly" (1.2.10–13). Henry angrily dismisses him. Worcester, Northumberland, and Hotspur plot to join the Welsh and the Scots in a rebellion against the King in support of Mortimer's claim to the throne.

At Gadshill, Falstaff and his crew are successful in robbing the wealthy travelers: "Hang ye, gorbellied knaves, are ye undone? No, ye fat chuffs: I would your store were here! On, bacons, on! What, ye knaves! young men must live. You are Grand-jurors, are ye? we'll jure ye, 'faith" (2.2.82.85).

This reference to grand jurors is somewhat puzzling. Under the common law, up to twenty-three laymen would be summoned to serve as the county grand jury to return indictments against those accused of committing felonies. The petit jury of twelve would then determine the guilt or innocence of the accused. Perhaps Falstaff is responding to an outcry by one of the travelers.

Falstaff and his crew are then surprised and robbed of their booty by the disguised Hal and Poins. Falstaff and the others run away. Hal and Poins wait for them at the Boar's-Head Tavern in

---

[12] Ephesians 5:15–16

Eastcheap. When Falstaff and his robbing crew arrive, Falstaff accuses Hal and Poins of cowardice for not joining them in the robbery on Gadshill. As Hal expected, Falstaff then begins telling an elaborate lie about what happened.

PRINCE HENRY   What's the matter?

FALSTAFF   What's the matter! there be four of us here have ta'en a thousand pound this day morning.

PRINCE HENRY   Where is it, Jack? where is it?

FALSTAFF   Where is it! taken from us it is: a hundred upon poor four of us.

PRINCE HENRY   What, a hundred, man?

FALSTAFF   I am a rogue, if I were not at half-sword with a dozen of them two hours together. I have 'scaped by miracle. I am eight times thrust through the doublet, four through the hose; my buckler cut through and through; my sword hacked like a hand-saw—ecce signum! I never dealt better since I was a man: all would not do. A plague of all cowards! Let them speak: if they speak more or less than truth, they are villains and the sons of darkness.

PRINCE HENRY   Speak, sirs; how was it?

GADSHILL   We four set upon some dozen—

FALSTAFF   Sixteen at least, my lord.

GADSHILL   And bound them.

PETO   No, no, they were not bound.

FALSTAFF   You rogue, they were bound, every man of them; or
I am a Jew else, an Ebrew Jew.

GADSHILL   As we were sharing, some six or seven fresh men set
upon us–

FALSTAFF   And unbound the rest, and then come in the other.

PRINCE HENRY   What, fought you with them all?

FALSTAFF   All! I know not what you call all; but if I fought
not with fifty of them, I am a bunch of radish: if
there were not two or three and fifty upon poor old
Jack, then am I no two-legged creature.

PRINCE HENRY   Pray God you have not murdered some of them.
(2.4.150–180)

As Falstaff begins telling his tale, the number of men assaulting
him grows each time he opens his mouth. Impeaching a witness by
confronting him with a prior inconsistent statement (usually made in
a deposition during the discovery process) is the stock-in-trade (some
judges might even say the obsession) of modern American litigators.
Falstaff just makes the whole endeavor appear to be ridiculous.

FALSTAFF   Nay, that's past praying for: I have peppered two
of them; two I am sure I have paid, two rogues
in buckram suits. I tell thee what, Hal, if I tell
thee a lie, spit in my face, call me horse. Thou
knowest my old ward; here I lay and thus I bore my
point. Four rogues in buckram let drive at me–

PRINCE HENRY   What, four? thou saidst but two even now.

FALSTAFF   Four, Hal; I told thee four.

POINS   Ay, ay, he said four.

FALSTAFF   These four came all a-front, and mainly thrust at
    me. I made me no more ado but took all their seven
    points in my target, thus.

PRINCE HENRY   Seven? why, there were but four even now.

FALSTAFF   In buckram?

POINS   Ay, four, in buckram suits.

FALSTAFF   Seven, by these hilts, or I am a villain else.

PRINCE HENRY   Prithee, let him alone; we shall have more
    anon.

FALSTAFF   Dost thou hear me, Hal?

PRINCE HENRY   Ay, and mark thee too, Jack.

FALSTAFF   Do so, for it is worth the listening to. These nine
    in buckram that I told thee of–

PRINCE HENRY   So, two more already.

FALSTAFF   Their points being broken,–

POINS   Down fell their hose.

FALSTAFF   Began to give me ground: but I followed me close,
    came in foot and hand; and with a thought seven of
    the eleven I paid.

PRINCE HENRY   O monstrous! eleven buckram men grown out
of two!

FALSTAFF   But, as the devil would have it, three misbegotten
knaves in Kendal green came at my back and let drive
at me; for it was so dark, Hal, that thou couldst
not see thy hand.

PRINCE HENRY   These lies are like their father that begets them;
gross as a mountain, open, palpable. Why, thou
clay-brained guts, thou knotty-pated fool, thou
whoreson, obscene, grease tallow-keech,–

FALSTAFF   What, art thou mad? art thou mad? is not the truth
the truth?

PRINCE HENRY   Why, how couldst thou know these men in Kendal
green, when it was so dark thou couldst not see thy
hand? come, tell us your reason: what sayest thou to this?
(2.4.181–221)

Falstaff refuses to explain himself "upon compulsion." When Hal
begins to insult him, Falstaff gives as good as he gets.

PRINCE HENRY   I'll be no longer guilty of this sin; this san-
guine coward, this bed-presser, this horseback-breaker,
this huge hill of flesh,–

FALSTAFF   'Sblood, you starveling, you elf-skin, you dried
neat's tongue, you bull's pizzle, you stock-fish! O
for breath to utter what is like thee! you
tailor's-yard, you sheath, you bowcase; you vile
standing-tuck,–

PRINCE HENRY   Well, breathe awhile, and then to it again: and

when thou hast tired thyself in base comparisons,
hear me speak but this.

POINS   Mark, Jack.

PRINCE HENRY   We two saw you four set on four and bound
them, and were masters of their wealth. Mark now, how a plain
tale shall put you down. Then did we two set on you
four; and, with a word, out-faced you from your
prize, and have it; yea, and can show it you here in
the house: and, Falstaff, you carried your guts
away as nimbly, with as quick dexterity, and roared
for mercy and still run and roared, as ever I heard
bull-calf. What a slave art thou, to hack thy sword
as thou hast done, and then say it was in fight!
What trick, what device, what starting-hole, canst
thou now find out to hide thee from this open and
apparent shame?

                    (2.4.229–253)

With extraordinary quickness of wit, Falstaff replies: "By the
Lord, I knew ye as well as he that made ye" (2.4.255). He claims to
have known "on instinct" that it was the Prince and that he could
not strike the heir to the throne.

The lying and storytelling at the Boar's-Head is interrupted by
a messenger from the King, who tells of Hotspur's rebellion and
summons Prince Hal to the court the next morning. Falstaff warns
Hal that his father will "be horribly chid tomorrow" (2.4.357) and
urges him to practice an answer for when his father puts him on
trial at the court in the morning.

PRINCE HENRY   Do thou stand for my father, and examine me
upon the particulars of my life.

FALSTAFF   Shall I? content: this chair shall be my state,

this dagger my sceptre, and this cushion my crown.

PRINCE HENRY   Thy state is taken for a joined-stool, thy golden
sceptre for a leaden dagger, and thy precious rich
crown for a pitiful bald crown!

FALSTAFF   Well, an the fire of grace be not quite out of thee,
now shalt thou be moved. Give me a cup of sack to
make my eyes look red, that it may be thought I have
wept; for I must speak in passion, and I will do it
in King Cambyses' vein.

PRINCE HENRY   Well, here is my leg.

FALSTAFF   And here is my speech. Stand aside, nobility.

HOSTESS   O Jesu, this is excellent sport, i' faith!

FALSTAFF   Weep not, sweet queen; for trickling tears are vain.

HOSTESS   O, the father, how he holds his countenance!

FALSTAFF   For God's sake, lords, convey my tristful queen;
For tears do stop the flood-gates of her eyes.

HOSTESS   O Jesu, he doth it as like one of these harlotry
players as ever I see!

FALSTAFF   Peace, good pint-pot; peace, good tickle-brain.
Harry, I do not only marvel where thou spendest thy
time, but also how thou art accompanied: for though
the camomile, the more it is trodden on the faster
it grows, yet youth, the more it is wasted the
sooner it wears. That thou art my son, I have
partly thy mother's word, partly my own opinion,

but chiefly a villanous trick of thine eye and a
foolish-hanging of thy nether lip, that doth warrant
me. If then thou be son to me, here lies the point;
why, being son to me, art thou so pointed at? Shall
the blessed sun of heaven prove a micher and eat
blackberries? a question not to be asked. Shall
the sun of England prove a thief and take purses? a
question to be asked. There is a thing, Harry,
which thou hast often heard of and it is known to
many in our land by the name of pitch: this pitch,
as ancient writers do report, doth defile; so doth
the company thou keepest: for, Harry, now I do not
speak to thee in drink but in tears, not in
pleasure but in passion, not in words only, but in
woes also: and yet there is a virtuous man whom I
have often noted in thy company, but I know not his name.

PRINCE HENRY   What manner of man, an it like your majesty?

FALSTAFF   A goodly portly man, i' faith, and a corpulent; of a
cheerful look, a pleasing eye and a most noble
carriage; and, as I think, his age some fifty, or,
by'r lady, inclining to three score; and now I
remember me, his name is Falstaff: if that man
should be lewdly given, he deceiveth me; for, Harry,
I see virtue in his looks. If then the tree may be
known by the fruit, as the fruit by the tree, then,
peremptorily I speak it, there is virtue in that
Falstaff: him keep with, the rest banish. And tell
me now, thou naughty varlet, tell me, where hast
thou been this month?

(2.4.359–415)

When well-acted, this mock trial scene is a hilarious performance by Falstaff. But Hal turns the tables on the fat old knight

and demands that Falstaff play the part of the Prince while Hal plays the King.

PRINCE HENRY   Dost thou speak like a king? Do thou stand for me, and I'll play my father.

FALSTAFF   Depose me? if thou dost it half so gravely, so majestically, both in word and matter, hang me up by the heels for a rabbit-sucker or a poulter's hare.

PRINCE HENRY   Well, here I am set.

FALSTAFF   And here I stand: judge, my masters.

PRINCE HENRY   Now, Harry, whence come you?

FALSTAFF   My noble lord, from Eastcheap.

PRINCE HENRY   The complaints I hear of thee are grievous.

FALSTAFF   'Sblood, my lord, they are false: nay, I'll tickle ye for a young prince, i' faith.

PRINCE HENRY   Swearest thou, ungracious boy? henceforth ne'er look, on me. Thou art violently carried away from grace: there is a devil haunts thee in the likeness of an old fat man; a tun of man is thy companion. Why dost thou converse with that trunk of humours, that bolting-hutch of beastliness, that swollen parcel of dropsies, that huge bombard of sack, that stuffed cloak-bag of guts, that roasted Manningtree ox with the pudding in his belly, that reverend vice, that grey iniquity, that father ruffian, that vanity in years? Wherein is he good, but to taste sack and drink it? wherein neat and cleanly, but to carve a

capon and eat it? wherein cunning, but in craft?
wherein crafty, but in villany? wherein villanous,
but in all things? wherein worthy, but in nothing?

FALSTAFF   I would your grace would take me with you: whom
means your grace?

PRINCE HENRY   That villanous abominable misleader of youth,
Falstaff, that old white-bearded Satan.

FALSTAFF   My lord, the man I know.

PRINCE HENRY   I know thou dost.

FALSTAFF   But to say I know more harm in him than in myself,
were to say more than I know. That he is old, the
more the pity, his white hairs do witness it; but
that he is, saving your reverence, a whoremaster,
that I utterly deny. If sack and sugar be a fault,
God help the wicked! if to be old and merry be a
sin, then many an old host that I know is damned: if
to be fat be to be hated, then Pharaoh's lean kine
are to be loved. No, my good lord; banish Peto,
banish Bardolph, banish Poins: but for sweet Jack
Falstaff, kind Jack Falstaff, true Jack Falstaff,
valiant Jack Falstaff, and therefore more valiant,
being, as he is, old Jack Falstaff, banish not him
thy Harry's company, banish not him thy Harry's
company: banish plump Jack, and banish all the world.

PRINCE HENRY   I do, I will.
                    (4.2.416–64)

Hal's final words in this mock trial are chilling and foreboding.
Falstaff's defense of himself is interrupted by the appearance at the

door of the Sheriff with a posse seeking the Gadshill robbers. "First, pardon me, my lord. A hue and cry / Hath follow'd certain men unto this house" (4.2.489–90).

A "hue and cry" was the pursuit of someone who had committed a felony. The constable was to call upon his parishioners to join him in pursuit of the felon as he was pursued from parish to parish and county to county. A private citizen engaged in the "hue and cry" was entitled to arrest the felon and receive forfeiture of the felon's property as a reward.

Falstaff and his crew hide themselves, and the Sheriff leaves after Hal promises to surrender the robbers. Falstaff falls asleep behind an arras. This extraordinarily long scene ends with a hilarious examination of and commentary by Hal on the contents of the sleeping Falstaff's pockets.

In the morning at court, Hal is horribly chided by the King. When Hal asks for pardon, the King explodes.

KING HENRY IV   God pardon thee! yet let me wonder, Harry,
At thy affections, which do hold a wing
Quite from the flight of all thy ancestors.
Thy place in council thou hast rudely lost.
Which by thy younger brother is supplied,
And art almost an alien to the hearts
Of all the court and princes of my blood:
The hope and expectation of thy time
Is ruin'd, and the soul of every man
Prophetically doth forethink thy fall.
(3.2.29–38)

The King compares Hal's behavior to that of Richard II who "[e]nfeoff'd himself to popularity" (3.2.69). "Enfeoffment" was the grant of land in fee simple, the most unqualified title to real property under the common law. Enfeoffment was accomplished by a ceremony known as "livery of seisin" whereby the donor delivered to the donee a handful of dirt on the land in the presence of numerous witnesses.

The King is saying that Richard gave himself to popularity and lost the aura of majesty. By constantly exposing himself, Richard had made himself seem like less than a king. The King accuses Hal of doing the same. Hal promises that "I shall hereafter, my thrice gracious lord, / Be more myself" (3.2.92–93). But the King continues his tirade and even accuses Hal of disloyalty. Hal cannot let this last accusation pass: "Do not think so; you shall not find it so: / And God forgive them that so much have sway'd / Your majesty's good thoughts away from me! / I will redeem all this on Percy's head" (3.2.130–33). The King finally relents and instructs Hal to take a portion of his forces and march toward the rebels gathered at Shrewsbury.

Hal pays back the money stolen by Falstaff and procures for him a commission to raise a company of soldiers for the battle. He tells Falstaff, "Jack, meet me to-morrow in the temple hall at two o'clock in the afternoon. / There shalt thou know thy charge" (3.3.196–97). Temple Hall was a structure connected to the Inner and Middle Temples of the Inns of Court.

In the rebel camp, Hotspur learns that his father and Owen Glendower's Welshmen will not arrive in time for the battle. But he is determined to give battle to the King's approaching forces. Fortunately for the King, Falstaff is in charge of only one company. He describes his recruiting methods as follows.

FALSTAFF   If I be not ashamed of my soldiers, I am a soused
    gurnet. I have misused the king's press damnably.
    I have got, in exchange of a hundred and fifty
    soldiers, three hundred and odd pounds. I press me
    none but good house-holders, yeoman's sons; inquire
    me out contracted bachelors, such as had been asked
    twice on the banns; such a commodity of warm slaves,
    as had as lieve hear the devil as a drum; such as
    fear the report of a caliver worse than a struck
    fowl or a hurt wild-duck. I pressed me none but such
    toasts-and-butter, with hearts in their bellies no

bigger than pins' heads, and they have bought out
their services; and now my whole charge consists of
ancients, corporals, lieutenants, gentlemen of
companies, slaves as ragged as Lazarus in the
painted cloth, where the glutton's dogs licked his
sores; and such as indeed were never soldiers,
but discarded unjust serving-men, younger sons to
younger brothers, revolted tapsters and ostlers
trade-fallen, the cankers of a calm world and a
long peace, ten times more dishonourable ragged than
an old faced ancient: and such have I, to fill up
the rooms of them that have bought out their
services, that you would think that I had a hundred
and fifty tattered prodigals lately come from
swine-keeping, from eating draff and husks. A mad
fellow met me on the way and told me I had unloaded
all the gibbets and pressed the dead bodies. No eye
hath seen such scarecrows. I'll not march through
Coventry with them, that's flat: nay, and the
villains march wide betwixt the legs, as if they had
gyves on; for indeed I had the most of them out of
prison.

(4.2.11–43)

Shakespeare's description of the corruption of conscription and
the widespread extent of bribery to avoid service was an accurate
description of the process that produced such poor common soldiers.
When he sees Falstaff's men, Hal exclaims: "I did never see such
pitiful rascals" (4.2.65). Falstaff cynically responds: "good enough
to toss; food for powder, food for powder; they'll fill a pit as well as
better: tush, man, mortal men, mortal men" (4.2.66–68). Cynical,
yes, but a realistic commentary upon the brutality of war, one that
is not shared by Hal or Hotspur.

At Shrewsbury, the King summons an emissary from the rebels
to discuss an end to the conflict. When Worcester comes to the King,

Hal issues a challenge to meet Hotspur in a man-to-man fight to settle the rebellion. Of course, the King cannot risk his crown on a single fight. He offers general amnesty to end the rebellion. Hal and Falstaff are then left alone on the stage. Falstaff says to the Prince: "Hal, if thou see me down in the battle and bestride me, so; 'tis a point of friendship" (5.1.122–23).

When the Prince tells him to say his prayers, Falstaff responds: "I would 'twere bed-time, Hal, and all well" (5.1.126). Falstaff is no seeker of glory on the battlefield. Hal then exclaims: "Why, thou owest God a death" (5.1.128). After Hal rides off to the battle, Falstaff has an extraordinary soliloquy on the nature of military glory as honor.

FALSTAFF 'Tis [*his death*] not due yet; I would be loath to pay
   him before his day. What need I be so forward with him that
   calls not on me? Well, 'tis no matter; honour pricks
   me on. Yea, but how if honour prick me off when I
   come on? how then? Can honour set to a leg? no: or
   an arm? no: or take away the grief of a wound? no.
   Honour hath no skill in surgery, then? no. What is
   honour? a word. What is in that word honour? what
   is that honour? air. A trim reckoning! Who hath it?
   he that died o' Wednesday. Doth he feel it? no.
   Doth he hear it? no. 'Tis insensible, then. Yea,
   to the dead. But will it not live with the living?
   no. Why? detraction will not suffer it. Therefore
   I'll none of it. Honour is a mere scutcheon: and so
   ends my catechism.
                  (5.1.129–142)

This speech of Falstaff is a radical rejection of Hotspur's devotion to honor and chivalry. Hal must negotiate between the polar opposites of Hotspur and Falstaff. Hotspur is so obsessed with honor and glory that he can think of nothing else. He rashly fights a battle he cannot win. Falstaff doesn't fight at all.

But the loveable old reprobate Falstaff at least never lies to himself. "Give me life, which if I can save, so: if not, honour comes unlooked for, and there's an end" (5.3.60–61). The contrast between Falstaff and Hotspur could not be starker. On the eve of the battle, Hotspur exclaims: "Doomsday is near; die all, die merrily" (4.1.141).

To Falstaff, the desire for military glory is nothing but sheer nonsense. To Falstaff there is joy and vitality in life. It is this quality of Falstaff that led Harold Goddard to say: "Falstaff lives. And where he is, life becomes bright, active, enthralling."[13]

In the rebel camp, Worcester believes he cannot trust the King. He lies to his nephew about the King's offer of clemency. "There is no seeming mercy in the king" (5.2.36). He does tell Hotspur of Prince Hal's challenge to single combat. On the battlefield, Hal saves his father from the murderous rebel Douglas. Hal is urged to leave the field because of a wound, but he refuses.

Hal and Hotspur meet. The collision of the two great hearts is the climax of the play. Falstaff comes on the scene and falls down and pretends to be dead after he is attacked by Douglas. Hal strikes down Hotspur.

HOTSPUR   O, Harry, thou hast robb'd me of my youth!
I better brook the loss of brittle life
Than those proud titles thou hast won of me;
They wound my thoughts worse than sword my flesh:
But thought's the slave of life, and life time's fool;
And time, that takes survey of all the world,
Must have a stop. O, I could prophesy,
But that the earthy and cold hand of death
Lies on my tongue: no, Percy, thou art dust
And food for–

[*Dies*]

---

[13] Harold Goddard, *The Meaning of Shakespeare* (University of Chicago Press, 1960), Vol. 1, 179.

PRINCE HENRY   For worms, brave Percy: fare thee well, great
heart!

(5.4.79–89)

In his tribute to Hotspur, Hal belies the charges of cynicism and
opportunism. "But let my favours hide thy mangled face" (5.4.98).
Hal then sees Falstaff lying on the ground and thinks that he is dead.
"What, old acquaintance! could not all this flesh / Keep in a little
life? Poor Jack, farewell!" (5.4.104–05). When Hal leaves, Falstaff
gets up. "'Sblood, 'twas time to counterfeit, or that hot termagant
Scot had paid me scot and lot too" (5.4.115–16). In criminal law,
a counterfeit is an imitation of a true article, such as counterfeit
currency or designer merchandise. Falstaff has counterfeited death
to save his life: "The better part of valour is discretion; in the which
better part I have saved my life" (5.4.122–23).

Seeing the body of Hotspur, Falstaff stabs it in the thigh and
drags it away. When he sees Hal, he claims to have killed Hotspur.
Hal is incredulous at this enormous lie: "Why, Percy I killed myself
and saw thee dead" (5.4.148).

It is Falstaff's extraordinary ability to make up a story that led
Harold Goddard to say of him: "Falstaff is immortal because he is
a symbol of the supremacy of imagination over fact. He forecasts
man's final victory over Fate itself." [14]

The King has defeated Hotspur and Douglas. "Thus ever did
rebellion find rebuke" (5.5.1). His noble captives are condemned
to death on the spot without judicial process: "Bear Worcester to
the death and Vernon too: / Other offenders we will pause upon"
(5.5.14–15). King Henry is exercising the prerogative of the victor
on the field of ordering the summary execution of Worcester and
Vernon as traitors. The lessor offenders will at least receive some
sort of trial. The King and his sons leave the field to pursue the
other rebels.

---

[14] Goddard, *The Meaning of Shakespeare*, Vol 1, 179.

KING HENRY IV   Then this remains, that we divide our power.
You, son John, and my cousin Westmoreland
Towards York shall bend you with your dearest speed,
To meet Northumberland and the prelate Scroop,
Who, as we hear, are busily in arms:
Myself and you, son Harry, will towards Wales,
To fight with Glendower and the Earl of March.
Rebellion in this land shall lose his sway,
Meeting the cheque of such another day:
And since this business so fair is done,
Let us not leave till all our own be won.
(5.1.35–45)

This is Shakespeare's most famous history play. In the fat knight Falstaff, Shakespeare created one of the most notable characters in dramatic literature. Falstaff is the breakthrough of Shakespeare's genius for comedy as Hamlet will be the breakthrough of his genius for tragedy. The politics of kingship takes second place to fat Jack, who steals the show. He eats, drinks, jokes, lies, steals, and fornicates through life. He is charming, witty, irreverent, guiltless, charismatic, and full of life. He doesn't worry about the state of his soul or the state of the kingdom. He is literature's greatest drinking buddy.

But Hal knows the time must come when he will have to abandon Falstaff: "I do, I will." To be a king requires virtues that Falstaff disdains. At the end of the play, Prince Hal and his father are momentarily reconciled.

The story could have ended there. But Shakespeare had a character in Falstaff who was too good to use up in a single play. So the story of the wastrel Prince Hal and the fat knight Falstaff continues in *Henry IV, Part 2.*

CHAPTER 11

Henry IV, Part 2

Henry IV, Part 2 begins immediately after the battle of Shrewsbury with the allegorical character Rumor, who declares: "Upon my tongues continual slanders ride, / The which in every language I pronounce, / Stuffing the ears of men with false reports" (*Henry IV, Part 2*, 1.1.6–8). Rumor appears before the castle of the Earl of Northumberland. He has been spreading the false tale that at the battle of Shrewsbury Hotspur has killed Prince Hal, and Douglas has killed the King. Lord Bardolph delivers this false report to Northumberland. But immediately a servant gives Northumberland a report that "rebellion had bad luck / And that young Harry Percy's spur was cold" (1.1.41–42). Lord Morton not only confirms this report but adds that the King with his army is on the way north. Northumberland responds with a cataclysmic vow: "Let heaven kiss earth! now let not Nature's hand / Keep the wild flood confined! let order die!" (1.1.153–54).

Northumberland is advised to quell his stormy passion and join forces with the Archbishop of York, who has turned "insurrection to religion" (1.1.201). York is claiming that the latest rebellion is God's punishment of King Henry for murdering Richard II. Thus, the question of whether Henry IV is a legitimate king continues to haunt him. Ultimately, Northumberland decides to flee to Scotland.

In his first appearance in the play, Falstaff asks his page for a report from a doctor who has examined his urine. The page responds that the water was good, "but, for the party that owed it, he might have more diseases than he knew for" (1.2.3–5). Falstaff is having trouble getting material for a cloak on credit. His page tells him that Master Dombeldon "liked not the security" (1.2.26).

FALSTAFF   Let him be damned, like the glutton! pray God his
tongue be hotter! A whoreson Achitophel! a rascally
yea-forsooth knave! to bear a gentleman in hand,
and then stand upon security! The whoreson
smooth-pates do now wear nothing but high shoes, and
bunches of keys at their girdles; and if a man is
through with them in honest taking up, then they
must stand upon security. I had as lief they would
put ratsbane in my mouth as offer to stop it with
security. I looked a' should have sent me two and
twenty yards of satin, as I am a true knight, and he
sends me security.

(1.2.27–38)

Achitophel of the Biblical Old Testament was a counselor of King David who betrayed him and joined the rebellion of David's son, Absalom. When the rebellion failed, Achitophel committed suicide by hanging himself.

On the street in London, Falstaff seeks to avoid an unpleasant encounter with the Lord Chief Justice of England. He claims to be deaf and cannot hear his name when it is called.

[Enter the LORD CHIEF-JUSTICE and Servant]

PAGE   Sir, here comes the nobleman that committed the
Prince for striking him about Bardolph.

FALSTAFF   Wait, close; I will not see him.

LORD CHIEF-JUSTICE   What's he that goes there?

SERVANT   Falstaff, an't please your lordship.

LORD CHIEF-JUSTICE   He that was in question for the robbery?

SERVANT   He, my lord: but he hath since done good service at
Shrewsbury; and, as I hear, is now going with some
charge to the Lord John of Lancaster.

LORD CHIEF-JUSTICE   What, to York? Call him back again.

SERVANT   Sir John Falstaff!

FALSTAFF   Boy, tell him I am deaf.

PAGE   You must speak louder; my master is deaf.

LORD CHIEF-JUSTICE   I am sure he is, to the hearing of any
thing good. Go, pluck him by the elbow; I must speak with
him.

SERVANT   Sir John!

(1.2.42–57)

Falstaff wants to avoid the encounter because of the robbery on
Gads Hill that has never been resolved. Although Prince Hal repaid
the money, Falstaff was still liable for the assault on the pilgrims. He
pretends to think that the Chief Justice's servant is a beggar.

FALSTAFF   What! a young knave, and begging! Is there not
wars? is there not employment? doth not the king
lack subjects? do not the rebels need soldiers?
Though it be a shame to be on any side but one, it
is worse shame to beg than to be on the worst side,
were it worse than the name of rebellion can tell
how to make it.

SERVANT   You mistake me, sir.

FALSTAFF   Why, sir, did I say you were an honest man? setting
   my knighthood and my soldiership aside, I had lied
   in my throat, if I had said so.

SERVANT   I pray you, sir, then set your knighthood and our
   soldiership aside; and give me leave to tell you,
   you lie in your throat, if you say I am any other
   than an honest man.

FALSTAFF   I give thee leave to tell me so! I lay aside that
   which grows to me! if thou gettest any leave of me,
   hang me; if thou takest leave, thou wert better be
   hanged. You hunt counter: hence! avaunt!

SERVANT   Sir, my lord would speak with you.

LORD CHIEF-JUSTICE   Sir John Falstaff, a word with you.

FALSTAFF   My good lord! God give your lordship good time of
   day. I am glad to see your lordship abroad: I heard
   say your lordship was sick: I hope your lordship
   goes abroad by advice. Your lordship, though not
   clean past your youth, hath yet some smack of age in
   you, some relish of the saltness of time; and I must
   humbly beseech your lordship to have a reverent care
   of your health.

(1.2.57–84)

The Chief Justice tells Falstaff that "[t]o punish you by the heels
would amend the attention of your ears" (1.2.106). He is threatening
Falstaff with putting him in the "stocks," a wooden apparatus used
to punish offenders against English law. The offender sat on a bench

with his feet fastened in holes under a moveable board. The length of time for the confinement would vary with the severity of the offense.

Falstaff abandons the pretense of being deaf in order to engage the Chief Justice in unrestrained verbal combat.

LORD CHIEF-JUSTICE   I sent for you, when there were matters against you for your life, to come speak with me.

FALSTAFF   As I was then advised by my learned counsel in the laws of this land-service, I did not come.

LORD CHIEF-JUSTICE   Well, the truth is, Sir John, you live in great infamy.

FALSTAFF   He that buckles him in my belt cannot live in less.

LORD CHIEF-JUSTICE   Your means are very slender, and your waste is great.

FALSTAFF   I would it were otherwise; I would my means were greater, and my waist slenderer.

LORD CHIEF-JUSTICE   You have misled the youthful prince.

FALSTAFF   The young prince hath misled me: I am the fellow with the great belly, and he my dog.

LORD CHIEF-JUSTICE   Well, I am loath to gall a new-healed wound: your day's service at Shrewsbury hath a little gilded over your night's exploit on Gad's-hill: you may thank the unquiet time for your quiet o'er-posting that action.

FALSTAFF   My lord?

LORD CHIEF-JUSTICE   But since all is well, keep it so: wake not a sleeping wolf.

FALSTAFF   To wake a wolf is as bad as to smell a fox.

LORD CHIEF-JUSTICE   What! you are as a candle, the better part burnt out.

FALSTAFF   A wassail candle, my lord, all tallow: if I did say of wax, my growth would approve the truth.

LORD CHIEF-JUSTICE   There is not a white hair on your face but should have his effect of gravity.

FALSTAFF   His effect of gravy, gravy, gravy.

LORD CHIEF-JUSTICE   You follow the young prince up and down, like his ill angel.

FALSTAFF   Not so, my lord; your ill angel is light; but I hope he that looks upon me will take me without weighing: and yet, in some respects, I grant, I cannot go: I cannot tell. . . .

LORD CHIEF-JUSTICE   Well, God send the prince a better companion!

FALSTAFF   God send the companion a better prince! I cannot rid my hands of him.

(1.2.114–45, 176–178)

Falstaff ends the ribald dialogue by outrageously asking the Chief Justice to loan him a thousand pounds. This scene of Falstaff verbally jousting with the Chief Justice shows him at his witty, irreverent best. Falstaff shows himself to be utterly unrestrained by law and its institutions. After the Chief Justice leaves, we hear one of Falstaff's rare lamentations that he is old, sick, and broke.

As the King and the Archbishop of York gather their forces for the contest, Falstaff is embroiled in a more domestic and farcical conflict. Mistress Quickly is determined to have him arrested for his overdue tavern bill. She and certain officers are waiting for him on a street in London.

MISTRESS QUICKLY   Master Fang, have you entered the action?

FANG   It is entered.

MISTRESS QUICKLY   Where's your yeoman? Is't a lusty yeoman? will a' stand to 't?

FANG   Sirrah, where's Snare?

MISTRESS QUICKLY   O Lord, ay! good Master Snare.

SNARE   Here, here.

FANG   Snare, we must arrest Sir John Falstaff.
                           (2.1.1–7)

The "action" refers to the formal initiation of a complaint in a court of law. In this case it would be an action for debt for which Mistress Quickly could have Falstaff arrested. As a "poor widow of Eastcheap" (2.1.61). Mistress Quickly was not subject to the law of coverture and could sue in her own name. When Falstaff enters, he and Bardolph get into a brawl with Mistress Quickly and her officers, and she shows her talent for malapropisms.

FANG   Sir John, I arrest you at the suit of Mistress Quickly.

FALSTAFF   Away, varlets! Draw, Bardolph: cut me off the villain's head: throw the quean [*whore*] in the channel.

MISTRESS QUICKLY   Throw me in the channel! I'll throw thee
in the channel. Wilt thou? wilt thou? thou bastardly rogue!
Murder, murder! Ah, thou honeysuckle [*homicidal*] villain!
wilt thou kill God's officers and the king's? Ah, thou honey-seed [*homicidal*] rogue! thou art a honey-seed [*homicide*],
a man-queller [*killer*], and a woman-queller [*killer*].

FALSTAFF   Keep them off, Bardolph.

FANG   A rescue! a rescue!

MISTRESS QUICKLY   Good people, bring a rescue or two. Thou
wo't, wo't thou? Thou wo't, wo't ta? do, do, thou rogue! do,
thou hemp-seed!

FALSTAFF   Away, you scullion! you rampallion! You fustilarian!
I'll tickle your catastrophe.
(2.1.39–53)

At this moment the Chief Justice and his men return and see the
street fight between Falstaff and Mistress Quickly's officers.

LORD CHIEF-JUSTICE   What is the matter? keep the peace here,
ho!

MISTRESS QUICKLY   Good my lord, be good to me. I beseech
you, stand to me.

LORD CHIEF-JUSTICE   How now, Sir John! what are you brawl-
ing here? Doth this become your place, your time and business? You should have been well on your way to York.
Stand from him, fellow: wherefore hang'st upon him?

MISTRESS QUICKLY   O most worshipful lord, an't please your grace, I am a poor widow of Eastcheap, and he is arrested at my suit.

LORD CHIEF-JUSTICE   For what sum?

MISTRESS QUICKLY   It is more than for some, my lord; it is for all, all I have. He hath eaten me out of house and home; he hath put all my substance into that fat belly of his: but I will have some of it out again, or I will ride thee o' nights like the mare.

FALSTAFF   I think I am as like to ride the mare, if I have any vantage of ground to get up.

LORD CHIEF-JUSTICE   How comes this, Sir John? Fie! what man of good temper would endure this tempest of exclamation? Are you not ashamed to enforce a poor widow to so rough a course to come by her own?

FALSTAFF   What is the gross sum that I owe thee?

MISTRESS QUICKLY   Marry, if thou wert an honest man, thyself and the money too. Thou didst swear to me upon a parcel-gilt goblet, sitting in my Dolphin-chamber, at the round table, by a sea-coal fire, upon Wednesday in Wheeson week, when the prince broke thy head for liking his father to a singing-man of Windsor, thou didst swear to me then, as I was washing thy wound, to marry me and make me my lady thy wife. Canst thou deny it. . . . And didst thou not kiss me and bid me fetch thee thirty shillings? I put thee now to thy bookoath: deny it, if thou canst.

FALSTAFF   My lord, this is a poor mad soul; and she says up and down the town that the eldest son is like you: she hath been in good case, and the truth is, poverty hath distracted her. But for these foolish officers, I beseech you I may have redress against them.

LORD CHIEF-JUSTICE   Sir John, Sir John, I am well acquainted with your manner of wrenching the true cause the false way. It is not a confident brow, nor the throng of words that come with such more than impudent sauciness from you, can thrust me from a level consideration: you have, as it appears to me, practised upon the easy-yielding spirit of this woman, and made her serve your uses both in purse and in person.

MISTRESS QUICKLY   Yea, in truth, my lord.

LORD CHIEF-JUSTICE   Pray thee, peace. Pay her the debt you owe her, and unpay the villany you have done her: the one you may do with sterling money, and the other with current repentance.

(2.1.54–81, 87–106)

As Chief Justice of the Court of King's Bench, he could order Falstaff to pay a debt. But only a church court could enforce the promise to marry. Seduction based upon a promise to marry would commonly result in a parish court ordering the defendant to perform some act of penance. But more promises from Falstaff convince Mistress Quickly to withdraw her suit and pawn her silver to loan him ten pounds. And so, the hilarious scene ends.

At the Boar's Head Tavern, Falstaff and Pistol get in a fight over a whore. At Westminster, the King is sick and cannot sleep. He gives an unexpectedly beautiful speech about how sickness—insomnia—affects even kings. King Henry: "How many thousand of my poorest subjects / Are at this hour asleep! O sleep, O gentle sleep, / Nature's soft nurse, how have I frighted thee, / That thou no more wilt weigh my eyelids down / And steep my senses in forgetfulness?" (3.1.5–9). Even the ship-boy tossed in a gale on the high seas can sleep. But not the King in the stillest night: "Uneasy lies the head that wears a crown" (3.1.32).

Prince Hal gets the King to give Falstaff a commission to raise a company of the militia. In Gloucestershire, Falstaff comes to the home of Justice of the Peace Shallow to recruit his company of soldiers.

The part-time, unsalaried office of the Justice of the Peace was created by statute in 1327. The Justices of the Peace were knights and substantial gentry (not necessarily lawyers) in each county who were given a royal commission to enforce the law. They were appointed by the king on the recommendation of the Lord Chancellor. They could order the arrest of criminal suspects and commit them to jail or allow bail.

The Marian Committal Statute of 1555 was an important innovation in pretrial criminal procedure. The Act required the Justice of the Peace to examine the accused and his accusers about the charges before committing a defendant to pretrial detention or allowing release on bail. The Justice of the Peace was required to summarize in writing these examinations and present them at the next assize of "gaol delivery." These depositions, often including a confession by the accused, could be read to the jury at trial. The Justice of the Peace could also order the accusing witnesses to appear at trial.

Justices of the Peace (Shakespeare's father served as one in the borough of Stratford for a year in the 1560s) had important local administrative responsibilities. For example, they were responsible for enforcing price limits on commodities such as ale, bread, and fuel. Under the Labourers Act of 1563, they were also responsible for enforcing the maximum wages that could be received for each occupation. They also licensed ale houses and kept the muster roll for pressing eligible men into military service. The system of Justices of the Peace was a powerful tool for Tudor monarchs to increase administrative control over the entire country.

Shakespeare's Justice Shallow, however, is a doddering old fool. Before Falstaff arrives, he reminisces with his imbecilic cousin Silence about youthful adventures at the Inns of Court.

SHALLOW   By yea and nay, sir, I dare say my cousin William is
become a good scholar: he is at Oxford still, is he not?

SILENCE   Indeed, sir, to my cost.

SHALLOW   A' must, then, to the inns o' court shortly. I was
once of Clement's Inn, where I think they will
talk of mad Shallow yet.

SILENCE   You were called 'lusty Shallow' then, cousin.

SHALLOW   By the mass, I was called any thing; and I would
have done any thing indeed too, and roundly too.
There was I, and little John Doit of Staffordshire,
and black George Barnes, and Francis Pickbone, and
Will Squele, a Cotswold man; you had not four such
swinge-bucklers in all the inns o' court again: and
I may say to you, we knew where the bona-robas were
and had the best of them all at commandment. Then
was Jack Falstaff, now Sir John, a boy, and page to
Thomas Mowbray, Duke of Norfolk.

SILENCE   This Sir John, cousin, that comes hither anon about
soldiers?

SHALLOW   The same Sir John, the very same. I see him break
Skogan's head at the court-gate, when a' was a
crack not thus high: and the very same day did I
fight with one Sampson Stockfish, a fruiterer,
behind Gray's Inn. Jesu, Jesu, the mad days that I
have spent! and to see how many of my old
acquaintance are dead!

(3.2.9–33)

In addition to the principal Inns of Court, there were the lesser Chancery Inns. One of the Chancery Inns was Clement's Inn. If the teenage Shakespeare attended an Inn of Court, it may well have been Clement's Inn.

When the character Bardolph now enters in advance of Falstaff, we are astonished to learn that Falstaff at one time had a wife.

BARDOLPH   Good morrow, honest gentlemen: I beseech you, which is Justice Shallow?

SHALLOW   I am Robert Shallow, sir; a poor esquire of this county, and one of the king's justices of the peace: What is your good pleasure with me?

BARDOLPH   My captain, sir, commends him to you; my captain, Sir John Falstaff, a tall gentleman, by heaven, and a most gallant leader.

SHALLOW   He greets me well, sir. I knew him a good backsword man. How doth the good knight? may I ask how my lady his wife doth?

BARDOLPH   Sir, pardon; a soldier is better accommodated than with a wife.

SHALLOW   It is well said, in faith, sir; and it is well said indeed too. Better accommodated! it is good; yea, indeed, is it: good phrases are surely, and ever were, very commendable. Accommodated! it comes of 'accommodo' very good; a good phrase.

(3.2.53–70)

But we learn nothing more of Falstaff's wife. Upon entering, Falstaff immediately proceeds to the business of impressing soldiers for his company. Bardolf and Falstaff allow the best of the men to pay bribes to escape from service, leaving only the feeble and penniless to enter the King's army.

As he leaves, Falstaff cannot resist the temptation to confide in us his true opinion of Justice Shallow when Shallow was a young country bumpkin. Falstaff: "This same starved justice hath done nothing but prate to me of the wildness of his youth, and the feats he hath done about Turnbull Street: and every third word a lie" (3.2.284–87). He was so skinny he looked like a victim of famine, but "yet lecherous as a monkey, and the whores called him man-drake" (3.2.294–95).

In Yorkshire, the Archbishop of York and Lord Hastings learn that their confederate Northumberland has fled to Scotland. The King's forces under Prince John, Duke of Lancaster, are nearby, and the Earl of Westmoreland comes to parley. York and Hastings give Westmoreland a schedule of their grievances. Prince John agrees to their demands and the rebel army is disbanded. But York and Hastings have fallen into a trap and will pay for it with their lives.

WESTMORELAND   Good tidings, my Lord Hastings; for the which
I do arrest thee, traitor, of high treason:
And you, lord archbishop, and you, Lord Mowbray,
Of capitol treason I attach you both.

MOWBRAY   Is this proceeding just and honourable?

WESTMORELAND   Is your assembly so?

ARCHBISHOP OF YORK   Will you thus break your faith?

LANCASTER   I pawn'd thee none:
I promised you redress of these same grievances

Whereof you did complain; which, by mine honour,
I will perform with a most Christian care.
But for you, rebels, look to taste the due
Meet for rebellion and such acts as yours.
Most shallowly did you these arms commence,
Fondly brought here and foolishly sent hence.
Strike up our drums, pursue the scatter'd stray:
God, and not we, hath safely fought to-day.
Some guard these traitors to the block of death,
Treason's true bed and yielder up of breath.
(4.2.113–131)

At the palace in Westminster, the King is sick. His younger sons
are with him. He is told that Prince Hal is not at Windsor but is in
London. The King greets this news with despair. Westmoreland enters
and reports that the rebellion has been crushed. Northumberland
and the Scots have been defeated in the north. The good news is
too much for Henry, who collapses in a fit of apoplexy. He is taken
to another chamber and is asleep in bed when Prince Hal enters.
Thinking his father is dead, Hal picks up the crown from the pillow
and places it upon his head.

PRINCE HENRY   My due from thee is this imperial crown,
    Which, as immediate as thy place and blood,
    Derives itself to me. Lo, here it sits,
    Which God shall guard: and put the world's whole strength
    Into one giant arm, it shall not force
    This lineal honour from me: this from thee
    Will I to mine leave, as 'tis left to me.
(4.5.44–50)

This is the essence of the doctrine of hereditary succession of the
Crown. Prince Hal has no doubt that he becomes the legitimate king
as of right by succession upon the death of his father.

Hal leaves the room. The King wakes up and demands to know who has taken his crown. Hal returns, and the King in his anger rebukes him for wishing him to be dead. He also reveals what kind of king he thinks Hal will be: "O my poor kingdom, sick with civil blows! / When that my care could not withhold thy riots, / What wilt thou do when riot is thy care? / O, thou wilt be a wilderness again, / Peopled with wolves, thy old inhabitants!" (4.5.137–41).

Hal eloquently explains his mistake in thinking his father was dead and accused the crown of killing him. The King and Hal are reconciled. To the very end, however, Henry IV is tormented by the shroud of illegitimacy that has darkened his kingship.

The Prince is confident of his right to wear the crown: "My gracious liege, / You won it, wore it, kept it, gave it me; / Then plain and right must my possession be" (4.5.224–226). Hal does not claim to be the best man to be King; he claims the kingship as his right under the law of hereditary succession. But under that law, should not the Crown go to the closest male heir of Richard II? That happens to be Mortimer, who was last seen doting upon the daughter of a Welsh chieftain. The King is taken back to the palace's Chamber of Jerusalem to die.

In Gloucestershire, Falstaff returns to the house of Justice Shallow. Falstaff amuses himself by thinking of all the funny stories he will tell Hal of foolish old Justice Shallow, who is as thin and witless as Falstaff is fat and witty. "O, you shall see him laugh till his face be like a wet cloak ill laid up!" (5.1.79–80).

Back at Westminster Palace, the Chief Justice is told the King has died. The news is received by him with great apprehension.

LORD CHIEF-JUSTICE   How doth the king?

WARWICK   Exceeding well; his cares are now all ended.

LORD CHIEF-JUSTICE   I hope, not dead.
Warwick   He's walk'd the way of nature;
And to our purposes he lives no more.

LORD CHIEF-JUSTICE   I would his majesty had call'd me
   with him:
   The service that I truly did his life
   Hath left me open to all injuries.

WARWICK   Indeed I think the young king loves you not.

LORD CHIEF-JUSTICE   I know he doth not, and do arm myself
   To welcome the condition of the time,
   Which cannot look more hideously upon me
   Than I have drawn it in my fantasy.

[Enter LANCASTER, CLARENCE, Gloucester,
WESTMORELAND]

WARWICK   Here come the heavy issue of dead Harry:
   O that the living Harry had the temper
   Of him, the worst of these three gentlemen!
   How many nobles then should hold their places
   That must strike sail to spirits of vile sort!

LORD CHIEF-JUSTICE   O God, I fear all will be overturn'd!
                  (5.2.2–21)

   Warwick and the Chief Justice both fear that Hal's reign as King
will not be a happy one for them. Henry IV's younger sons enter,
and then Prince Hal—now King Henry V—arrives and assures his
brothers that they have no reason to fear him. He then turns to the
Chief Justice.

KING HENRY V   You all look strangely on me: and you most;
   You are, I think, assured I love you not.

LORD CHIEF-JUSTICE   I am assured, if I be measured rightly,
   Your majesty hath no just cause to hate me.

KING HENRY V   No!
    How might a prince of my great hopes forget
    So great indignities you laid upon me?
    What! rate, rebuke, and roughly send to prison
    The immediate heir of England! Was this easy?
    May this be wash'd in Lethe, and forgotten?

LORD CHIEF-JUSTICE   I then did use the person of your father;
    The image of his power lay then in me:
    And, in the administration of his law,
    Whiles I was busy for the commonwealth,
    Your highness pleased to forget my place,
    The majesty and power of law and justice,
    The image of the king whom I presented,
    And struck me in my very seat of judgment;
    Whereon, as an offender to your father,
    I gave bold way to my authority
    And did commit you. If the deed were ill,
    Be you contented, wearing now the garland,
    To have a son set your decrees at nought,
    To pluck down justice from your awful bench,
    To trip the course of law and blunt the sword
    That guards the peace and safety of your person;
    Nay, more, to spurn at your most royal image
    And mock your workings in a second body.
    Question your royal thoughts, make the case yours;
    Be now the father and propose a son,
    Hear your own dignity so much profaned,
    See your most dreadful laws so loosely slighted,
    Behold yourself so by a son disdain'd;
    And then imagine me taking your part
    And in your power soft silencing your son:
    After this cold considerance, sentence me;
    And, as you are a king, speak in your state

What I have done that misbecame my place,
My person, or my liege's sovereignty.
(5.2.67–105)

Once again, Shakespeare gives forceful eloquence to one speaking in praise of the rule of law. It is about as close as Shakespeare gets to the debate in the sixteenth century about whether the King of England was bound by the law. Hal's response is a surprise to everyone on stage, but perhaps not to the audience.

KING HENRY V   You are right, justice, and you weigh this well;
   Therefore still bear the balance and the sword:
   And I do wish your honours may increase,
   Till you do live to see a son of mine
   Offend you and obey you, as I did.
   So shall I live to speak my father's words:
   'Happy am I, that have a man so bold,
   That dares do justice on my proper son;
   And not less happy, having such a son,
   That would deliver up his greatness so
   Into the hands of justice.' You did commit me:
   For which, I do commit into your hand
   The unstained sword that you have used to bear;
   With this remembrance, that you use the same
   With the like bold, just and impartial spirit
   As you have done 'gainst me. There is my hand.
   You shall be as a father to my youth:
   My voice shall sound as you do prompt mine ear,
   And I will stoop and humble my intents
   To your well-practised wise directions.
(5.2.105–125)

Henry promises to rule as a traditional English king who respects the law and not as an Eastern tyrant: "Now call we our high court of parliament: / And let us choose such limbs of noble counsel, / That the great body of our state may go / In equal rank with the best govern'd nation" (5.2.138–41).

This scene is justly famous as an argument for the "impartial" rule of law. In performance, Shakespeare sets up his audience to appreciate it as such by an odd little verbal exchange between Justice Shallow and his servant Davy in an earlier scene. Instead of going about his business of getting supper ready, Davy tries to intervene in a case before Justice of the Peace Shallow.

DAVY   I beseech you, sir, to countenance William Visor of Woncot against Clement Perkes of the hill.

SHALLOW   There is many complaints, Davy, against that Visor: that Visor is an arrant knave, on my knowledge.

DAVY   I grant your worship that he is a knave, sir; but yet, God forbid, sir, but a knave should have some countenance at his friend's request. An honest man, sir, is able to speak for himself, when a knave is not. I have served your worship truly, sir, this eight years; and if I cannot once or twice in a quarter bear out a knave against an honest man, I have but a very little credit with your worship.
(5.1.33–44)

Shallow apparently agrees to provide the favor: "Go to; I say he shall have no wrong" (5.1.47). This is very different from the impartial justice of the Lord Chief Justice.

Back at Justice Shallow's house, a great deal of sack has been drunk with supper. The scene is one of convivial Falstaffian merriment. As Shallow, Silence, and Falstaff sing and drink, Pistol rushes in with unexpected news.

PISTOL   Sir John, God save you!

FALSTAFF   What wind blew you hither, Pistol?

PISTOL   Not the ill wind which blows no man to good. Sweet
knight, thou art now one of the greatest men in this realm.

SILENCE   By'r lady, I think a' be, but goodman Puff of
Barson. . . .

SHALLOW   Give me pardon, sir: if, sir, you come with news
from the court, I take it there's but two ways,
either to utter them, or to conceal them. I am,
sir, under the king, in some authority.

PISTOL   Under which king, Besonian? speak, or die.

SHALLOW   Under King Harry.

PISTOL   Harry the Fourth? or Fifth?

SHALLOW   Harry the Fourth.

PISTOL   A foutre for thine office!
Sir John, thy tender lambkin now is king;
Harry the Fifth's the man. I speak the truth:
When Pistol lies, do this; and fig me, like
The bragging Spaniard.

FALSTAFF   What, is the old king dead?

PISTOL   As nail in door: the things I speak are just.

FALSTAFF   Away, Bardolph! saddle my horse. Master Robert
Shallow, choose what office thou wilt in the land,
'tis thine. Pistol, I will double-charge thee with dignities.

BARDOLPH   O joyful day!
I would not take a knighthood for my fortune.

PISTOL   What! I do bring good news.

FALSTAFF   Carry Master Silence to bed. Master Shallow, my
Lord Shallow,–be what thou wilt; I am fortune's
Steward–get on thy boots: we'll ride all night.
O sweet Pistol! Away, Bardolph!

[Exit BARDOLPH]

Come, Pistol, utter more to me; and withal devise
something to do thyself good. Boot, boot, Master
Shallow: I know the young king is sick for me. Let
us take any man's horses; the laws of England are at
my commandment. Blessed are they that have been my
friends; and woe to my lord chief-justice!
(5.3.78–82, 99–130)

Now that Hal is king, Falstaff believes he will be above the law.
The play, however, hints that all may not be well in Falstaff's world.
In the next little scene constables drag Doll Tearsheet and Mistress
Quickly off to jail. "Come, I charge you both go with me; for the man
is dead that you and Pistol beat amongst you" (5.4.17–19).

Falstaff, Justice Shallow (who has just loaned Falstaff a thousand
pounds), and Pistol rush off to London. They are in the crowd outside
Westminster Abbey when the new King's coronation procession
begins. The King enters accompanied by the Chief Justice. Falstaff
calls out to Hal, but the response is not what he expected.

FALSTAFF   God save thy grace, King Hal! my royal Hal!

PISTOL   The heavens thee guard and keep, most royal imp
of fame!

FALSTAFF   God save thee, my sweet boy!

KING HENRY V   My lord chief-justice, speak to that vain man.

LORD CHIEF-JUSTICE   Have you your wits? know you what 'tis
   to speak?

FALSTAFF   My king! my Jove! I speak to thee, my heart!

KING HENRY V   I know thee not, old man: fall to thy prayers;
   How ill white hairs become a fool and jester!
   I have long dream'd of such a kind of man,
   So surfeit-swell'd, so old and so profane;
   But, being awaked, I do despise my dream.
   Make less thy body hence, and more thy grace;
   Leave gormandizing; know the grave doth gape
   For thee thrice wider than for other men.
   Reply not to me with a fool-born jest:
   Presume not that I am the thing I was;
   For God doth know, so shall the world perceive,
   That I have turn'd away my former self;
   So will I those that kept me company.
   When thou dost hear I am as I have been,
   Approach me, and thou shalt be as thou wast,
   The tutor and the feeder of my riots:
   Till then, I banish thee, on pain of death,
   As I have done the rest of my misleaders,
   Not to come near our person by ten mile.
   For competence of life I will allow you,
   That lack of means enforce you not to evil:
   And, as we hear you do reform yourselves,
   We will, according to your strengths and qualities,
   Give you advancement. Be it your charge, my lord,
   To see perform'd the tenor of our word.

                    (5.5.43–73)

Shakespeare has shown us two systems of justice. One is that of Justice Shallow, who dispenses judgment based upon friendships and relationships. The other is that of the Chief Justice, who upholds the rule of law even when the offender is of the highest rank. As King, Hal has clearly chosen the latter.

After the procession moves on, the Chief Justice returns with Prince John and orders Falstaff and the others confined in "the fleet" (5.5.92), that is, the Fleet Street Prison.

In the epilogue we are promised that the story of Hal and Falstaff will continue in France. However, it also states cryptically "this is not the man" (5.5.142–143).

The previous encounters between Falstaff and the Chief Justice have shown us that Falstaff was outside the bounds of the law and its institutions. Hal must govern as King within those institutions. With the death of his father, Hal must choose between Falstaff's bawdy world of the tavern and the world of the court.

I think that for Hal to be the king that he wishes to be, Falstaff must be rejected and utterly banished from his company. But did he have to do it so publicly and so brutally? Shakespeare doesn't tell us what we are to think about this. For four hundred years, lovers of Shakespeare have debated the morality of Hal's rejection of Falstaff. It is a measure of Shakespeare's genius that the debate has lasted so long and continues to this day.

A word about the common law courts in Shakespeare's day. By about 1200, the judges of the royal courts were professional judges rather than the politicians and courtiers of the royal court (the *Curia Regis*) who traveled around the country with the king. The five judges of the Court of Common Pleas and five judges of King's Bench (or Queen's Bench under Mary and Elizabeth) were chosen by the king from the serjeants-at-law. In general, the Court of Common Pleas heard cases involving title to real property and other civil cases. The Court of King's Bench had civil and criminal jurisdiction.

The Chief Judge of King's Bench was the Chief Justice of England. The judges were paid by the Crown and were not allowed to continue practicing law. In theory, they were removeable at the pleasure of the King. It is true that upon the death of a king, each of the royal judges had to receive a new commission from the Chancellor. Thus, Henry V could have ordered his new Chancellor not to issue a new Commission to the Chief Justice in *Henry IV, Part 2*. In the play, his ability to remove the Chief Justice is clearly recognized. But this almost never happened, and for three hundred years the common law judiciary grew increasingly independent of the Crown.

As a result, judges such as Chief Justice Sir John Fortescue saw the judiciary as an institution within a constitutional monarchy. He was Chief Justice of the Court of King's Bench from1442 to 1461. A supporter of the House of Lancaster, he fled to France with Queen Margaret in 1461 when Edward, Duke of York, overthrew King Henry VI. He was attainted for treason by the Yorkists. While in exile he composed the influential treatise *De Laudibus Legum Anglia* for the education of the exiled Prince Edward. Fortescue believed in a constitutional monarchy in which natural law limited the powers of the monarch. He praised the English legal system for the use of juries to try cases rather than the continental system of having evidence gathered by judges.

Judges such as Fortescue believed their loyalty was to the common law rather than the person of the king. This began to change under the Stuart kings. In 1616, the year of Shakespeare's death, the clash between King James and Chief Justice Coke exploded, resulting in the King's dismissal of Coke.

Removal of judges continued at an accelerating pace under the Stuarts until the Glorious Revolution brought William III to the throne. He appointed all judges for life during "good behavior"—the same standard that is incorporated in Article III of the Constitution of the United States.

CHAPTER 12

Much Ado About Nothing

Beatrice ("one who blesses") and Benedick ("one who is blessed") in *Much Ado About Nothing* are two of Shakespeare's most appealing characters. Their witty banter dominates the dialogue of the play. And in the character of Dogberry, legal malapropism rises to the level of comic genius.

The play is set in the Sicilian town of Messina at the house of Leonato, the governor of Messina and father to Hero. Word comes that Don Pedro, Prince of Aragon, is on his way to Messina after some slight military action. Leonato's niece Beatrice asks about Benedick, who has been in the army with Don Pedro.

BEATRICE   I pray you, is Signior Mountanto returned from the wars or no?

MESSENGER   I know none of that name, lady: there was none such in the army of any sort.

LEONATO   What is he that you ask for, niece?

HERO   My cousin means Signior Benedick of Padua.

MESSENGER   O, he's returned; and as pleasant as ever he was.

BEATRICE   He set up his bills here in Messina and challenged
   Cupid at the flight; and my uncle's fool, reading
   the challenge, subscribed for Cupid, and challenged
   him at the bird-bolt. I pray you, how many hath he
   killed and eaten in these wars? But how many hath
   he killed? for indeed I promised to eat all of his killing.

LEONATO   Faith, niece, you tax Signior Benedick too much;
   but he'll be meet with you, I doubt it not.

MESSENGER   He hath done good service, lady, in these wars.
   (*Much Ado About Nothing*, 1.1.28–44)

Leonato tells the messenger not to pay too much attention to his
niece: "You must not, sir, mistake my niece. There is a kind of merry
war betwixt Signior Benedick and her: they never meet but there's
a skirmish of wit between them" (1.1.55–58).

Beatrice learns that Benedick's new best friend is Claudio, a
young Florentine officer. Don Pedro enters with Benedick and
Claudio. Beatrice and Benedick at once resume their skirmish
of wit.

DON PEDRO   I think this [*Hero*]
   is your daughter.

LEONATO   Her mother hath many times told me so.

BENEDICK   Were you in doubt, sir, that you asked her?

LEONATO   Signior Benedick, no; for then were you a child.

DON PEDRO   You have it full, Benedick: we may guess by this
   what you are, being a man. Truly, the lady fathers
   herself. Be happy, lady; for you are like an
   honourable father.

BENEDICK   If Signior Leonato be her father, she would not
    have his head on her shoulders for all Messina, as
    like him as she is.

BEATRICE   I wonder that you will still be talking, Signior
    Benedick: nobody marks you.

BENEDICK   What, my dear Lady Disdain! are you yet living?

BEATRICE   Is it possible disdain should die while she hath
    such meet food to feed it as Signior Benedick?
    Courtesy itself must convert to disdain, if you come
    in her presence.

BENEDICK   Then is courtesy a turncoat. But it is certain I
    am loved of all ladies, only you excepted: and I
    would I could find in my heart that I had not a hard
    heart; for, truly, I love none.

BEATRICE   A dear happiness to women: they would else have
    been troubled with a pernicious suitor. I thank God
    and my cold blood, I am of your humour for that: I
    had rather hear my dog bark at a crow than a man
    swear he loves me.

BENEDICK   God keep your ladyship still in that mind! so some
    gentleman or other shall 'scape a predestinate
    scratched face.

BEATRICE   Scratching could not make it worse, an't were such
    a face as yours were.

(1.1.96–128)

As we see here, Beatrice almost always triumphs in these
verbal skirmishes.

Leonato welcomes everyone into his house, including Don Pedro's bastard brother Don John. Claudio confesses to Benedick that he is in love with Hero. When Don Pedro returns, Benedick tells him of Claudio's secret. Benedick swears he will never be in love and will live as a bachelor. Don Pedro responds: "I shall see thee, ere I die, look pale with love" (1.1.227). Don Pedro then promises to approach Hero and her father on Claudio's behalf.

At supper, Leonato chides Beatrice for her sharp tongue. Leonato: "By my troth, niece, thou wilt never get thee a husband, if thou be so shrewd of thy tongue" (2.1.16). Beatrice swears she does not want a husband—with a beard or without one. When Leonato says he hopes to see Beatrice "fitted" with a husband, she responds: "Not till God make men of some other metal than earth" (2.1.52).

Benedick declares to Don Pedro of Beatrice: "I would not marry her, though she were endowed with all that Adam had left him before he transgressed" (2.1.223). To be "endowed" was to receive a settlement, such as an inheritance or a dowry, that a wife might receive upon her marriage. Benedick is saying he would not marry Beatrice for the whole world. But we shortly learn there has been some prior attachment between Beatrice and Benedick, one that did not end well.

DON PEDRO   Come, lady, come; you have lost the heart of Signior Benedick.

BEATRICE   Indeed, my lord, he lent it me awhile; and I gave him use for it, a double heart for his single one: marry, once before he won it of me with false dice, therefore your grace may well say I have lost it.

DON PEDRO   You have put him down, lady, you have put him down.

BEATRICE   So I would not he should do me, my lord, lest I should prove the mother of fools.

(2.1.251–59)

Meanwhile, Don Pedro has succeeded in getting Hero and her father's consent for her to marry Claudio. When told of this, Claudio is momentarily speechless. Beatrice says he must state his consent to marry Hero. Claudio responds to Hero: "Silence is the perfectest herald of joy: I were but little happy, if I could say how much. Lady, as you are mine, I am yours: I give away myself for you and dote upon the exchange" (2.1.279–82).

Claudio's words are sufficient to express his present intent to be married to Hero. Her consent could be expressed by words or a gesture such as a kiss. There is some ambiguity here about whether they now have a spousal marriage, because we do not hear what she whispers in Claudio's ear. This ambiguity is typical of Shakespeare when it comes to what ceremony is required for a valid marriage.

Don Pedro declares Beatrice would make an excellent wife for Benedick. Leonato responds: "O Lord, my lord, if they were but a week married, they would talk themselves mad" (2.1.322–23). Don Pedro promises to devise a plan to bring the two together. All seems to be going well.

But the villainous Don John ("it must not be denied but I am a plain-dealing villain") (1.3.30) seeks revenge against Claudio for gaining from "my overthrow" (1.3.62). He has a plan to break up the marriage of Hero and Claudio. Don John will accuse Hero of unchastity to Claudio. To prove it, Margaret, Hero's maid, will appear at Hero's window at night disguised as Hero and admit her lover Borachio into Hero's bedroom. Claudio and Don Pedro will be hidden nearby to observe Hero's infidelity. We naturally think of this in terms of Don John slandering Hero. However, it is also a slander of Claudio by saying that he is a cuckhold, the worst insult at the time to a man's honor.

Meanwhile, Don Pedro puts into motion his plan for Beatrice and Benedict. Pretending to be unaware that Benedick is nearby in the garden, Don Pedro allows Benedick to overhear a conversation between him and Leonato in which they say Beatrice is in love with him.

DON PEDRO   Hath she made her affection known to Benedick?

LEONATO   No; and swears she never will: that's her torment.

CLAUDIO   'Tis true, indeed; so your daughter says: 'Shall
I,' says she, 'that have so oft encountered him
with scorn, write to him that I love him?'

LEONATO   This says she now when she is beginning to write to
him; for she'll be up twenty times a night, and
there will she sit in her smock till she have writ a
sheet of paper: my daughter tells us all.
(2.3.120–29)

They say they fear telling Benedict, because he will scorn Beatrice's love, then leave Benedick alone in the orchard. Benedick thinks that because Beatrice is in love with him, he must be in love with her. Benedict: "They have the truth of this from Hero. They seem to pity the lady: it seems her affections have their full bent. Love me! why, it must be requited" (2.3.205–07).

Half of Don Pedro's plan has worked. In the next scene, Hero and Margaret lure Beatrice into the garden. There, she overhears them say Benedick is in love with her, but she would respond to his love with scorn and disdain. Hero: "If I should speak, / She would mock me into air; O, she would laugh me / Out of myself, press me to death with wit" (3.1.74–76). This "press me to death" is a reference to the practice, adopted after trial by ordeal was abolished in England, of pressing to death with heavy weights a person accused of a felony who would not enter a lawful plea upon arraignment agreeing to trial by jury.

After Beatrice is left alone, we see that Don Pedro's plan has worked all around.

BEATRICE   [*Coming forward.*]
What fire is in mine ears? Can this be true?

Stand I condemn'd for pride and scorn so much?
Contempt, farewell! and maiden pride, adieu!
No glory lives behind the back of such.
And, Benedick, love on; I will requite thee,
Taming my wild heart to thy loving hand:
If thou dost love, my kindness shall incite thee
To bind our loves up in a holy band;
For others say thou dost deserve, and I
Believe it better than reportingly.

(3.1.107–16)

At night on the street, the constable Dogberry, who is the master of malapropism, organizes his band of watchmen. He is told by the parish headborough to give the men of the watch their charge. Dogberry first asks who is the most "desertless" [*deserving*] man to be constable of the watch. (3.3.8). In England at this time, a constable was a minor public civil officer whose general duty was to maintain the peace within his district. Dogberry is told that the watchman Seacole can read and write.

DOGBERRY   Come hither, neighbour Seacole. God hath blessed
    you with a good name: to be a well-favoured man is
    the gift of fortune; but to write and read comes by nature [*edu-
    cation, training*].

SECOND WATCHMAN   Both which, master constable,–

DOGBERRY   You have: I knew it would be your answer. Well,
    for your favour, sir, why, give God thanks, and make
    no boast of it; and for your writing and reading,
    let that appear when there is no need of such
    vanity. You are thought here to be the most
    senseless [*sensible*] and fit man for the constable of the
    watch; therefore bear you the lantern. This is your
    charge: you shall comprehend [*apprehend*] all vagrom [*vagrant*]
    men; you are

to bid any man stand [*stop*], in the prince's name.

SECOND WATCHMAN   How if a' will not stand?

DOGBERRY   Why, then, take no note of him, but let him go; and
presently call the rest of the watch together and
thank God you are rid of a knave.
(3.3.12–29)

The watchmen are fools, and Dogberry gives them an absurd
charge that is a hilarious parody of the duties of constables and
night watchmen.

DOGBERRY   If you meet a thief, you may suspect [*arrest*] him,
by virtue of your office, to be no true man; and, for such
kind of men, the less you meddle or make with them,
why the more is for your honesty.

WATCHMAN   If we know him to be a thief, shall we not lay
hands on him?

DOGBERRY   Truly, by your office, you may; but I think they
that touch pitch will be defiled: the most peaceable [*practical*]
way for you, if you do take a thief, is to let him
show himself what he is and steal out of your company.

VERGES   You have been always called a merciful man, partner.

DOGBERRY   Truly, I would not hang a dog by my will, much
more [*less*] a man who hath any honesty in him.

VERGES   If you hear a child cry in the night, you must call
to the nurse and bid her still it.

WATCHMAN   How if the nurse be asleep and will not hear us?

DOGBERRY   Why, then, depart in peace, and let the child wake
  her with crying; for the ewe that will not hear her
  lamb when it baes will never answer a calf when he bleats.

VERGES   'Tis very true.

DOGBERRY   This is the end of the charge:–you, constable, are
  to present [*represent*] the prince's own person: if you meet the
  prince in the night, you may stay him.

VERGES   Nay, by'r our lady, that I think a' cannot.

DOGBERRY   Five shillings to one on't, with any man that knows
  the statues [*statutes*], he may stay him: marry, not without
  the prince be willing; for, indeed, the watch ought
  to offend no man; and it is an offence to stay a
  man against his will.

VERGES   By'r lady, I think it be so.
  (3.3.48–78)

The deception witnessed by Claudio and Don Pedro at Hero's
window occurs offstage. But the audience learns it has succeeded
in smearing Hero's honor. Claudio and Don Pedro are fooled into
thinking they saw what they expected to see.

For all of Dogberry's bumbling, it is two of his watchmen who
overhear Borachio telling Conrade that Don John has paid him
a thousand ducats to deceive Claudio into believing that Hero is
unchaste. The watchmen arrest Borachio and Conrade. The Second
Watchman proclaims: "We have here recovered [*discovered*] the
most dangerous piece of lechery [*treachery*] that ever was known
in the commonwealth" (3.3.153–54).

The next day is Hero's wedding day. Dogberry goes to Leonato's
house with his prisoners to have them examined by Leonato. But his
explanation of the case is so convoluted and tedious that Leonato

refuses to hear any more. Leonato must go to the church for Hero's wedding. He instructs Dogberry to conduct the examination of the prisoners and bring him the record of it.

DOGBERRY   One word, sir: our watch, sir, have indeed comprehended [*apprehended*] two aspicious [*suspicious*] persons, and we would have them this morning examined before your worship.

LEONATO   Take their examination yourself and bring it me: I
   am now in great haste, as it may appear unto you.

DOGBERRY   It shall be suffigance [*sufficient*].
               (3.5.43–48)

Dogberry takes the prisoners back to the jail. There, Francis Seacole, who can read and write, will record the examination.

DOGBERRY   Go, good partner, go, get you to Francis Seacole;
   bid him bring his pen and inkhorn to the gaol: we
   are now to examination [*examine*] these men.

VERGES   And we must do it wisely.

DOGBERRY   We will spare for no wit, I warrant you; here's
   that shall drive some of them to a non-come[*non compos*]: only
   get the learned writer to set down our excommunication [*examination*] and meet me at the gaol.
               (3.5.52–59)

At the common law, a person of unsound mind was *non-compos mentis*. Dogberry is saying his wit will drive the prisoners to extreme madness.

At the church, Hero and Claudio are standing to take their vows. The priest asks: "If either of you know any inward impediment why you should not be conjoined, charge you, on your souls, to utter it." (4.1.11–13). This refers to "dirimentary impediments," such as consanguinity (blood kinship), which could result in annulment of a marriage. Claudio shocks everyone when he declares he will not be married to "an approved wanton" (4.1.43). Hero protests her innocence; when told she was seen the night before admitting a man to her bedroom, she vehemently denies it.

HERO   I talk'd with no man at that hour, my lord.

DON PEDRO   Why, then are you no maiden. Leonato,
    I am sorry you must hear: upon mine honour,
    Myself, my brother and this grieved count
    Did see her, hear her, at that hour last night
    Talk with a ruffian at her chamber-window
    Who hath indeed, most like a liberal villain,
    Confess'd the vile encounters they have had
    A thousand times in secret.

(4.1.78–98)

This is Shakespeare dramatizing the problem of relying upon circumstantial evidence (evidence of a chain of circumstances to prove guilt or innocence) to determine guilt in this case of unchastity. Neither Don Pedro nor Claudio saw Hero at her window. They saw a woman and assumed it was Hero because she was at Hero's window. This is like Othello seeing Desdemona's handkerchief in Cassio's possession and drawing the wrong inference from this circumstantial evidence.

So too, is Iachimo's knowledge of the mole on Imogen's breast in *Cymbeline*. So too, is Lady Macbeth's smearing of blood on the faces of Duncan's attendants. In each of these instances, circumstantial evidence points to guilt, but there is a reasonable explanation. As the audience, we know this and watch with horror as the innocent are condemned.

The false accusation is a threat to the honor both of Claudio, Hero's betrothed, and Leonato, her father. When Leonato asks for a dagger to kill himself, Hero swoons and appears to be dead. Leonato says to the Friar: "Thou seest that all the grace that she hath left / Is that she will not add to her damnation / A sin of perjury; she not denies it" (4.1.167–69).

But Hero has been silent throughout the play. Again, a witness draws the wrong conclusion from ambiguous evidence. Leonato succinctly states the difficulty that women of the period had in defending themselves against accusations of unchastity: "Would the two princes lie, and Claudio lie, / Who loved her so, that, speaking of her foulness, / Wash'd it with tears? Hence from her! let her die" (4.1.148–50). After most have left, Friar Francis proclaims Hero's innocence based upon his perceptions as a witness.

FRIAR FRANCIS   Hear me a little; for I have only been
   Silent so long and given way unto
   This course of fortune
   By noting of the lady: I have mark'd
   A thousand blushing apparitions
   To start into her face; a thousand innocent shames
   In angel whiteness beat away those blushes;
   And in her eye there hath appear'd a fire,
   To burn the errors that these princes hold
   Against her maiden truth.
              (4.1.151–60)

There is here a nice contrast between Friar Francis' reliability as a witness and that of Claudio and Don Pedro. Friar Francis "counsels" Leonato to allow Hero to be hidden until the truth can be determined. In the meantime, Leonato is to act as if she has died.

Most leave. Beatrice and Benedick remain behind.

[Exeunt all but BENEDICK and BEATRICE.]

BENEDICK   Lady Beatrice, have you wept all this while?

BEATRICE   Yea, and I will weep a while longer.

BENEDICK   I will not desire that.

BEATRICE   You have no reason; I do it freely.

BENEDICK   Surely I do believe your fair cousin is wronged.

BEATRICE   Ah, how much might the man deserve of me that
would right her!

BENEDICK   Is there any way to show such friendship?

BEATRICE   A very even way, but no such friend.

BENEDICK   May a man do it?

BEATRICE   It is a man's office, but not yours.

BENEDICK   I do love nothing in the world so well as you: is
not that strange?

BEATRICE   As strange as the thing I know not. It were as
possible for me to say I loved nothing so well as
you: but believe me not; and yet I lie not; I
confess nothing, nor I deny nothing. I am sorry for my cousin.

BENEDICK   By my sword, Beatrice, thou lovest me.
                    (4.1.251–68)

Beatrice confesses that she does love Benedick: "I love you with
so much of my heart that none is left to protest" (4.1.280–81). But
amid this talk of love, when he asks what he can do for her, Beatrice
makes a shocking demand of Benedick: "Kill Claudio" (4.1.283).
Reluctantly, Benedick agrees to challenge Claudio.

At the jail, Dogberry begins the examination of Borachio and Conrade by asking, "Is our whole dissembly [*assembly*] appeared?" (4.2.1). When the sexton asks who are the "malefactors," Dogberry replies: "Marry, that am I and my partner" (4.2.4). Dogberry makes a totally inept attempt to get the prisoners to confess that they are knaves. The sexton tells him he is mishandling the proceeding. "Master constable, you go not the way to examine: you must call forth the watch that are their accusers" (4.2.30–31).

At the common law, the justice of the peace or magistrate would first examine the witnesses to determine if a crime had been committed. Dogberry had the entire process of examination backward. This is a parody of the Marian commitment procedure. The watchmen are called to testify.

FIRST WATCHMAN   This man said, sir, that Don John, the prince's brother, was a villain.

DOGBERRY   Write down Prince John a villain. Why, this is flat Perjury [*slander*], to call a prince's brother villain.

BORACHIO   Master constable,–

DOGBERRY   Pray thee, fellow, peace: I do not like thy look, I promise thee.

SEXTON   What heard you him say else?

SECOND WATCHMAN   Marry, that he had received a thousand ducats of Don John for accusing the Lady Hero wrongfully.

DOGBERRY   Flat burglary [*perjury*] as ever was committed.

VERGES   Yea, by mass, that it is.

SEXTON   What else, fellow?

FIRST WATCHMAN   And that Count Claudio did mean, upon
his words, to disgrace Hero before the whole assembly and
not marry her.

DOGBERRY   O villain! thou wilt be condemned into everlasting
Redemption [*perdition*] for this.
(4.2.35–52)

The sexton directs Dogberry to bind the prisoners and take them
to Leonato. The sexton leaves. Conrade resists and insults Dogberry,
whose response is hilarious.

CONRADE   Away! you are an ass, you are an ass.

DOGBERRY   Dost thou not suspect [*respect*] my place? dost thou
not Suspect [*respect*] my years? O that he were here to write
me down an ass! But, masters, remember that I am an
ass; though it be not written down, yet forget not
that I am an ass. No, thou villain, thou art full of
piety [*impiety*], as shall be proved upon thee by good witness.
I am a wise fellow, and, which is more, an officer,
and, which is more, a householder, and, which is
more, as pretty a piece of flesh as any is in
Messina, and one that knows the law, go to; and a
rich fellow enough, go to; and a fellow that hath
had losses, and one that hath two gowns and every
thing handsome about him. Bring him away. O that
I had been writ down an ass!
(4.2.68–81)

Dogberry is asking Conrade if he disrespects Dogberry's office.
Like many petty officials of the law, Dogberry is quick to take offense
at a slight.

Thus ends one of the strangest court scenes in literature. As he does in several of the plays, Shakespeare uses the pretensions, pomposity, and verbosity of petty legal officers to create comedy of a high order.

At Leonato's house, as Don Pedro is preparing to leave, Leonato accuses Claudio of slandering his innocent daughter and challenges him to fight. Don Pedro defends Claudio in lawyerly fashion: "My heart is sorry for your daughter's death: / But, on my honour, she was charged with nothing / But what was true and very full of proof" (5.1.103–05).

Benedick enters and challenges Claudio to fight. After they leave, Dogberry enters with his prisoners. Dogberry: "Come you, sir: if justice cannot tame you, she shall ne'er weigh more reasons in her balance" (5.1.199–200). Another reference to the popular image of a blindfolded Justice holding a balance and a sword in either hand. Don Pedro recognizes that they are his brother's men.

DON PEDRO   How now? two of my brother's men bound! Borachio one!

CLAUDIO   Hearken after their offence, my lord.

DON PEDRO   Officers, what offence have these men done?

DOGBERRY   Marry, sir, they have committed false report; moreover, they have spoken untruths; secondarily, they are slanders; sixth and lastly, they have belied a lady; thirdly, they have verified unjust things; and, to conclude, they are lying knaves.

DON PEDRO   First, I ask thee what they have done; thirdly, I ask thee what's their offence; sixth and lastly, why they are committed; and, to conclude, what you lay to their charge.

(5.1.202–14)

Borachio confesses to Don Pedro his participation in the plot to deceive Don Pedro and Claudio about Hero. Claudio is shocked.

CLAUDIO Sweet Hero! now thy image doth appear
In the rare semblance that I loved it first.

DOGBERRY Come, bring away the plaintiffs [*defendants*]:
by this time our sexton hath reformed [*informed*] Signior
Leonato of the matter: and, masters, do not forget to specify
[*testify*], when time and place shall serve, that I am an ass.
(5.1.240–45)

Claudio and Don Pedro are aghast at what they have done to poor Hero. Claudio says to Leonato: "Choose your revenge yourself; / Impose me to what penance your invention / Can lay upon my sin" (5.1.259–61).

In the ecclesiastical courts of the time, the punishment for slander was frequently a public apology to the victim or another form of public penance such as being lead through the streets walking barefoot and wearing only a white sheet for a garment. Actions for slander could be brought in both the secular and the church courts. But a public apology and penance were probably more likely to restore the victim's reputation than an award of monetary damages by a secular court.

Leonato says they must compose for Hero's tomb an epitaph that will proclaim her innocence to Messina, and Claudio must marry Leonato's niece the next morning. The next day, Claudio comes to Leonato's house to be married to his niece. Hero appears with her face covered with a veil.

CLAUDIO Give me your hand: before this holy friar,
I am your husband, if you like of me.

HERO And when I lived, I was your other wife:

[Unmasking]

And when you loved, you were my other husband.

CLAUDIO   Another Hero!

HERO   Nothing certainer:
One Hero died defiled, but I do live,
And surely as I live, I am a maid.

DON PEDRO   The former Hero! Hero that is dead!

LEONATO   She died, my lord, but whiles her slander lived.
(5.4.60–69)

Under pre-Reformation English law, hand-holding and words or gestures of present consent were sufficient to make a valid marriage. It appears Shakespeare did not intend this to be the case here.

Friar Francis says, "to the chapel let us presently" (5.4.74) to perform holy rites (5.4.74). And Benedick, a few lines later, says to Beatrice, "let's have a dance ere we are married" (5.4.122).

Again, Shakespeare does not show the ceremony on stage. Before they go off to be married, a kiss ends one last skirmish in the war of wits between Beatrice and Benedict.

CHAPTER 13

As You Like It

As *You Like It* is one of Shakespeare's most popular comedies. This pastoral comedy, based upon the novella *Rosalynd* by Thomas Lodge of Lincoln's Inn, was written around 1599. It was not published until it appeared in the *First Folio* in 1623.

The heroine, Rosalind, is another of Shakespeare's magnificent women who overshadow their male lovers. Rosalind, disguised as the boy Ganymede, is the pinnacle (perhaps along with Portia in *The Merchant of Venice*) of Shakespeare's use of the comic device of the girl disguised as a boy.

The play begins in the orchard of Oliver de Boys's house. Orlando, Oliver's younger brother, is complaining to Adam, a servant of Oliver's, that his older brother, who inherited the estate of their father, is neglecting Orlando's education and mode of living. Thus, the play begins with the problem of an inheritance which, in accordance with the English custom of the times, went disproportionally to the eldest son.

ORLANDO   As I remember, Adam, it was upon this fashion
    bequeathed me by will but poor a thousand crowns,
    and, as thou sayest, charged my brother, on his
    blessing, to breed me well: and there begins my
    sadness. My brother Jaques he keeps at school, and
    report speaks goldenly of his profit: for my part,
    he keeps me rustically at home, or, to speak more

properly, stays me here at home unkept; for call you
that keeping for a gentleman of my birth, that
differs not from the stalling of an ox?

(As You Like It, 1.1.1–10)

Under the early common law of England, real property could not
be conveyed by will but descended by the laws of inheritance to the
eldest male heir based on the law of primogeniture. Personal property,
in this case a thousand crowns, could be given by bequest in a will. By
the middle of the sixteenth century, land could also be devised by will.
But the practice of primogeniture continued through the centuries
in order to keep large estates intact. That's what has happened here.

Orlando complains that his older brother is not complying with
the terms of their father's will. I find it significant that Shakespeare
grounds Orlando's complaint against his brother in a legal obligation
derived from the father's will rather than natural affinity.

Oliver enters the garden. Orlando protests that he has as much of
their father in him as does Oliver although the "courtesy of nations"
gives preference to the firstborn (1.1.43). When Oliver insults him
by calling him "boy," Orlando grabs his older brother by the throat.

OLIVER   Wilt thou lay hands on me, villain?

ORLANDO   I am no villain; I am the youngest son of Sir
Rowland de Boys; he was my father, and he is thrice
a villain that says such a father begot villains.
Wert thou not my brother, I would not take this hand
from thy throat till this other had pulled out thy
tongue for saying so: thou hast railed on thyself.

(1.1.51–57)

Orlando charges his brother with violating their father's will by
neglecting his education. He demands to receive "the poor allottery
my father left me by testament" (1.1.68) so that he may leave and
seek his fortune elsewhere.

After Orlando and Adam leave, Oliver vows to "physic" [punish] (1.1.82) Orlando's offense, and without giving him the thousand crowns. The proper relationship between the older and younger brothers has completely broken down.

Charles, the Duke's wrestler, comes to talk to Oliver of the wrestling match to take place at court the next day. Oliver asks him:

OLIVER   Good Monsieur Charles, what's the new news at the
new court?

CHARLES   There's no news at the court, sir, but the old news:
that is, the old duke is banished by his younger
brother the new duke; and three or four loving lords
have put themselves into voluntary exile with him,
whose lands and revenues enrich the new duke;
therefore he gives them good leave to wander.

OLIVER   Can you tell if Rosalind, the duke's daughter, be
banished with her father?

CHARLES   O, no; for the duke's daughter, her cousin, so loves
her, being ever from their cradles bred together,
that she would have followed her exile, or have died
to stay behind her. She is at the court, and no
less beloved of her uncle than his own daughter; and
never two ladies loved as they do.

OLIVER   Where will the old duke live?

CHARLES   They say he is already in the forest of Arden, and
a many merry men with him; and there they live like
the old Robin Hood of England: they say many young
gentlemen flock to him every day, and fleet the time
carelessly, as they did in the golden world.
                    (1.1.90–112)

At court, the relationship between the older and younger brothers has also broken down. But it is the younger brother, Ferdinand, who has overturned the law of primogenitor and usurped the inheritance of the older brother, Duke Senior.

Charles tells Oliver he has heard that Orlando intends to challenge him at the wrestling match tomorrow, and warns Oliver that Orlando is likely to get hurt. Oliver says his younger brother is a villain and Charles is free to break his neck. After Charles leaves, Oliver admits that he hates his brother.

At the Duke's palace, Rosalind tells Celia, Ferdinand's daughter, of her sorrow at the banishment of her father, the Old Duke. Celia attempts to sooth her.

ROSALIND   Well, I will forget the condition of my estate, to
   rejoice in yours.

CELIA   You know my father hath no child but I, nor none is
   like to have: and, truly, when he dies, thou shalt
   be his heir, for what he hath taken away from thy
   father perforce, I will render thee again in
   affection; by mine honour, I will; and when I break
   that oath, let me turn monster: therefore, my
   sweet Rose, my dear Rose, be merry.
                    (1.2.13–21)

Under the English common law, a daughter could inherit property if a father died without having a living male heir. Under the Salic law of France, land and titles did not descend through females. Of course, Shakespeare knew about the Salic law, which was said in an earlier play to be a bar to Henry V's claim to the throne of France.

But the problem here is that Rosalind could not be her uncle's heir as long as Celia lives. Celia is saying she will return the inheritance that Rosalind lost when her uncle usurped her father's title and lands. The girls agree that they will try to amuse themselves.

Celia suggests that they mock what was commonly referred to as the "wheel of fortune" (1.2.29).

Touchstone the fool comes to summon Celia to her father. Celia tells him, "since the little wit that fools have was silenced, the little foolery that wise men have makes a great show" (1.2.82–84). The courtier Le Beau enters and tells the girls of the wrestling match. Charles has already thrown and maimed three challengers.

Duke Frederick, Charles, and Orlando enter. The Duke urges the girls to dissuade Orlando from challenging Charles and withdraw from the contest. Orlando replies that if he is killed it will do no wrong to his friends, for he has none.

When they wrestle, to everyone's astonishment, Orlando throws Charles so hard that he is knocked unconscious. Duke Frederick congratulates Orlando but is dismayed to learn that he is the youngest son of Sir Rowland de Boys, who was the Duke's enemy. Duke Frederick: "But fare thee well; thou art a gallant youth: / I would thou hadst told me of another father" (1.2.222–23).

Rosalind says her father, the Old Duke, loved Sir Rowland. She encourages Orlando and gives him a chain to wear around his neck. Orlando and Rosalind are mutually infatuated.

Orlando is warned that Duke Fredrick is displeased with him and he should leave the palace. Orlando: "Thus must I from the smoke into the smother; / From tyrant duke unto a tyrant brother: / But heavenly Rosalind!" (1.2.279–81).

Duke Frederick is angry—and not only with Orlando. He suddenly orders Rosalind to leave court, threatening her with death if she comes within twenty miles of the palace. Rosalind begs to know the cause of her disgrace. The Duke replies that he does not trust her; she is a traitor. It is enough for him that she is her father's daughter. She protests that treason is not inherited. Celia protests in vain that her cousin is no traitor.

After the Duke exits the stage, Celia says she is banished too and will go with Rosalind to seek out the Old Duke in the Forest of Arden. Rosalind—who is tall—will dress as a man to protect them.

She will call herself Ganymede. Celia will persuade Touchstone the clown to accompany them.

In the Forest of Arden, the Old Duke cheers his companions by idealizing the state of nature they occupy. He proclaims: "Sweet are the uses of adversity" (2.1.12).

Back at the palace, Duke Frederick learns that his daughter and her cousin have fled in the night with the fool and that Orlando may be with them. At Sir Rowland's house, the old servant Adam warns Orlando that his brother intends to kill him. They both flee the house.

In the forest, Rosalind, Celia, and Touchstone soon weary of the journey. They encounter Corin, an old man, and Silvius, a young shepherd. Silvius is in love with Phebe. Corin agrees to take the travelers to the cottage of his master where they hope to get food and drink.

Orlando and Adam are also hungry and fatigued. Adam can go no farther. Orlando leaves to seek food for them both. He bursts into the Old Duke's camp. Thinking they are outlaws, Orlando has his sword drawn and demands food. The Old Duke says Orlando is welcome to join them and share their food. Orlando begs pardon for drawing his sword. He leaves to get Adam, and the Old Duke reminds his fellows that they are not the only unfortunate ones.

This prompts Jacques to deliver his famous "stages of man" speech. To appreciate the reference to the mature man as a Justice of the Peace, I will quote it in full.

JAQUES   All the world's a stage,
    And all the men and women merely players:
    They have their exits and their entrances;
    And one man in his time plays many parts,
    His acts being seven ages. At first the infant,
    Mewling and puking in the nurse's arms.
    And then the whining school-boy, with his satchel
    And shining morning face, creeping like snail
    Unwillingly to school. And then the lover,
    Sighing like furnace, with a woeful ballad

Made to his mistress' eyebrow. Then a soldier,
Full of strange oaths and bearded like the pard,
Jealous in honour, sudden and quick in quarrel,
Seeking the bubble reputation
Even in the cannon's mouth. And then the justice,
In fair round belly with good capon lined,
With eyes severe and beard of formal cut,
Full of wise saws and modern instances;
And so he plays his part. The sixth age shifts
Into the lean and slipper'd pantaloon,
With spectacles on nose and pouch on side,
His youthful hose, well saved, a world too wide
For his shrunk shank; and his big manly voice,
Turning again toward childish treble, pipes
And whistles in his sound. Last scene of all,
That ends this strange eventful history,
Is second childishness and mere oblivion,
Sans teeth, sans eyes, sans taste, sans everything.

(2.7.138–65)

The "justice" refers to a non-lawyer member of the gentry serving as a justice of the peace. This portrayal of the middle-aged justice of the peace as a man of "wise saws and modern instances" is by far the most favorable of Shakespeare's depictions in the plays of a country gentleman justice of the peace.

Duke Frederick, in his palace, is furious that Orlando has disappeared and orders Oliver to find him. In the Forest of Arden, Orlando is writing sonnets to Rosalind and pinning them onto trees. Rosalind finds the poems and shows them to Touchstone, who thinks they are bad poetry: "Truly, the tree yields bad fruit" (3.2.91).

Celia tells Rosalind it is Orlando who has written the verses about loving her. Orlando meets Rosalind disguised as Ganymede, and she shows her wit by talking of how time is relative: To the maid waiting on her wedding day, it trots . . . "Time's pace is so hard that

it seems the length of seven year" (3.2.286–87). Rosalind adds that
to a rich man with no gout, "time ambles" (3.2.325).

ORLANDO   Who doth he gallop withal?

ROSALIND   With a thief to the gallows, for though he go as
softly as foot can fall, he thinks himself too soon there.

ORLANDO   Who stays it still withal?

ROSALIND   With lawyers in the vacation, for they sleep
between term and term and then they perceive not how Time
moves.

(3.2.297–302)

Hanging was the prescribed punishment for theft of property
above the value of a shilling. In Shakespeare's day, the royal courts
sat in session each year during four terms. The period between terms
was referred to as the "vacation" when no fees could be earned by
appearing in court.

Orlando confesses to Rosalind/Ganymede to being the author
of the poems she has found on the trees. Rosalind/Ganymede
replies that she can cure Orlando of love if he comes to her every
day and woos her as if she were Rosalind. Orlando vows he will
die of lovesickness if he cannot have Rosalind. She responds: "[M]
en have died from time to time and worms have eaten them, but
not for love" (4.1.81–82). She clearly is the cleverer of the two; this
is a startlingly realistic statement by a young heroine of a romantic
comedy. They then practice a marriage ceremony.

ROSALIND   Come, sister, you shall be the priest and marry us.
Give me your hand, Orlando. What do you say, sister?

ORLANDO   Pray thee, marry us.

CELIA   I cannot say the words.

ROSALIND   You must begin, 'Will you, Orlando–'

CELIA   Go to. Will you, Orlando, have to wife this Rosalind?

ORLANDO   I will.

ROSALIND   Ay, but when?

ORLANDO   Why now; as fast as she can marry us.

ROSALIND   Then you must say 'I take thee, Rosalind, for wife.'

ORLANDO   I take thee, Rosalind, for wife.

ROSALIND   I might ask you for your commission; but I do take
thee, Orlando, for my husband: there's a girl goes
before the priest; and certainly a woman's thought
runs before her actions.

(4.1.97–113)

Here, Rosalind is accurately recognizing the sophisticated legal
difference between a promise to marry in the future ("I will") and
a present consent ("I take thee") to be married.

Early canon law stated that marriage was the union of a man
and a woman consummated by sexual intercourse. This was the
theory of marriage by consent, with no religious ceremony such as
endowment at the church door required.

Later, it was held that a marriage could be effected without a
church ceremony by agreement—provided that the agreement was
stated in words of the present tense (*per verba de praesenti*) generally
accompanied by holding of hands in the presence of two witnesses.
No particular words were required to create such a "spousal" marriage (also known as troth-plight). It was valid and binding as long
as there was present consent to be married by both parties. "A simple
rule, that the formation of a contract by the present mutual consent

of bride and groom (as long as they were eligible to marry) made an indissoluble marriage certainly applied. But that very simplicity brought in almost innumerable quandaries."[15]

This marriage by present consent contrasted with a promise to marry in the future (*per verba de futuo*). This would result in marriage if consummated but could be dissolved before that by mutual consent. The uncertainty created by these fine distinctions spawned much litigation and attempts at marriage reform by legislation and church convocations. These controversies are the backdrop to marriage contract issues in more than a dozen of Shakespeare's plays.

Another theory was that marriage was a sacrament of the Roman Church and efforts to require a ceremony were made. After the Reformation, marriage was dropped as one of the sacraments of the English Church. Disagreements among Puritans, Catholics, and Anglicans prevented any agreed-upon solution to the form of marriage.

The common law in Elizabethan England until the mid-sixteenth century recognized a valid marriage if the two parties expressed consent to be married even without the presence of a priest to solemnize the marriage. The recognition of spousal marriages became further muddled by the Act of Uniformity in 1559, which seemed to require solemnization of marriage by the liturgy set forth in the Book of Common Prayer. This itself was controversial.

For example, the Puritans objected vociferously to any obligation to exchange rings (idolatry) or taking communion during the ceremony (popery). Nevertheless, the church applied enormous pressure to have marriages solemnized in a church ceremony. So called "clandestine" marriages, although valid in the eyes of the law, could be punished by the church courts, typically with fines and penance.

A church-sanctioned marriage required the proclamation of the banns in church three times on successive Sundays or Holy

---

[15] B. J. Sokol and Mary Sokol, *Shakespeare, Law, and Marriage* (Cambridge University Press, 2003), 10.

Days before the ceremony. This allowed anyone who knew of an impediment (such as bigamy or incest) to the marriage to have an opportunity to object to it going forward. Then, a ceremony would be performed in the presence of family and friends, typically in the bride's parish church.

Rosalind and Orlando would be legally married by the words used here. This is one of the few depictions in the plays of an actual (although pretend) marriage ceremony.

There is much witty banter between Rosalind and Orlando. When Orlando is late for one of their meetings, Rosalind/Ganymede says she would rather marry a snail: "Ay, of a snail; for though he comes slowly, he carries his house on his head; a better jointure, I think, than you make a woman" (4.1.49–50). A "jointure" was a contractual agreement whereby a widow would receive certain property upon the death of her husband in lieu of her dower rights to a life interest in a third of her husband's real property. Since Orlando had no property, he was not able to offer his wife a jointure.

At the command of Duke Frederick, Oliver has gone to the Forest of Arden to find his brother. In a wildly improbable chain of events, Orlando rescues Oliver from a lioness, and the brothers are reconciled. Celia and Oliver immediately fall in love. Oliver gives his estate to Orlando and intends to live in the forest as a shepherd with Celia. Oliver: "it shall be to your good; for my father's house and all the revenue that was old Sir Rowland's will I estate upon you, and here live and die a shepherd" (5.2.9–12).

Celia and Oliver are to be married the next day. Rosalind/Ganymede promises Orlando that he will marry Rosalind the same day. Duke Frederick has a religious conversion and restores to the Old Duke his title and lands. The wedding ceremonies for Rosalind and Orlando and the other lovers begin, and the play ends.

As you Like It is a bright romantic comedy. Rosalind is one of Shakespeare's memorable female characters. And yet there is a Shakespearean fatalism that keeps popping up in the play. Duke Senior famously says: "Sweet are the uses of adversity." In the Duke

Senior's camp, Jacques tells of meeting a fool (Touchstone) in the forest.

JAQUES   A fool, a fool! I met a fool i' the forest. . . .
　　'Good morrow, fool,' quoth I. 'No, sir,' quoth he,
　　'Call me not fool till heaven hath sent me fortune:'
　　And then he drew a dial from his poke,
　　And, looking on it with lack-lustre eye,
　　Says very wisely, 'It is ten o'clock:
　　Thus we may see,' quoth he, 'how the world wags:
　　'Tis but an hour ago since it was nine,
　　And after one hour more 'twill be eleven;
　　And so, from hour to hour, we ripe and ripe,
　　And then, from hour to hour, we rot and rot;
　　And thereby hangs a tale.'
　　　　　　　　(2.7.12, 18–28)

Jacques' seven ages of man speech seems oddly out of place in a light romantic comedy. Yet there is more here than conventional romanticized lover behavior. Touchstone makes no pretense that he is looking for romantic love with Audrey, a shepherd girl: "Come, sweet Audrey: / We must be married, or we must live in bawdry" (3.3.77–78). Ganymede/ Rosalind tells Phoebe she should accept Silvius as her lover: "Sell when you can; you are not for all markets" (3.5.60).

When Orlando tells Ganymede/Rosalind that he will die "in mine own person" if Rosalind does not love him, she responds: "No, faith, die by attorney . . . men have died from time to time and worms have eaten them, but not for love" (4.1.69–70, 81–82).

To me, these intimations of a more human and less idealized love between men and women show the variety and richness of Shakespeare at this stage of his career as a playwright.

CHAPTER 14

HAMLET

Shakespeare probably completed *Hamlet* in 1601, the year it was first performed. Many consider it his greatest play. If performance is the measure of greatness, it has no equal in the four hundred–plus years since its creation. From my perspective, it is the story of a young intellectual, whose natural mode of responding to the world is to engage in thought and reflection. He is charged by the ghost of his father with revenging the father's murder by Hamlet's uncle, who has also married Hamlet's mother.

The Hamlet we meet at the beginning of the play is most unsuited for this task. For a man of action like Othello, it would have been but the work of a moment. Not so for Hamlet. In Hamlet's soliloquies, Shakespeare takes us through the inner workings of Hamlet's mind as he wrestles with doubt and uncertainty as the action plays out. In the brilliance and richness of his imagery, Shakespeare reached the height of his greatness as a dramatic poet.

The play begins at night on the battlements of the castle of Elsinore in Denmark. The opening line: "Who's there?" (*Hamlet* 1.1.1), sets the tone for the play. It is a drama with many questions.

Two guards of the watch have the night before seen a ghostly apparition that resembles the dead King Hamlet. They ask Hamlet's friend Horatio, a young scholar who is visiting Elsinore, to accompany them to the castle walls and to address the apparition if it appears again. It does.

[Enter Ghost]

MARCELLUS   Peace, break thee off; look, where it comes again!

BERNARDO   In the same figure, like the king that's dead.

MARCELLUS   Thou art a scholar; speak to it, Horatio.

BERNARDO   Looks it not like the king? mark it, Horatio.

HORATIO   Most like: it harrows me with fear and wonder.

BERNARDO   It would be spoke to.

MARCELLUS   Question it, Horatio.

HORATIO   What art thou that usurp'st this time of night,
Together with that fair and warlike form
In which the majesty of buried Denmark
Did sometimes march? by heaven I charge thee, speak!

MARCELLUS   It is offended.

BERNARDO   See, it stalks away!

HORATIO   Stay! speak, speak! I charge thee, speak!

[Exit Ghost]

(1.1.40–51)

After the Ghost leaves, Marcellus asks if anyone can explain the feverish preparations for war in the Danish kingdom. Horatio responds that Young Fortinbras, with a band of "lawless resolutes" (1.1.98), threatens to reclaim by force the land that was lawfully won by Hamlet's father in a trial by single combat with Old Fortinbras of Norway.

The Ghost appears again, but disappears as the dawn breaks with the crow of the cock. The men on the wall resolve to tell young Hamlet what they have seen.

In Scene 2, with Queen Gertrude (Hamlet's mother) by his side, we see King Claudius (the brother of Old Hamlet) at his court in all his regal glory. In medieval Europe, succession to the kingship did not necessarily go automatically to the oldest surviving son. It could go to an adult male from the royal family. Shakespeare's audience would have understood this from the example of King John, who was declared King rather than the twelve-year-old Arthur of Brittainy.

Claudius's first speech suggests that something is not as it should be.

KING CLAUDIUS   Therefore our sometime sister, now our
   queen,
   The imperial jointress to this warlike state,
   Have we, as 'twere with a defeated joy,–
   With an auspicious and a dropping eye,
   With mirth in funeral and with dirge in marriage,
   In equal scale weighing delight and dole,–
   Taken to wife: nor have we herein barr'd
   Your better wisdoms, which have freely gone
   With this affair along. For all, our thanks.
                (1.2.8–16)

Originally, a "jointure" referred to property jointly owned by a husband and wife for life. It is certainly this sense of the word that Shakespeare is using here. He cannot be referring to jointure in the sense of property settled on the widow in lieu of dower. Gertrude's position in the kingdom is derived from her marriage to Claudius and not as the widow of Old Hamlet. Could Claudius's former sister-in-law now be his lawful wife and Queen?

Shakespeare's audience would certainly remember that Queen Elizabeth's father had married Katherine of Aragon, who had briefly been married to Arthur, Henry's older brother, before the teenage

Arthur's death in 1501. When Henry became King eight years later, he married Katherine. When Katherine failed to produce a male heir and Henry wanted to marry Anne Boleyn, he claimed in his divorce case, which led to the break with Rome and the English Reformation, that the marriage with Katherine was in violation of the biblical prohibition upon incest.

Claudius seems aware that all may not appear to be quite right when he speaks of "mirth in funeral and with dirge in marriage." Nevertheless, he goes about the business of being King with apparent relish. He sends ambassadors to Norway to protest the preparations for war by Young Fortinbras. Polonius, the King's counselor, seeks permission for his son, Laertes, to return to France, which the King grants. Claudius, and then Gertrude, address Hamlet.

KING CLAUDIUS   But now, my cousin Hamlet, and my son,-

HAMLET   [*Aside*] A little more than kin, and less than kind.

KING CLAUDIUS   How is it that the clouds still hang on you?

HAMLET   Not so, my lord; I am too much i' the sun.

QUEEN GERTRUDE   Good Hamlet, cast thy nighted colour off,
    And let thine eye look like a friend on Denmark.
    Do not for ever with thy vailed lids
    Seek for thy noble father in the dust:
    Thou know'st 'tis common; all that lives must die,
    Passing through nature to eternity.

HAMLET   Ay, madam, 'tis common.

QUEEN GERTRUDE   If it be,
    Why seems it so particular with thee?

HAMLET   Seems, madam! nay it is; I know not 'seems.'

'Tis not alone my inky cloak, good mother,
Nor customary suits of solemn black,
Nor windy suspiration of forced breath,
No, nor the fruitful river in the eye,
Nor the dejected 'haviour of the visage,
Together with all forms, modes, shapes of grief,
That can denote me truly: these indeed seem,
For they are actions that a man might play:
But I have that within which passeth show;
These but the trappings and the suits of woe.

(1.2.65–88)

These few lines of dialogue introduce two themes that will recur throughout the play. One is the universality of human mortality. "Thou know'st 'tis common; all that lives must die, / Passing through nature to eternity." The other is Hamlet's search for the truth that lies behind appearances. This distinction between being and seeming is one of most pervasive themes of Shakespeare's plays. It is there in all of the references to man's life as playing a role upon a stage. As a former trial lawyer and now a judge, I am very conscious of the distinction. (For example, the haughty prosecutor who appears in my courtroom in November, then becomes a criminal defense lawyer to earn more money, and returns in December, pleading for leniency for his unfortunate client who endured a troubled childhood.)

The King reminds Hamlet that all men lose their fathers. "We pray you, throw to earth / This unprevailing woe, and think of us / As of a father: for let the world take note, / You are the most immediate to our throne; / And with no less nobility of love / Than that which dearest father bears his son, / Do I impart toward you" (1.2.106–12). On the surface, this seems to be good, practical advice. But are we to believe that Claudius is sincere about his affection for Hamlet? If so, this belief will not last long.

At the urging of Claudius and Gertrude, Hamlet agrees not to return to school at Wittenberg. (The University of Wittenberg was founded in 1502, long after the time in which Hamlet is set. It was there that Martin Luther began the Protestant Reformation.)

Hamlet is left alone on the stage to deliver his first great soliloquy. He has not yet seen the Ghost. It is his mother's marriage to his uncle that tortures his heart.

HAMLET   O, that this too too solid flesh would melt
Thaw and resolve itself into a dew!
Or that the Everlasting had not fix'd
His canon 'gainst self-slaughter! O God! God!
How weary, stale, flat and unprofitable,
Seem to me all the uses of this world!
Fie on't! ah fie! 'tis an unweeded garden,
That grows to seed; things rank and gross in nature
Possess it merely. That it should come to this!
But two months dead: nay, not so much, not two:
So excellent a king; that was, to this,
Hyperion to a satyr; so loving to my mother
That he might not beteem the winds of heaven
Visit her face too roughly. Heaven and earth!
Must I remember? why, she would hang on him,
As if crease of appetite had grown
By what it fed on: and yet, within a month–
Let me not think on't–Frailty, thy name is woman!–
A little month, or ere those shoes were old
With which she follow'd my poor father's body,
Like Niobe, all tears:–why she, even she–
O, God! a beast, that wants discourse of reason,
Would have mourn'd longer–married with my uncle,
My father's brother, but no more like my father
Than I to Hercules: within a month:
Ere yet the salt of most unrighteous tears
Had left the flushing in her galled eyes,
She married. O, most wicked speed, to post
With such dexterity to incestuous sheets!

It is not nor it cannot come to good:
But break, my heart; for I must hold my tongue.
                    (1.2.129–59)

Under canon (church) law, suicide was a crime. Incest is—and
was—the crime of sexual relations or marriage taking place between
a male and female who are so closely linked by blood or affinity that
the act is prohibited by law. Gertrude's marriage to Claudius was
technically incestuous under the rules of the Roman Church. But
the rules could be bent for reasons of state, as they were for young
Prince Henry (later Henry VIII) and Katherine of Aragon.

It is while he is in this state of depression and disillusionment
that fate strikes young Hamlet a horrible blow. His reverie is broken
by the entrance of Horatio, Marcellus, and Bernardo. They talk of
Hamlet's father. Hamlet: "He was a man, take him for all in all, / I
shall not look upon his like again" (1.2.187–88). Horatio tells him
of the appearance of the Ghost the previous night. Hamlet agrees
to meet them on the wall that night to see if the Ghost reappears:
"I will watch to-night; / Perchance 'twill walk again" (1.2.240–41).

In Scene III, Polonius and his daughter, Ophelia, bid farewell to
his son, Laertes, who is returning to Wittenberg. Polonius's father-
to-son advice, which might pass for wisdom from another, is one
cliché tacked on to another.

LORD POLONIUS   Yet here, Laertes! aboard, aboard, for shame!
  The wind sits in the shoulder of your sail,
  And you are stay'd for. There; my blessing with thee!
  And these few precepts in thy memory
  See thou character. Give thy thoughts no tongue,
  Nor any unproportioned thought his act.
  Be thou familiar, but by no means vulgar.
  Those friends thou hast, and their adoption tried,
  Grapple them to thy soul with hoops of steel;
  But do not dull thy palm with entertainment
  Of each new-hatch'd, unfledged comrade. Beware

Of entrance to a quarrel, but being in,
Bear't that the opposed may beware of thee.
Give every man thy ear, but few thy voice;
Take each man's censure, but reserve thy judgment.
Costly thy habit as thy purse can buy,
But not express'd in fancy; rich, not gaudy;
For the apparel oft proclaims the man,
And they in France of the best rank and station
Are of a most select and generous chief in that.
Neither a borrower nor a lender be;
For loan oft loses both itself and friend,
And borrowing dulls the edge of husbandry.
This above all: to thine ownself be true,
And it must follow, as the night the day,
Thou canst not then be false to any man.

(1.3.55–80)

Ophelia is warned by both her brother and her father against accepting Hamlet as her lover. After Ophelia admits to Polonius that Hamlet has spoken of his love for her, he forbids her to talk to the young Prince.

The next scene of Act I begins with Hamlet, Horatio, and Marcellus at night on the castle wall where the Ghost has appeared. Around midnight, as they are talking of the King's excessive drinking, the Ghost appears.

HORATIO   Look, my lord, it comes!

[Enter Ghost]

HAMLET   Angels and ministers of grace defend us!
Be thou a spirit of health or goblin damn'd,
Bring with thee airs from heaven or blasts from hell,
Be thy intents wicked or charitable,
Thou comest in such a questionable shape

That I will speak to thee: I'll call thee Hamlet,
King, father, royal Dane: O, answer me!
Let me not burst in ignorance; but tell
Why thy canonized bones, hearsed in death,
Have burst their cerements; why the sepulchre,
Wherein we saw thee quietly inurn'd,
Hath oped his ponderous and marble jaws,
To cast thee up again.
                        (1.4.38–51)

The Ghost refuses to speak but gestures to Hamlet to follow it. Over the protests of Marcellus and Horatio, Hamlet follows the Ghost offstage. Marcellus proclaims: "Something is rotten in the state of Denmark" (1.4.90).

In the last scene of Act I, Hamlet and the Ghost are alone on the castle wall. Hamlet has no idea whether the Ghost is "a spirit of health or goblin damned" (1.4.40).

A central feature of Reformation doctrine was the denial of Purgatory, where the souls of the dead would go before ascending to Heaven or descending to Hell. There was, however, still a widespread popular belief in ghosts who would wander about the world due to some accident connected with their death. Thus, Shakespeare was not necessarily offending Church of England doctrine by having a ghost return from the dead. Hamlet asks the Ghost to speak.

HAMLET   Speak; I am bound to hear.

GHOST   So art thou to revenge, when thou shalt hear.

HAMLET   What?

GHOST   I am thy father's spirit,
    Doom'd for a certain term to walk the night,
    And for the day confined to fast in fires,
    Till the foul crimes done in my days of nature

Are burnt and purged away. But that I am forbid
To tell the secrets of my prison-house,
I could a tale unfold whose lightest word
Would harrow up thy soul, freeze thy young blood,
Make thy two eyes, like stars, start from their spheres,
Thy knotted and combined locks to part
And each particular hair to stand on end,
Like quills upon the fretful porpentine:
But this eternal blazon must not be
To ears of flesh and blood. List, list, O, list!
If thou didst ever thy dear father love–

HAMLET   O God!

GHOST   Revenge his foul and most unnatural murder.

HAMLET   Murder!

GHOST   Murder most foul, as in the best it is;
But this most foul, strange and unnatural.

HAMLET   Haste me to know't, that I, with wings as swift
As meditation or the thoughts of love,
May sweep to my revenge.

(1.5.6–31)

The Ghost tells Hamlet that his uncle the King committed the murder by pouring poison in the ear of the sleeping Hamlet Senior.

GHOST   'Tis given out that, sleeping in my orchard,
A serpent stung me; so the whole ear of Denmark
Is by a forged process of my death
Rankly abused: but know, thou noble youth,
The serpent that did sting thy father's life
Now wears his crown.

HAMLET   O my prophetic soul! My uncle!

GHOST   Ay, that incestuous, that adulterate beast,
With witchcraft of his wit, with traitorous gifts,–
O wicked wit and gifts, that have the power
So to seduce!–won to his shameful lust
The will of my most seeming-virtuous queen:
O Hamlet, what a falling-off was there!
                        (1.5.34–46)

As the dawn begins to break, the Ghost must disappear. He bids
Hamlet farewell: "Adieu, adieu! Hamlet, remember me." (1.5.91) The
great Shakespearean critic A.C. Bradley says of the Ghost that he is
"the messenger of divine justice set upon the expiation of offenses
which it appeared impossible for man to discover and avenge. . . ."[16]
Hamlet vows to revenge the foul murder of his father.

HAMLET   O all you host of heaven! O earth! what else?
And shall I couple hell? O, fie! Hold, hold, my heart;
And you, my sinews, grow not instant old,
But bear me stiffly up. Remember thee!
Ay, thou poor ghost, while memory holds a seat
In this distracted globe. Remember thee!
Yea, from the table of my memory
I'll wipe away all trivial fond records,
All saws of books, all forms, all pressures past,
That youth and observation copied there;
And thy commandment all alone shall live
Within the book and volume of my brain,
Unmix'd with baser matter: yes, by heaven!
O most pernicious woman!
O villain, villain, smiling, damned villain!
My tables,–meet it is I set it down,

---

[16] A.C. Bradley, *Shakespearean Tragedy* (Fawcett Publications, 2006), 146.

That one may smile, and smile, and be a villain;
At least I'm sure it may be so in Denmark:

[Writing]

So, uncle, there you are. Now to my word;
It is 'Adieu, adieu! remember me.'
I have sworn't.

(1.5.92–112)

When his companions find Hamlet, he refuses to say what he has been told by the Ghost. They swear not to tell anyone what they have seen. They must be silent, even if Hamlet acts as if he is a little mad ("an antic disposition") (1.5.172).

Hamlet recognizes the difficulty he will have in revenging his father's murder: "The time is out of joint: O cursed spite, / That ever I was born to set it right!" (1.5.189–90). Hamlet must choose his course of action carefully if he is both to revenge the murder of his father and claim the kingship that should have been his. When Horatio remarks upon the strange events of the night, Hamlet famously responds: "There are more things in heaven and earth, Horatio, / Than are dreamt of in your philosophy" (1.5.167–68).

The Ghost has charged young Hamlet with revenging his murder. In the Denmark of the play, there appears to be no law other than the will of the King. Thus, Hamlet has no remedy for the murder of his father other than an act of private revenge.

The play explores many of the problems that arise as a result. What evidence does Hamlet need to be sure Claudius murdered his father? Is the word of the Ghost enough? Should Hamlet confront Claudius with the accusation before he takes any action? Is Fortinbras justified in the revenge he seeks? Is the law a better means of seeking justice than acts of private revenge? In Shakespeare's time, most thought that it was.

Early in the reign of James I, Francis Bacon had written in his *Essays*: "Revenge is a kind of Wilde Justice; which the more man's nature runs to, the more ought Law to weed it out. For as the first Wrong, it doth but offend the Law; but the Revenge of that wrong putteth the Law out of Office." In a sense, Hamlet is a tragedy about the consequences of private revenge in a society where there is no rule of law.

In the next scene, Ophelia tells her father of an encounter with the "mad" Hamlet, who looked disheveled and displayed other symptoms of melancholy. Polonius asks her if Hamlet is mad for her love. She responds: "My lord, I do not know; / But truly, I do fear it" (2.1.84–85). Others have also observed Hamlet's mad behavior.

The suspicious King has summoned Rosencrantz and Guildenstern, friends from Hamlet's youth, to the court; and he charges them with finding out from Hamlet what afflicts him. They agree to act as the King's spies. But Polonius tells the King that he has discovered the "very cause of Hamlet's lunacy" (2.2.49).

After the ambassadors Voltemand and Cornelius report on their mission to Norway (the King of Norway has forbidden Young Fortinbras's expedition against Denmark), Polonius begins his tedious explanation of Hamlet's madness.

LORD POLONIUS   This business is well ended.
   My liege, and madam, to expostulate
   What majesty should be, what duty is,
   Why day is day, night night, and time is time,
   Were nothing but to waste night, day and time.
   Therefore, since brevity is the soul of wit,
   And tediousness the limbs and outward flourishes,
   I will be brief: your noble son is mad:
   Mad call I it; for, to define true madness,
   What is't but to be nothing else but mad?
   But let that go.

QUEEN GERTRUDE   More matter, with less art.

LORD POLONIUS   Madam, I swear I use no art at all.
That he is mad, 'tis true: 'tis true 'tis pity;
And pity 'tis 'tis true: a foolish figure;
But farewell it, for I will use no art.
Mad let us grant him, then: and now remains
That we find out the cause of this effect,
Or rather say, the cause of this defect,
For this effect defective comes by cause:
Thus it remains, and the remainder thus. Perpend.
I have a daughter–have while she is mine–
Who, in her duty and obedience, mark,
Hath given me this: now gather, and surmise.

[Reads]

'To the celestial and my soul's idol, the most
beautified Ophelia,'– That's an ill phrase, a vile phrase; 'beauti-
    fied' is a vile phrase: but you shall hear. Thus:

[Reads]

'In her excellent white bosom, these, &c.'

QUEEN GERTRUDE   Came this from Hamlet to her?

LORD POLONIUS   Good madam, stay awhile; I will be faithful.
                 (2.2.86–115)

Gertrude here speaks for all the judges (jurors, voters) who have had to endure a lawyer (witness, politician, orator) in love with the sound of his or her own voice, and who simply will not get to the point of their argument. Endless digressions pile up: wave after wave of verbosity.

Shakespeare uses this rhetorical technique to great effect when he wishes to make a character appear foolish and ridiculous. We also see this in the speeches of Elbow in *Measure for Measure* and Dogberry in *Much Ado About Nothing*.

Polonius eventually tells Gertrude and Claudius that he instructed Ophelia to spurn Hamlet's love and this has caused his madness. To test the theory, Polonius and Claudius plan to hide behind an arras and eavesdrop on Hamlet and Ophelia. Before they do, Polonius has a wicked encounter with Hamlet.

[Enter HAMLET, reading]

LORD POLONIUS   O, give me leave:
How does my good Lord Hamlet?

HAMLET   Well, God-a-mercy.

LORD POLONIUS   Do you know me, my lord?

HAMLET   Excellent well; you are a fishmonger.

LORD POLONIUS   Not I, my lord.

HAMLET   Then I would you were so honest a man.

LORD POLONIUS   Honest, my lord!

HAMLET   Ay, sir; to be honest, as this world goes, is to be one man picked out of ten thousand.

LORD POLONIUS   That's very true, my lord.

HAMLET   For if the sun breed maggots in a dead dog, being a god kissing carrion,–Have you a daughter?

LORD POLONIUS   I have, my lord.

HAMLET   Let her not walk i' the sun: conception is a blessing: but not as your daughter may conceive. Friend, look to 't.

LORD POLONIUS   [*Aside*] How say you by that? Still harping on
my daughter: yet he knew me not at first; he said I
was a fishmonger: he is far gone, far gone: and
truly in my youth I suffered much extremity for
love; very near this. I'll speak to him again.
What do you read, my lord?

HAMLET   Words, words, words.

LORD POLONIUS   What is the matter, my lord?

HAMLET   Between who?

LORD POLONIUS   I mean, the matter that you read, my lord.

HAMLET   Slanders, sir: for the satirical rogue says here
that old men have grey beards, that their faces are
wrinkled, their eyes purging thick amber and
plum-tree gum and that they have a plentiful lack of
wit, together with most weak hams: all which, sir,
though I most powerfully and potently believe, yet
I hold it not honesty to have it thus set down, for
yourself, sir, should be old as I am, if like a crab
you could go backward.

LORD POLONIUS   [*Aside*] Though this be madness, yet there is
method in 't. Will you walk out of the air, my lord?

HAMLET   Into my grave.

LORD POLONIUS   Indeed, that is out o' the air.

[*Aside*]

How pregnant sometimes his replies are! a happiness
that often madness hits on, which reason and sanity

could not so prosperously be delivered of. I will
leave him, and suddenly contrive the means of
meeting between him and my daughter.–My honourable
lord, I will most humbly take my leave of you.

HAMLET   You cannot, sir, take from me any thing that I will
more willingly part withal: except my life, except
my life, except my life.

LORD POLONIUS   Fare you well, my lord.

HAMLET   These tedious old fools!
(2.2.169–216)

Hamlet then sees Rosencrantz and Guildenstern. After some
bawdy banter, Hamlet tells them that Denmark is a prison. When
Rosencrantz denies this, Hamlet responds: "Why, then, 'tis none
to you; for there is nothing either good or bad, but thinking
makes it so: to me it is a prison" (2.2.241–243). Hamlet denies
that it is his ambition that makes him think of Denmark as a
prison. "O God, I could be bounded in a nut shell and count
myself a king of infinite space, were it not that I have bad dreams"
(2.2.246–49).

Hamlet gets them to confess that they have come to Elsinore
at the King's request to spy on him. Hamlet then makes one of the
most beautiful—but melancholy—speeches of the play.

GUILDENSTERN   My lord, we were sent for.

HAMLET   I will tell you why; so shall my anticipation
prevent your discovery, and your secrecy to the king
and queen moult no feather. I have of late–but
wherefore I know not–lost all my mirth, forgone all
custom of exercises; and indeed it goes so heavily
with my disposition that this goodly frame, the

earth, seems to me a sterile promontory, this most
excellent canopy, the air, look you, this brave
o'erhanging firmament, this majestical roof fretted
with golden fire, why, it appears no other thing to
me than a foul and pestilent congregation of vapours.
What a piece of work is a man! how noble in reason!
how infinite in faculty! in form and moving how
express and admirable! in action how like an angel!
in apprehension how like a god! the beauty of the
world! the paragon of animals! And yet, to me,
what is this quintessence of dust? man delights not
me: no, nor woman neither, though by your smiling
you seem to say so.

(2.2.280–302)

Rosencrantz responds that Hamlet will delight in the players
known to Hamlet ("the tragedians of the city") (2.2.314), who are
coming to Elsinore. Hamlet is happy to renew his acquaintance
with the players. Polonius returns and tells Hamlet the players have
arrived. He praises their ability to perform all forms of drama.

LORD POLONIUS   The best actors in the world, either for tragedy, comedy, history, pastoral, pastoral-comical,
historical-pastoral, tragical-historical, tragical-
comical-historical-pastoral, scene individable, or
poem unlimited: Seneca cannot be too heavy, nor
Plautus too light. For the law of writ and the
liberty, these are the only men.

HAMLET   O Jephthah, judge of Israel, what a treasure hadst
thou!

LORD POLONIUS   What a treasure had he, my lord?

HAMLET   Why,

'One fair daughter and no more,
The which he loved passing well.'

LORD POLONIUS   [*Aside*] Still on my daughter.

HAMLET   Am I not i' the right, old Jephthah?
                        (2.2.375–88)

The story of Jephthah is told in the Old Testament Book of Judges.
Jephthah led an Israelite army against the Ammonites. During a
battle, he swore to God to sacrifice the first person to greet him on
his return home if he won the battle, which he did. The first person
to greet him on his return was his daughter—he had her killed as
a sacrifice to God.

The players enter. After a spirited dialogue concerning the state
of the theater world, Hamlet begs the first player to give a speech
that he had heard once ("for the play, I remember, pleased not the
million") (2.2.413) about the murder of old Priam by Achilles' son
Pyrrhus during the sack of Troy. The player delivers the speech—
notwithstanding repeated interruptions by the foolish Polonius—
with sincere emotion. And then Hamlet and Polonius have a classic
Shakespearean confrontation.

LORD POLONIUS   Look, whether he has not turned his colour
    and has tears in's eyes. Pray you, no more.

HAMLET   'Tis well: I'll have thee speak out the rest soon.
    Good my lord [*Polonius*], will you see the players well
    bestowed? Do you hear, let them be well used; for
    they are the abstract and brief chronicles of the
    time: after your death you were better have a bad
    epitaph than their ill report while you live.

LORD POLONIUS   My lord, I will use them according to their desert.

HAMLET   God's bodykins, man, much better: use every man
after his desert, and who should 'scape whipping?
Use them after your own honour and dignity: the less
they deserve, the more merit is in your bounty.
Take them in.

LORD POLONIUS   Come, sirs.
                                            (2.2.495–507)

This essentially Protestant Christian idea that we are all sinners
in the eyes of God and will be judged harshly if we get exactly what
we deserve is a recurrent theme in Shakespeare. We see it in the
plea for mercy of Isabella before Angelo in *Measure for Measure*.
And we see it most powerfully in mad Lear's commentaries upon
the limitations and hypocrisy of human justice.

Hamlet then arranges with the players to have a play performed for the King the following evening: It is about a king who
is murdered by his nephew who then seduces the widowed queen.
Hamlet hopes that Claudius's guilty response to the play will
confirm the tale of the Ghost. He has heard "That guilty creatures
sitting at a play / Have by the very cunning of the scene / Been
struck so to the soul that presently / They have proclaim'd their
malefactions" (2.2.563–67). From the reaction of the King to
the play, Hamlet hopes to know whether he is guilty of murder.
"[T]he play 's the thing / Wherein I'll catch the conscience of the
king" (2.2.578–79).

Hamlet wants to act. But he also wants more evidence than the
word of the Ghost—who may be the Devil tempting him to commit
an evil, malicious murder. When is the evidence sufficient when
private revenge must substitute for the rule of law? Who makes
that determination?

At the beginning of Act III, Claudius interrogates Rosencrantz
and Guildenstern without much satisfaction as to the cause of
Hamlet's apparent madness. Claudius and Polonius then conceal
themselves to eavesdrop on Hamlet and Ophelia. In response to an

offhand comment by Polonius, Claudius admits to us, the audience, that he is guilty of a great offense.

LORD POLONIUS   Ophelia, walk you here. Gracious, so please you,
We will bestow ourselves.

[To OPHELIA]

Read on this book;
That show of such an exercise may colour
Your loneliness. We are oft to blame in this,–
'Tis too much proved–that with devotion's visage
And pious action we do sugar o'er
The devil himself.

KING CLAUDIUS   *[Aside]* O, 'tis too true!
How smart a lash that speech doth give my conscience!
The harlot's cheek, beautied with plastering art,
Is not more ugly to the thing that helps it
Than is my deed to my most painted word:
O heavy burthen!

LORD POLONIUS   I hear him coming: let's withdraw, my lord.
(3.1.44–55)

Thus, we know that the Ghost is an honest spirit that is telling the truth. But Hamlet does not know this yet. Hamlet then enters and delivers the most famous speech in all of Western literature.

[Enter HAMLET]

HAMLET   To be, or not to be: that is the question:
Whether 'tis nobler in the mind to suffer
The slings and arrows of outrageous fortune,

Or to take arms against a sea of troubles,
And by opposing end them? To die: to sleep;
No more; and by a sleep to say we end
The heart-ache and the thousand natural shocks
That flesh is heir to, 'tis a consummation
Devoutly to be wish'd. To die, to sleep;
To sleep: perchance to dream: ay, there's the rub;
For in that sleep of death what dreams may come
When we have shuffled off this mortal coil,
Must give us pause: there's the respect
That makes calamity of so long life;
For who would bear the whips and scorns of time,
The oppressor's wrong, the proud man's contumely,
The pangs of despised love, the law's delay,
The insolence of office and the spurns
That patient merit of the unworthy takes,
When he himself might his quietus make
With a bare bodkin? who would fardels bear,
To grunt and sweat under a weary life,
But that the dread of something after death,
The undiscover'd country from whose bourn
No traveller returns, puzzles the will
And makes us rather bear those ills we have
Than fly to others that we know not of?
Thus conscience does make cowards of us all;
And thus the native hue of resolution
Is sicklied o'er with the pale cast of thought,
And enterprises of great pith and moment
With this regard their currents turn awry,
And lose the name of action.

(3.1.56–88)

Hamlet says that the "law's delay" is one of the things that can make a calamity of a long life.

Complaints about "justice delayed, justice denied" are not new. The royal courts at Westminster were in session for only a few months of the year. The Court of Chancery would become notorious for the delay in resolving cases, as Charles Dickens famously described in his novel *Bleak House*.

Hamlet then sees Ophelia where she walks. She has become a sacrifice, like the daughter of Jephthah. The unfortunate girl betrays her lover by following her father's instructions to return Hamlet's letters to him. Hamlet says he never loved her and delivers his brutal "Get thee to a nunnery" (3.1.121) speech. He then leaves her.

Having overheard this, Claudius says Hamlet is dangerous and he is to be sent to England. Polonius suggests more eavesdropping, this time on Hamlet and his mother, to further determine the cause of his madness. Claudius agrees: "It shall be so: / Madness in great ones must not unwatch'd go" (3.1.188–89).

In the next scene, Hamlet famously tells the players how he wants his play to be performed: "Speak the speech, I pray you, as I pronounced it to you, trippingly on the tongue" (3.2.1–3). Hamlet recruits Horatio to observe the king's reaction to the play, which is performed at court that night. When the player king is murdered by his nephew pouring poison in his ear, Claudius suddenly rises, calls for lights, and rushes off the stage. Hamlet is satisfied with this as proof of the Ghost's tale of Old Hamlet's murder.

HAMLET   O good Horatio, I'll take the ghost's word for a
    thousand pound. Didst perceive?

HORATIO   Very well, my lord.

HAMLET   Upon the talk of the poisoning?

HORATIO   I did very well note him.
                    (3.2.281–85)

After retiring, Claudius tells Rosencrantz and Guildenstern he plans to send Hamlet to England; they are to go also and take a commission for him. Claudius: "I like him not, nor stands it safe with us / To let his madness rage" (3.3.1–2). Claudius is then alone on stage and begins to speak from the heart.

KING CLAUDIUS   O, my offence is rank it smells to heaven;
It hath the primal eldest curse upon't,
A brother's murder. Pray can I not,
Though inclination be as sharp as will:
My stronger guilt defeats my strong intent;
And, like a man to double business bound,
I stand in pause where I shall first begin,
And both neglect. What if this cursed hand
Were thicker than itself with brother's blood,
Is there not rain enough in the sweet heavens
To wash it white as snow? Whereto serves mercy
But to confront the visage of offence?
And what's in prayer but this two-fold force,
To be forestalled ere we come to fall,
Or pardon'd being down? Then I'll look up;
My fault is past. But, O, what form of prayer
Can serve my turn? 'Forgive me my foul murder'?
That cannot be; since I am still possess'd
Of those effects for which I did the murder,
My crown, mine own ambition and my queen.
May one be pardon'd and retain the offence?
In the corrupted currents of this world
Offence's gilded hand may shove by justice,
And oft 'tis seen the wicked prize itself
Buys out the law: but 'tis not so above;
There is no shuffling, there the action lies
In his true nature; and we ourselves compell'd,
Even to the teeth and forehead of our faults,
To give in evidence. What then? what rests?

Try what repentance can: what can it not?
Yet what can it when one can not repent?
O wretched state! O bosom black as death!
O limed soul, that, struggling to be free,
Art more engaged! Help, angels! Make assay!
Bow, stubborn knees; and, heart with strings of steel,
Be soft as sinews of the newborn babe!
All may be well.

(3.3.36–72)

Claudius kneels as if in prayer. Hamlet enters unseen behind him. He sees that this is his opportunity to kill Claudius. But he thinks Claudius is praying and seeking forgiveness for his sins. If he kills him now, Claudius will go to heaven, whereas his father was condemned to Purgatory. Hamlet leaves without acting. Claudius rises: "My words fly up, my thoughts remain below: / Words without thoughts never to heaven go" (3.3.100–01).

This powerful, eloquent speech is often overlooked and, indeed, often omitted in contemporary performances. Claudius meditates upon corrupt earthly justice where the offender's "gilded hand may shove by justice" (3.3.58) and buy out the law. It will not be like that in the court of Divine Justice where there will be no "shuffling," no evasion. He will be compelled to confess his own guilt. He tries prayer as a form of penitence, but it does not work.

British literary critic Frank Kermode says of this speech that "the persistent but not expansive legal references testify not only to a different range of metaphorical usage but to a different, dramatic manner of representing a man thinking, under the stress of guilt and fear."[17]

Abraham Lincoln preferred Claudius's "Oh my offense is rank" speech to the "To be or not to be" soliloquy of Hamlet. It was included in one of the primers, William Scott's *Lessons in Elocution* (1811), that the teenage Lincoln read in his effort to self-educate himself

---

[17] Frank Kermode, *Shakespeare's Language* (Penguin 2001), 120.

on his father's farm on the Indiana frontier. One Lincoln scholar offers this explanation for why Lincoln may have preferred the speech of Claudius:

> Claudius's soliloquy, in contrast, has the immediacy and drama of a mind in turmoil; it is a remarkably human speech, in which a man who has killed his own brother, thereby gaining the latter's throne and wife, nevertheless both wishes for some expiation of his sin and at the same time realizes that he cannot give up what his crime has gained for him. Lincoln, whose love of Shakespeare had much to do, I believe, with the drama of men caught up in powerful emotions, found Claudius's immediate struggle with his conscience more compelling than Hamlet's generalized speculations on suicide.[18]

I often use Claudius's speech in my continuing legal education talks on professionalism to advance the argument that actions have consequences that often cannot be reversed. It is a beautiful and powerful speech for the retired trial lawyer in me to give to audiences that almost certainly have never heard it before.

After Claudius's soliloquy, Rosencrantz and Polonius tell Hamlet his mother wants to see him; he says he will go to her. In her bedroom, Polonius hides behind a curtain to spy on Gertrude's confrontation with Hamlet about his offensive behavior toward the King. But when he enters, Hamlet immediately turns the accusation of bad behavior back on his mother.

[Enter HAMLET]

HAMLET   Now, mother, what's the matter?

QUEEN GERTRUDE   Hamlet, thou hast thy father much offended.

---

[18] Michael Anderegg, *Lincoln and Shakespeare* (University Press of Kansas, 2015), 43.

HAMLET   Mother, you have my father much offended.

QUEEN GERTRUDE   Come, come, you answer with an idle
   tongue.

HAMLET   Go, go, you question with a wicked tongue.

QUEEN GERTRUDE   Why, how now, Hamlet!

HAMLET   What's the matter now?

QUEEN GERTRUDE   Have you forgot me?

HAMLET   No, by the rood, not so:
   You are the queen, your husband's brother's wife;
   And—would it were not so!—you are my mother.
                          (3.4.8–18)

As Hamlet's language becomes more violent, Gertrude loses her
composure. Thinking he might murder her, she cries out for help.
When Polonius also calls for help from behind the curtain, Hamlet
draws his sword and stabs him through the curtain thinking it is the
King. "How now! a rat? Dead, for a ducat, dead!" (3.4.24). Gertrude is
horrified at the slaughter of the old man: "O, what a rash and bloody
deed is this!" (3.4.26). But Hamlet is not deterred from confronting
her for marrying her husband's murderer: "A bloody deed! almost
as bad, good mother, / As kill a king, and marry with his brother"
(3.4.27–28).

Hamlet speaks of her betrayal of his father in such damning
vividness that she begs him to stop. The Ghost appears to Hamlet
and tells him that "this visitation / Is but to whet thy almost blunted
purpose" (3.4.107–08). In other words, Hamlet must remember
that the Ghost seeks vengeance against Claudius, not Gertrude.
Gertrude cannot see the Ghost and thinks Hamlet is mad when
he speaks to the vacant air. Hamlet urges his mother not to return

to Claudius's bed. He says goodbye and lugs the body of Polonius out of the room.

In Act IV, Scene 1, Gertrude tells Claudius Hamlet is mad and has killed Polonius. The King resolves to send Hamlet to England immediately. He sends Rosencrantz and Guildenstern to find Hamlet and Polonius's body. Because of Hamlet's popularity with the people, Claudius is reluctant to condemn Hamlet.

KING CLAUDIUS   I have sent to seek him, and to find the body.
How dangerous is it that this man goes loose!
Yet must not we put the strong law on him:
He's loved of the distracted multitude,
Who like not in their judgment, but their eyes;
And where tis so, the offender's scourge is weigh'd,
But never the offence. To bear all smooth and even,
This sudden sending him away must seem
Deliberate pause: diseases desperate grown
By desperate appliance are relieved,
Or not at all.

                        (4.3.1–11)

Hamlet is brought before the King, who demands to know where the body of Polonius is. Hamlet replies that Polonius is at supper, where he is being eaten by "a certain convocation of politic worms" (4.3.21). He then tells Claudius where Polonius's body may be found.

Hamlet leaves for England. Alone on the stage, Claudius reveals to us that he is sending secret instructions to the King of England to have Hamlet murdered.

After her father's death at the hands of Hamlet, Ophelia has gone truly mad. Laertes returns and accuses the King of complicity in Polonius's murder. The King persuades Laertes that he can prove himself blameless and promises justice will be done. "And where the offence is, let the great axe fall" (4.5.197).

In Scene 6 of Act IV, Horatio receives a letter from Hamlet saying he has returned to Denmark after having been captured by pirates on the way to England. Hamlet has also seen Claudius's secret letter commanding his death, and he has substituted the names of the messengers—Rosencrantz and Guildenstern—for his own. "I sat me down, / Devised a new commission, wrote it fair: / I once did hold it, as our statists do, / A baseness to write fair and labour'd much / How to forget that learning, but, sir, now / It did me yeoman's service" (5.2.31–36).

To write "fair" is apparently a reference to "court hand," the stylized mode of cursive handwriting used to produce legal documents and record court proceedings.

Claudius is with Laertes when letters arrive with news of Hamlet's return to Denmark. Laertes swears he will have revenge for the murder of his father: "To cut his throat i' the church" (4.7.127). Claudius responds: "No place, indeed, should murder sanctuarize; / Revenge should have no bounds" (4.7.128–29).

Claudius tells him of a plan to make Hamlet's death appear to be an accident. Laertes will challenge Hamlet to a fencing match. Unknown to Hamlet, Laertes's rapier will not be blunted, and he will kill Hamlet during the match. Laertes agrees and embellishes the plan: He'll apply poison to the point of his blade. Claudius adds that he will have a goblet of poisoned wine for Hamlet to drink. So they have a threefold plan for Hamlet's death.

Gertrude enters and adds to Laertes's woe; she says Ophelia has died by drowning, having fallen into a brook when a willow limb she was holding on to broke.

Act V opens in a churchyard with two men digging a grave—it is Ophelia's. The gravediggers discuss whether she is to receive a Christian burial. She could not be buried in consecrated ground if she committed suicide. Suicide, as a form of homicide, was a felony in early modern England. A coroner's jury would be convened to investigate the cause of any suspicious death. If the verdict was suicide (*felo de se*), the property of the deceased was forfeited to the King.

FIRST CLOWN   Is she to be buried in Christian burial that wilfully seeks her own salvation?

SECOND CLOWN   I tell thee she is: and therefore make her grave straight: the crowner [*coroner*] hath sat on her [*heard her case*], and finds it Christian burial.

FIRST CLOWN   How can that be, unless she drowned herself in her own defence?

SECOND CLOWN   Why, 'tis found so.

FIRST CLOWN   It must be 'se offendendo' [*se defendendo*]; it cannot be else. For here lies the point: if I drown myself wittingly, it argues an act: and an act hath three branches: it is, to act, to do, to perform: argal [*ergo*], she drowned herself wittingly.

SECOND CLOWN   Nay, but hear you, goodman delver,–

FIRST CLOWN   Give me leave. Here lies the water; good: here stands the man; good; if the man go to this water, and drown himself, it is, will he[*willy*], nill he [*nilly*], he goes,–mark you that; but if the water come to him and drown him, he drowns not himself: argal [*ergo*], he that is not guilty of his own death shortens not his own life.

SECOND CLOWN   But is this law?

FIRST CLOWN   Ay, marry, is't; crowner's [*coroner's*] quest [*inquest*] law.

(5.1.1–20)

The lawyers and law students in the audience would have immediately recognized this as a parody of the famous case of *Hales v. Petit* (decided almost forty years before the first performance of *Hamlet*), involving a property dispute and a claim of suicide by drowning. Lady Margaret Hales brought suit against Petit to recover a leasehold that had been forfeited to the Crown after a coroner's jury found that her husband, Sir James Hales (a Justice of the Court of Common Pleas), had committed suicide by drowning.

This raises the question of how Shakespeare would have known about *Hales v. Petit*. Certainly, he could have heard it discussed in the taverns and barrooms around the Globe. But is it more likely that the teenage Shakespeare was at least briefly enrolled in one of the Inns of Court and heard the case discussed in a reading?

Hamlet and Horatio enter at a distance and listen to the grave-diggers' banter. The first gravedigger throws out a skull. Hamlet and Horatio speculate whether it might be the "pate of a politician" (5.1.74) or a lord. A second skull is thrown up out of the grave.

HAMLET There's another: why may not that be the skull of a
 lawyer? Where be his quiddities now, his quillets,
 his cases, his tenures, and his tricks? why does he
 suffer this rude knave now to knock him about the
 sconce with a dirty shovel, and will not tell him of
 his action of battery? Hum! This fellow might be
 in's time a great buyer of land, with his statutes,
 his recognizances, his fines, his double vouchers,
 his recoveries: is this the fine of his fines, and
 the recovery of his recoveries, to have his fine
 pate full of fine dirt? will his vouchers vouch him
 no more of his purchases, and double ones too, than
 the length and breadth of a pair of indentures? The
 very conveyances of his lands will hardly lie in
 this box; and must the inheritor himself have no more, ha?
 (5.1.91–109)

"Quiddities and quillets" refer to subtle distinctions in a lawyer's argument. We might refer to them as quips or quibbles. "Tenures" refers to different types of interest in real property, such as fee simple or a life estate. At common law, an action for battery could be maintained for striking or unlawfully touching another person. The writ would allege that the defendant did "assault, beat and wound with force and arms namely with swords and staves" threatening the life of the plaintiff. Of course, a dead person cannot bring an action for battery because a gravedigger strikes his skull with a shovel. Hamlet is saying that even the judgment of the courts will not protect against human mortality.

"Statutes" were a form of written evidence of indebtedness containing strong protections for the creditor, entered into before special registries in certain towns. They declined in popularity during Shakespeare's time as bonds became more useful. "Fines and recoveries" were means of conveying land outside of the law of primogeniture or avoiding feudal duties upon the inheritance of land. "Fines" were settlements of fictitious disputes over the title to land. "Recoveries" were sham lawsuits brought to convey title to land.

"Recognizances" were bonds acknowledging a debt. A "voucher" was a warranty of title to land used in a collusive lawsuit to cut off the rights of heirs to land held entail. A minor court official would be paid to issue the warranty of title in himself. The purchaser would sue him under a fictious title to the land. The vouching party would allow the lawsuit to go into default and the court would award title to the land to the purchaser. This would cut off the rights of the seller's heirs. A double voucher would provide even more protection against the claims of the seller's heirs.

"Indentures" could refer to any number of legal documents. The term was often used to refer to a written agreement that would be torn or cut in half with one half going to each party. If the two parts matched, that would be a guarantee of authenticity.

The larger point is that the lawyer's remains are now in a small bit of dirt. This passage again shows Shakespeare's easy familiarity with the language of the law. In the celebrated BBC production of *Hamlet* starring Derek Jacobi, Claire Booth, and Patrick Stewart, this entire speech is omitted. Apparently, the BBC expected fewer lawyers in the audience than did Shakespeare.

After Hamlet's "Alas poor Yorick" (5.1.171) speech, Ophelia's funeral procession (including a priest) appears on stage. When Laertes protests that Ophelia should receive more ceremony, the priest responds: "No more be done! / We should profane the service of the dead / To sing a requiem and such rest to her / As to peace-parted souls" (5.1.222–25). Gertrude tosses flowers on the grave and makes another of her pithy comments: "Sweets to the sweet: farewell!" (5.1.229). Hamlet appears and he and Laertes fight in Ophelia's grave. Gertrude sensibly proclaims: "This is mere madness." (5.1.270). Gertrude and Claudius tell Laertes that Hamlet is mad. Hamlet leaves with Horatio, and Claudius tells Gertrude to put a watch over her son.

In the final scene of the play, the King's messenger summons Hamlet to the fencing match with Laertes. Hamlet is reluctant to engage in such "foolery" (5.2.201) but insists upon accepting the challenge.

HORATIO   If your mind dislike any thing, obey it: I will
    forestall their repair hither, and say you are not
    fit.

HAMLET   Not a whit, we defy augury: there's a special
    providence in the fall of a sparrow. If it be now,
    'tis not to come; if it be not to come, it will be
    now; if it be not now, yet it will come: the
    readiness is all: since no man has aught of what he
    leaves, what is't to leave betimes?
                        (5.2.203–10)

This stoic philosophy marks a maturity in the hero that was not present at the beginning of the play. Hamlet reminds Horatio of all the evil the King has done to him.

HAMLET   Does it not, think'st thee, stand me now upon—
    He that hath kill'd my king and whored my mother,

Popp'd in between the election and my hopes,
Thrown out his angle for my proper life,
And with such cozenage–is't not perfect conscience,
To quit him with this arm?

(5.2.63–68)

So Hamlet admits after all that he was ambitious for the Crown.

In all but name, the fencing match is a trial by battle with Laertes accusing Hamlet of the murder of Polonius. By staging it as a fencing match, Shakespeare has more flexibility of action than if it were a single fight to the death with lethal weapons. When the court assembles for the match, Hamlet first makes his apologies to Laertes.

HAMLET   Give me your pardon, sir: I've done you wrong;
    But pardon't, as you are a gentleman.
    This presence knows,
    And you must needs have heard, how I am punish'd
    With sore distraction. What I have done,
    That might your nature, honour and exception
    Roughly awake, I here proclaim was madness.
    Was't Hamlet wrong'd Laertes? Never Hamlet:
    If Hamlet from himself be ta'en away,
    And when he's not himself does wrong Laertes,
    Then Hamlet does it not, Hamlet denies it.
    Who does it, then? His madness: if't be so,
    Hamlet is of the faction that is wrong'd;
    His madness is poor Hamlet's enemy.
    Sir, in this audience,
    Let my disclaiming from a purposed evil
    Free me so far in your most generous thoughts,
    That I have shot mine arrow o'er the house,
    And hurt my brother.

(5.2.211–229)

This is a classic plea of not guilty by reason of insanity.

During the match, Laertes stabs Hamlet with the poisoned foil. In the melee, they switch swords. Hamlet then stabs Laertes with the poisoned sword. Gertrude drinks from the poisoned wine goblet. She collapses and cries out, "The drink, the drink! I am poison'd" (5.2.296).

The dying Laertes confesses that it was the King's plan to murder Hamlet with the poisoned foil and wine. Hamlet stabs the King and forces him to drink the poisoned wine.

HAMLET Here, thou incestuous, murderous, damned Dane,
  Drink off this potion. Is thy union here?
  Follow my mother.

[KING CLAUDIUS dies.]

LAERTES He is justly served;
  It is a poison temper'd by himself.
                    (5.2.310–14)

Laertes asks Hamlet for forgiveness and dies. As he dies, Hamlet begs Horatio to live and tell his story.

HAMLET Heaven make thee free of it! I follow thee.
  I am dead, Horatio. Wretched queen, adieu!
  You that look pale and tremble at this chance,
  That are but mutes or audience to this act,
  Had I but time–as this fell sergeant, death,
  Is strict in his arrest–O, I could tell you–
  But let it be. Horatio, I am dead;
  Thou livest; report me and my cause aright
  To the unsatisfied.

HORATIO Never believe it:
  I am more an antique Roman than a Dane:
  Here's yet some liquor left.

HAMLET   As thou'rt a man,
　　Give me the cup: let go; by heaven, I'll have't.
　　O good Horatio, what a wounded name,
　　Things standing thus unknown, shall live behind me!
　　If thou didst ever hold me in thy heart
　　Absent thee from felicity awhile,
　　And in this harsh world draw thy breath in pain,
　　To tell my story.
(5.2.318–34)

To the dead Prince, Horatio speaks the immortal lines: "Now cracks a noble heart. Good night sweet prince: / And flights of angels sing thee to thy rest!" (5.2.344–45).

There had never been anything like *Hamlet* before. As Frank Kermode has written, "the whole idea of dramatic character is changed forever by this play."[19]

---

[19] Kermode, *Shakespeare's Language*, 125.

CHAPTER 15

ALL'S WELL THAT ENDS WELL

Although classified as a comedy, most of *All's Well That Ends Well* has a dark mood, much like *Troilus and Cressida*. Fittingly, it opens with everyone dressed in black. Bertram, the Count of Rousillon (a region of France on the coast of the Mediterranean Sea just north of the Pyrenees), and his mother, the Countess, are in mourning for the death of Bertram's father. With them is Helena, a "virtuous" young gentlewoman who is the ward of the Countess, and Lord Lafeu, an old French nobleman and friend to the Countess.

Bertram says he must leave Rousillon to attend the King of France "to whom I am now in ward, evermore in subjection" (*All's Well That Ends Well*, 1.1.4).

A ward is someone under the guardianship of another. In England, the heirs of large fortunes were wards of the king. This was a holdover from the feudal system where, at least in theory, the king held the ultimate title to all property. Bertram's father had been a soldier for the King of France. His wardship is an incident of military service due to the King by the Count of Rousillon.

In general, the holder of a wardship was entitled to the custody of the person and lands of the ward until he or she reached the age of majority: twenty-one for males and sixteen for unmarried females. The holder of the wardship was also able to direct the marriage of his ward. Although the ward could refuse an arranged marriage, the holder of the wardship could impose a heavy fine for disobedience.

Shakespeare's patron, the Earl of Southampton, was the ward of Queen Elizabeth's Secretary of State, Lord Burghley, who wanted Southampton to marry his granddaughter. When Southampton refused, he had to pay a ruinous fine when he came of age.

Lord Lafeu says the King is sick and has abandoned his physicians. The Countess comments that were Helena's deceased father, Gerard de Narbon, a famous physician, still alive, he could have cured the King. The Countess praises Helena for her many virtues, including her honesty, goodness, and love of her late father.

Before he leaves for Paris, Bertram asks his mother for a blessing. She says, "Be thou blest, Bertram, and succeed thy father / In manners, as in shape!" (1.1.56–57).

Alone on the stage, Helena confesses to us that she is in love with Bertram. As a doctor's daughter, she knows she can never be the young Count's wife because "he is so above me" (1.1.84).

Bertram's companion Parolles enters. Helena knows him to be "a notorious liar" (1.1.97), a great fool, and a coward. Under the common law, "parol" (a Law French term for speech) evidence was oral testimony about the terms or meaning of a contract. Parol evidence was generally inadmissible to alter the terms of a written contract. Parrolles is aptly named because although he pretends to be a fierce warrior, he is all talk.

Helena and Parrolles have an amusing dialogue on the virtue of female virginity. Parolles is of the view that "There's little can be said in 't; 'tis against the rule of nature" (1.1.131–32). In this sentiment, he joins that other disreputable moral philosopher, Pompey Bum in *Measure for Measure*, in declaring that sexual desire is a natural human trait.

Shakespeare was on pretty safe ground here, because the Reformation had overturned the medieval Catholic Church's exaltation of virginity and celibacy.

In Paris at the King's palace, Bertram is welcomed as the son of his father, whom the King remembers as a valiant soldier and trusted friend. Significantly, the King remembers how honorably Bertram's father had behaved to those below him in rank.

Back in Rousillon, the Countess's steward tells her Helena is in love with Bertram. The Countess confronts Helena, who confesses as much.

COUNTESS Do you love my son?

HELENA Your pardon, noble mistress!

COUNTESS Love you my son?

HELENA Do not you love him, madam?

COUNTESS Go not about; my love hath in't a bond,
Whereof the world takes note: come, come, disclose
The state of your affection; for your passions
Have to the full appeach'd.

HELENA Then, I confess,
Here on my knee, before high heaven and you,
That before you, and next unto high heaven,
I love your son.

(1.3.183–94)

The Countess is not offended by her confession. Helena explains her plan to go to Paris with some "prescriptions" left to her by her father that she will offer to the King to heal his illness. The Countess blesses this scheme. Up to this point, it seems that Helena is another of Shakespeare's admirable female characters.

In Paris, the Lords are preparing to leave for the war between Florence and Siena in Italy. Bertram is ordered to stay in Paris: "I am commanded here, and kept a coil with / 'Too young' and 'the next year' and ''tis too early' " (2.1.30–31).

The King is told that a young woman has arrived with a medicine that can cure his illness. Helena introduces herself as the daughter of the famous Gerard de Narbon. She promises the King that he will be cured in twenty-four hours if he accepts her treatment. He agrees: "Sweet practiser, thy physic I will try, / That ministers thine own death if I die" (2.1.196–97). Helena asks for a favor in return if she succeeds: "Then shalt thou give me with thy kingly hand / What husband in thy power I will command" (2.1.205–06). The King agrees. Miraculously, Helena cures the King of his deadly malady.

The King offers to fulfill his side of the bargain. Of all the lords of France, Helena takes Bertram. The King approves: "Why, then, young Bertram, take her; she's thy wife" (2.3.109). But the snobbish Bertram will not have her.

KING   Know'st thou not, Bertram,
What she has done for me?

BERTRAM   Yes, my good lord;
But never hope to know why I should marry her.

KING   Thou know'st she has raised me from my sickly bed.

BERTRAM   But follows it, my lord, to bring me down
Must answer for your raising? I know her well:
She had her breeding at my father's charge.
A poor physician's daughter my wife! Disdain
Rather corrupt me ever!
(2.3.113–22)

In England at the time, a physician was considered of the "middling" class—far below that of a count. In Magna Carta, a lord was prohibited from "disparaging" a ward by forcing him to marry a person of lower class.

The King's response to this snobbish rejection of Helena is remarkable for its egalitarianism. "She is young, wise, fair; / In these to nature she's immediate heir, / And these breed honour" (2.3.137–39). The King vows to raise Helena to a station worthy to be the wife of a count: "If thou canst like this creature as a maid, /

I can create the rest: virtue and she / Is her own dower; honour and wealth from me" (2.3.148–50).

The haughty Bertram replies scornfully:

BERTRAM   I cannot love her, nor will strive to do't.

KING   Thou wrong'st thyself, if thou shouldst strive to choose.

HELENA   That you are well restored, my lord, I'm glad:
    Let the rest go.

KING   My honour's at the stake; which to defeat,
    I must produce my power. Here, take her hand,
    Proud scornful boy, unworthy this good gift;
    That dost in vile misprision shackle up
    My love and her desert.

(2.3.151–59)

The word "misprision" is most often used in the sense of concealment of a crime. Here, Shakespeare seems to be using it in the general sense of committing an offense. Helena responds with becoming humility: "That you are well restored, my lord, I'm glad: Let the rest go" (2.3.153–54). But the King insists he will have his way and act with revenge and hate upon the disobedient young man: "Loosing upon thee, in the name of justice, / Without all terms of pity" (2.3.171–72). Under this extreme pressure Bertram relents.

BERTRAM   I take her hand.

KING   Good fortune and the favour of the king
    Smile upon this contract; whose ceremony
    Shall seem expedient on the now-born brief,
    And be perform'd to-night: the solemn feast
    Shall more attend upon the coming space,
    Expecting absent friends.

(2.3.184–90)

As usual in Shakespeare's plays, the marriage ceremony is performed offstage. But Bertram comes onstage and vows he will not consummate the marriage.

BERTRAM   Although before the solemn priest I have sworn,
I will not bed her.

PAROLLES   What, what, sweet-heart?

BERTRAM   O my Parolles, they have married me!
I'll to the Tuscan wars, and never bed her.
(2.3.271–75)

Bertram says he will send Helena to his house and acquaint his mother of his "hate" (2.3.289). He will flee immediately to the war, away from the King's wrath. Helena tells Bertram she will comply: "Sir, I can nothing say, / But that I am your most obedient servant" (2.5.70–71). The lout refuses even to kiss her when she leaves.

HELENA   Pray, sir, your pardon.

BERTRAM   Well, what would you say?

HELENA   I am not worthy of the wealth I owe,
Nor dare I say 'tis mine, and yet it is;
But, like a timorous thief, most fain would steal
What law does vouch mine own.

BERTRAM   What would you have?

HELENA   Something; and scarce so much: nothing, indeed.
I would not tell you what I would, my lord:
Faith yes;
Strangers and foes do sunder, and not kiss.

BERTRAM   I pray you, stay not, but in haste to horse.
(2.5.79–90)

A thief cannot steal her own property. This is modest Helena's way of saying she has the right to be treated by Bertram as his wife. Bertram sends her a letter. It says: "When thou canst get the ring upon my finger which never shall come off and show me a child begotten of thy body that I am father to, then call me husband: but in such a 'then' I write a 'never' " (3.2.55–58). These seem impossible conditions for Helena to satisfy. Once again, a Shakespearean heroine has fallen in love not only with someone beneath her in admirable qualities, but with a loutish knave.

In Italy, the Duke of Florence laments that the King of France will not join him in the war against Austria, even as the young men of France rush to fight on the side of Florence. In Rousillon, the Countess receives her son's letter declaring that he has run away and will not accept Helena as his wife. She is dismayed: "This is not well, rash and unbridled boy. / To fly the favours of so good a king; / To pluck his indignation on thy head / By the misprising of a maid too virtuous / For the contempt of empire" (3.2.25–30).

The Countess vows that Helena deserves twenty men such as her unworthy son, thus showing herself to be far above her snobbish offspring. But Helena believes she has sent Bertram to be killed in the war, and she must flee Rousillon so that he can return home.

The Duke of Florence has appointed Bertram as his "general of our horse" (3.3.1). In Rousillon, the Countess receives a letter from Helena urging her to write to her son to return home now that Helena is far away. The Countess thinks Helena has shown her worth for sacrificing herself for Bertram. She asks: "What angel shall / Bless this unworthy husband?" (3.4.28–29).

In Florence, Bertram has shown himself to be a better soldier than a husband. Helena arrives in Florence disguised as a pilgrim. The cad Bertram has been unsuccessfully employing Parrolles to seduce Diana, a Florentine maiden.

Helena and Diana's mother come up with a scheme to trick Bertram into bedding Helena (the bed trick from *Measure for Measure*) thinking she is Diana. Helena will prove she is the one who slept with Bertram by getting his ring. The old Widow of Florence, her daughter Diana, and Helena agree to carry out the plan that night.

At this point we begin to wonder about Helena. How far is she willing to go to get the lout Bertram to acknowledge her as his wife?

HELENA   Why then to-night
Let us assay our plot; which, if it speed,
Is wicked meaning in a lawful deed
And lawful meaning in a lawful act,
Where both not sin, and yet a sinful fact:
But let's about it.

(3.7.50–54)

Ordinarily, the commission of a crime requires an unlawful intent to commit an unlawful act. Although Bertram's intent is to seduce Diana, it is neither immoral nor illegal for him to have sexual intercourse with Helena, who is his lawful wife.

Bertram tells Diana his marriage was coerced and swears that he loves her. She is skeptical: "'Tis not the many oaths that makes the truth, / But the plain single vow that is vow'd true" (4.2.27–28). Diana demands to have Bertram's ancestral ring and tells him to come to her chamber at midnight. He may stay for only one hour and will not be allowed to speak to her. When she has submitted to him, she will give him a ring. Meanwhile, a story spreads in the French camp that Bertram's wife has died of grief.

After his midnight assignation with Helena (thinking that she is Diana), Bertram returns to France with a letter to the King from the Duke of Florence. The King himself goes to Rousillon and laments to the Countess the death of Helena. The King has heard good things about Bertram from Florence: "I have letters sent me /

That set him high in fame" (5.3.35–36). Bertram is summoned to the presence of the King and begs his pardon: "My high-repented blames, / Dear sovereign, pardon to me" (5.3.43–44).

The King consents to Bertram's marriage to the daughter of Lord Lafeu. But when Bertram gives her a ring, the Countess recognizes it as Helena's. The King also recognizes it, because he gifted it to her for healing him. Bertram vehemently denies that he got the ring from Helena.

Believing Bertram has killed Helena and taken the ring, the King has him arrested. As Bertram is taken away by the guards, a letter arrives for the King from one who is coming to Rousillon: Diana from Florence.

KING   [*Reads*] Upon his many protestations to marry me
    when his wife was dead, I blush to say it, he won
    me. Now is the Count Rousillon a widower: his vows
    are forfeited to me, and my honour's paid to him. He
    stole from Florence, taking no leave, and I follow
    him to his country for justice: grant it me, O
    king! in you it best lies; otherwise a seducer
    flourishes, and a poor maid is undone.

                                   Diana Capilet.

LAFEU   I will buy me a son-in-law in a fair, and toll for
    this: I'll none of him.

KING   The heavens have thought well on thee Lafeu,
    To bring forth this discovery.
                (5.3.158–70)

Bertram is again summoned before the King. The play then becomes the proceedings of a "bawdy court," as the church courts that tried offenses against morality such as fornication and adultery were known. Diana and the Widow appear. Diana claims to be Bertram's wife. As proof, she produces Bertram's ring, which the

Countess recognizes. The King is outraged that Bertram has the ring the King gave to Helena.

KING   This ring was mine; I gave it his first wife.

DIANA   It might be yours or hers, for aught I know.

KING   Take her away; I do not like her now;
To prison with her: and away with him.
Unless thou tell'st me where thou hadst this ring,
Thou diest within this hour.

DIANA   I'll never tell you.

KING   Take her away.

DIANA   I'll put in bail, my liege.
                    (5.3.312–20)

She summons Helena as her "bail." The King is amazed and asks if this is really Helena or a work of sorcery.

KING   Is there no exorcist
Beguiles the truer office of mine eyes?
Is't real that I see?

HELENA   No, my good lord;
'Tis but the shadow of a wife you see,
The name and not the thing.

BERTRAM   Both, both. O, pardon!

HELENA   O my good lord, when I was like this maid,
I found you wondrous kind. There is your ring;
And, look you, here's your letter; this it says:

'When from my finger you can get this ring
And are by me with child,' &c. This is done:
Will you be mine, now you are doubly won?

BERTRAM   If she, my liege, can make me know this clearly,
I'll love her dearly, ever, ever dearly.

HELENA   If it appear not plain and prove untrue,
Deadly divorce step between me and you!
                    (5.3.340–56)

The common law did not recognize an action for divorce; it was
exclusively a matter for the ecclesiastical courts. In the ordinary
case, marriage ended only with the death of a spouse. Bertram has
agreed to accept Helena as his wife. And so, all's well that ends well.
At least, so it appears.

In the end, Bertram redeems himself by declaring that he will
love Helena. She joins Portia, Rosalind, Juliet, and Beatrice in
seeming more deserving of our admiration than her lover.

CHAPTER 16

Measure for Measure

Measure for Measure is Shakespeare's second (after *The Merchant of Venice*) great legalistic play. The title is taken from the Gospel of Matthew. It is a play about judging, morality, and the law. In it, Shakespeare confronts the tension between strict enforcement of the law and the need to achieve justice. Because the play is set in Vienna, Shakespeare is free to create an imaginary legal system and imaginary laws and punishments.

The Duke or his delegate is the chief magistrate, at least for capital offenses. The play begins with Duke Vincentio telling his deputies, Angelo and Escalus, he is leaving them in charge during an absence from the city. Angelo is to be the senior of the two, although it appears that Escalus has more experience in the administration of justice. The Duke addresses Escalus thus: "For common justice, you're as pregnant in / As art and practise hath enriched any / That we remember. There is our commission, / From which we would not have you warp" (*Measure for Measure*, 1.1.11–14).

Lord Angelo is a younger man but one with a stellar reputation. Is this why the Duke gives all his power to Angelo? Endorsement of the Duke's choice by Escalus should be reassuring. Angelo enters and the Duke tells him:

DUKE VINCENTIO   Angelo,
> There is a kind of character in thy life,
> That to the observer doth thy history
> Fully unfold. Thyself and thy belongings
> Are not thine own so proper as to waste
> Thyself upon thy virtues, they on thee. . . .
> Hold therefore, Angelo:–
> In our remove be thou at full ourself;
> Mortality and mercy in Vienna
> Live in thy tongue and heart: old Escalus,
> Though first in question, is thy secondary.
> Take thy commission.
>
> (1.1.1.27–31, 43–47)

Therefore, the full power of the Duke is invested in Angelo because of "thy virtues." Notably, he is given both the power to condemn and to show mercy. What effect will this unlimited power have upon Angelo? We are left to ask if it had not been better to reverse the roles and make the older and wiser Escalus the senior and Angelo the junior deputy in charge. It might have been a better decision. But that would have made for a dull play.

In the next scene, we learn that with the Duke absent, justice under Angelo has taken a turn toward extreme severity. Mistress Overdone (the madame of a brothel) tells the foppish Lucio that young Claudio has been arrested and is to be executed in three days for getting Juliet "with child" (1.2.74).

In Shakespeare's day fornication was not a crime that could be prosecuted in the English royal courts. It was a moral offense that could be punished in the parish church courts (the "bawdy" courts). However, the most severe punishment that could be inflicted in the church courts was excommunication. This led to some Puritan agitation to make fornication a capital felony. The effort failed until the establishment of the Commonwealth after Shakespeare's death. Shakespeare's audience would have appreciated the folly of imposing draconian punishments for offenses against morality.

Mistress Overdone's tapster Pompey enters and asks if she has heard the proclamation that all the brothels in the suburbs are to be torn down on Angelo's orders.

MISTRESS OVERDONE   What proclamation, man?

POMPEY   All houses in the suburbs of Vienna must be plucked down.

MISTRESS OVERDONE   And what shall become of those in the city?

POMPEY   They shall stand for seed: they had gone down too, but that a wise burgher put in for them.

MISTRESS OVERDONE   But shall all our houses of resort in the suburbs be pulled down?

POMPEY   To the ground, mistress.

MISTRESS OVERDONE   Why, here's a change indeed in the commonwealth! What shall become of me?

POMPEY   Come; fear you not: good counsellors lack no clients: though you change your place, you need not change your trade; I'll be your tapster still. Courage! there will be pity taken on you: you that have worn your eyes almost out in the service, you will be considered.

(1.2.98–112)

Pompey is telling Mistress Overdone she will always have plenty of clients for her brothels. "[G]ood counsellors lack no clients" is a wonderful example of Shakespeare's use of the law as a metaphor for life. In Shakespeare's time, the main playhouses—and many brothels—were located in the London suburbs on the south bank of the Thames where they could escape the restraint of the Puritans in control of London's city government. Vice flourished on the south bank. Thus, it seems that a policy of Puritanism (although the word is never used in the play) has come to rule in Vienna. Is this what Duke Vincentio intended?

The libertine Lucio sees his friend Claudio led through the street under arrest. Lucio: "Why, how now, Claudio! whence comes this restraint?" (1.2.116). Claudio responds: "From too much liberty, my Lucio, liberty: / As surfeit is the father of much fast, / So every scope by the immoderate use / Turns to restraint" (1.2.117–20).

When asked if he has committed murder, Claudio denies it. We learn from Claudio himself that his only offense has been to have sex with Juliet before they were legally married: "Thus stands it with me: upon a true contract / I got possession of Juliet's bed: / You know the lady; she is fast my wife" (1.2.136–38). Claudio seems to be saying they had a contract to marry in the future, although he also says Juliet is his wife. Juliet had not obtained her dowry. However, under English law, there was no legal requirement that the bride's family or friends provide her with a dowry to have a valid marriage. So lack of a dowry would not have prevented Claudio and Juliet from marrying. Also, a contract to marry was considered by some to authorize conjugal relations.

Shakespeare himself had hurriedly married Anne Hathaway after getting her pregnant. Nonetheless, in Shakespeare's imaginary Vienna, there was a law against fornication, one that had not been enforced under the Duke. Claudio and Juliet are both unmarried. There is no question about the sex being nonconsensual or Juliet being underage. Thus, the crime is purely one of an offense against the morality of the time.

Claudio has tried to appeal to the Duke, but he cannot be found. As Claudio is led away to prison, he begs Lucio to have his sister appeal for mercy on his behalf to Angelo. Lucio promises to do so.

In the next scene, we learn that the Duke has not gone abroad. He is at a nearby monastery where he explains to Friar Thomas why he has put Angelo in charge of Vienna in his temporary absence.

DUKE VINCENTIO   We have strict statutes and most biting laws.
   The needful bits and curbs to headstrong steeds,
   Which for this nineteen years we have let slip;
   Even like an o'ergrown lion in a cave,
   That goes not out to prey. Now, as fond fathers,
   Having bound up the threatening twigs of birch,
   Only to stick it in their children's sight
   For terror, not to use, in time the rod
   Becomes more mock'd than fear'd; so our decrees,
   Dead to infliction, to themselves are dead;
   And liberty plucks justice by the nose;
   The baby beats the nurse, and quite athwart
   Goes all decorum.

(1.3.19–31)

The Duke is saying that the deterrence function of the law was not working because the laws were not being enforced. Order (what Ulysses in *Troilus and Cressida* called "degree") has become disorder. In theory, when the law is enforced with sufficient regularity the punishment inflicted upon wrongdoers will deter others from committing the same offense. This modern, essentially utilitarian idea is to be contrasted to the idea of punishment as retribution ("An eye for an eye") for injury to another.

Friar Thomas points out to the Duke that it was in his power to undo this excessive lenity.

FRIAR THOMAS   It rested in your grace
   To unloose this tied-up justice when you pleased:
   And it in you more dreadful would have seem'd
   Than in Lord Angelo.

DUKE VINCENTIO   I do fear, too dreadful:

Sith 'twas my fault to give the people scope,
'Twould be my tyranny to strike and gall them
For what I bid them do: for we bid this be done,
When evil deeds have their permissive pass
And not the punishment. Therefore indeed, my father,
I have on Angelo imposed the office;
Who may, in the ambush of my name, strike home,
And yet my nature never in the fight
To do in slander.
(1.3.29–43)

For nineteen years, the Duke has neglected to enforce Vienna's strict laws, and disorder is now rampant ("liberty plucks justice by the nose"). But the Duke does not want to be the one to do the actual hard work of administering harsh laws. He leaves that to Angelo. The Duke will assume a disguise that will allow him to hang around and see how things work out.

DUKE VINCENTIO   And to behold his sway,
I will, as 'twere a brother of your order,
Visit both prince and people: therefore, I prithee,
Supply me with the habit and instruct me
How I may formally in person bear me
Like a true friar. More reasons for this action
At our more leisure shall I render you;
Only, this one: Lord Angelo is precise;
Stands at a guard with envy; scarce confesses
That his blood flows, or that his appetite
Is more to bread than stone: hence shall we see,
If power change purpose, what our seemers be.
(1.3.44–54)

The Duke will sneak around in a friar's garb to see if Angelo is as pure and morally upright as he appears.

I am starting to think the Duke is a bad ruler. In his portrait of the Duke, Shakespeare shows us an over-lenient magistrate who values popularity over fidelity to the law. At the other extreme, we already know that Angelo, as the supreme judge in the absence of the Duke, is not exercising the traits of humanity and mercy that were to be in his "tongue and heart."

Claudio's sister, Isabella, seeks to withdraw from the pervasive immorality and vice of Viennese life. She is about to take a vow of chastity and enter into holy orders at a convent. She seeks "a more strict restraint" (1.4.4) than the existing rules of the order of St. Clare, the order of nuns in Isabella's convent.

This is straight out of the Gospel of Matthew. "For I say unto you, except your righteousness shall exceed the righteousness of the scribes and Pharisees, ye shall in no case enter into the kingdom of heaven."[20] An alternative explanation, that she is entering the convent because she has no dowry, seems improbable to me.

The "jester" Lucio tells her of her brother's imprisonment under orders of Lord Angelo for getting Juliet pregnant. Isabella's response is direct and immediate: "O, let him marry her" (1.4.52). Lucio explains that Angelo wants to make an example of Claudio by condemning him to death.

LUCIO   Governs Lord Angelo; a man whose blood
        Is very snow-broth; one who never feels
        The wanton stings and motions of the sense,
        But doth rebate and blunt his natural edge
        With profits of the mind, study and fast.
        He–to give fear to use and liberty,
        Which have for long run by the hideous law,
        As mice by lions–hath pick'd out an act,
        Under whose heavy sense your brother's life
        Falls into forfeit: he arrests him on it;
        And follows close the rigour of the statute,

---

[20] Matthew 5:20 (Authorized Version).

To make him an example. All hope is gone,
Unless you have the grace by your fair prayer
To soften Angelo: and that's my pith of business
'Twixt you and your poor brother.

ISABELLA   Doth he so seek his life?

LUCIO   Has censured him
Already; and, as I hear, the provost hath
A warrant for his execution.

(1.4.57–75)

Isabella agrees to plead her brother's cause to Angelo. Before
she arrives, we hear Escalus urge Angelo to have mercy on young
Claudio. Confessing no weakness in himself, Angelo is determined
to enforce the law in all of its rigor.

ANGELO   We must not make a scarecrow of the law,
Setting it up to fear the birds of prey,
And let it keep one shape, till custom make it
Their perch and not their terror.

ESCALUS   Ay, but yet
Let us be keen, and rather cut a little,
Than fall, and bruise to death. Alas, this gentleman
Whom I would save, had a most noble father!
Let but your honour know,
Whom I believe to be most strait in virtue,
That, in the working of your own affections,
Had time cohered with place or place with wishing,
Or that the resolute acting of your blood
Could have attain'd the effect of your own purpose,
Whether you had not sometime in your life
Err'd in this point which now you censure him,
And pull'd the law upon you.

ANGELO 'Tis one thing to be tempted, Escalus,
Another thing to fall. I not deny,
The jury, passing on the prisoner's life,
May in the sworn twelve have a thief or two
Guiltier than him they try. What's open made to justice,
That justice seizes: what know the laws
That thieves do pass on thieves? 'Tis very pregnant,
The jewel that we find, we stoop and take't
Because we see it; but what we do not see
We tread upon, and never think of it.
You may not so extenuate his offence
For I have had such faults; but rather tell me,
When I, that censure him, do so offend,
Let mine own judgment pattern out my death,
And nothing come in partial. Sir, he must die.

(2.1.1–31)

Angelo is making the cogent argument that faults in the character of the judge are irrelevant if the judgment is right and just under the law. But in early modern Vienna, under the Civil Law there would have been no juries. All judgments in the play are rendered by the Duke or by Angelo and Escalus acting as his deputies.

Trial by jury, however, would have been well-known to English theatergoers of the day, and the reference would not have been startling. Escalus is making the same argument made by Bassanio in *The Merchant of Venice*: "And I beseech you, / Wrest once the law to your authority: / To do a great right, do a little wrong, / And curb this cruel devil of his will" (*The Merchant of Venice*, 4.1.214–17).

This tension between the rule of law and justice was a continuing concern for Shakespeare. Angelo's view of the law is that it must be fixed and unbending. To do otherwise is to make a "scarecrow" of the law. Escalus urges a more nuanced approach to the law and judging that is grounded in the Golden Rule of doing unto others as you would have them do unto you. Escalus says, "Well, heaven forgive him, and forgive us all!" (2.1.37). Angelo turns this upside down and says he would sentence himself to die if he yielded to temptations of the flesh. Angelo refuses to acknowledge his own mortality and humanity. This will make it all the harder for him to resist temptation when it comes along. This is in contrast to the Duke, who "above all other strifes contended especially to know himself" (3.2.209–10).

At this moment, a befuddled constable, Elbow, enters the court to accuse Pompey Bum, Mistress Overdone's clown and servant, of running a brothel. Like Dogberry in *Much Ado About Nothing*, Elbow is a master of malapropism.

ELBOW   Come, bring them away [*forward*]: if these be good [*bad*] people in a commonweal that do nothing but use [*permit*] their abuses in common [*bawdy*] houses, I know no law: bring them away [*forward*].

ANGELO   How now, sir! What's your name? and what's the matter?

ELBOW   If it Please your honour, I am the poor duke's constable, and my name is Elbow: I do lean upon [*uphold*] justice, sir, and do bring in here before your good honour two notorious benefactors [*malefactors*].

ANGELO   Benefactors? Well; what benefactors are they? are they not malefactors?

ELBOW   If it? please your honour, I know not well what they are: but precise [*loose*] villains they are, that I am sure of; and void of all profanation [*reverence*] in the world that good Christians ought to have.

ESCALUS   This comes off well; here's a wise officer.

ANGELO   Go to: what quality are they of? Elbow is your name? why dost thou not speak, Elbow?

POMPEY   He cannot, sir; he's out at elbow.

ANGELO   What are you, sir?

ELBOW   He, sir! a tapster, sir; parcel [*pander*]-bawd; one that
serves a bad woman; whose house, sir, was, as they
say, plucked down in the suburbs; and now she
professes a hot [*whore*]-house, which, I think, is a very ill house too.

ESCALUS   How know you that?

ELBOW   My wife, sir, whom I detest [*protest*] before heaven and
your honour,–

ESCALUS   How? thy wife?

ELBOW   Ay, sir; whom, I thank heaven, is an honest woman,–

ESCALUS   Dost thou detest her therefore?

ELBOW   I say, sir, I will detest [*protest*] myself also, as well as
she, that this house, if it be not a bawd's house,
it is pity of her life, for it is a naughty house.

ESCALUS   How dost thou know that, constable?

ELBOW   Marry, sir, by my wife; who, if she had been a woman
Cardinally [*carnally*] given, might have been accused in
fornication, adultery, and all uncleanliness there.

(2.1.41–78)

It seems that Elbow's pregnant wife mistakenly entered the brothel
in search of prunes and was mistaken for a prostitute. Pompey denies
the charge and proceeds with an elaborate and tedious argument in
which he constantly strays off the main point.

This is a parody of the Marian commitment procedure adopted in the mid-sixteenth century. As in *Much Ado About Nothing*, it is the bumbling constable—the sixteenth century Barney Fife—who provides the comic element. Every trial judge recognizes the type: the petty law enforcement officer who tries to impress everyone with his stilted legal jargon and small knowledge of the law.

Finally, Angelo—showing extreme impatience as a judge—can stand it no more.

ANGELO   This will last out a night in Russia,
When nights are longest there: I'll take my leave.
And leave you to the hearing of the cause;
Hoping you'll find good cause to whip them all.

ESCALUS   I think no less. Good morrow to your lordship.

[Exit ANGELO]

(2.1.128–32)

It seems that humanity, mercy, and patience—three qualities essential to a good judge—are lacking in Angelo. In the ensuing dialogue between Escalus and Pompey, Pompey defends himself by arguing against strict enforcement of the laws against prostitution.

ESCALUS   Come you hither to me, Master tapster. What's your name, Master tapster?

POMPEY   Pompey.

ESCALUS   What else?

POMPEY   Bum, sir.

ESCALUS   Troth, and your bum is the greatest thing about you; so that in the beastliest sense you are Pompey the

Great. Pompey, you are partly a bawd, Pompey,
howsoever you colour it in being a tapster, are you
not? come, tell me true: it shall be the better for you.

POMPEY   Truly, sir, I am a poor fellow that would live.

ESCALUS   How would you live, Pompey? by being a bawd?
What do you think of the trade, Pompey? is it a lawful trade?

POMPEY   If the law would allow it, sir.

ESCALUS   But the law will not allow it, Pompey; nor it shall
not be allowed in Vienna.

POMPEY   Does your worship mean to geld and spay all the
youth of the city?

ESCALUS   No, Pompey.

POMPEY   Truly, sir, in my poor opinion, they will to't then.
If your worship will take order for the drabs and
the knaves, you need not to fear the bawds.

ESCALUS   There are pretty orders beginning, I can tell you:
it is but heading and hanging.

POMPEY   If you head and hang all that offend that way but
for ten year together, you'll be glad to give out a
commission for more heads: if this law hold in
Vienna ten year, I'll rent the fairest house in it
after three-pence a bay: if you live to see this
come to pass, say Pompey told you so.

ESCALUS   Thank you, good Pompey; and, in requital of your
prophecy, hark you: I advise you, let me not find

you before me again upon any complaint whatsoever;
no, not for dwelling where you do: if I do, Pompey,
I shall beat you to your tent, and prove a shrewd
Caesar to you; in plain dealing, Pompey, I shall
have you whipt: so, for this time, Pompey, fare you well.

POMPEY   I thank your worship for your good counsel.

[Aside.]

but I shall follow it as the flesh and fortune shall
better determine. Whip me? No, no; let carman whip his jade:
The valiant heart is not whipt out of his trade.

[Exit.]

(2.1.201–41)

Pompey the Great was Julius Caesar's great rival in the last days
of the Roman Republic. Unlike the repressed Angelo and Isabella,
Pompey Bum understands that sexual desire is natural and cannot
be entirely suppressed. Escalus exercises a degree of moderation not
shown by Angelo. He puts Pompey on probation and threatens him
with whipping if he again offends.

Here is the dilemma: It appears that the strictest enforcement of
the law will not change natural behavior, including sexual desire,
and extreme leniency only encourages more bad behavior. Escalus
comes closest to following the true path of justice. He certainly recognizes Elbow's incompetence. At the end of the scene, he questions
Elbow about how long he has been a constable.

ESCALUS   Come hither to me, Master Elbow; come hither,
Master constable. How long have you been in this place of
constable?

ELBOW   Seven year and a half, sir.

ESCALUS I thought, by your readiness in the office, you had
continued in it some time. You say, seven years together?

ELBOW And a half, sir.

ESCALUS Alas, it hath been great pains to you. They do you
wrong to put you so oft upon 't: are there not men
in your ward sufficient to serve it?

ELBOW Faith, sir, few of any wit in such matters: as they
are chosen, they are glad to choose me for them; I
do it for some piece of money, and go through with
all.

ESCALUS Look you bring me in the names of some six or
seven, the most sufficient of your parish.

ELBOW To your worship's house, sir?

ESCALUS To my house. Fare you well.
                    (2.1.244–60)

It was common practice in Tudor England for those called to
serve a turn in their parish as constable to pay a small fee to another
(usually the least capable) to serve instead. Escalus intends to replace
the bumbling, incompetent Elbow with more intelligent and efficient
citizens of the parish. Escalus again wishes that Claudio could be
saved from execution.

ESCALUS It grieves me for the death of Claudio;
But there's no remedy.

JUSTICE Lord Angelo is severe.

ESCALUS   It is but needful:
  Mercy is not itself, that oft looks so;
  Pardon is still the nurse of second woe:
  But yet,–poor Claudio! There is no remedy.
                   (2.1.264–70)

In the next scene, Isabella comes before Angelo to plead for her brother's life. Accompanied by the foppish Lucio, she at first struggles to plead for mercy for Claudio without acknowledging his sin and guilt. Angelo responds that he cannot condemn the act without punishing the actor.

[Enter ISABELLA and LUCIO]

PROVOST   God save your honour!

ANGELO   Stay a little while.

[To ISABELLA]

You're welcome: what's your will?

ISABELLA   I am a woeful suitor to your honour,
  Please but your honour hear me.

ANGELO   Well; what's your suit?

ISABELLA   There is a vice [*fornication*] that most I do abhor,
  And most desire should meet the blow of justice;
  For which I would not plead, but that I must;
  For which I must not plead, but that I am
  At war 'twixt will and will not.

ANGELO   Well; the matter?

ISABELLA   I have a brother is condemn'd to die:

I do beseech you, let it be his fault,
And not my brother.

PROVOST   [*Aside.*] Heaven give thee moving graces!

ANGELO   Condemn the fault and not the actor of it?
Why, every fault's condemn'd ere it be done:
Mine were the very cipher of a function,
To fine the faults whose fine stands in record,
And let go by the actor.

ISABELLA   O just but severe law!
I had a brother, then. Heaven keep your honour!
(2.2.25–43)

Isabella seeming to be at a loss for words, Lucio urges her to renew her argument with greater warmth: "You are too cold; if you should need a pin, / You could not with more tame a tongue desire it: To him, I say!" (2.2.47–49). Isabella renews the argument with greater warmth.

ISABELLA   Must he needs die?

ANGELO   Maiden, no remedy.

ISABELLA   Yes; I do think that you might pardon him,
And neither heaven nor man grieve at the mercy.

ANGELO   I will not do't.

ISABELLA   But can you, if you would?

ANGELO   Look, what I will not, that I cannot do.

ISABELLA   But might you do't, and do the world no wrong,

If so your heart were touch'd with that remorse
As mine is to him?

ANGELO   He's sentenced; 'tis too late.

LUCIO   [*Aside to ISABELLA*] You are too cold.

ISABELLA   Too late? why, no; I, that do speak a word.
May call it back again. Well, believe this,
No ceremony that to great ones 'longs,
Not the king's crown, nor the deputed sword,
The marshal's truncheon, nor the judge's robe,
Become them with one half so good a grace
As mercy does.
If he had been as you and you as he,
You would have slipt like him; but he, like you,
Would not have been so stern.

(2.2.47–66)

Here Isabella invokes, but without quoting, the verse in the Sermon on the Mount from the Gospel of Matthew that gives the play its title: "Judge not, that ye be not judged. For with what judgment ye judge, ye shall be judged, and with what measure ye mete, it shall be measured to you again."[21]

Every judge of the Christian faith must reflect upon what this means. In civilized society, it cannot mean that no one can judge another. Without the act of judging, the rule of law would collapse into anarchy or tyranny.

"The issue is, as the title of the play suggests, the more fundamental one of whether judgment—in the sense of assigning punishment for offenses against the law—is in itself a desirable thing.

---

[21] Matthew 7:1–2.

If the answer to this question is negative, then it is hard to see how there can be a legal system."[22]

I would go further and say that it is impossible to have a legal system without judgment. For me, it means judge not without those qualities of humanity and mercy which Angelo lacks. In other words, "Judge not unjustly." Angelo rejects out of hand Isabella's appeal.

ANGELO   Pray you, be gone.

ISABELLA   I would to heaven I had your potency,
And you were Isabel! should it then be thus?
No; I would tell what 'twere to be a judge,
And what a prisoner.

LUCIO   [Aside to ISABELLA]
Ay, touch him; there's the vein.

ANGELO   Your brother is a forfeit of the law,
And you but waste your words.

ISABELLA   Alas, alas!
Why, all the souls that were were forfeit once;
And He that might the vantage best have took
Found out the remedy. How would you be,
If He, which is the top of judgment, should
But judge you as you are? O, think on that;
And mercy then will breathe within your lips,
Like man new made.

(2.2.67–78)

Here Isabella comes even closer to an explicit appeal to the words of Christ in the Gospel of Matthew. She eloquently appeals to Angelo

[22] Eds. Cormack, Nussbaum, and Strier, *Shakespeare and the Law* (University of Chicago Press 2013), 184.

to think how he will be judged by Christ upon the ultimate judgment day. But Angelo rejects her argument with the trite response that it is the law that condemns her brother and not the judge. He fails to use the power given to him by the Duke of exercising mercy. His conception of the law is that it is an abstraction apart from the very human instruments that administer it.

ANGELO   Be you content, fair maid;
    It is the law, not I condemn your brother:
    Were he my kinsman, brother, or my son,
    It should be thus with him: he must die tomorrow.
                (2.2.79-82)

Isabella skillfully argues that the sentence of death is totally out of proportion for an offence so many have committed with no punishment at all: "Good, good my lord, bethink you; / Who is it that hath died for this offence? / There's many have committed it" (2.2.86–88).

ISABELLA   To-morrow! O, that's sudden! Spare him, spare him!
    He's not prepared for death. . . . Good, good my lord, bethink you;
    Who is it that hath died for this offence?
    There's many have committed it.

LUCIO   [*Aside to ISABELLA*] Ay, well said.
                (2.2.79–87)

Angelo responds with the prosecutor's argument that strict enforcement of the law will do more good than ill by deterring others from the temptation to break the law. This is an articulate statement of general deterrence as a justification of criminal punishment. Angelo shares the Duke's understanding that this is an important justification for proper enforcement of the law.

In response, Isabella is magnificent.

ANGELO   The law hath not been dead, though it hath slept:

Those many had not dared to do that evil,
If the first that did the edict infringe
Had answer'd for his deed: now 'tis awake
Takes note of what is done; and, like a prophet,
Looks in a glass, that shows what future evils,
Either new, or by remissness new-conceived,
And so in progress to be hatch'd and born,
Are now to have no successive degrees,
But, ere they live, to end.

ISABELLA   Yet show some pity.

ANGELO   I show it most of all when I show justice;
For then I pity those I do not know,
Which a dismiss'd offence would after gall;
And do him right that, answering one foul wrong,
Lives not to act another. Be satisfied;
Your brother dies to-morrow; be content.

ISABELLA   So you must be the first that gives this sentence,
And he, that suffer's. O, it is excellent
To have a giant's strength; but it is tyrannous
To use it like a giant!

LUCIO   [Aside to ISABELLA] That's well said. . . .

ANGELO   Why do you put these sayings upon me?

ISABELLA   Because authority, though it err like others,
Hath yet a kind of medicine in itself,
That skins the vice o' the top. Go to your bosom;
Knock there, and ask your heart what it doth know
That's like my brother's fault: if it confess
A natural guiltiness such as is his,
Let it not sound a thought upon your tongue
Against my brother's life.

ANGELO   [*Aside*] She speaks, and 'tis
       Such sense, that my sense breeds with it. Fare you well.

ISABELLA   Gentle my lord, turn back.

ANGELO   I will bethink me: come again tomorrow.

ISABELLA   Hark how I'll bribe you: good my lord, turn back.

ANGELO   How! bribe me?

ISABELLA   Ay, with such gifts that heaven shall share with you.

LUCIO   [*Aside to ISABELLA*] You had marr'd all else.

ISABELLA   Not with fond shekels of the tested gold,
       Or stones whose rates are either rich or poor
       As fancy values them; but with true prayers
       That shall be up at heaven and enter there
       Ere sun-rise, prayers from preserved souls,
       From fasting maids whose minds are dedicate
       To nothing temporal.

ANGELO   Well; come to me to-morrow.

LUCIO   [*Aside to ISABELLA*] Go to: 'tis well. Away!

ISABELLA   Heaven keep your honour safe!

ANGELO   [*Aside*] Amen!
       For I am that way going to temptation,
       Where prayers cross.

ISABELLA   At what hour to-morrow
       Shall I attend your lordship?

ANGELO   At any time 'fore noon.
                    (2.2.90–109, 133–160)

Isabella's eloquent plea for mercy has gained her brother a reprieve
of one day. But it also has had a startling effect upon Angelo. His
cold blood has become hot. He is human after all.

ISABELLA   'Save your honour!

[Exeunt ISABELLA, LUCIO, and Provost]

ANGELO   From thee, even from thy virtue!
    What's this, what's this? Is this her fault or mine?
    The tempter or the tempted, who sins most?
    Ha!
    Not she: nor doth she tempt: but it is I
    That, lying by the violet in the sun,
    Do as the carrion does, not as the flower,
    Corrupt with virtuous season. Can it be
    That modesty may more betray our sense
    Than woman's lightness? Having waste ground enough,
    Shall we desire to raze the sanctuary
    And pitch our evils there? O, fie, fie, fie!
    What dost thou, or what art thou, Angelo?
    Dost thou desire her foully for those things
    That make her good? O, let her brother live!
    Thieves for their robbery have authority
    When judges steal themselves. What, do I love her,
    That I desire to hear her speak again,
    And feast upon her eyes? What is't I dream on?
    O cunning enemy, that, to catch a saint,
    With saints dost bait thy hook! Most dangerous
    Is that temptation that doth goad us on
    To sin in loving virtue: never could the strumpet,
    With all her double vigour, art and nature,

Once stir my temper; but this virtuous maid
Subdues me quite. Even till now,
When men were fond, I smiled and wonder'd how.
                    (2.2.160–186)

Angelo confesses his desire for Isabella. But in this, does he not seek to commit the same crime for which he has condemned Claudio? Having never been tempted, Angelo has no experience in resisting temptation. I frequently see something similar in my courtroom. For example, the successful financial advisor who starts stealing money from his clients to support a lavish lifestyle.

The Duke, disguised as a friar, meets Juliet in the prison. He says, "Repent you, fair one, of the sin you carry?" (2.3.20). She responds, "I do; and bear the shame most patiently" (2.3.21). She laments the "injurious law" that condemns her lover to death. The following day, Angelo, in soliloquy, admits that he is consumed by his illicit passion for Isabella.

ANGELO   When I would pray and think, I think and pray
        To several subjects. Heaven hath my empty words;
        Whilst my invention, hearing not my tongue,
        Anchors on Isabel: Heaven in my mouth,
        As if I did but only chew his name;
        And in my heart the strong and swelling evil
        Of my conception.
                    (2.4.1–7)

When Isabella returns and renews her plea for her brother's life, Angelo offers to save him if she will yield her chastity to his lust.

ANGELO   Which had you rather, that the most just law
        Now took your brother's life; or, to redeem him,
        Give up your body to such sweet uncleanness
        As she that he hath stain'd?

ISABELLA   Sir, believe this,
   I had rather give my body than my soul.

ANGELO   I talk not of your soul: our compell'd sins
   Stand more for number than for accompt.

ISABELLA   How say you?

ANGELO   Nay, I'll not warrant that; for I can speak
   Against the thing I say. Answer to this:
   I, now the voice of the recorded law,
   Pronounce a sentence on your brother's life:
   Might there not be a charity in sin
   To save this brother's life?

                    (2.4.51–64)

Angelo is guilty of the grossest hypocrisy and corruption. It is unclear at the beginning whether Isabella understands the proposition that Angelo is making. So he is more explicit.

ANGELO   But mark me;
   To be received plain, I'll speak more gross:
   Your brother is to die.

ISABELLA   So.

ANGELO   And his offence is so, as it appears,
   Accountant to the law upon that pain.

ISABELLA   True.

ANGELO   Admit no other way to save his life,–
   As I subscribe not that, nor any other,
   But in the loss of question,–that you, his sister,
   Finding yourself desired of such a person,

Whose credit with the judge, or own great place,
Could fetch your brother from the manacles
Of the all-building law; and that there were
No earthly mean to save him, but that either
You must lay down the treasures of your body
To this supposed, or else to let him suffer;
What would you do?

ISABELLA   As much for my poor brother as myself:
That is, were I under the terms of death,
The impression of keen whips I'ld wear as rubies,
And strip myself to death, as to a bed
That longing have been sick for, ere I'ld yield
My body up to shame.

ANGELO   Then must your brother die.

ISABELLA   And 'twere the cheaper way:
Better it were a brother died at once,
Than that a sister, by redeeming him,
Should die for ever.

ANGELO   Were not you then as cruel as the sentence
That you have slander'd so?

ISABELLA   Ignomy in ransom and free pardon
Are of two houses: lawful mercy
Is nothing kin to foul redemption.
                    (2.4.81–113)

A man in a position of power or authority ("but man, proud man, / Drest in a little brief authority") (2.2.117–18) over a woman demands sexual gratification in exchange for something she wants or needs. It seems nothing much has changed in four hundred years. This is the genius of Shakespeare. Isabella will allow her brother to die rather than commit what she considers a mortal sin.

When Isabella threatens to expose Angelo for his corrupt proposal, he confidently responds that no one will accept her story because of his spotless reputation: "Who will believe thee, Isabel? / My unsoil'd name, the austereness of my life" (2.4.155–56). The imagery is that of the scales of justice unfairly tipped in favor of Angelo: "As for you, / Say what you can, my false o'erweighs your true" (2.4.169–70).

Thus, we have the familiar scenario of a powerful man seeking sexual gratification as a quid pro quo, confident that her accusations of his misconduct will not be believed when it is her word against his. Angelo gives her another day to respond to his proposition. Isabella vows to go to her brother, confident that he will die rather than sacrifice his sister's honor.

The Duke—still disguised as a friar—enters the prison again, and counsels Claudio to accept death as the fate that eventually comes to all men. Claudio seems to accept his fate. "I humbly thank you. To sue to live, I find I seek to die; And, seeking death, find life: let it come on" (3.1.42–44). Isabella then enters, and the Duke conceals himself in order to overhear the conversation between brother and sister. When first told of Angelo's "devilish mercy" (3.1.65), Claudio is resolute that Isabella must not submit to satisfy Angelo's lust. But then, fear of death overcomes him.

ISABELLA   What says my brother?

CLAUDIO   Death is a fearful thing.

ISABELLA   And shamed life a hateful.

CLAUDIO   Ay, but to die, and go we know not where;
   To lie in cold obstruction and to rot;
   This sensible warm motion to become
   A kneaded clod; and the delighted spirit
   To bathe in fiery floods, or to reside

In thrilling region of thick-ribbed ice;
To be imprison'd in the viewless winds,
And blown with restless violence round about
The pendent world; or to be worse than worst
Of those that lawless and incertain thought
Imagine howling: 'tis too horrible!
The weariest and most loathed worldly life
That age, ache, penury and imprisonment
Can lay on nature is a paradise
To what we fear of death.

ISABELLA   Alas, alas!

CLAUDIO   Sweet sister, let me live:
What sin you do to save a brother's life,
Nature dispenses with the deed so far
That it becomes a virtue.
(3.1.115–36)

This is beautiful language; it sounds more like tragedy than comedy. Although generally included in the comedies, the play is hard to classify according to the usual standard. But Isabella is unmoved. Indeed, she responds with contempt.

ISABELLA   O you beast!
O faithless coward! O dishonest wretch!
Wilt thou be made a man out of my vice?
Is't not a kind of incest, to take life
From thine own sister's shame? What should I think?
Heaven shield my mother play'd my father fair!
For such a warped slip of wilderness
Ne'er issued from his blood. Take my defiance!
Die, perish!
(3.1.137–43)

To many in the audience, Isabella's self-righteous condemnation of her brother's weakness may seem excessively cruel. She does not demonstrate the qualities of mercy and pity she had urged upon Angelo. This is Shakespeare's genius: His characterization of Isabella is so rich that many likely think her right to condemn her brother's cowardice.

After Isabella leaves, the Duke enters Claudio's cell and concocts a story that Angelo is merely testing Isabella's virtue. He convinces Claudio that there is no hope for him. Duke Vincentio: "I am confessor to Angelo, and I know this to be true; therefore prepare yourself to death" (3.1.163–64). This is an outright lie. Claudio responds: "Let me ask my sister pardon. I am so out of love with life that I will sue to be rid of it" (3.1.168–69).

The Duke then talks to Isabella alone. He explains his plan to have Angelo's jilted fiancé, Mariana, substitute herself in the dead of night for Isabella in Angelo's bed. Isabella readily agrees. She describes the plan as a "a most prosperous perfection" (3.1.247), although it involves Mariana sacrificing her chastity when Isabella will not.

Outside the prison, the Duke encounters Lucio and Pompey. The latter has again been arrested for keeping a bawdy house. When Pompey is led away to prison, Lucio and the disguised Duke speak of affairs in Vienna.

LUCIO   What news, friar, of the duke?

DUKE VINCENTIO   I know none. Can you tell me of any?

LUCIO   Some say he is with the Emperor of Russia; other some, he is in Rome: but where is he, think you?

DUKE VINCENTIO   I know not where; but wheresoever, I wish him well.

LUCIO   It was a mad fantastical trick of him to steal from the state, and usurp the beggary he was never born

to. Lord Angelo dukes it well in his absence; he
puts transgression to 't.

DUKE VINCENTIO   He does well in 't.

LUCIO   A little more lenity to lechery would do no harm in
him: something too crabbed that way, friar.

DUKE VINCENTIO   It is too general a vice, and severity must cure it.

LUCIO   Yes, in good sooth, the vice is of a great kindred;
it is well allied: but it is impossible to extirp
it quite, friar, till eating and drinking be put
down. They say this Angelo was not made by man and
woman after this downright way of creation: is it
true, think you?

DUKE VINCENTIO   How should he be made, then?

LUCIO   Some report a sea-maid spawned him; some, that he
was begot between two stock-fishes. But it is
certain that when he makes water his urine is
congealed ice; that I know to be true: and he is a
motion generative; that's infallible.

DUKE VINCENTIO   You are pleasant, sir, and speak apace.

LUCIO   Why, what a ruthless thing is this in him, for the
rebellion of a codpiece to take away the life of a
man! Would the duke that is absent have done this?
Ere he would have hanged a man for the getting a
hundred bastards, he would have paid for the nursing
a thousand: he had some feeling of the sport: he
knew the service, and that instructed him to mercy.

(3.2.78–107)

While wishing for his return, Lucio foolishly accuses the Duke of having many vices. Meanwhile, the Duke has arranged the bed swap of Mariana—her identity concealed by the night—to get Isabella out of her dilemma.

ISABELLA   Little have you to say
When you depart from him, but, soft and low,
'Remember now my brother.'

MARIANA   Fear me not.

DUKE VINCENTIO   Nor, gentle daughter, fear you not at all.
He is your husband on a pre-contract:
To bring you thus together, 'tis no sin,
Sith that the justice of your title to him
Doth flourish the deceit. Come, let us go:
Our corn's to reap, for yet our tilth's to sow.
                    (4.1.66–75)

Thus, the Duke assures Mariana she will not be committing a sin: She is already legally contracted to be Angelo's wife and will become so in the eyes of God when the promise to marry is consummated by sexual intercourse. It is ironic in the extreme that the Duke is encouraging Mariana to do what had been condemned as a sin in Juliet.

At the prison, Pompey agrees to become the assistant to the executioner in mitigation of his punishment. The Provost asks Pompey if he can cut off a man's head. Pompey responds: "If the man be a bachelor, sir, I can; but if he be married man, he's his wife's head, and I can never cut off a woman's head" (4.2.1–5). This is a joke based upon the common law doctrine that a husband and wife were one person under the law.

Near dawn, the still disguised Duke and the Provost await Claudio's pardon. A messenger comes from Angelo.

DUKE VINCENTIO   And here comes Claudio's pardon.

MESSENGER   [*Giving a paper.*]
My lord hath sent you this note; and by me this
further charge, that you swerve not from the
smallest article of it, neither in time, matter, or
other circumstance. Good morrow; for, as I take it,
it is almost day.

PROVOST   I shall obey him.

[*Exit Messenger.*]

DUKE VINCENTIO   [*Aside.*] This is his pardon, purchas'd by such sin
For which the pardoner himself is in.
Hence hath offence his quick celerity,
When it is born in high authority:
When vice makes mercy, mercy's so extended,
That for the fault's love is the offender friended.
Now, sir, what news?

PROVOST   I told you. Lord Angelo, belike thinking me remiss
in mine office, awakens me with this unwonted
putting-on; methinks strangely, for he hath not used it before.

DUKE VINCENTIO   Pray you, let's hear.

PROVOST   [*Reads.*]
'Whatsoever you may hear to the contrary, let
Claudio be executed by four of the clock; and in the
afternoon Barnardine: for my better satisfaction,
let me have Claudio's head sent me by five. Let
this be duly performed; with a thought that more
depends on it than we must yet deliver. Thus fail
not to do your office, as you will answer it at your peril.'
What say you to this, sir?

(4.2.97–121)

So Isabella is to be betrayed and her brother executed. The Duke asks who is this Barnardine who is to be executed. The Provost explains: "A Bohemian born, but here nursed up and bred; one that is a prisoner nine years old" (4.2.124–25).

DUKE VINCENTIO   How came it that the absent duke had not either delivered him to his liberty or executed him? I have heard it was ever his manner to do so.

PROVOST   His friends still wrought reprieves for him: and, indeed, his fact, till now in the government of Lord Angelo, came not to an undoubtful proof.

DUKE VINCENTIO   It is now apparent?

PROVOST   Most manifest, and not denied by himself.

DUKE VINCENTIO   Hath he born himself penitently in prison? how seems he to be touched?

PROVOST   A man that apprehends death no more dreadfully but as a drunken sleep; careless, reckless, and fearless of what's past, present, or to come; insensible of mortality, and desperately mortal.

DUKE VINCENTIO   He wants advice.

PROVOST   He will hear none: he hath evermore had the liberty of the prison; give him leave to escape hence, he would not: drunk many times a day, if not many days entirely drunk. We have very oft awaked him, as if to carry him to execution, and showed him a seeming warrant for it: it hath not moved him at all.

                              (4.2.126–46)

To save Claudio, the Duke suggests: "Let this Barnardine be this morning executed, and his head born to Angelo" (4.2.163–64). The disguised Duke persuades the Provost to delay Claudio's execution for a time until the return of the Duke who will "avouch the justice of your dealing" (4.2.178). The absurdity of the situation is highlighted when Bernadine is summoned to be executed. He refuses to get out of his cell on the grounds that he has been drinking all night and is not fit to be executed. However, a notorious pirate has died that night in the prison and his head can be sent to Angelo.

The Provost is given letters for Angelo advising him of the Duke's return to Vienna in two days. When Isabella comes to the prison, the disguised Duke tells her Claudio has been executed. At first reading, this seems an act of inexplicable cruelty. And it is. But it seems to me that Shakespeare does it in order to give sufficient reason for Isabella to appear before the returned Duke to denounce Angelo as a seducer and a murdering judge.

Escalus and Angelo receive letters from the Duke saying to meet him at the city gates the following day. Unaware of the Duke's plan to have Isabella denounce him, Angelo finds the Duke's messages puzzling.

In the final scene of the play, the Duke enters the city gate and warmly greets Angelo and Escalus. He congratulates them on what he has heard of their administration of justice in his absence.

DUKE VINCENTIO   My very worthy cousin, fairly met!
Our old and faithful friend, we are glad to see you.

ANGELO AND ESCALUS   Happy return be to your royal grace!

DUKE VINCENTIO   Many and hearty thankings to you both.
We have made inquiry of you; and we hear
Such goodness of your justice, that our soul
Cannot but yield you forth to public thanks,
Forerunning more requital.

(5.1.1–10)

Isabella comes forward and demands to be heard. She kneels before the Duke and cries out:

ISABELLA   Justice, O royal duke! Vail your regard
Upon a wrong'd, I would fain have said, a maid!
O worthy prince, dishonour not your eye
By throwing it on any other object
Till you have heard me in my true complaint
And given me justice, justice, justice, justice!
(5.1.24–29)

In feigned ignorance of her grievance, the Duke bids her make her complaint to Lord Angelo. Because the Duke knows that Angelo is guilty—and we know that he knows—this is the manifest injustice of letting the accused be his own judge. Allowing the accused or the accuser to be the judge in his own case was a frequent concern in Shakespeare's plays.

DUKE VINCENTIO   Relate your wrongs; in what? by whom? be brief.
Here is Lord Angelo shall give you justice:
Reveal yourself to him.

ISABELLA   O worthy duke,
You bid me seek redemption of the devil:
Hear me yourself; for that which I must speak
Must either punish me, not being believed,
Or wring redress from you. Hear me, O hear me, here!

ANGELO   My lord, her wits, I fear me, are not firm:
She hath been a suitor to me for her brother
Cut off by course of justice,–

ISABELLA   By course of justice!

ANGELO   And she will speak most bitterly and strange.

ISABELLA   Most strange, but yet most truly, will I speak:
That Angelo's forsworn; is it not strange?
That Angelo's a murderer; is 't not strange?
That Angelo is an adulterous thief,
An hypocrite, a virgin-violator;
Is it not strange and strange?

DUKE VINCENTIO   Nay, it is ten times strange.

ISABELLA   It is not truer he is Angelo
Than this is all as true as it is strange:
Nay, it is ten times true; for truth is truth
To the end of reckoning.

DUKE VINCENTIO   Away with her! Poor soul,
She speaks this in the infirmity of sense.
(5.1.30–55)

But the Duke relents and allows Isabella to tell her tale. As a good judge would, the Duke puts down with a firm hand the officious interruptions of Lucio.

ISABELLA   I am the sister of one Claudio,
Condemn'd upon the act of fornication
To lose his head; condemn'd by Angelo:
I, in probation of a sisterhood,
Was sent to by my brother; one Lucio
As then the messenger,—

LUCIO   That's I, an't like your grace:
I came to her from Claudio, and desired her
To try her gracious fortune with Lord Angelo
For her poor brother's pardon.

ISABELLA   That's he indeed.

DUKE VINCENTIO   You were not bid to speak.

LUCIO   No, my good lord;
　　　Nor wish'd to hold my peace.

DUKE VINCENTIO   I wish you now, then;
　　　Pray you, take note of it: and when you have
　　　A business for yourself, pray heaven you then
　　　Be perfect.

LUCIO   I warrant your honour.

DUKE VINCENTIO   The warrants for yourself; take heed to't.

ISABELLA   This gentleman told somewhat of my tale,—

LUCIO   Right.

DUKE VINCENTIO   It may be right; but you are i' the wrong
　　　To speak before your time. Proceed.

ISABELLA   I went
　　　To this pernicious caitiff deputy–

DUKE VINCENTIO   That's somewhat madly spoken.

ISABELLA   Pardon it;
　　　The phrase is to the matter.

DUKE VINCENTIO   Mended again. The matter; proceed.

ISABELLA   In brief, to set the needless process by,
　　　How I persuaded, how I pray'd, and kneel'd,

How he refell'd me, and how I replied,–
For this was of much length,–the vile conclusion
I now begin with grief and shame to utter:
He would not, but by gift of my chaste body
To his concupiscible intemperate lust,
Release my brother; and, after much debatement,
My sisterly remorse confutes mine honour,
And I did yield to him: but the next morn betimes,
His purpose surfeiting, he sends a warrant
For my poor brother's head.

DUKE VINCENTIO   This is most likely!

ISABELLA   O, that it were as like as it is true!
(5.1.80–123)

The Duke pretends to refuse to believe her complaints against a man of Angelo's "integrity." Isabella is resigned that she must look to heaven for divine justice. But the Duke demands to know who has prompted her to make this false accusation. She says Friar Lodowick knew of her intent to appear before the Duke and accuse Angelo. Isabella is carried off to prison. Mariana then comes forward and accuses Angelo of sleeping with her, thinking she was Isabella.

The Duke again tells Angelo to be his own judge: "Come, cousin Angelo; / In this I'll be impartial; be you judge / Of your own cause" (5.1.187–89). But the Duke instead questions Mariana about her accusations against Angelo. Angelo scoffs at the accusations: "These poor informal women are no more / But instruments of some more mightier member / That sets them on" (5.1.260–62).

Seeming to agree, the Duke asks Angelo and Escalus to inquire into why these women are making false accusations against Angelo. The friar that set them on is sent for, and the Duke leaves.

Escalus sends for Isabella and the Duke returns, disguised as Friar Lodowick. He is confronted by Escalus.

ESCALUS   Come, sir: did you set these women on to slander
   Lord Angelo? they have confessed you did.

DUKE VINCENTIO   'Tis false.

ESCALUS   How! know you where you are?

DUKE VINCENTIO   Respect to your great place! and let the devil
   Be sometime honour'd for his burning throne!
   Where is the duke? 'tis he should hear me speak.

ESCALUS   The duke's in us; and we will hear you speak:
   Look you speak justly.

DUKE VINCENTIO   Boldly, at least. But, O, poor souls,
   Come you to seek the lamb here of the fox?
   Good night to your redress! Is the duke gone?
   Then is your cause gone too. The duke's unjust,
   Thus to retort your manifest appeal,
   And put your trial in the villain's mouth
   Which here you come to accuse.

LUCIO   This is the rascal; this is he I spoke of.

ESCALUS   Why, thou unreverend and unhallow'd friar,
   Is't not enough thou hast suborn'd these women
   To accuse this worthy man, but, in foul mouth
   And in the witness of his proper ear,
   To call him villain? and then to glance from him
   To the duke himself, to tax him with injustice?
   Take him hence; to the rack with him! We'll touse you
   Joint by joint, but we will know his purpose.
   What 'unjust'!

                    (5.1.314–38)

Thinking all is going well for him, Angelo encourages the officious Lucio to slander the absent Duke by lying about the friar. When Escalus tells the provost to take the friar to prison, Lucio rashly pulls away the frier's hood, revealing him to be the Duke. The provost is ordered to "bail" Lucio before he can run away. The Duke then takes Angelo's seat and addresses him. Angelo immediately confesses that the accusations by the women are true.

DUKE VINCENTIO   [*To ESCALUS*]
We'll borrow place of him.

[To ANGELO]

Sir, by your leave.
Hast thou or word, or wit, or impudence,
That yet can do thee office? If thou hast,
Rely upon it till my tale be heard,
And hold no longer out.

ANGELO   O my dread lord,
I should be guiltier than my guiltiness,
To think I can be undiscernible,
When I perceive your grace, like power divine,
Hath look'd upon my passes. Then, good prince,
No longer session hold upon my shame,
But let my trial be mine own confession:
Immediate sentence then and sequent death
Is all the grace I beg.
                        (5.1.384–98)

Angelo is at least consistent. "When I, that censure him, do so offend, / Let mine own judgment pattern out my death, / And nothing come in partial" (2.1.29–31). He does not ask for mercy. The Duke orders Angelo to be taken away to marry Mariana immediately. Escalus is astonished.

ESCALUS   My lord, I am more amazed at his dishonour
   Than at the strangeness of it.

DUKE VINCENTIO   Come hither, Isabel.
   Your friar is now your prince: as I was then
   Advertising and holy to your business,
   Not changing heart with habit, I am still
   Attorney'd at your service.

                  (5.1.405–10)

Angelo returns to the stage after having married Mariana.
Without further ado, the Duke condemns Angelo to die for the
death of Claudio.

DUKE VINCENTIO   For this new-married man approaching
   here,
   Whose salt imagination yet hath wrong'd
   Your well defended honour, you must pardon
   For Mariana's sake: but as he adjudged your brother,–
   Being criminal, in double violation
   Of sacred chastity and of promise-breach
   Thereon dependent, for your brother's life,–
   The very mercy of the law cries out
   Most audible, even from his proper tongue,
   'An Angelo for Claudio, death for death!'
   Haste still pays haste, and leisure answers leisure;
   Like doth quit like, and MEASURE still FOR MEASURE.
   Then, Angelo, thy fault's thus manifested;
   Which, though thou wouldst deny, denies thee vantage.
   We do condemn thee to the very block
   Where Claudio stoop'd to death, and with like haste.
   Away with him!

                  (5.1.429–45)

Here, the reference to the Gospel of Matthew is explicit. Angelo has confessed and waived a trial. The Duke condemns him to die. But this seems a bit hasty. The Duke orders Angelo's property to be confiscated and given to Mariana. She pleads for mercy for her new husband. When the Duke rejects her plea, Mariana turns to Isabella and seeks her help in saving Angelo. Isabella responds.

ISABELLA   Most bounteous sir,

[Kneeling]

Look, if it please you, on this man condemn'd,
As if my brother lived: I partly think
A due sincerity govern'd his deeds,
Till he did look on me: since it is so,
Let him not die. My brother had but justice,
In that he did the thing for which he died:
For Angelo,
His act did not o'ertake his bad intent,
And must be buried but as an intent
That perish'd by the way: thoughts are no subjects;
Intents but merely thoughts.

MARIANA   Merely, my lord.

DUKE VINCENTIO   Your suit's unprofitable; stand up, I say.
I have bethought me of another fault.
(5.1.478–490)

Isabella is arguing that a mere intent should not be punished as a crime. She is arguing for the modern law of attempt and conspiracy which require more than mere intent to impose criminal liability. Portia was not so merciful in *The Merchant of Venice*. Shylock is punished for his intent to murder Antonio.

Claudio is led on stage with his head covered. The Duke pardons Barnardine, and then the hood is removed from Claudio's head. Everyone is amazed to see Claudio alive. The Duke then pardons Claudio and Angelo. He is not so generous to Lucio.

VINCENTIO   [*To LUCIO*]
> You, sirrah, that knew me for a fool, a coward,
> One all of luxury, an ass, a madman;
> Wherein have I so deserved of you,
> That you extol me thus?

LUCIO   'Faith, my lord. I spoke it but according to the
> trick. If you will hang me for it, you may; but I
> had rather it would please you I might be whipt.

DUKE VINCENTIO   Whipt first, sir, and hanged after.
> (5.1.540–47)

Lucio is also forced to marry a whore. "Marrying a punk, my lord, is pressing to death, whipping, and hanging" (5.1.61–62). Pressing to death ("*peine forte et dure*") was the punishment for one accused of a felony who would not "put himself upon the country" and submit to a trial by jury.

Is hanging Lucio justice? Under the common law, a judge could summarily convict an offender for a crime committed in the judge's presence. Yet even conceding the procedural issue, is hanging a just sentence for slandering the Duke? Is this not as arbitrary and unjust as Angelo's condemnation of Claudio?

Eventually, the Duke pardons Lucio of the slanders. He has manipulated the plot and the characters to see that no great injustice has been done. But he has not done this in the context of orderly legal and magisterial procedures. The pardon of Barnardine the murderer is inexplicable. The problem of the lax enforcement of the laws has not gotten better. It may have gotten worse.

After the Duke pardons Claudio, he makes a startling proposal to Isabella.

DUKE VINCENTIO   [*To ISABELLA.*]
> Is he pardon'd; and, for your lovely sake,
> Give me your hand and say you will be mine.
> He is my brother too: but fitter time for that.
> By this Lord Angelo perceives he's safe;
> Methinks I see a quickening in his eye.
> Well, Angelo, your evil quits you well:
> Look that you love your wife; her worth worth yours.
> (5.1.531–37)

After brief commendations to Escalus and the Provost, the play ends with the Duke's extraordinary proposal to Isabella.

DUKE VINCENTIO   Dear Isabel,
> I have a motion much imports your good;
> Whereto if you'll a willing ear incline,
> What's mine is yours and what is yours is mine.
> So, bring us to our palace; where we'll show
> What's yet behind, that's meet you all should know.

[Exeunt.]

(5.1.573–78)

In the legal sense, a motion is a formal request for a court to take some action. The play ends with no response from Isabella to the Duke's proposal. Indeed, she does not speak for the last 88 lines of the play. Some directors have Isabella take the Duke's hand, indicating consent to his proposal. Others leave the play with a more ambiguous ending.

In a sense, *Measure for Measure* is a play in which Shakespeare through the Duke arranges a series of trials for all the other characters. As a magistrate, Angelo is tried and fails to exercise mercy and observe justice. He grossly abuses his power as a judge. His virtue is tried by the passion and sexual desire he feels for Isabella. Claudio is tried to see if he will sacrifice his sister's chastity to save his life. Lucio and Pompey are tried for their many violations of law and morality.

For Isabella, the play is one trial after another. She must plead for mercy for her brother, whom she believes has committed a sin against God. She must then choose between committing the same mortal sin and saving her brother's life. In the last act, she is the accuser in the trial of Angelo. After his confession, she is put to the trial of whether she will plead for mercy for the man who attempted to seduce her and whom she believes has murdered her brother. And then there is the final trial brought about by the Duke's extraordinary proposal of marriage.

But what is her response to this "motion"? We do not know. Of course, the Duke is making an honorable proposal. But unlike all the other heroines in Shakespeare's comedies, Isabella was not seeking love and marriage. From the beginning, she was seeking to escape from the world of sexual desire. Is a return to the convent still an option for Isabella? Is she again being forced to submit against her will to another powerful man who wants to sleep with her? Are there three forced marriages at the end of the play?

According to the conventions of Shakespearean comedy, the Duke and Isabella should marry and live happily ever after. But we do not know. Is justice restored in Vienna? Has the Duke learned that excessive lenity can be just as destructive as excessive hardness? We do not know. Many nineteenth century readers thought there was something morally or artistically untrue about the play because sin was not adequately punished. Maybe so. In any event, this "problem play" was the end of comedy for Shakespeare.

CHAPTER 17

King Lear

In *King Lear*, Shakespeare gives us a vision of human and divine justice that is rich—and dark. The play was performed for King James at Whitehall Palace the night after Christmas in 1606 with the renowned actor Richard Burbage playing the part of Lear.

The play begins at the court of old King Lear in pagan Britain, before the Roman conquest of the island and before its division into the kingdoms of England, Scotland, and Wales. Lear has already made the calamitous decision to divide his kingdom among his three daughters. The two older daughters, Goneril and Regan, are married to the Dukes of Albany and Cornwall. The youngest daughter, Cordelia, is unmarried.

The action begins (typical of Shakespeare) with a seemingly innocuous conversation between the Earl of Kent and the Earl of Gloucester.

KENT   I thought the king had more affected the Duke of Albany than Cornwall.

GLOUCESTER   It did always seem so to us: but now, in the division of the kingdom, it appears not which of the dukes he values most; for equalities are so weighed, that curiosity in neither can make choice of either's moiety.
(King Lear, 1.1.1–5)

At this moment, Gloucester introduces Kent to his bastard son Edmund. Kent: "Is not this your son my lord?" (1.1.6). Gloucester replies: "His breeding, sir, hath been at my charge: I have so often blushed to acknowledge him, that now I am brazed to it" (1.1.10–12).

This ambiguous response may reflect a change in attitudes from the early sixteenth century when concubinage and bastardy in the upper classes were generally tolerated and Shakespeare's time when they were more likely to be condemned.

At this moment, King Lear enters in all his regal glory. He announces his intention to divide his kingdom into three parts. The absence of a clear motive to do this has baffled some critics (Tolstoy for one), who have not understood the difference between a prose narrative meant to be read and a play meant to be performed on a stage in front of an audience. Lear acknowledges that this is in anticipation of his death.

KING LEAR   Attend the lords of France and Burgundy, Gloucester.

GLOUCESTER   I shall, my liege.

[Exeunt Gloucester and EDMUND.]

KING LEAR   Meantime we shall express our darker purpose.
Give me the map there. Know that we have divided
In three our kingdom: and 'tis our fast intent
To shake all cares and business from our age;
Conferring them on younger strengths, while we
Unburthen'd crawl toward death. Our son of Cornwall,
And you, our no less loving son of Albany,
We have this hour a constant will to publish
Our daughters' several dowers, that future strife
May be prevented now.

(1.1.35–46)

This reference to "dowers" is puzzling here—and throughout this scene. It clearly is not a reference to his daughters' "dowries," which would be property given by the father to the daughter's husband at the time of marriage. Arguably, Cordelia could receive her one-third of the kingdom as her dowry when she is betrothed. But the two older daughters are already married. If they received a dowry, it has already been delivered.

As I have mentioned before, "dower" was the provision the law made for a widow out of the lands of her husband, for her support and the nurture of her children. It was a life estate a woman was by law entitled to claim on the death of her husband, in the lands and tenements which he possessed during the marriage, and which her issue, if any, might have inherited. It was generally one-third in value of all real property. Dower rights came to a married woman by law and from her husband—not from her father. Lear could not by "will" give dower rights to his daughters. He is making a gift to his daughters during his lifetime.

By referring to dowers, is Shakespeare suggesting that Lear has confused the love his daughters owe him with the love they owe their husbands? This might explain the "love test" he then inflicts upon his daughters.

Of course, this division of the kingdom will not prevent future strife—it will cause it. And the strife will be aggravated by the continued presence of Lear, who retains the name of King—and wants to be treated like one—but has given up his authority. Before he divides his kingdom among his daughters, he first puts them to a test. Each of them must tell him how much she loves him.

KING LEAR   Tell me, my daughters,—
   Since now we will divest us both of rule,
   Interest of territory, cares of state,—
   Which of you shall we say doth love us most?
   That we our largest bounty may extend
   Where nature doth with merit challenge.
               (1.1.49–54)

Here, Shakespeare has clearly forecast the dark themes of the play. The two older daughters—Goneril and Regan—respond to the test with extravagant expressions of love for Lear: It is greater than language can express, exceeding all other loves. Goneril: "A love that makes breath poor, and speech unable; / Beyond all manner of so much I love you" (1.1.61–62).

In essence, they play along and humor the old man. He gives each of them one-third of his kingdom. Lear then turns to the youngest daughter, Cordelia, whom he loves best.

KING LEAR   Now, our joy,
　　Although the last, not least; to whose young love
　　The vines of France and milk of Burgundy
　　Strive to be interess'd; what can you say to draw
　　A third more opulent than your sisters? Speak.

CORDELIA   Nothing, my lord.

KING LEAR   Nothing!

CORDELIA   Nothing.

KING LEAR   Nothing will come of nothing: speak again.

CORDELIA   Unhappy that I am, I cannot heave
　　My heart into my mouth: I love your majesty
　　According to my bond; nor more nor less.

KING LEAR   How, how, Cordelia! mend your speech a little,
　　Lest it may mar your fortunes.

CORDELIA   Good my lord,
　　You have begot me, bred me, loved me: I
　　Return those duties back as are right fit,
　　Obey you, love you, and most honour you.

Why have my sisters husbands, if they say
They love you all? Haply, when I shall wed,
That lord whose hand must take my plight shall carry
Half my love with him, half my care and duty:
Sure, I shall never marry like my sisters,
To love my father all.

KING LEAR   But goes thy heart with this?

CORDELIA   Ay, good my lord.

KING LEAR   So young, and so untender?

CORDELIA   So young, my lord, and true.

KING LEAR   Let it be so; thy truth, then, be thy dower:
For, by the sacred radiance of the sun,
The mysteries of Hecate, and the night;
By all the operation of the orbs
From whom we do exist, and cease to be;
Here I disclaim all my paternal care,
Propinquity and property of blood,
And as a stranger to my heart and me
Hold thee, from this, for ever.

(1.1.84–121)

Cordelia's silence has been baffling to some. To me, it seems quite understandable. Lear has come up with this love test to determine if Cordelia, in particular, will remain ultimately loyal to him and love him more than any other. He wants to marry Cordelia off to Burgundy but will not let her go and live with him as a true wife. She is to remain in England and take care of Lear. Cordelia loves her father but wants to love him as a daughter and not to be his pseudo-widow, taking her third of his kingdom as her dower/dowry. "Sure, I shall never marry like my sisters, / To love my father all"

(1.1.106–07). She refuses to go along with the love test; like Juliet, she refuses to submit to the will of the older generation.

Lacking any self-awareness and consumed by hubris, Lear (like Capulet) is enraged because Cordelia has told him the truth. Cordelia is remarkable for always speaking the truth. Of all of Shakespeare's extraordinary women, her only rival for purity of spirit is Desdemona. The loyal Kent protests this cruel treatment of Cordelia, but Lear is consumed by his rage.

KING LEAR   Peace, Kent!
    Come not between the dragon and his wrath.
    I loved her most, and thought to set my rest
    On her kind nursery. Hence, and avoid my sight!
    So be my grave my peace, as here I give
    Her father's heart from her! Call France; who stirs?
    Call Burgundy. Cornwall and Albany,
    With my two daughters' dowers digest this third:
    Let pride, which she calls plainness, marry her.
    I do invest you jointly with my power,
    Pre-eminence, and all the large effects
    That troop with majesty. Ourself, by monthly course,
    With reservation of an hundred knights,
    By you to be sustain'd, shall our abode
    Make with you by due turns. Only we still retain
    The name, and all the additions to a king;
    The sway, revenue, execution of the rest,
    Beloved sons, be yours: which to confirm,
    This coronet part betwixt you.
               (1.1.126–144)

Kent is banished after he persists in warning Lear against his blind folly.

KENT   [B]e Kent unmannerly,
    When Lear is mad. What wilt thou do, old man?

Think'st thou that duty shall have dread to speak,
When power to flattery bows? To plainness honour's bound,
When majesty stoops to folly.

(1.1.150–55)

"Out of my sight!" (1.1.165) rages Lear at Kent. "See better, Lear" (1.1.166), responds Kent. In Lear's ancient Britain, there are no institutions to check or ameliorate the will of the King, even when he is mad.

Lear then offers Cordelia to the Duke of Burgundy but tells him she will have no dowry. Burgundy protests: "Royal Lear, / Give but that portion which yourself proposed, / And here I take Cordelia by the hand" (1.1.260–62). Lear responds: "Nothing: I have sworn; I am firm" (1.1.265). The Duke of Burgundy rejects the dowryless Cordelia. Her hand is then claimed by the King of France.

KING OF FRANCE   Fairest Cordelia, that art most rich, being poor;
Most choice, forsaken; and most loved, despised!
Thee and thy virtues here I seize upon:
Be it lawful I take up what's cast away.
Gods, gods! 'tis strange that from their cold'st neglect
My love should kindle to inflamed respect.
Thy dowerless daughter, king, thrown to my chance,
Is queen of us, of ours, and our fair France:
Not all the dukes of waterish Burgundy
Can buy this unprized precious maid of me.
Bid them farewell, Cordelia, though unkind:
Thou losest here, a better where to find.

(1.1.271–82)

In 1606, Parliament passed "An Act to Restrain Abuses of Players" that prohibited references on the stage to God, Jesus Christ, or the Trinity. Here, France seems to be referring to the gods of antiquity rather than the Christian God. The cruel treatment of Lear by the two older sisters is foreshadowed by the revelation of their true feelings toward their aged father after he leaves the stage.

GONERIL   Sister, it is not a little I have to say of what
   most nearly appertains to us both. I think our
   father will hence to-night.

REGAN   That's most certain, and with you; next month with us.

GONERIL   You see how full of changes his age is; the
   observation we have made of it hath not been
   little: he always loved our sister most; and
   with what poor judgment he hath now cast her off
   appears too grossly.

REGAN   'Tis the infirmity of his age: yet he hath ever
   but slenderly known himself.

GONERIL   The best and soundest of his time hath been but
   rash; then must we look to receive from his age,
   not alone the imperfections of long-engraffed
   condition, but therewithal the unruly waywardness
   that infirm and choleric years bring with them.
                    (1.1.306–21)

Cordelia and Kent spoke out against Lear's tyrannous behavior out of loyalty and love for him. Goneril and Regan kept silent out of entirely different motives. The stage is now set for the tragedy to follow.

As Lear is making the calamitous decision to divide his kingdom between his two cruel, ungrateful daughters, Gloucester is acting with equal blindness in choosing between his legitimate and illegitimate sons. It is worth giving the complete introduction of Edmund and his half-brother, the legitimate son, Edgar.

KENT   Is not this your son, my lord?

GLOUCESTER   His breeding, sir, hath been at my charge: I have
so often blushed to acknowledge him, that now I am brazed
to it.

KENT   I cannot conceive you.

GLOUCESTER   Sir, this young fellow's mother could: whereupon
she grew round-wombed, and had, indeed, sir, a son for her
cradle ere she had a husband for her bed. Do you smell a fault?

KENT   I cannot wish the fault undone, the issue of it
being so proper.

GLOUCESTER   But I have, sir, a son by order of law, some year
elder than this, who yet is no dearer in my account:
though this knave came something saucily into the
world before he was sent for, yet was his mother
fair; there was good sport at his making, and the
whoreson must be acknowledged. Do you know this
noble gentleman, Edmund?

EDMUND   No, my lord.

GLOUCESTER   My lord of Kent: remember him hereafter as my
honourable friend.

EDMUND   My services to your lordship.
(1.1.9–27)

Gloucester has two sons. We are introduced to a "proper" young
man whom the law defines as illegitimate—a bastard. This is in contrast to Gloucester's other son, Edgar, a son by "order of law," who is
also the elder son. He, under the law of primogeniture, will inherit
all of the Earl's titles and property. This is one of many dualities that
will drive the structure of the drama.

We learn quickly that Edmund is not willing to submit to the fate dealt him by the law. He rejects what he calls the plague of custom and celebrates his bastardy.

EDMUND   Thou, nature, art my goddess; to thy law
My services are bound. Wherefore should I
Stand in the plague of custom, and permit
The curiosity of nations to deprive me,
For that I am some twelve or fourteen moon-shines
Lag of a brother? Why bastard? wherefore base?
When my dimensions are as well compact,
My mind as generous, and my shape as true,
As honest madam's issue? Why brand they us
With base? with baseness? bastardy? base, base?
Who, in the lusty stealth of nature, take
More composition and fierce quality
Than doth, within a dull, stale, tired bed,
Go to the creating a whole tribe of fops,
Got 'tween asleep and wake? Well, then,
Legitimate Edgar, I must have your land:
Our father's love is to the bastard Edmund
As to the legitimate: fine word,–legitimate!
Well, my legitimate, if this letter speed,
And my invention thrive, Edmund the base
Shall top the legitimate. I grow; I prosper:
Now, gods, stand up for bastards!
                    (1.2.1–23)

Edmund is rejecting the law of the state (the common law) which declares him illegitimate. He is asserting that he will be governed only by the law of nature, which does not recognize such distinctions.

In Scene 2, Edmund has forged a letter in which Edgar appears to seek his father's early death in order to claim his inheritance. Edmund contrives to have his father see the letter. Like Lear,

Gloucester fails to "see better." Edmund cleverly fans the flames of Gloucester's rage at his innocent son.

GLOUCESTER   Hath he never heretofore sounded you in this
     business?

EDMUND   Never, my lord: but I have heard him oft
     maintain it to be fit, that, sons at perfect age,
     and fathers declining, the father should be as
     ward to the son, and the son manage his revenue.

GLOUCESTER   O villain, villain! His very opinion in the letter!
     Abhorred villain! Unnatural, detested, brutish villain! worse
     than brutish! Go, sirrah, seek him; I'll apprehend him: abom-
     inable villain!

                              (1.2.71–78)

Edmund cannot take the risk of having Edgar reveal his treachery. He cunningly convinces Edgar to flee his father's castle on pain of his life. On the heath, Edgar disguises himself as "Tom of Bedlam," that is, an insane beggar begrimed with filth and in tattered clothes who wanders about aimlessly. Gloucester attributes these unfortunate events to divine displeasure: "These late eclipses in the sun and moon portend no good to us" (1.2.106–07). On stage alone, Edmund responds:

EDMUND   This is the excellent foppery of the world, that,
     when we are sick in fortune,–often the surfeit
     of our own behavior,–we make guilty of our
     disasters the sun, the moon, and the stars: as
     if we were villains by necessity; fools by
     heavenly compulsion; knaves, thieves, and
     treachers, by spherical predominance; drunkards,
     liars, and adulterers, by an enforced obedience of
     planetary influence; and all that we are evil in,

by a divine thrusting on: an admirable evasion
of whoremaster man, to lay his goatish
disposition to the charge of a star!
                    (1.2.123–34)

At Albany's castle, things have gone bad quickly between Lear and his eldest daughter. As she abuses Lear to her steward, it is clear that she and Reagan are of "like mind" that their father is an idle old fool.

[Enter GONERIL, and OSWALD, her steward]

GONERIL   Did my father strike my gentleman for chiding of his fool?

OSWALD   Yes, madam.

GONERIL   By day and night he wrongs me; every hour
He flashes into one gross crime or other,
That sets us all at odds: I'll not endure it:
His knights grow riotous, and himself upbraids us
On every trifle. . . .

OSWALD   He's coming, madam; I hear him.

[Horns within]

GONERIL   Put on what weary negligence you please,
You and your fellows; I'll have it come to question:
If he dislike it, let him to our sister,
Whose mind and mine, I know, in that are one,
Not to be over-ruled. Idle old man,
That still would manage those authorities
That he hath given away! Now, by my life,
Old fools are babes again; and must be used
With cheques as flatteries,–when they are seen abused.
Remember what I tell you.

OSWALD   Well, madam.

(1.3.1–7, 11–22)

After Lear arrives, the disguised Kent convinces Lear to take him into his service. After a bitter quarrel with his daughter in which he curses her: "Blasts and fogs upon thee! / The untented woundings of a father's curse / Pierce every sense about thee!" (1.4.298–300), Lear storms out of Goneril's castle on his way to Regan. Goneril sends Oswald to warn Regan that trouble is on its way.

Throughout Act I, legal images and metaphors are employed with great effect. When Kent accuses Lear's Fool of saying nothing, the Fool responds: "Then 'tis like the breath of an unfee'd lawyer; you gave me nothing for't" (1.4.122).

Lear also sends the disguised Kent ahead to prepare Regan for his coming. Oswald and the loyal Kent meet at Gloucester's castle. Before they come to blows, Kent confronts Oswald for his insults to Lear.

KENT   Fellow, I know thee.

OSWALD   What dost thou know me for?

KENT   A knave; a rascal; an eater of broken meats; a base, proud, shallow, beggarly, three-suited, hundred-pound, filthy, worsted-stocking knave; a lily-livered, action-taking knave, a whoreson, glass-gazing, super-serviceable finical rogue; one-trunk-inheriting slave; one that wouldst be a bawd, in way of good service, and art nothing but the composition of a knave, beggar, coward, pandar, and the son and heir of a mongrel bitch: one whom I will beat into clamorous whining, if thou deniest the least syllable of thy addition.

(2.2.11–23)

Kent draws his sword and begins to beat Oswald who cries out: "Help, ho! murder! murder!" (2.2.37). Cornwall hears the fight and quickly takes Oswald's part in the quarrel.

CORNWALL   Fetch forth the stocks!
You stubborn ancient knave, you reverend braggart,
We'll teach you–

KENT   Sir, I am too old to learn:
Call not your stocks for me: I serve the king;
On whose employment I was sent to you:
You shall do small respect, show too bold malice
Against the grace and person of my master,
Stocking his messenger.

CORNWALL   Fetch forth the stocks! As I have life and honour,
There shall he sit till noon.
(2.2.126–36)

Stocks consisted of a heavy timber frame with holes for confining the ankles and sometimes the wrists, used for punishment of minor crimes. The offender was made to sit in a public place with his ankles or wrists confined in the device.

Lear arrives at Gloucester's castle and sees that his man Kent has been humiliated by being put in the stocks. He quickly quarrels with both his daughters. Ultimately, the cruel sisters insist that Lear give up all but fifty of his knights, then all but twenty-five, and then all. Their ingratitude—"I gave you all" (2.4.273)—drives Lear to the verge of madness.

GONERIL   Hear me, my lord;
What need you five and twenty, ten, or five,
To follow in a house where twice so many
Have a command to tend you?

REGAN   What need one?

KING LEAR   O, reason not the need: our basest beggars
   Are in the poorest thing superfluous:
   Allow not nature more than nature needs,
   Man's life's as cheap as beast's: thou art a lady;
   If only to go warm were gorgeous,
   Why, nature needs not what thou gorgeous wear'st,
   Which scarcely keeps thee warm. But, for true need,–
   You heavens, give me that patience, patience I need!
   You see me here, you gods, a poor old man,
   As full of grief as age; wretched in both!
   If it be you that stir these daughters' hearts
   Against their father, fool me not so much
   To bear it tamely; touch me with noble anger,
   And let not women's weapons, water-drops,
   Stain my man's cheeks! No, you unnatural hags,
   I will have such revenges on you both,
   That all the world shall–I will do such things,–
   What they are, yet I know not: but they shall be
   The terrors of the earth. You think I'll weep
   No, I'll not weep:
   I have full cause of weeping; but this heart
   Shall break into a hundred thousand flaws,
   Or ere I'll weep. O fool, I shall go mad!

[*Storm and tempest*]
(2.4.286–313)

Lear rages away into the heath. The cruel sisters order Gloucester to lock the doors to his castle, shutting Lear and his Fool out in a ferocious storm.

Acts I and II have structured the drama largely in terms of relationships between father and daughters, and between father and sons. Of course, in sixteenth century England, these relationships were governed in large part by law.

In Act III, the drama pivots to focus upon larger themes. The action begins on a heath. The weather is stormy and foul. An unnamed gentleman tells Kent the King is in a rage as he "[s]trives in his little world of man to out-scorn / The to-and-fro-conflicting wind and rain" (3.1.10–11).

In Scene 2, Lear enters accompanied only by his Fool. Lear urges the storm to do its worst.

KING LEAR   Blow, winds, and crack your cheeks! rage! blow!
   You cataracts and hurricanoes, spout
   Till you have drench'd our steeples, drown'd the cocks!
   You sulphurous and thought-executing fires,
   Vaunt-couriers to oak-cleaving thunderbolts,
   Singe my white head! And thou, all-shaking thunder,
   Smite flat the thick rotundity o' the world!
   Crack nature's moulds, an germens spill at once,
   That make ingrateful man!

FOOL   O nuncle, court holy-water in a dry
   house is better than this rain-water out o' door.
   Good nuncle, in, and ask thy daughters' blessing:
   here's a night pities neither wise man nor fool.

KING LEAR   Rumble thy bellyful! Spit, fire! spout, rain!
   Nor rain, wind, thunder, fire, are my daughters:
   I tax not you, you elements, with unkindness;
   I never gave you kingdom, call'd you children,
   You owe me no subscription: then let fall
   Your horrible pleasure: here I stand, your slave,
   A poor, infirm, weak, and despised old man:
   But yet I call you servile ministers,
   That have with two pernicious daughters join'd
   Your high engender'd battles 'gainst a head

So old and white as this. O! O! 'tis foul!
(3.2.1–24)

The storm here functions much like the storm in Julius Caesar. It mirrors the passions and turbulence of human relationships. It is also a profoundly dark view of what A.C. Bradley refers to as the "divine power." When the disguised Kent finds the King, Lear cries to the gods to administer justice to those who are guilty of hidden crimes.

KING LEAR   Let the great gods,
That keep this dreadful pother o'er our heads,
Find out their enemies now. Tremble, thou wretch,
That hast within thee undivulged crimes,
Unwhipp'd of justice: hide thee, thou bloody hand;
Thou perjured, and thou simular man of virtue
That art incestuous: caitiff, to pieces shake,
That under covert and convenient seeming
Hast practised on man's life: close pent-up guilts,
Rive your concealing continents, and cry
These dreadful summoners grace. I am a man
More sinn'd against than sinning.
(3.2.50–61)

Here, Lear calls upon the gods to punish those who have escaped earthly justice. For himself, Lear begins the process of recognizing his own humanity: "I am a man / More sinn'd against than sinning." (3.2.60–61). The Fool asks Lear to go into a nearby hovel to get out of the storm. For the first time in the play, Lear thinks of someone other than himself: He asks the Fool if he is cold.

In Scene 3, we return to the parallel story of Gloucester and Edmund. Gloucester, blind to his bastard son's villainy, tells him he has received a letter that tells of forces loyal to the King (Cordelia and her army) that have landed in England. As Gloucester leaves in secrecy to find the King, Edmund, in soliloquy, says he will betray his father to the Duke of Cornwall. "The younger rises when the old doth fall" (3.3.25).

Lear, out in the cold and rain and on the verge of madness, astonishingly, begins to feel sympathy for the first time for his subjects.

KING LEAR   Poor naked wretches, whereso'er you are,
That bide the pelting of this pitiless storm,
How shall your houseless heads and unfed sides,
Your loop'd and window'd raggedness, defend you
From seasons such as these? O, I have ta'en
Too little care of this! Take physic, pomp;
Expose thyself to feel what wretches feel,
That thou mayst shake the superflux to them,
And show the heavens more just.
(3.4.32–40)

Thus, the play now begins its central concern with the nature of justice. The inquiry does not end well. In a hovel, the Fool comes upon Edgar disguised as Poor Tom. Mad Lear and Poor Tom have a crazy conversation in which Lear asks the nearly naked man if he became a beggar after giving everything to his daughters. Lear then famously concludes: "Thou art the thing itself: unaccommodated man is no more but such a poor bare, forked animal as thou art" (3.4.107–09).

But Lear's madness has overtaken him. He thinks Poor Tom is a philosopher who can tell him the cause of thunder. He decides to put Goneril and Regan on trial in the "farmhouse" where they have sought shelter. In the imaginary trial, he insists upon an orderly proceeding.

KING LEAR   It shall be done; I will arraign them straight.

[To EDGAR]

Come, sit thou here, most learned justicer;

[To the Fool]

Thou, sapient sir, sit here. Now, you she foxes!

EDGAR   Look, where he stands and glares!
Wantest thou eyes at trial, madam?
Come o'er the bourn, Bessy, to me,–

FOOL   Her boat hath a leak,
And she must not speak
Why she dares not come over to thee. . . .

KENT   How do you, sir? Stand you not so amazed:
Will you lie down and rest upon the cushions?

KING LEAR   I'll see their trial first. Bring in the evidence.

[To EDGAR]

Thou robed man of justice, take thy place;

[To the Fool]

And thou, his yoke-fellow of equity,
Bench by his side:

[To KENT]

you are o' the commission,
Sit you too. . . .

KING LEAR   Arraign her first; 'tis Goneril. I here take my
oath before this honourable assembly, she kicked the
poor king her father.

FOOL   Come hither, mistress. Is your name Goneril?

KING LEAR   She cannot deny it.

FOOL   Cry you mercy, I took you for a joint-stool.

KING LEAR   And here's another, whose warp'd looks proclaim
What store her heart is made on. Stop her there!
Arms, arms, sword, fire! Corruption in the place!
False justicer, why hast thou let her 'scape?

EDGAR   Bless thy five wits!

KENT   O pity! Sir, where is the patience now,
That thou so oft have boasted to retain?
(3.6.20–59)

Arraignment is the early proceeding in a criminal case to bring
a criminal defendant before the court. The charges are presented
to the defendant, the opportunity to enter a plea is given, a determination of whether the party has a lawyer is made (or whether
a lawyer needs to be appointed), the amount of bail is set, and
future appearances are scheduled. The "robed man of justice" is
a reference to a judge of the common law courts. The reference to
"his yoke-fellow of equity" is a reference to the Court of Chancery,
which had jurisdiction as to equitable claims and relief.

By the middle of the fourteenth century, the Court of Chancery
became the great rival of the common law courts. In its beginning,
the Chancery was the royal secretariat. The Lord Chancellor had once
been second to the King in prestige and influence. He had custody
of the Great Seal and used it to authenticate documents prepared by
clerks in the Chancery. In theory, the Chancellor exercised judicial
power as the deputy of the King. In the turmoil of the fourteenth
and fifteenth centuries, the Chancellor began hearing more and
more petitions involving allegations of intimidation, corruption,
and bribery in the common law courts.

Gradually, Chancery's judicial duties eclipsed its administrative
responsibilities. By the mid-fifteenth century, the Court of Chancery
was the fourth law court to sit in Westminster Hall; it sat in the upper
end of Westminster Hall across from the Court of King's Bench. It did
not observe the terms of the common law courts and sat year-round.

The "equity" jurisdiction of the Court of Chancery developed haphazardly, as an alternative to the common law courts. By the fifteenth century, the Lord Chancellor was primarily a judicial officer, hearing and granting petitions where the remedies provided by the common law courts were inadequate.

For example, the Lord Chancellor could grant a petition for specific performance of a contract where the common law courts could award only money damages. The Court of Chancery exercised its equitable jurisdiction to relieve litigants of forfeitures and penalties that were enforced in the common law courts until the middle of the seventeenth century.

Lear is combining the courts of law and equity to achieve maximum potency in his imaginary trial. Of course, there was no such court in pre-Roman Britain. But the lawyers and law students in Shakespeare's audience would have understood the reference.

In Lear's trial of Goneril and Regan, the imaginary defendants escape with no punishment. Thus, the deluded King's attempt to obtain justice from the courts of law is a miserable failure. The law is a poor instrument to prevent or punish cruelty and ingratitude. The failed effort drives Lear further into madness and nihilism.

Gloucester arrives and warns Kent of the plot to murder the old King. Kent then gets the King on the way to Dover to meet Cordelia and her army.

Act III ends with the horrific scene in which Cornwall seizes Gloucester, has him bound to a chair, and declares him a traitor based upon Edmund's treachery. Even so, Cornwall does not follow Goneril's advice to hang Gloucester, which in Shakespeare's time, could not be done without a jury trial. Cornwall's punishment of Gloucester is more horrifying than a hanging.

CORNWALL Edmund, farewell.

[Exeunt GONERIL, EDMUND, and OSWALD]

Go seek the traitor Gloucester,
Pinion him like a thief, bring him before us.

[Exeunt other Servants]

Though well we may not pass upon his life
Without the form of justice, yet our power
Shall do a courtesy to our wrath, which men
May blame, but not control. Who's there? the traitor?

[Enter Gloucester, brought in by two or three]

REGAN   Ingrateful fox! 'tis he.

CORNWALL   Bind fast his corky arms.

GLOUCESTER   What mean your graces? Good my friends, consider
You are my guests: do me no foul play, friends.

CORNWALL   Bind him, I say.

[Servants bind him]

REGAN   Hard, hard. O filthy traitor!

GLOUCESTER   Unmerciful lady as you are, I'm none.
                                    (3.7.23–36)

After Cornwall gouges out one of Gloucester's eyes, a servant attempts to prevent him from doing the same to his remaining eye. Cornwall and the servant fight, and the servant is killed. Although fatally wounded, Cornwall gouges out Gloucester's other eye.

FIRST SERVANT   O, I am slain! My lord, you have one eye left
To see some mischief on him. O!

[Dies]

CORNWALL   Lest it see more, prevent it. Out, vile jelly!
Where is thy lustre now?

GLOUCESTER   All dark and comfortless. Where's my son
Edmund?
Edmund, enkindle all the sparks of nature,
To quit this horrid act.

REGAN   Out, treacherous villain!
Thou call'st on him that hates thee: it was he
That made the overture of thy treasons to us;
Who is too good to pity thee.

GLOUCESTER   O my follies! then Edgar was abused.
Kind gods, forgive me that, and prosper him!

REGAN   Go thrust him out at gates, and let him smell
His way to Dover.

(3.7.89–103)

Although blind, Gloucester now knows it was his bastard son
Edmund who betrayed him. After blinding Gloucester, Cornwall
dies of his wound. This appalling scene ends Act III.

As Act IV begins, the blind Gloucester is led onto the heath by
an elderly tenant, and they encounter Poor Tom.

OLD MAN   O, my good lord, I have been your tenant, and
your father's tenant, these fourscore years.

GLOUCESTER   Away, get thee away; good friend, be gone:
Thy comforts can do me no good at all;
Thee they may hurt.

OLD MAN   Alack, sir, you cannot see your way.

GLOUCESTER   I have no way, and therefore want no eyes;
I stumbled when I saw: full oft 'tis seen,
Our means secure us, and our mere defects
Prove our commodities. O dear son Edgar,
The food of thy abused father's wrath!
Might I but live to see thee in my touch,
I'd say I had eyes again!

OLD MAN   How now! Who's there?

EDGAR   [*Aside*] O gods! Who is't can say 'I am at
the worst'?
I am worse than e'er I was.

OLD MAN   'Tis poor mad Tom.

EDGAR   [*Aside*] And worse I may be yet: the worst is not
So long as we can say 'This is the worst.'
(4.1.13–32)

Gloucester is in the depths of his despair and determined to end
his life at the cliffs of Dover. Famously, he declares: "As flies to wanton
boys, are we to the gods. / They kill us for their sport" (4.1.42–43).
On stage, we see Edgar pretend to lead his father to the cliffs. In a flat
field, Gloucester falls down, thinking he is falling off the cliff. Edgar,
in a new persona, declares to Gloucester that he has miraculously
fallen from the heights of the cliff to the beach and yet lives.

At Dover, Cordelia has landed with a French army determined to
restore her father to his throne. "No blown ambition doth our arms
incite, / But love, dear love, and our aged father's right" (4.4.30–31).

In a field near Dover, the blind Gloucester and the mad Lear
meet. Gloucester asks if the voice that he hears is that of the King.

GLOUCESTER   The trick of that voice I do well remember: Is 't
not the king?

KING LEAR   Ay, every inch a king:
When I do stare, see how the subject quakes.
I pardon that man's life. What was thy cause? Adultery?
Thou shalt not die: die for adultery! No:
The wren goes to 't, and the small gilded fly
Does lecher in my sight.
Let copulation thrive; for Gloucester's bastard son
Was kinder to his father than my daughters
Got 'tween the lawful sheets.
                    (4.6.120–130)

Yes, this is the King. But not the old King. The old pride and arrogance are gone. Through his suffering, Lear has gained in his humanity and grants pardon even before it is asked. We see how far Lear has come when Gloucester asks to kiss his hand.

GLOUCESTER   O, let me kiss that hand!

KING LEAR   Let me wipe it first; it smells of mortality.

GLOUCESTER   O ruin'd piece of nature! This great world
Shall so wear out to nought.
                    (4.6.148–151)

Lear asks the blind Gloucester to read a letter. When Gloucester responds that he can only read it "feelingly," Lear delivers his final terrible condemnation of the hypocrisy of worldly justice.

KING LEAR   What, art mad? A man may see how this world
goes with no eyes. Look with thine ears: see how yond
justice rails upon yond simple thief. Hark, in
thine ear: change places; and, handy-dandy, which
is the justice, which is the thief? Thou hast seen
a farmer's dog bark at a beggar?

GLOUCESTER   Ay, sir.

KING LEAR   And the creature run from the cur? There thou
    mightst behold the great image of authority: a
    dog's obeyed in office.
    Thou rascal beadle, hold thy bloody hand!
    Why dost thou lash that whore? Strip thine own back;
    Thou hotly lust'st to use her in that kind
    For which thou whipp'st her. The usurer hangs the cozener.
    Through tatter'd clothes small vices do appear;
    Robes and furr'd gowns hide all. Plate sin with gold,
    And the strong lance of justice hurtless breaks:
    Arm it in rags, a pigmy's straw does pierce it.
    None does offend, none, I say, none; I'll able 'em:
    Take that of me, my friend, who have the power
    To seal the accuser's lips. Get thee glass eyes;
    And like a scurvy politician, seem
    To see the things thou dost not. . . .

EDGAR   O, matter and impertinency mix'd! Reason in
    madness!

                        (4.6.165–190)

In the depths of his madness, Lear now sees the irony of seeking
justice in a world where the rich and powerful hold all authority.
This is as close as Shakespeare ever gets to condemning the English
justice system as wholly corrupted by those with money. Perhaps he
got away with it because the words are spoke by a madman.

Edmund and Albany have joined forces to defeat the invading
French forces lead by Cordelia. On the eve of the battle, Cordelia's
attendants find Lear and bring him to her camp. He is given medicine and sleeps. When the doctor says she may wake him, Cordelia
calls for music and speaks to her father.

CORDELIA   How does my royal lord? How fares your majesty?

KING LEAR   You do me wrong to take me out o' the grave:
 Thou art a soul in bliss; but I am bound
 Upon a wheel of fire, that mine own tears
 Do scald like moulten lead.

CORDELIA   Sir, do you know me?

KING LEAR   You are a spirit, I know: when did you die?

CORDELIA   Still, still, far wide!

DOCTOR   He's scarce awake: let him alone awhile.

KING LEAR   Where have I been? Where am I? Fair daylight?
 I am mightily abused. I should e'en die with pity,
 To see another thus. I know not what to say.
(4.7.50–61)

But sleep has begun the process of Lear regaining his sanity.
It begins when Lear recognizes Cordelia as his daughter. And he
knows he must beg her forgiveness. He attempts to kneel before her.

CORDELIA   O, look upon me, sir,
 And hold your hands in benediction o'er me:
 No, sir, you must not kneel.

KING LEAR   Pray, do not mock me:
 I am a very foolish fond old man,
 Fourscore and upward, not an hour more nor less;
 And, to deal plainly,
 I fear I am not in my perfect mind.
 Methinks I should know you, and know this man;
 Yet I am doubtful for I am mainly ignorant
 What place this is; and all the skill I have
 Remembers not these garments; nor I know not

Where I did lodge last night. Do not laugh at me;
For, as I am a man, I think this lady
To be my child Cordelia.

CORDELIA   And so I am, I am.

KING LEAR   Be your tears wet? yes, 'faith. I pray, weep not:
If you have poison for me, I will drink it.
I know you do not love me; for your sisters
Have, as I do remember, done me wrong:
You have some cause, they have not.

CORDELIA   No cause, no cause.

(4.7.65–85)

In Cordelia's unqualified love and forgiveness, Lear the man is redeemed. It is in this sense that the play is a profound statement of the Christian belief in redemption through love and sacrifice.

In the other camp, lust, jealousy, and ambition reign supreme. Goneril and Regan are both in love with Edmund, and he encourages them both. On the eve of the battle, Edgar obtains a letter from Goneril to Edmund pledging to be his wife should Albany fall in the fighting. A disguised Edgar gives the letter to Albany just before the battle. We anticipate that good will defeat evil on the field of war. But it is not to be so. Near the battlefield, Edgar tells his father of the tragic outcome of the fight.

EDGAR   Away, old man; give me thy hand; away!
King Lear hath lost, he and his daughter ta'en:
Give me thy hand; come on.

GLOUCESTER   No farther, sir; a man may rot even here.

EDGAR   What, in ill thoughts again? Men must endure
Their going hence, even as their coming hither;

Ripeness is all: come on.

GLOUCESTER   And that's true too.
(5.2.6–13)

In Act V, Scene 3, Edmund orders Lear and Cordelia to prison. Lear's response shows how he has been transformed by Cordelia's unqualified love.

EDMUND   Some officers take them away: good guard,
Until their greater pleasures first be known
That are to censure them.

CORDELIA   We are not the first
Who, with best meaning, have incurr'd the worst.
For thee, oppressed king, am I cast down;
Myself could else out-frown false fortune's frown.
Shall we not see these daughters and these sisters?

KING LEAR   No, no, no, no! Come, let's away to prison:
We two alone will sing like birds I' the cage:
When thou dost ask me blessing, I'll kneel down,
And ask of thee forgiveness: so we'll live,
And pray, and sing, and tell old tales, and laugh
At gilded butterflies, and hear poor rogues
Talk of court news; and we'll talk with them too,
Who loses and who wins; who's in, who's out;
And take upon's the mystery of things,
As if we were God's spies: and we'll wear out,
In a wall'd prison, packs and sects of great ones,
That ebb and flow by the moon.

EDMUND   Take them away.
(5.3.9–21)

Ironically, Lear has gotten what he wanted in the beginning. Cordelia has sacrificed everything for him, and now will be his nurse in prison. Lear is the fool now for thinking he and Cordelia will be allowed to live happily in prison. Cordelia weeps because she suspects their true fate. Edmund gives secret instructions to the captain of the guard that Lear and Cordelia are to be murdered.

After the captives are led away, Albany, Goneril, and Regan join Edmund on stage. When Albany refuses to address Edmund as a brother, Regan declares that he must do so when Edmund becomes her husband. The quarreling of the jealous sisters is interrupted by Albany.

ALBANY   Stay yet; hear reason. Edmund, I arrest thee
On capital treason; and, in thine attaint,
This gilded serpent

[Pointing to Goneril]

For your claim, fair sister,
I bar it in the interest of my wife:
'Tis she is sub-contracted to this lord,
And I, her husband, contradict your bans.
If you will marry, make your loves to me,
My lady is bespoke.

GONERIL   An interlude!

ALBANY   Thou art arm'd, Gloucester: let the trumpet sound:
If none appear to prove upon thy head
Thy heinous, manifest, and many treasons,
There is my pledge;
[Throwing down a glove]
I'll prove it on thy heart,
Ere I taste bread, thou art in nothing less
Than I have here proclaim'd thee.

                    (5.2.95–109)

Albany has challenged Edmund to trial by battle, and Edmund accepts. Albany commands the trumpet to blow three times. A herald reads the challenge: "If any man of quality or degree within the lists of the army will maintain upon Edmund, supposed Earl of Gloucester, that he is a manifold traitor, let him appear by the third sound of the trumpet: he is bold in his defence" (5.2.130–134). Thus, Edmund's guilt is to be determined through trial by combat, according to the laws of chivalry.

At the third sound of the trumpet, Edgar enters on stage in armor with his face concealed. In the etiquette of trial by combat, Albany demands his name and his cause. Under the common law right to trial by battle upon an appeal of felony or treason, the accused was required to accept a challenge only from someone of equal rank.

ALBANY   Ask him his purposes, why he appears
Upon this call o' the trumpet.

HERALD   What are you?
Your name, your quality? and why you answer
This present summons?

EDGAR   Know, my name is lost;
By treason's tooth bare-gnawn and canker-bit:
Yet am I noble as the adversary
I come to cope.

ALBANY   Which is that adversary?

EDGAR   What's he that speaks for Edmund Earl of Gloucester?

EDMUND   Himself: what say'st thou to him?

EDGAR   Draw thy sword,
That, if my speech offend a noble heart,

Thy arm may do thee justice: here is mine.
                    (5.2.138–152)
They fight and Edgar mortally wounds Edmund. Albany confronts Goneril with her treachery and she flees the stage.

ALBANY   Go after her: she's desperate; govern her.

EDMUND   What you have charged me with, that have I done;
    And more, much more; the time will bring it out:
    'Tis past, and so am I. But what art thou
    That hast this fortune on me? If thou'rt noble,
    I do forgive thee.

EDGAR   Let's exchange charity.
    I am no less in blood than thou art, Edmund;
    If more, the more thou hast wrong'd me.
    My name is Edgar, and thy father's son.
    The gods are just, and of our pleasant vices
    Make instruments to plague us:
    The dark and vicious place where thee he got
    Cost him his eyes.

EDMUND   Thou hast spoken right, 'tis true;
    The wheel is come full circle: I am here.
                    (5.2.190–205)

Goneril has poisoned Regan and then kills herself offstage. As Edmund dies, he confesses to ordering the murder of Lear and Cordelia. He begs for them to be saved before the order can be carried out. But it is too late.

*[Re-enter KING LEAR, with CORDELIA dead in his arms;
EDGAR, Captain, and others following]*

KING LEAR   Howl, howl, howl, howl! O, you are men of stones:

Had I your tongues and eyes, I'ld use them so
That heaven's vault should crack. She's gone for ever!
I know when one is dead, and when one lives;
She's dead as earth. Lend me a looking-glass;
If that her breath will mist or stain the stone,
Why, then she lives.

KENT   Is this the promised end

EDGAR   Or image of that horror?
                    (5.2.302–310)

Lear has killed Cordelia's hangman, but too late. His darker purpose has been fulfilled. Lear's final lament over his dead daughter
is heartbreaking.

KING LEAR   And my poor fool [*Cordelia*] is hang'd! No, no, no
   life!
Why should a dog, a horse, a rat, have life,
And thou no breath at all? Thou'lt come no more,
Never, never, never, never, never!
Pray you, undo this button: thank you, sir.
Do you see this? Look on her, look, her lips,
Look there, look there!

[Dies]

EDGAR   He faints! My lord, my lord!

KENT   Break, heart; I prithee, break!

EDGAR   Look up, my lord.

KENT   Vex not his ghost: O, let him pass! he hates him much
   That would upon the rack of this tough world
   Stretch him out longer.

EDGAR   He is gone, indeed.

KENT   The wonder is, he hath endured so long:
  He but usurp'd his life.

                    (5.2.361–376)

Arthur Kirsch says of this final scene of the play: "There is no scene in Shakespeare that represents the finality of death more absolutely or more harshly; and the scene is not merely the conclusion of the action, it is its recapitulation, the moment toward which the whole of it has been directed."[23]

Albany speaks the last words of the play:

ALBANY   Bear them from hence. Our present business
  Is general woe.

  [To KENT and EDGAR]

  Friends of my soul, you twain
  Rule in this realm, and the gored state sustain.

KENT   I have a journey, sir, shortly to go;
  My master calls me, I must not say no.

ALBANY   The weight of this sad time we must obey;
  Speak what we feel, not what we ought to say.
  The oldest hath borne most: we that are young
  Shall never see so much, nor live so long.

  [Exeunt, with a dead march]
                    (5.2.377–386)

The immoral characters are all dead as well as some of the moral ones. Albany, Edgar, and Kent live. But in the end, it seems that

---

[23] Arthur Kirsch, *Shakespeare's Tragedies*, in John F. Andrews, ed., *William Shakespeare: His World, His Work, His Influence* (Charles Scribner's Sons, 1985), 525.

the Stoic philosophy of enduring suffering and misfortune with patience has failed. Albany says: "Speak what we feel, not what we ought to say."

I will conclude my discussion of King Lear by asking two related questions: First, reading the play as a whole, do we agree with Edgar that "The gods are just, and of our pleasant vices / Make instruments to plague us" (5.2.200–201)? Albany expresses the same idea when told of the death of Cornwall: "This shows you are above, / You justicers, that these our nether crimes / So speedily can venge! But, O poor Gloucester!" (4.2.88–90). This is essentially the idea of the Christian God who is all powerful and only good. Is the death of Cordelia just? Is her honesty in Act I a vice for which she must die?

This is not the only view expressed in the play about divine power. Gloucester himself says that "As flies to wanton boys, are we to the gods. / They kill us for their sport" (4.1.42–43). This is the idea of the pagan gods of Homer who intervene in human affairs to fulfill their own whims and desires.

Man's fate is arbitrary and out of human control. There is at least a third point of view, one expressed by Edmund: "Thou, nature, art my goddess; to thy law / My services are bound" (1.2.1–2). There is no divine justice, and Edmund is free to pursue whatever action is in his self-interest, even if it includes betraying his father and brother. Regan and Goneril are his soulmates in this.

The second, final question is: Why must Cordelia die? If Shakespeare's King Lear is interpreted purely as a parable about justice, this is a profoundly pessimistic ending. By any measure of justice—earthly or heavenly—Cordelia is innocent. We all must die, but killing Cordelia when she should live is killing innocence itself. Is this what Albany says we must feel at the end?

If so, the end of the play leaves us with nothing but pity and sorrow. If, however, King Lear is interpreted as a parable of the redeeming power of love and forgiveness, and the triumph, however imperfectly, of courage and virtue, it is a profoundly uplifting drama. I choose the second interpretation. For those in any position to administer justice, the play should be read often.

CHAPTER 18

MACBETH

"Fair is foul, and foul is fair" (*Macbeth*, 1.1.12). Three witches announce the theme of the play in the first scene of *Macbeth*.

On March 24, 1603, King James VI of Scotland succeeded Queen Elizabeth as King James I of England. At this time, the theaters were facing increasing pressure from the Puritans. Fortunately for Shakespeare, King James and Queen Anne loved the theater. When James arrived in London, he insisted that Shakespeare's theatrical company, the Lord Chamberlain's Men, become the King's Men. In its patent, Shakespeare was listed second among the actors in the company.

It has been said that *Macbeth* was written to show appreciation for the favor shown by its new patron. It was the first play Shakespeare wrote for the new sovereign, and the interests of King James pervade it. One of these was witchcraft. James thought of himself as a scholar; while he was King of Scotland he wrote a book about witchcraft, *Demonology*. So a play about a man who is destroyed by ambiguous prophesies made by witches would have appealed to James. He also had a horror of assassination. His father, husband of Mary, Queen of Scots, was assassinated less than a year after James's birth.

Shakespeare's *Macbeth* opens with three witches announcing that they will meet with Macbeth after a battle on the heath.

FIRST WITCH   When shall we three meet again
      In thunder, lightning, or in rain?

SECOND WITCH   When the hurlyburly's done,
      When the battle's lost and won.

THIRD WITCH   That will be ere the set of sun.

FIRST WITCH   Where the place?

SECOND WITCH   Upon the heath.

THIRD WITCH   There to meet with Macbeth. . . .

ALL   Fair is foul, and foul is fair:
      Hover through the fog and filthy air.
                    (1.1.1–13)

Thus, the play begins with ambiguity, a difference between
appearance and reality: "Fair is foul, and foul is fair" (1.1.12). This
will lead us directly into what the Shakespearean audience would
understand as "equivocation."

At a camp near Forres, a little town in the northern Lowlands,
King Duncan of Scotland, his sons, Malcolm and Donalbain, and
other attendants meet a bleeding soldier who gives them news of
a rebellion led by Macdonwald.

SERGEANT   Doubtful it stood;
      As two spent swimmers, that do cling together
      And choke their art. The merciless Macdonwald–
      Worthy to be a rebel, for to that
      The multiplying villanies of nature
      Do swarm upon him–from the Western Isles
      Of kerns and gallowglasses is supplied;
      And fortune, on his damned quarrel smiling,

Show'd like a rebel's whore: but all's too weak:
For brave Macbeth–well he deserves that name–
Disdaining fortune, with his brandish'd steel,
Which smoked with bloody execution,
Like valour's minion carved out his passage
Till he faced the slave;
Which ne'er shook hands, nor bade farewell to him,
Till he unseam'd him from the nave to the chaps,
And fix'd his head upon our battlements.

DUNCAN   O valiant cousin! worthy gentleman!
                    (1.2.9–26)

But the soldier also brings news of a Norwegian invasion that
Duncan's generals Macbeth and Banquo must meet. The Norwegians
are aided by the traitorous Thane of Cawdor. The Thane of Ross
enters and announces the victory of the forces loyal to Duncan.
Duncan summarily condemns Cawdor to death and gives his title
and lands to Macbeth. "No more that thane of Cawdor shall deceive
our bosom interest: go pronounce his present death, / And with his
former title greet Macbeth" (1.2.72–74).

The scene shifts to the heath near Forres where the three witches
appear. Macbeth and Banquo enter, and Macbeth says: "So foul
and fair a day I have not seen" (1.3.39). They then see the witches.
When Banquo and then Macbeth demand to know what they are,
the witches respond with fateful prophesies.

MACBETH   Speak, if you can: what are you?

FIRST WITCH   All hail, Macbeth! hail to thee, thane of Glamis!

SECOND WITCH   All hail, Macbeth, hail to thee, thane of
    Cawdor!

THIRD WITCH   All hail, Macbeth, thou shalt be king hereafter!

BANQUO   Good sir, why do you start; and seem to fear
  Things that do sound so fair? I' the name of truth,
  Are ye fantastical, or that indeed
  Which outwardly ye show? My noble partner
  You greet with present grace and great prediction
  Of noble having and of royal hope,
  That he seems rapt withal: to me you speak not.
  If you can look into the seeds of time,
  And say which grain will grow and which will not,
  Speak then to me, who neither beg nor fear
  Your favours nor your hate.

FIRST WITCH   [*To Banquo*] Hail!

SECOND WITCH   Hail!

THIRD WITCH   Hail!

FIRST WITCH   Lesser than Macbeth, and greater.

SECOND WITCH   Not so happy, yet much happier.

THIRD WITCH   Thou shalt get kings, though thou be none:
  So all hail, Macbeth and Banquo!

FIRST WITCH   Banquo and Macbeth, all hail!
                    (1.3.49–71)

Macbeth does not understand this; he thinks he is Thane of
Glamis, not of Cawdor. "Stay, you imperfect speakers, tell me more: /
By Sinel's death I know I am thane of Glamis; / But how of Cawdor?
the thane of Cawdor lives" (1.3.72–74). Sinel was Macbeth's father
from whom he inherited Glamis.

The witches vanish before answering his question. We are left
to ask: How are these things to happen? Lords Ross and Angus

enter and tell them of the King's joy at their success. Ross salutes
Macbeth as Thane of Cawdor. He says Cawdor has been condemned
to die for treason. Macbeth is now Thane of Cawdor by decree of
the King. Macbeth is astonished that the witches' first prophesy
has already come true. Will the others as well?

MACBETH   [*Aside.*]
   Two truths are told,
   As happy prologues to the swelling act
   Of the imperial theme. – I thank you, gentlemen.

   [*Aside.*]

   This supernatural soliciting
   Cannot be ill, cannot be good: if ill,
   Why hath it given me earnest of success,
   Commencing in a truth? I am thane of Cawdor:
   If good, why do I yield to that suggestion
   Whose horrid image doth unfix my hair
   And make my seated heart knock at my ribs,
   Against the use of nature? Present fears
   Are less than horrible imaginings:
   My thought, whose murder yet is but fantastical,
   Shakes so my single state of man that function
   Is smother'd in surmise, and nothing is
   But what is not.

BANQUO   Look, how our partner's rapt.

MACBETH   [*Aside.*]
   If chance will have me king, why, chance may crown me,
   Without my stir.
                    (1.3.136–152)

The prophecy that Macbeth will become King is ambiguous,
equivocal. Does it mean he will become King in the normal course

of events? If so, there is nothing he must do to become King. But clearly, the witches' prophecy has triggered thoughts in Macbeth of another way to become King.

Tenth-century Lowland Scotland had just undergone several centuries of endless tribal warfare and revolts by the thanes against whoever called himself king. The nobility elected the king, and there was no rigid hereditary succession. Thus, the kingdom was in a state of chronic political instability. The idea of the divine right of kings emerged later—when kings were made by birth (as under the Tudors and the Stuarts) and not by election.

Duncan is an old man. As a member of the royal family, Macbeth had the right to assume he would be considered a legitimate successor to Duncan. But by murder? That is his own guilty thought. The idea of killing a king selected by God would have been a "horrible imagining" in the early seventeenth century.

At the palace, Duncan is impatient to know if Cawdor has been executed. Indeed, he has been.

DUNCAN   Is execution done on Cawdor? Are not
Those in commission yet return'd?

MALCOLM   My liege,
They are not yet come back. But I have spoke
With one that saw him die: who did report
That very frankly he confess'd his treasons,
Implored your highness' pardon and set forth
A deep repentance: nothing in his life
Became him like the leaving it; he died
As one that had been studied in his death
To throw away the dearest thing he owed,
As 'twere a careless trifle.

(1.4.1–12)

This is the typical formula for scaffold confessions of sixteenth and seventeenth century England. On the scaffold, the condemned man would confess his treason and beg pardon of the King. All the property of a condemned traitor was forfeit to the Crown. The condemned man might confess and beg pardon in the hope that some of his property might be spared for a wife or children. Or he might be promised divine forgiveness in exchange for an earthly confession. Often, scaffold confessions were printed up as pamphlets and distributed to bolster the legitimacy of the sitting monarch.

Duncan responds to the news of Cawdor's execution: "There's no art / To find the mind's construction in the face: / He was a gentleman on whom I built / An absolute trust" (1.4.12–15).

Is Duncan about to make the same mistake again?

Macbeth and Banquo enter and are saluted with thanks by Duncan. Ominously for Macbeth however, Duncan announces he will name his son Malcolm as Prince of Cumberland and his successor.

As I said earlier, the Scottish kingship did not necessarily descend according to the laws of primogeniture. Indeed, the historical Duncan succeeded his maternal grandfather as King. So this is a serious blow to Macbeth's ambitions. Duncan has chosen an impolitic time to cut off the capable and ambitious Macbeth from further advancement. Macbeth immediately understands the implications of this sudden check upon his aspirations.

MACBETH   [*Aside.*]
    The Prince of Cumberland! that is a step
    On which I must fall down, or else o'erleap,
    For in my way it lies. Stars, hide your fires;
    Let not light see my black and deep desires:
    The eye wink at the hand; yet let that be,
    Which the eye fears, when it is done, to see.
              (1.4.48–53)

The King is going to Inverness and will stop at Macbeth's castle of Dunsinane to spend the night on the way. Has Duncan made a fatal political error?

At Dunsinane, Lady Macbeth has received a letter from her husband relating the prophesies of the three witches. From her reaction, it's clear she will be a willing, even eager party to her husband's ambitions.

LADY MACBETH   Glamis thou art, and Cawdor; and shalt be
What thou art promised: yet do I fear thy nature;
It is too full o' the milk of human kindness
To catch the nearest way: thou wouldst be great;
Art not without ambition, but without
The illness should attend it: what thou wouldst highly,
That wouldst thou holily; wouldst not play false,
And yet wouldst wrongly win: thou'ldst have, great Glamis,
That which cries 'Thus thou must do, if thou have it;
And that which rather thou dost fear to do
Than wishest should be undone.' Hie thee hither,
That I may pour my spirits in thine ear;
And chastise with the valour of my tongue
All that impedes thee from the golden round,
Which fate and metaphysical aid doth seem
To have thee crown'd withal.
                    (1.5.16–31)

A messenger arrives to tell Lady Macbeth that Duncan will spend the night Dunsinane. She prays to evil spirits to assist her in the murder of Duncan to make her husband King.

Then Macbeth arrives. Without speaking of the deed, both know what they are thinking of doing. Lady Macbeth says, "Leave all the rest to me" (1.5.75). It seems clear that murdering Duncan is something they have talked about.

Duncan arrives and is welcomed to Macbeth's castle. In a soliloquy, Macbeth expresses grave doubts about the plan to murder Duncan. If the murder would be "the be-all and the end-all here" (1.7.5) he would do it. But he is afraid that by "even-handed justice" (1.7.13) similar means might lead to his deposition as king. "Bloody

instructions, which, being taught, return / To plague the inventor"
(1.7.11–12).

Unlike the naïve Brutus in *Julius Caesar*, Macbeth understands
that one political murder will lead to another and then another. He
knows he owes loyalty to Duncan as his subject, as his kinsman, and
as his host. Macbeth: "He's here in double trust" (1.7.15). Duncan
has been a meek, virtuous King, and Macbeth has nothing but
ambition to spur him to the awful deed. But unlike Richard III, he
acknowledges moral restraints upon his ambition. "My thought,
whose murder yet is but fantastical, / Shakes so my single state of
man that function / Is smother'd in surmise, and nothing is / But
what is not" (1.3.146–49).

It is this temporary triumph of conscience that makes Macbeth
seem a tragic character who at first has the sympathy of the audience. He tells Lady Macbeth, "We will proceed no further in this
business" (1.7.31). She responds with scorn:

LADY MACBETH   Was the hope drunk
  Wherein you dress'd yourself? hath it slept since?
  And wakes it now, to look so green and pale
  At what it did so freely? From this time
  Such I account thy love. Art thou afeard
  To be the same in thine own act and valour
  As thou art in desire? Wouldst thou have that
  Which thou esteem'st the ornament of life,
  And live a coward in thine own esteem,
  Letting 'I dare not' wait upon 'I would,'
  Like the poor cat i' the adage?

MACBETH   Prithee, peace:
  I dare do all that may become a man;
  Who dares do more is none.

LADY MACBETH   What beast was't, then,
  That made you break this enterprise to me?

When you durst do it, then you were a man;
And, to be more than what you were, you would
Be so much more the man. Nor time nor place
Did then adhere, and yet you would make both:
They have made themselves, and that their fitness now
Does unmake you. I have given suck, and know
How tender 'tis to love the babe that milks me:
I would, while it was smiling in my face,
Have pluck'd my nipple from his boneless gums,
And dash'd the brains out, had I so sworn as you
Have done to this.

MACBETH   If we should fail?

LADY MACBETH   We fail!
But screw your courage to the sticking-place,
And we'll not fail.

(1.7.35–61)

The tragedy of Macbeth is that he cannot resist his wife's assault upon his manhood. He will suppress his conscience and murder Duncan.

Lady Macbeth's plan is to make Duncan's attendants drunk while he sleeps, then blame the murder on them. Macbeth is resolved to proceed with the murder. "Away, and mock the time with fairest show: / False face must hide what the false heart doth know" (1.7.81–82). Macbeth has a vision of a dagger magically suspended in mid-air. "It is the bloody business which informs / Thus to mine eyes" (2.1.48–49).

When Lady Macbeth rings a bell from inside the castle, Macbeth knows it is time to do the "bloody business." Macbeth: "I go, and it is done; the bell invites me. / Hear it not, Duncan; for it is a knell / That summons thee to heaven or to hell" (2.1.62–64).

Lady Macbeth has drugged the drink of Duncan's attendants. The murder itself occurs offstage. Macbeth returns with bloody hands and says he has done the deed. "My husband!" (2.2.17) she exclaims. Macbeth begins to think on the enormity of his murder of Duncan. But Lady Macbeth is relentless.

MACBETH   Methought I heard a voice cry 'Sleep no more!
   Macbeth does murder sleep', the innocent sleep,
   Sleep that knits up the ravell'd sleeve of care,
   The death of each day's life, sore labour's bath,
   Balm of hurt minds, great nature's second course,
   Chief nourisher in life's feast,–

LADY MACBETH   What do you mean?

MACBETH   Still it cried 'Sleep no more!' to all the house:
   'Glamis hath murder'd sleep, and therefore Cawdor
   Shall sleep no more; Macbeth shall sleep no more.'

LADY MACBETH   Who was it that thus cried? Why, worthy
   thane,
   You do unbend your noble strength, to think
   So brainsickly of things. Go get some water,
   And wash this filthy witness from your hand.
   Why did you bring these daggers from the place?
   They must lie there: go carry them; and smear
   The sleepy grooms with blood.
                          (2.2.46–62)

Macbeth refuses to return to Duncan's quarters. Lady Macbeth says she will do it. The sleeping and the dead are no more than pictures. "If he do bleed, / I'll gild the faces of the grooms withal; / For it must seem their guilt" (2.2.69–71). Macbeth looks at his bloody hands, and asks himself, "Will all great Neptune's ocean wash this blood / Clean from my hand? No, this my hand will rather / The multitudinous seas in incarnadine, / Making the green one red" (2.2.75–78).

Lady Macbeth returns with her own bloody hands. They hear a loud knocking from the south entry of the castle. Despite this, they retire to wash away the blood. Lady Macbeth: "A little water clears us of this deed" (2.2.83). It is her fate to learn that moral responsibility for murder is not so easily washed away. Macbeth wishes the knocking could waken Duncan, but he knows it cannot. The deed cannot be undone.

The knocking is that of Macduff and Lennox, who have come to see the King. But before we see them, a porter, who is drunk, enters. He imagines he is the gatekeeper of Hell and is welcoming new arrivals.

[Knocking within. Enter a Porter.]

PORTER   Here's a knocking indeed! If a man were porter of hell-gate, he should have old turning the key. *[Knocking within.]* Knock, knock, knock! Who's there, i' the name of Beelzebub? Here's a farmer, that hanged himself on the expectation of plenty: come in time; have napkins enow about you; here you'll sweat for't. *[Knocking within.]* Knock, knock! Who's there, in th'other devil's name? Faith, here's an equivocator, that could swear in both the scales against either scale; who committed treason enough for God's sake, yet could not equivocate to heaven: O, come in, equivocator. *[Knocking within.]* Knock, knock, knock! Who's there? Faith, here's an English tailor come hither, for stealing out of a French hose: come in, tailor; here you may roast your goose. *[Knocking within.]* Knock, knock; never at quiet! What are you? But this place is too cold for hell. I'll devil-porter it no further: I had thought to have let in some of all professions that go the prim-rose way to the everlasting bonfire. *[Knocking within.]* Anon, anon! I pray you, remember the porter. *[Opens the gate.]*
                                        (2.3.1–14)

"Equivocation" was a technique used by Jesuit priests to evade questions of their loyalty to the pope when they were in England illegally seeking converts to Catholicism. It was generally understood to mean saying one thing while thinking another thing was the truth. Or saying something in an ambiguous way that was subject to more than one interpretation.

The leader of the clandestine Jesuit mission in England was the Jesuit priest Henry Garnet who had written *A Treatise of Equivocation*. Sir Edward Coke found a manuscript copy of the treatise in the Inner Temple rooms of one of the Gunpowder Plot conspirators. Garnet went on trial for treason in March 1606 for his role in the failed 1605 Gunpowder Plot to assassinate King James and the members of Parliament. In prosecuting Garnet, Attorney General Edward Coke soundly condemned the Jesuit teaching of equivocation as nothing more than lying. Garnet defended equivocation by saying: "So then no man may equivocate, when he ought to tell the truth, otherwise he may."

Garnet was convicted, hanged, drawn and quartered. His head was set on a pole on London Bridge. The porter is probably referring to Garnet entering the gates of Hell. To Shakespeare's audience the reference to equivocation would have been obvious. The word appears once more in Act V.

After he is told that Burnam Wood is moving toward Dunsinane, Macbeth exclaims: "I pull in resolution, and begin / To doubt the equivocation of the fiend / That lies like truth" (5.5.42–43).

Macduff and Lennox enter. Macduff asks the porter why he was sleeping so late. The porter's response is the only comic moment in the play.

PORTER   'Faith sir, we were carousing till the second cock: and drink, sir, is a great provoker of three things.

MACDUFF   What three things does drink especially provoke?

PORTER   Marry, sir, nose-painting, sleep, and urine. Lechery, sir, it provokes, and unprovokes; it provokes the desire, but it takes away the performance: therefore, much drink may be said to be an equivocator with lechery: it makes him, and it mars him; it sets him on, and it takes him off; it persuades him, and disheartens him; makes him stand to, and not stand to; in conclusion, equivocates him in a sleep, and, giving him the lie, leaves him.

MACDUFF I believe drink gave thee the lie last night.

PORTER That it did, sir.

(2.3.33–43)

Macbeth joins them after he has cleaned off all the blood. After Macduff goes in to see Duncan, Lennox tells Macbeth of the strange things that have happened during the night. Macbeth laconically remarks, "'Twas a rough night" (2.3.67). Macduff returns horrified at what he has found. Macduff: "O horror, horror, horror! Tongue nor heart / Cannot conceive nor name thee!" (2.3.68–69). Macbeth goes into the King's quarters. Lady Macbeth enters and is told of Duncan's murder. She asks nervously, "What, in our house?" (2.3.95). Macbeth returns and speaks of regret with an irony only he and the audience can fully appreciate.

[Re-enter MACBETH and LENNOX, with ROSS.]

MACBETH Had I but died an hour before this chance,
I had lived a blessed time; for, from this instant,
There 's nothing serious in mortality:
All is but toys: renown and grace is dead;
The wine of life is drawn, and the mere lees
Is left this vault to brag of.

(2.3.96–101)

Malcolm and Donalbain are awakened and told of their father's murder. Lennox says Duncan's attendants must have done it because they were found with bloody hands and faces and bloody daggers on their pillows. In a "fury" (2.3.112) Macbeth enters the King's chambers and kills the attendants. Macduff immediately questions this: "Wherefore did you so?" (2.3.114). Further questions are preempted when Lady Macbeth faints.

Malcolm and Donalbain, fearing they too may be murdered, decide to flee. Malcolm will go to England and Donalbain to Ireland. Their flight is taken by some at the court to be evidence of guilt in the murder of their father. Macbeth is named King and goes to Scone to be crowned. He now appears to be the legitimate King of Scotland. Nothing good happens to him thereafter.

At the Palace in Forres, Banquo muses upon the prophesies of the three witches. The prophecies to Macbeth have all been fulfilled. He suspects Macbeth of the murder of Duncan. "Thou hast it now: king, Cawdor, Glamis, all, / As the weird women promised, and, I fear, / Thou play'dst most foully for't" (3.1.1–3). Will the prophecy as to Banquo fathering a line of kings be also fulfilled?

Macbeth invites Banquo to a banquet that evening. Before dinner, Banquo and his son Fleance will go riding. Macbeth remembers the prophecy about Banquo. He fears this means no son of his will inherit the Scottish throne. Macbeth tells Lady Macbeth he has scorpions in his mind as long as Banquo and Fleance live.

Defying fate, he arranges to have Banquo and Fleance murdered as they return to the castle. Macbeth: "It is concluded. Banquo, thy soul's flight, / If it find heaven, must find it out to-night" (3.1.155–56). But the murderers bungle the job, killing Banquo but allowing Fleance to escape. That night, as the banquet begins, one of the murderers tells Macbeth that Banquo is dead in a ditch, but his son has fled.

The bloody ghost of Banquo enters the banquet room and sits at Macbeth's seat. Only Macbeth can see the ghost, and his fearful outbursts alarm Lady Macbeth and the other guests. After the ghost disappears, Lady Macbeth tells the guests to go. "At once, good night: / Stand not upon the order of your going, / But go at once" (3.4.117–19). When Macbeth calms down and remembers that Macduff has not obeyed his summons to attend the banquet, he recognizes there must be more bloodshed if he is to hold on to his crown. "It will have blood; they say, blood will have blood" (3.4.123). He will revisit the three witches the next day to know his fate. Macbeth: "All causes shall give way: I am in blood / Stepp'd in so far that, should I wade no more, / Returning were as tedious as go o'er" (3.4.136–38).

Lady Macbeth says they should go to bed. This is the last time they speak to each other on the stage. Killing Banquo has not made Macbeth easy and secure on the throne. Unlike Richard II, Macbeth never refers to himself as a king anointed by God. Indeed, that would seem a form of blasphemy. Macbeth has cast away his moral scruples against killing to gain and now keep the crown. This bodes ill. As I see in my daily work, crime begets more crime. A lawyer steals money from a client to support a lifestyle he cannot quite afford. He then steals from a second client to conceal his first offense, and so on until it all collapses and he ends up in federal prison.

Suspecting Macbeth of the murder of Duncan, Macduff has fled to join Malcolm in England. They seek the aid of King Edward to make war against Macbeth. By rebelling against Macbeth the King, they are committing treason. Technically, they are just as guilty as the Earl of Cawdor. Knowing Macbeth obtained the throne by the unprovoked murder of Duncan, we do not question the legitimacy of their rebellion.

The three witches appear again on the heath. Hecate tells them Macbeth will come to the pit of Acheron "to know his destiny" (3.5.17). The witches are then seen in a cave where they are mixing an evil brew in a caldron. All: "Double, double toil and trouble; / Fire burn, and cauldron bubble" (4.1.10–11). Macbeth enters and demands to know his fate. A first apparition appears and says, "beware Macduff; / Beware the thane of Fife" (4.1.71–72). A second apparition comes and says, "Be bloody, bold, and resolute; laugh to scorn / The power of man, for none of woman born / Shall harm Macbeth" (4.1.79–81). A third apparition adds, "Macbeth shall never vanquish'd be until / Great Birnam wood to high Dunsinane hill / Shall come against him" (4.1.92–94).

Macbeth is reassured by these prophesies. In their first encounter with the weird sisters, Banquo had warned Macbeth: "And oftentimes, to win us to our harm, / The instruments of darkness tell us truths, / Win us with honest trifles, to betray's / In deepest consequence" (1.3.130–33). That is what is happening now. The prophecy is ambiguous. It is another equivocation. Macbeth chooses to believe what he wants to believe—with disastrous results. Then the witches show him an apparition of a line of eight kings followed by the ghost of Banquo. According to legend, James I was a descendant of Banquo. Told that Macduff has fled to England, Macbeth sends men to capture his castle at Fife and murder his wife and children.

In England, young Malcolm tells Macduff the English King has given him ten thousand men to invade Scotland. But then Ross tells Macduff his castle has been captured and his wife and children slaughtered. Macduff is shocked and blames the catastrophe on himself. Malcolm says, "Be this the whetstone of your sword: let grief / Convert to anger; blunt not the heart, enrage it" (4.3.228–29).

Macbeth is at his castle Dunsinane. Lady Macbeth's guilty conscience has driven her insane. She is observed sleepwalking by one of her women and a doctor. They hear her say, "Yet who would have thought the old man to have had so much blood in him" (5.1.38). She says she and Macbeth have nothing to fear because no one can hold them accountable. But she knows what they did. Lady Macbeth: "Here's the smell of the blood still: all the perfumes of Arabia will not sweeten this little hand. Oh, oh, oh!" (5.1.57–59). The doctor suspects what we in the audience know. But he is silent, as are we.

Outside the castle, Malcolm and his forces gather in Birnam Wood. Inside, Macbeth is told there are ten thousand men ready to storm the castle. But Macbeth remembers the prophesies of the witches and is unafraid. He says, "The mind I sway by and the heart I bear / Shall never sag with doubt nor shake with fear" (5.3.9–10). Yet Macbeth understands and appreciates what his murderous course has cost him.

MACBETH   Seyton!–I am sick at heart,
When I behold–Seyton, I say!–This push
Will cheer me ever, or disseat me now.
I have lived long enough: my way of life
Is fall'n into the sear, the yellow leaf,
And that which should accompany old age,
As honour, love, obedience, troops of friends,
I must not look to have; but, in their stead,
Curses, not loud but deep, mouth-honour, breath,
Which the poor heart would fain deny, and dare not. Seyton!
                                    (5.3.19–28)

Here, Macbeth seems fully aware of what his ambition and dreadful murders have cost him. In this he seems to me to retain more of a sense of consciousness of guilt than Claudius in *Hamlet*. Nevertheless, he will bravely meet his fate. He says he will fight until all his flesh is hacked off his bones. Macbeth will not be afraid "Till Birnam forest come to Dunsinane" (5.3.60).

In the wood, Malcom orders his soldiers to cut down leafy boughs and hold them up to conceal the number of their troops as they advance. In the castle, Macbeth is confident he can withstand a siege. Seyton and Macbeth hear a cry of women. Seyton investigates. He returns and tells Macbeth that Lady Macbeth is dead. He responds, "She should have died hereafter; / There would have been a time for such a word" (5.5.17–18). Macbeth reflects upon what his life means. It is the ultimate in nihilistic despair.

MACBETH   To-morrow, and to-morrow, and to-morrow,
Creeps in this petty pace from day to day
To the last syllable of recorded time,
And all our yesterdays have lighted fools
The way to dusty death. Out, out, brief candle!
Life's but a walking shadow, a poor player
That struts and frets his hour upon the stage
And then is heard no more: it is a tale

Told by an idiot, full of sound and fury,
Signifying nothing.

(5.5.19–28)

President Lincoln is said to have read this speech to the Secretary of the Senate during the bloody battle of Spotsylvania Courthouse and said the words came to him as a "consolation." Of course, the words express a profound pessimism.

According to author Michael Anderegg, "Lincoln turned to Shakespeare not for consolation in the usual sense of the word but, rather, for powerful imaginative expressions of pain and loss that echoed his own feelings."[24]

A messenger enters and tells Macbeth he has seen Birnam Wood moving toward Dunsinane. Macbeth responds: "I pull in resolution, and begin / To doubt the equivocation of the fiend / That lies like truth" (5.5.42–44). After threatening to hang the messenger if his story is false, Macbeth decides to leave the castle and go out and meet his foes. Macbeth: "Ring the alarum-bell! Blow, wind! come, wrack! / At least we'll die with harness on our back" (5.5.51–52). Macbeth fights bravely and slays a young soldier, Siward.

Macduff confronts Macbeth on the battlefield. Macbeth tells Macduff he has a charmed life because he cannot be killed by man of woman born. Macduff responds: "And let the angel whom thou still hast served / Tell thee, Macduff was from his mother's womb / Untimely ripp'd (5.8.15–17).

Macbeth has misconstrued the witches' prophesies, which now seem to condemn him to defeat and death. Macbeth does not run away from his fate. "Before my body / I throw my warlike shield. Lay on, Macduff, / And damn'd be him that first cries, 'Hold, enough!'" (5.8.32–34). Macbeth and Macduff exit fighting. Malcolm's forces capture the castle. He has won the battle, but what has happened to Macduff?

---

[24] Michael Anderegg, *Lincoln and Shakespeare* (University Press of Kansas, 2015), 44.

[Re-enter MACDUFF, with MACBETH's head]

MACDUFF   Hail, king! for so thou art: behold, where stands
The usurper's cursed head: the time is free:
I see thee compass'd with thy kingdom's pearl,
That speak my salutation in their minds;
Whose voices I desire aloud with mine:
Hail, King of Scotland!

ALL   Hail, King of Scotland!

[Flourish]

(5.8.55–61)

Another Scottish king has been killed offstage. The play ends with
Malcolm's triumphant promise to award new honors to his thanes
and to recall all those who fled Macbeth's tyranny.

MALCOLM   We shall not spend a large expense of time
Before we reckon with your several loves,
And make us even with you. My thanes and kinsmen,
Henceforth be earls, the first that ever Scotland
In such an honour named. What's more to do,
Which would be planted newly with the time,
As calling home our exiled friends abroad
That fled the snares of watchful tyranny;
Producing forth the cruel ministers
Of this dead butcher and his fiend-like queen,
Who, as 'tis thought, by self and violent hands
Took off her life; this, and what needful else
That calls upon us, by the grace of Grace,
We will perform in measure, time and place:
So, thanks to all at once and to each one,
Whom we invite to see us crown'd at Scone.

(5.8.60–75)

Thus, treason, murder, and tyranny are overthrown; justice and the moral order are restored. The witches' prophesy is that a new line of kings will be established on the Scottish throne that leads all the way through time to King James himself. But as the scholar Stephen Greenblatt has said, "the witches are dancing around the cauldron, and, the play seems to imply, the cauldron is in every one of us." [25]

Before Banquo's descendants can become kings, must there be another bloody overthrow of Malcolm or his heirs? Why did Shakespeare write a tragedy about a tyrant and a murderer? I think Harold Goddard answered that question when he wrote: "Macbeth is at bottom any man of noble intentions who gives way to his appetites. And who at one time or another has not been that man? Who, looking back over his life, cannot perceive some moral catastrophe that he escaped by inches? Or did not escape. *Macbeth* reveals how close we who thought ourselves safe may be to the precipice."[26]

In many ways, *Macbeth* is a puzzling play to have been written for performance before the new King. It is true that it shows the horror and carnage that result from the murder of a legitimate king. It was written just a year after the failed Gunpowder Plot aimed at killing James I. And the play predicts a long line of kings, including James himself, springing from the loins of Banquo.

But the play also depicts the transformation of Macbeth into a bloody tyrant who ignores English–Scottish legal traditions. No one in the play (unlike the Bishop of Carlisle in *Richard II*) questions the use of force to depose the tyrannical Macbeth.

While still James VI of Scotland, the King had published a treatise titled *The True Law of Free Monarchies*. In it, he preached a doctrine of absolutist rule of monarchs ordained by God and unchecked by legal restraints. If there are no legal restraints, is armed rebellion a morally acceptable alternative? What about political assassination?

---

[25] Stephen Greenblatt, ed., *The Norton Shakespeare*, (W. W. Norton & Co., 2015), 2717.
[26] Goddard, Vol. 2, pp. 109–10.

In the late fourteenth century, one of the early common law legal historians, Sir John Fortescue, in his *In Praise of the Laws of England*, stated the case against the doctrine later expressed in James's *True Law*:

> [A]mong the civil [Roman] laws there is a famous sentence, maxim or rule, which runs like this, "what pleased the prince has the force of law." The laws of England do not sanction any such maxim, since the king of that land rules his people not only royally but also politically, and so he is bound by oath at his coronation to the observance of his law.

Fortescue is making the argument that even the king is subject to the rule of law in England. The year after James's coronation, Sir Edward Coke wrote in his Reports:

> The king is under no man; but only God and the law, for the law makes the King: Therefore let the King attribute that to the law, which from the law he hath received, to witt power and dominion.

James had shown his ignorance or defiance of English law in 1603. On his way to London to be crowned as King, he ordered a thief to be hanged without giving him a trial by jury. One corollary of James' royal absolutism was that there could be no legitimate resistance to even the worst sort of king.

The paradox of Shakespeare's *Macbeth* is that according to *The True Law* there could be no resistance to a king ("an untitled tyrant bloody-sceptered") who obtained the throne by murder and kept it by murdering all who were perceived by him as a threat.

Within four years of the first performance of *Macbeth*, the conflict between Stuart absolutism and English constitutionalism would result in the Petition of Right protesting against the imposition of taxes without an act of Parliament. In less than forty years, the conflict would result in civil war and the beheading of a legitimate king—Charles I. The Act of Parliament creating a High Court of Justice in 1649 to try Charles accused him of having "a wicked design totally to subvert the ancient and fundamental laws and liberties of this nation, and in their place to introduce an arbitrary and tyrannical government."

After a brief republican interlude under Oliver Cromwell and the overthrow of the last Stuart king, England emerged as what it is today: a constitutional monarchy.

CHAPTER 19

Henry VIII

Although included in the *First Folio*, there has been considerable debate over the years about how much of this play was written by Shakespeare. The leading contender as co-author has been John Fletcher, who took over as the house dramatist for the King's Men when Shakespeare left London for retirement in 1610. However, Fletcher was still alive when Heminges and Condell attributed the play to Shakespeare in the *First Folio*. Certainly, the prologue that begins the play is a sad piece of writing compared to the prologue of *Henry V*, Shakespeare's last history play, written in 1599.

Henry VIII could not have been written and staged during the reign of Elizabeth, who is depicted as an infant at the end of the play. By 1613, when it was first performed, however, enough time had passed to escape the heavy hand of the censors. In addition, the play contains elaborate spectacles that would have appealed to King James.

On June 29, 1613, during one of the first performances of the play, a cannon was fired in the Globe Theater during the masque at Cardinal Woolsey's house upon the entrance of the actor playing Henry VIII. A spark from the cannon set the thatch roof on fire and the Globe burned to the ground. Only one person was injured—a gentleman whose pants caught fire and were doused with a bottle of ale.

Henry VIII begins at the palace in London. The Duke of Norfolk describes to the Duke of Buckingham the meeting between King

Henry VIII and Francis I, King of France in 1520, at what came to be called the Field of the Cloth of Gold. This fabulously lavish meeting was an effort by Francis I to obtain an alliance with England in France's war against Charles V of Spain and the Holy Roman Empire. Four thousand English noblemen accompanied King Henry to the field near Calais. There were tournaments and joisting. Henry and Francis swore eternal friendship. But an "untimely ague" kept Buckingham "my chamber's prisoner" (*Henry VIII*, 1.1.6–7).

Norfolk explains that the splendid affair was arranged by Thomas Woolsey, Cardinal of York. The son of a butcher from Ipswich, Woolsey graduated from Oxford University and was ordained as a priest. He became the royal chaplain to Henry VII. Due to his remarkable ability as an administrator and diplomat, he rose to be Henry VIII's Chancellor and ran the government in the King's early years. He was also Cardinal of York and a papal legate (a personal representative of the pope).

He accepted large sums of money from both Francis I and the Holy Roman Emperor Charles V. He also received large gratuities from dispensing ecclesiastical and political patronage. It took all his income to maintain an establishment of fabulous extravagance.

Norfolk and Buckingham agree that Woolsey has a great deal of pride and is the most powerful man in England. Buckingham: "Why the devil, / Upon this French going out, took he upon him, / Without the privity o' the king, to appoint / Who should attend on him?" (1.1.83–86). They question whether the peace with France Woolsey obtained was worth the cost. Norfolk warns Buckingham against becoming the victim of Woolsey's malice. When Woolsey and his train enter briefly on stage the Cardinal asks for the "examination" (1.1.136) of Buckingham's surveyor. We are led to think there is already at work a plan by Woolsey to destroy Buckingham.

After Woolsey leaves, Buckingham says he will denounce the Cardinal to the King as a traitor, accusing Woolsey of accepting a bribe from Charles V. But before Buckingham can leave, he is arrested by the King's officer and accused of "high treason" (1.1.234).

When he is shown the warrant and sees the others who are accused, Buckingham realizes the surveyor who managed his lands is the accuser, and he is doomed: "My surveyor is false; the o'er-great cardinal / Hath show'd him gold; my life is spann'd already: / I am the shadow of poor Buckingham" (1.1.263–65).

The second scene begins with the King and his Council in the Council Chamber. Henry thanks Woolsey for uncovering Buckingham's treachery. Queen Katharine complains to Henry of unrest in the country because of commissions issued by Woolsey requiring some to pay a sixth of their property in taxes to the State.

Woolsey claims to have done nothing other than get an opinion from the royal Judges: "And for me, / I have no further gone in this than by / A single voice; and that not pass'd me but / By learned approbation of the judges" (1.2.79–81). The King is amazed that such a crushing burden of taxation would be imposed in his name. When Henry orders the tax abated, Woolsey sends his man to the "grieved commons" (1.2.117) to spread the word that he, Woolsey, got the King to rescind the tax. Henry then proceeds to hear the accusation against Buckingham by his surveyor.

CARDINAL WOLSEY   Stand forth, and with bold spirit relate what you,
Most like a careful subject, have collected
Out of the Duke of Buckingham.

KING HENRY VIII   Speak freely.

SURVEYOR   First, it was usual with him, every day
It would infect his speech, that if the king
Should without issue die, he'll carry it so
To make the sceptre his: these very words
I've heard him utter to his son-in-law,
Lord Abergavenny; to whom by oath he menaced
Revenge upon the cardinal.
(1.2.143–153)

"Issue" is a legal term for children born into a marriage. For the first ten years or so, the marriage of Henry and Katharine was happy enough. But there was one problem. Katharine had given birth to four girls and two boys. All but one were stillborn or died shortly after birth. Only Princess Mary survived.

Buckingham was descended through the female line from the youngest son of Edward III. If Henry died, and Princess Mary was not accepted as heir to the throne because she was a woman, Buckingham could have had a creditable claim to the throne.

Although warned by the Queen against lying, when brought into the King's presence the surveyor accuses Buckingham of planning to stab Henry. The King is outraged.

KING HENRY VIII   There's his period,
    To sheathe his knife in us. He is attach'd;
    Call him to present trial: if he may
    Find mercy in the law, 'tis his: if none,
    Let him not seek 't of us: by day and night,
    He's traitor to the height.
                        (1.2.240–45)

Buckingham had been "attach'd" when he had been arrested by the King's officers in the earlier scene.

Woolsey has a grand banquet in his great palace at York Place. King Henry and others enter the hall disguised as shepherds. The King chooses Anne Bullen (Anne Boleyn in real life) as his partner for a dance. King Henry: "The fairest hand I ever touch'd! O beauty, / Till now I never knew thee!" (1.4.93–94).

Woolsey reveals the true identity of the King, who asks his chamberlain the name of his partner at the dance. Henry regrets letting her escape without a kiss.

Later, outside on the street, we learn at secondhand that Buckingham has been convicted of treason. A gentleman who was present describes for us Buckingham's trial:

SECOND GENTLEMAN   But, pray, how pass'd it?

FIRST GENTLEMAN   I'll tell you in a little. The great duke
Came to the bar; where to his accusations
He pleaded still not guilty and alleged
Many sharp reasons to defeat the law.
The king's attorney on the contrary
Urged on the examinations, proofs, confessions
Of divers witnesses; which the duke desired
To have brought viva voce to his face:
At which appear'd against him his surveyor;
Sir Gilbert Peck his chancellor; and John Car,
Confessor to him; with that devil-monk,
Hopkins, that made this mischief.

SECOND GENTLEMAN   That was he
That fed him with his prophecies?

FIRST GENTLEMAN   The same.
All these accused him strongly; which he fain
Would have flung from him, but, indeed, he could not:
And so his peers, upon this evidence,
Have found him guilty of high treason. Much
He spoke, and learnedly, for life; but all
Was either pitied in him or forgotten.
                        (2.1.12–37)

In Shakespeare's day, the "bar" referred to the railing that separated the court officers from where the lawyers stood to address
the court. They had no tables or chairs for the barristers until the
eighteenth century. Inside the bar was a table covered by a green
cloth where the court clerks sat and kept their records. The judges sat
on a raised platform against the wall of the chamber. Buckingham
would have gone up to the railing to argue his innocence.

Buckingham had to defend himself, because at the time those accused of a felony, including treason, were not allowed to have counsel to defend them. During his defense, Buckingham demands that his accusers confront him in person in court, which they did.

This right to confront one's accusers was not firmly grounded in English law at the time. The judges later formally declared that no witnesses were required under the Treason Act of 1352. This was a big issue in the 1603 trial of Sir Walter Raleigh. Shakespeare would almost certainly have been aware of Raleigh's claim that his trial was unfair—because Attorney General Sir Edward Coke did not call any of Raleigh's accusers to testify at trial. Instead he relied on out-of-court examinations and affidavits.

Treason was a crime at common law. But the substantive law of treason was unusual in that very early it was defined by statute. A statute of Edward III in 1352 defined treason as to "compass or imagine the death of our lord the king, of our lady his Queen, or of their eldest son and heir; . . . to levy war against the king in his realm or adhere to the king's enemies and be provably attaint of it by men of the offender's own condition. . . ."

The statue was intended by Parliament to limit what royal judges could charge as treason. By and large, the statute was adequate to deal with the many armed rebellions after the reign of Richard II. It was widely assumed that treason under the 1352 statute required "deeds" to be actionable. But during the reign of Henry VIII, the Duke of Buckingham was prosecuted under this statute for merely imagining the King's murder in order to succeed him on the throne. At his trial, Chief Justice Fineux declared that to intend the death of the King was high treason even if it was proven by words alone and no proof of an overt act was offered.

At his trial, Buckingham was condemned to death. In the play, as he is lead through the streets to his place of execution, Buckingham speaks eloquently: "The law I bear no malice for my death; / 'T has done, upon the premises, but justice: / But those that sought it I could wish more Christians" (2.1.78–80). At least he had a trial, unlike his father who was murdered by Richard III.

BUCKINGHAM   My noble father, Henry of Buckingham,
  Who first raised head against usurping Richard,
  Flying for succor to his servant Banister,
  Being distress'd, was by that wretch betray'd,
  And without trial fell; God's peace be with him!
  Henry the Seventh succeeding, truly pitying
  My father's loss, like a most royal prince,
  Restored me to my honours, and, out of ruins,
  Made my name once more noble. Now his son,
  Henry the Eighth, life, honour, name and all
  That made me happy at one stroke has taken
  For ever from the world. I had my trial,
  And, must needs say, a noble one; which makes me,
  A little happier than my wretched father:
  Yet thus far we are one in fortunes: both
  Fell by our servants, by those men we loved most;
  A most unnatural and faithless service!
                    (2.1.126–142)

The downfall of Buckingham is complete. Upon his execution on May 17, 1521, by beheading ("And, as the long divorce of steel falls on me") (2.1.92), no great peers with substantial Plantagenet blood remained alive. Therefore, the Tudor dynasty seemed secure—except for the troubling question of who would succeed Henry. Thus, the cycle begins in the play of those in high places falling out of favor with the King.

The downfall of Queen Katharine is about to begin. After Buckingham's execution, those left in the street speak quietly about the rumors that Woolsey has created a rift between King Henry and Queen Katharine. Indeed, in the next scene, the rumors are confirmed. Chamberlain: "It seems the marriage with his brother's wife / Has crept too near his conscience." (2.2.18–19) Another says, "No, his conscience / Has crept too near another lady" (2.2.20–21). Henry first met Anne Boleyn around 1522 after having had an affair with her older sister, Mary. Anne was present at the Field of the Cloth of Gold. They'd flirted back and forth for years.

By 1527, Henry was getting desperate about his marriage. Katharine was forty-two, unlikely to give Henry a son, and he was tired of her. Woolsey advised the King to divorce Katharine. The pope sent Cardinal Campeius to advise the King in this matter.

Henry orders the Queen summoned to the former abbey at Blackfriars for the trial of his divorce on the grounds that they were never legally married. Interestingly, this is the former abbey where Shakespeare and his acting company would establish their indoor theater in 1609. There is a beautiful replica of the Blackfriars Theater in Staunton, Virginia, where the American Shakespeare Center performs Shakespeare in his original performance conditions, including the lighting, stage positioning, actors playing multiple roles, and more.

In the Queen's apartment, Anne Bullen learns that King Henry has given her the title of Marchioness of Pembroke and a generous income.

At Blackfriars, there is a magnificent procession into the hall for the divorce trial. King Henry sits upon his throne. Cardinal Woolsey and Cardinal Campeius "sit below him as judges" (2.4.1).

Pope Clement I was not at first opposed to the divorce. The original plan was for the pope to delegate to Cardinal Woolsey the papal authority to annul the marriage after a legatine [Papal] trial. This could have happened quickly. But by the time of the play in 1529, the pope was virtually a prisoner of Holy Roman Emperor, Charles V, who was Katharine's nephew. The pope sent Cardinal Campeius to England with secret instructions to delay and obstruct the trial.

In Scene II, Queen Katharine sits at some distance from King Henry. Woolsey starts to read his commission from Rome, but Henry impatiently tells him to get on with the trial: "It [*the commission*] hath already publicly been read" (2.4.4). Henry and Katharine are formally summoned by name, as they would be in a normal trial. Henry answers but Katharine does not. Instead, she rises and kneels at his feet. She declares that she is Henry's true wife.

QUEEN KATHARINE   Sir, I desire you do me right and justice;
   And to bestow your pity on me: for
   I am a most poor woman, and a stranger,
   Born out of your dominions; having here
   No judge indifferent, nor no more assurance
   Of equal friendship and proceeding. Alas, sir,
   In what have I offended you? what cause
   Hath my behavior given to your displeasure,
   That thus you should proceed to put me off,
   And take your good grace from me? Heaven witness,
   I have been to you a true and humble wife,
   At all times to your will conformable;
   Ever in fear to kindle your dislike,
   Yea, subject to your countenance, glad or sorry
   As I saw it inclined: when was the hour
   I ever contradicted your desire,
   Or made it not mine too? . . . Sir, call to mind
   That I have been your wife, in this obedience,
   Upward of twenty years, and have been blest
   With many children by you: if, in the course
   And process of this time, you can report,
   And prove it too, against mine honour aught,
   My bond to wedlock, or my love and duty,
   Against your sacred person, in God's name,
   Turn me away; and let the foul'st contempt
   Shut door upon me, and so give me up
   To the sharp'st kind of justice.

(2.4.13–44)

Katharine's eloquence in her own defense is reminiscent of that of Hermione in *The Winter's Tale*. Woolsey tells Katharine the bishops are prepared to "plead your cause" (2.4.62), and she should not address the King. Katharine knows the outcome of the trial will be determined by Henry's will and not the merits of her defense. Campeius says it is time for the arguments to begin.

When Woolsey tells Katharine to be patient, she turns on him
ferociously.

CARDINAL WOLSEY   Be patient yet.

QUEEN KATHARINE   I will, when you are humble; nay, before,
Or God will punish me. I do believe,
Induced by potent circumstances, that
You are mine enemy, and make my challenge
You shall not be my judge: for it is you
Have blown this coal betwixt my lord and me;
Which God's dew quench! Therefore I say again,
I utterly abhor, yea, from my soul
Refuse you for my judge; whom, yet once more,
I hold my most malicious foe, and think not
At all a friend to truth.
                    (2.4.79–90)

At the time, the plea of *recusation* or lack of impartiality on the
part of the judge was allowed in the church courts. Woolsey protests:
"Madam, you do me wrong" (2.4.95). He has his commission from
the consistory of Rome. Katharine rebukes Woolsey for his arrogance
and pride: "You have, by fortune and his highness' favours, / Gone
slightly o'er low steps and now are mounted / Where powers are your
retainers, and your words, / Domestics to you, serve your will as't
please / Yourself pronounce their office" (2.4.120–24).

Katharine again tells Woolsey she will not submit to him
being her judge; she will appeal to the pope to be judged by him.
Katharine then leaves the court. "I will not tarry; no, nor ever
more / Upon this business my appearance make / In any of their
courts" (2.4.140–42).

After she has gone, Henry acquits Woolsey of the charge
of urging him to divorce Katharine. He says his conscience
first suggested that his marriage to his dead brother's wife
was illegitimate.

KING HENRY VIII   I meant to rectify my conscience,–which
    I then did feel full sick, and yet not well,–
    By all the reverend fathers of the land
    And doctors learn'd: first I began in private
    With you, my Lord of Lincoln; you remember
    How under my oppression I did reek,
    When I first moved you.
                     (2.4.216–22)

Katharine's inability to bear him a male heir was a judgment from heaven of his sin. Henry insists he has proceeded judicially in all aspects of the proceeding.

KING HENRY VIII   I then moved you,
    My Lord of Canterbury; and got your leave
    To make this present summons: unsolicited
    I left no reverend person in this court;
    But by particular consent proceeded
    Under your hands and seals: therefore, go on:
    For no dislike i' the world against the person
    Of the good queen, but the sharp thorny points
    Of my alleged reasons, drive this forward.
                     (2.4.233–41)

Cardinal Campeius insists that the court must be adjourned until Katharine's appeal to Rome can be called back. Henry suspects a trick ("This dilatory sloth and tricks of Rome") (2.4.256), but allows the court to adjourn. Katharine's downfall is almost complete; Woolsey's is about to begin.

Woolsey and Campeius go to Katharine and urge her to allow Henry to judge her cause rather than continuing the trial. She rejects their counsel.

CARDINAL CAMPEIUS   I would your grace
    Would leave your griefs, and take my counsel.

QUEEN KATHARINE   How, sir?

CARDINAL CAMPEIUS   Put your main cause into the king's
protection;
He's loving and most gracious: 'twill be much
Both for your honour better and your cause;
For if the trial of the law o'ertake ye,
You'll part away disgraced.

CARDINAL WOLSEY   He tells you rightly.

QUEEN KATHARINE   Ye tell me what ye wish for both,–my
ruin:
Is this your Christian counsel? out upon ye!
Heaven is above all yet; there sits a judge
That no king can corrupt.

(3.1.102–114)

Katharine says she will die before giving up the title as Henry's wife.

Secretly reversing course, Woolsey has advised the pope to stay Henry's divorce in order to prevent him from marrying Anne Bullen. Meanwhile, Woolsey's enemies learn that his letters to the pope have been intercepted and shown to the King, who is furious with the Cardinal.

The King has already secretly married Anne. Cardinal Campeius has fled to Rome to second Woolsey's scheme. Thomas Cranmer, Archbishop of Canterbury, has satisfied Henry as to the divorce, and Anne is soon to be crowned as Queen. Wolsey thinks Anne is a "spleeny Lutheran," and Cranmer is a "heretic" (3.2.130, 134).

The King has seen Woolsey's letters to the pope and an inventory of all the wealth Wolsey has accumulated. Woolsey proclaims his loyalty to the King. But Henry confronts him with the letters and the inventory. Reading them after Henry leaves, Woolsey knows he is undone. Norfolk returns with the King's command that Woolsey give up the Great Seal he holds as Chancellor of England.

NORFOLK   Hear the king's pleasure, cardinal: who commands
you
To render up the great seal presently
Into our hands; and to confine yourself
To Asher House, my Lord of Winchester's,
Till you hear further from his highness.

CARDINAL WOLSEY   Stay:
Where's your commission, lords? words cannot carry
Authority so weighty.

SUFFOLK   Who dare cross 'em,
Bearing the king's will from his mouth expressly?

CARDINAL WOLSEY   Till I find more than will or words to do
it,
I mean your malice, know, officious lords,
I dare and must deny it. . . . That seal,
You ask with such a violence, the king,
Mine and your master, with his own hand gave me;
Bade me enjoy it, with the place and honours,
During my life; and, to confirm his goodness,
Tied it by letters-patents: now, who'll take it?

SURREY   The king, that gave it.

CARDINAL WOLSEY   It must be himself, then.

SURREY   Thou art a proud traitor, priest.
                    (3.2.276–304)

Suffolk tells Woolsey the King has ordered a writ of praemunire to
be issued that will result in the forfeiture of all of Woolsey's property:
"To forfeit all your goods, lands, tenements, / Chattels, and whatsoever, and to be / Out of the king's protection" (3.2.407–09). The

writ of praemunire charged someone with the offence of resorting to a foreign jurisdiction, especially to that of the pope, in a matter determinable in a royal court.

To prevent the pope from assuming the supremacy in granting ecclesiastical livings, a number of statutes were enacted in England during the reigns of Edward I and his successors, punishing certain acts of submission to any authority outside of England, particularly the papal authority. In the writ for the execution of these statutes, the words *praemunire facias* were used. This gave the name of praemunire not only to the writ, but to the offence itself, of maintaining the papal power.

Henry is accusing Woolsey of violating the statute by urging the pope to stay the divorce proceeding. The King later threatened to charge all of the English clergy with writs of praemunire because their courts were subject to the jurisdiction of Rome. He used this threat to force the English clergy in convocation to acknowledge Henry as "sole protector and supreme head of the English Church and clergy."

Woolsey laments his fall from power. "Farewell! a long farewell, to all my greatness!" (3.2.416). Indeed, his fall has been quick. Henry has appointed Sir Thomas More as Chancellor in his place. Woolsey responds to this news by saying, "May he continue / Long in his highness' favour, and do justice / For truth's sake and his conscience" (3.2.467–69). As to his own fate, Woolsey laments, "Had I but served my God with half the zeal / I served my king, he would not in mine age / Have left me naked to mine enemies" (3.2.530–32).

Gentlemen in the street at Westminster describe Anne's coronation and the enormous coronation procession. The stage directions for the coronation procession are extraordinary and must have taxed the actors and personnel of the King's Men. The gentlemen in the street tell of Henry's official divorce of Katharine.

SECOND GENTLEMAN   But, I beseech you, what's become of
    Katharine,
    The princess dowager? how goes her business?

FIRST GENTLEMAN   That I can tell you too. The Archbishop

Of Canterbury [*Cranmer*], accompanied with other
Learned and reverend fathers of his order,
Held a late court at Dunstable, six miles off
From Ampthill where the princess lay; to which
She was often cited by them, but appear'd not:
And, to be short, for not appearance and
The king's late scruple, by the main assent
Of all these learned men she was divorced,
And the late marriage made of none effect
Since which she was removed to Kimbolton,
Where she remains now sick.

(4.1.26–39)

They gossip about who will be the King's new officers after the downfall of Woolsey. The Earl of Northumberland arrests Woolsey at York, and Woolsey's downfall is complete. On the road back to London for his trial, Wolsey becomes ill and dies.

Katharine has been sent to Kimbolton where Henry sends an ambassador to bid her to be of good comfort. Katharine responds: "O my good lord, that comfort comes too late; / 'Tis like a pardon after execution: / That gentle physic, given in time, had cured me; / But now I am past an comforts here, but prayers" (4.2.136–38). Katharine is sick and near death. In a letter, she asks Henry to take care of their daughter Mary.

Anne goes into labor and gives birth to a girl.

Chancellor More and Stephen Gardiner, the Bishop of Winchester, accuse Thomas Cranmer, the Archbishop of Canterbury, of being a Protestant heretic. Henry commits Cranmer to the Tower to make it appear that he is not interfering in the case. Is Cranmer the next to fall? Henry warns Cranmer that the outcome of the trial may not be determined by the "justice and truth 'o the question" (5.1.155). The accusation against Cranmer of heresy is brought before the Council. His principal accusers are Chancellor Thomas More and Gardiner, the Bishop of Winchester.

Cranmer, like Buckingham in his trial, demands to face his accusers. "I do beseech your lordships, / That, in this case of justice, my accusers, / Be what they will, may stand forth face to face, / And freely urge against me" (5.3.51–54). The request is refused by Suffolk: "Nay, my lord, / That cannot be: you are a counsellor, / And, by that virtue, no man dare accuse you" (5.3.55–57).

Gardiner orders Cranmer committed to the Tower to await his trial. Cranmer responds sarcastically: "Ah, my good Lord of Winchester, I thank you; / You are always my good friend; if your will pass, / I shall both find your lordship judge and juror, / You are so merciful" (5.3.67–70). Cranmer protests that Gardiner has already decided the case. Cranmer then brings the proceedings to a halt when he produces a ring the King has given him.

King Henry suddenly enters the council chamber and interrupts Cranmer's arraignment. He announces that Cranmer will be godfather to his newly born daughter. The last scene of the play is at the palace, where the infant Elizabeth is christened. Cranmer proclaims: "Heaven, from thy endless goodness, send prosperous / life, long, and ever happy, to the high and mighty / princess of England, Elizabeth!" (5.5.1–3).

The Epilogue that follows is as bad as the Prologue.

By the time Shakespeare wrote *Henry VIII*, England was a thoroughly Protestant kingdom. After the pope refused to grant his divorce from Katharine of Aragon, King Henry charged the entire clergy of England of usurping his authority over the administration of canon law. Under the threat of mass confiscations of church property, the clergy begged for pardon and admitted that the King was the supreme head of the English church "as far as the law of Christ allows." Sir Thomas More resigned as Chancellor the day after the Convocation of Canterbury in 1532 declared the King the supreme authority in England for the determination of canon law.

In 1533, the King's marriage to Katharine was declared null and void by Archbishop Cranmer, and Pope Clement VII excommunicated the King. In 1534, Parliament adopted what was known as the Act of Succession. The Act made Elizabeth the presumptive heir to the Crown by declaring that Mary, the daughter of Katharine, was a bastard. The Act also required all English subjects to swear an oath, if commanded, to recognize the Act and the supremacy of the King.

In 1533, Archbishop Cranmer declared King Henry VIII's marriage to Katharine null and void, leading Pope Clement VII to excommunicate the king. The following year, Parliament passed the Act of Succession, recognizing Henry VIII and his heirs as the Supreme Head of the Church of England. The Act also legitimized Elizabeth as the presumptive heir to the Crown while declaring Katharine's daughter, Mary, a bastard. Additionally, it required English subjects to swear an oath, if commanded, affirming the Act and the king's supremacy.

The Treason Act of 1534 made it a crime to disavow the Act of Supremacy or to deprive the king of his "dignity, title, or name." John Fisher, Bishop of Rochester, and Thomas More refused to take the oath and were executed in 1535.

Following Anne Boleyn's execution in 1536, the Second Succession Act declared Elizabeth illegitimate. However, the Third Succession Act of 1543 reinstated both Mary and Elizabeth in the royal line of succession.

During Queen Mary's reign, Parliament repealed the Act of Supremacy. Upon Elizabeth's accession, her first Parliament passed the 1558 Act of Supremacy, declaring her the Supreme Governor of the Church of England. This Act also required all public and church officials to swear an oath of allegiance to her as head of both church and state.

Thus, the Protestant Reformation was completed in England.

Afterward

When I began writing this book, my intention was to include a chapter on each of Shakespeare's plays. There is something to say about Shakespeare and the law in every play. After years of working in that direction, it became apparent that the manuscript was so large as to be unpublishable. The book you have before you is about half the size of my original manuscript. It includes half of the plays I began with—those I feel have the most to say about Shakespeare's use of the law in his plays.

Much good stuff has been left out. In *Two Gentlemen of Verona*, the play's most entertaining character is Proteus's servant Launce. At one point, Proteus sends Launce to take a puppy to Mistress Silvia as a present. Instead, Launce takes his dog Crab that he has raised from a puppy. The result is an unfortunate display of bad manners by the dog in the Duke's dining chamber.

LAUNCE   When a man's servant shall play the cur with him,
    look you, it goes hard. . . . I was sent to deliver
    him [*Crab*] as a present to Mistress Silvia from my master;
    and I came no sooner into the dining-chamber but he
    steps me to her trencher and steals her capon's leg:
    O, 'tis a foul thing when a cur cannot keep himself
    in all companies! . . . He thrusts me himself into the company
    of three or four gentlemanlike dogs under the duke's table: he
    had not been there–bless the mark!–a pissing while, but
    all the chamber smelt him. 'Out with the dog!' says
    one: 'What cur is that?' says another: 'Whip him

out' says the third: 'Hang him up' says the duke.
I, having been acquainted with the smell before,
knew it was Crab, and goes me to the fellow that whips the dogs:
'Friend,' quoth I, 'you mean to whip the dog?' 'Ay, marry, do I,'
quoth he. 'You do him the more wrong,' quoth I; ''twas I did the
thing you wot of.' He makes me no more ado, but whips me out
of the chamber. How many masters would do this for
his servant?

(Two Gentlemen of Verona, 4.4.1–30)

Launce then enumerates all the early modern forms of minor
punishments, in addition to whipping, that he has endured for the
sake of his dog.

Nay, I'll be sworn, I have sat in the
stocks for puddings he hath stolen, otherwise he had
been executed; I have stood on the pillory for geese
he hath killed, otherwise he had suffered for't.
Thou thinkest not of this now. Nay, I remember the
trick you served me when I took my leave of Madam
Silvia: did not I bid thee still mark me and do as I
do? when didst thou see me heave up my leg and make
water against a gentlewoman's farthingale? didst
thou ever see me do such a trick?

(4.4.30–39)

This hilarious passage describing the types of punishment for
criminal misdemeanors in Shakespeare's day was sacrificed for the
sake of economy since there is little else of interest in this very early
comedy.

Some of Shakespeare's most popular plays, however, were sacrificed for the same reason: *Julius Caesar* with the wonderful funeral
orations of Brutus and Antony; *Antony and Cleopatra*; *Henry V*
with its extraordinary battlefield speeches by the hero king; Justice
Shallow's threat to take a case of riot against Falstaff to the Court

of Star Chamber in *The Merry Wives of Windsor*; *The Winter's Tale* with its magnificent trial of Hermione; and Shakespeare's great crime melodrama *Othello*.

Notwithstanding these sacrifices, writing the book has been a great adventure and has broadened my understanding and appreciation of Shakespeare. As I said at the beginning, I hope the reader does not see it as much ado about nothing.

About the Author

Thomas W. Thrash is a federal trial judge in Atlanta, Georgia. He was born in 1951 in Birmingham, Alabama. As an adolescent and teenager in the Birmingham public schools, he lived through the turmoil that the resistance to equal rights for Blacks brought to the city. His freshman class at Woodlawn High School marked the first year of integration in the school system. After graduating first in his high school class, Judge Thrash went on to attend the University of Virginia on a DuPont Scholarship. He was President of the Virginia Debaters, and graduated with a Bachelor of Arts Degree in American Government with High Distinction. He received his Juris Doctor Cum Laude from Harvard Law School in 1976. After law school, he made his home in Atlanta, Georgia. He was a Fulton County Assistant District Attorney for three years, and was then in private practice as a civil and criminal trial attorney for seventeen years. He was an Adjunct Professor of Law at Georgia State University College of Law for nine years. In 1997, President Clinton appointed him as United States District Judge for the Northern District of Georgia. As a federal trial judge he has handled many high profile civil and criminal cases, including more than a dozen cases referred to him by the Judicial Panel on Multidistrict Litigation. He served as Chief Judge of the Northern District of Georgia from 2014 to 2021. Judge Thrash is a former Trustee of the American Shakespeare Center in Staunton, Virginia, and a former Director of the Atlanta Shakespeare Company. He is married to Margaret Lines Thrash, and has two adult children.